BELLY AND BODY IN THE PAULINE EPISTLES

The belly is today a matter of much concern. Modern cultures, particularly in the West, have developed means to cultivate this part of the body: corsets, exercises, revealing fashions. In this compelling exploration of the 'belly' motif, Karl Olav Sandnes asks whether St Paul might be addressing a culture in which the stomach is similarly high on the agenda. The result is a surprising new insight into this writings.

Paul twice mentions the enigmatic phrase 'belly-worship' (Phil. 3; Rom. 16). The proper context for these texts is the moral philosophy debate about mastering the desires, and the reputation of Epicurus' philosophy as promoting indulgence. The belly became a catchword for a life controlled by pleasures. Belly-worship was not only pejorative rhetoric, but developed from Paul's conviction that the body was destined to a future with Christ.

KARL OLAV SANDNES is Professor in New Testament Theology at The Norwegian Lutheran School of Theology, Oslo. He has published two books in English: *Paul – One of the Prophets? A Contribution to the Apostle's Self-Understanding* (1991), and *A New Family: Conversion and Ecclesiology in the Early Church with Cross-Cultural Comparisons* (1994).

SOCIETY FOR NEW TESTAMENT STUDIES

MONOGRAPH SERIES

General Editor: Richard Bauckham

120

BELLY AND BODY IN THE PAULINE EPISTLES

Belly and Body in the Pauline Epistles

KARL OLAV SANDNES

The Norwegian Lutheran School of Theology, Oslo

CAMBRIDGE
UNIVERSITY PRESS

PUBLISHED BY THE PRESS SYNDICATE OF THE UNIVERSITY OF CAMBRIDGE
The Pitt Building, Trumpington Street, Cambridge, United Kingdom

CAMBRIDGE UNIVERSITY PRESS
The Edinburgh Building, Cambridge CB2 2RU, UK
40 West 20th Street, New York, NY 10011-4211, USA
477 Williamstown Road, Port Melbourne, VIC 3207, Australia
Ruiz de Alarcón 13, 28014 Madrid, Spain
Dock House, The Waterfront, Cape Town 8001, South Africa

http://www.cambridge.org

First published 2002

Printed in the United Kingdom at the University Press, Cambridge

Typeface Times 10/12 pt   *System* LATEX 2ε   [TB]

A catalogue record for this book is available from the British Library

ISBN 0 521 81535 5 hardback

CONTENTS

Preface   *page* xi
Abbreviations   xiii

Part 1   Prolegomena

**1   Introduction, previous solutions, method and
     Pauline context**   **4**
     1.0   Introduction   4
     1.1   Bible translations   5
     1.2   The scholarly debate   7
     1.3   Methodological considerations   11
     1.4   Belly and body – the Pauline context of the study   14

Part 2   The Graeco-Roman belly

2   The belly as a sign – ancient physiognomics   **24**
     2.0   Introduction   24
     2.1   The stomach as a sign   27
     2.2   Summary   34

3   The belly in ancient moral philosophy   **35**
     3.0   Introduction   35
     3.1   Euripides (born probably in the 480s BC)   37
     3.2   Plato (c. 429–347 BC)   39
     3.3   Xenophon (born around 430 BC)   42
     3.4   Aristotle (384–322 BC)   45
     3.5   Dio Chrysostom (AD c. 40/50–110)   46
     3.6   Musonius Rufus (AD 30–AD 101/102)   47
     3.7   Epictetus (mid first century to second
           century AD)   49
     3.8   Plutarch (AD c. 50–c. 120)   52
     3.9   Athenaeus (flourished c. AD 200)   54
     3.10 Summary   57

4   Ancient critique of Epicureanism   **61**
4.0   Epicurus – the popularity and reputation of a doctrine   61
4.1   Cicero   65
4.2   Seneca   71
4.3   Plutarch   74
4.4   Summary   77

5   Banquets – opportunities for the belly   **79**
5.0   Introduction   79
5.1   Parties for pleasure   80
5.2   Seneca – the moral philosopher   83
5.3   Horace and Juvenal – two Roman satirists   86
5.4   Athenaeus and Alciphron   89
5.5   Summary   92

Part 3   The appropriated belly

6   The belly-*topos* in Jewish-Hellenistic sources   **97**
6.1   Sir. 23:6   97
6.2   *T. Rub.* 2:1–3:8   97
6.3   3 Macc. 7:10–11   98
6.4   4 Maccabees   101
6.5   *Aristeas to Philocrates* 140–1   104
6.6   *T. Mos.* 7:2–4   105
6.7   *Cairo Geniza Wisdom*   106

7   The belly in Philo's writings   **108**
7.0   Introduction   108
7.1   Anthropology   109
7.2   The 'geography' of the belly   112
7.3   The serpent crawling on its belly   113
7.4   Esau selling his birthright for the sake of his belly   117
7.5   Joseph and the servants of Pharaoh   121
7.6   Jewish customs as means of controlling
         the stomach   123
7.7   Fasts and Sabbaths   126
7.8   Food laws   128
7.9   Conversion – the safest way to rule the belly   130
7.10 Summary   131

Part 4   Belly-worship and body according to Paul

**8   The lifestyle of citizens of the heavenly
       politeuma – Phil. 3:17–21**   **136**
8.0   Introduction   136

8.1	'Stand firm' and the rhetoric of examples	138
8.2	'Whose god is the belly'	141
8.3	Opponents?	155
8.4	Belly-worship and body in Philippians	159
8.5	Summary	162

9 'Serving the belly' as kinship with Satan – Rom. 16:17–20   **165**

9.0	Introduction	165
9.1	Warning against deceivers	165
9.2	Worshipping the belly – Gen. 3:15, Satan and flattery	169
9.3	Why call the adversaries belly-worshippers?	172
9.4	'Serving the belly' and body in Romans	175
9.5	Summary	179

10 The Corinthian belly   **181**

10.0	Introduction	181
10.1	1 Cor. 15:32: Epicurean lifestyle versus faith in resurrection	181
10.2	1 Cor. 11:17–34: the Lord's Supper or stuffing one's own stomach?	187
10.3	1 Cor. 6:12–20: the Christian faith has implications for stomach and sex	191
10.4	1 Cor. 10:7 in context: the belly – a tempting force in Corinth as in the wilderness	199
10.5	Belly and body in 1 Corinthians	212
10.6	Summary	215

Part 5 The earliest expositors of Paul

11 The belly-dicta of Paul in Patristic literature   **219**

11.1	Clement of Alexandria (c. 150–c. 215)	219
11.2	Tertullian (c. 160–c. 225)	223
11.3	Origen (c. 185–c. 254)	226
11.4	Cyprian (d. 258)	230
11.5	Novatian (d. 257–8)	232
11.6	Methodius of Olympus (d. c. 311)	234
11.7	Ambrosiaster (c. 300)	235
11.8	Pelagius (late fourth and early fifth centuries)	237
11.9	Jerome (c. 345–420)	238
11.10	John Chrysostom (c. 347–407)	244
11.11	Augustine of Hippo (354–430)	252
11.12	Severian of Gabala (fl. c. 400)	256
11.13	Tyrannius Rufinus (c. 345–411)	256
11.14	Theodore of Mopsuestia (c. 350–428)	256

11.15 Theodoret of Cyrrhus (c. 393–c. 460)   258
11.16 Peter Chrysologus (c. 400–50)   259
11.17 Gennadius of Marseilles (fl. 470)   259
11.18 Antiochus, the Patriarch of Antioch (d. 598) 260
11.19 John Climacus (c. 570–c. 649)   261
11.20 Summary   261

Part 6   Conclusions

12   Concluding remarks   **265**
12.1   Paul's critique of belly-worship in an ancient setting   265
12.2   Belly-worship and body in Paul's letters   269

Bibliography   275
  Works of reference   275
  Sources   276
  Secondary literature   278
Index of modern authors   292
Index of Graeco-Roman sources   295
*Index of Old Testament, Apocrypha, Pseudepigrapha
  and other Jewish writings*   303
Index of New Testament and early Christian writings 311

PREFACE

I have incurred many debts in the course of this project. The present study was written during my sabbatical (1998/1999); I am grateful to the Norwegian Lutheran School of Theology (Det teologiske Menighets-fakultet, Oslo), where I teach, for this opportunity. I owe thanks to the library there for patiently providing me with the necessary material. Most of the work was, however, carried out in Cambridge. I am very grateful for the hospitality and access to the library which was given me at Tyndale House. This excellent library for Biblical research made it possible for me to finish most of the work during my time there. I owe special thanks to the head librarian at Tyndale House, Dr David I. Brewer as well as his staff. I am grateful for the fellowship I enjoyed at Tyndale House, and to the scholars who were there together with me. This fellowship stimulated and contributed in various ways to my investigation. I owe special thanks to the Warden, Dr Bruce W. Winter, for his willingness to share his knowledge with me and to bring relevant literature to my attention, and for having introduced me to the Cambridge University Library as well as the library of the Classical Faculty. Without access to these libraries and the kind assistance which I found there, this investigation would not have been possible. These Cambridge days bring to mind also the kind hospitality which I enjoyed in the house of my hostess Mrs Veronica Becho.

Many colleagues at my own school encouraged me in this work; some also read and commented upon my manuscripts. I am grateful for the help I received from Dr Hans Kvalbein, Dr Reidar Hvalvik, Dr Oskar Skarsaune, and Martin Synnes. Special thanks are owed to my colleagues Bjørn-Helge Sandvei and Jan Schumacher, whom I consulted regarding Greek and Latin. My Latin teacher from college, Bjørgulv Rian, kindly assisted me with some Latin passages.

I owe thanks to the Research Council of Norway (Norges Forskningsråd) for granting me the necessary support to improve my English. This work has been done with much enthusiasm and patience by Dr David Pugh, Bergen. His work included critical comments, fruitful suggestions and involvement. His contribution extends beyond working with the language. Although I have benefited from the help of many people, any faults or mistakes remain fully my own responsibility.

I am very grateful to Dr Richard Bauckham, editor of this series, for recommending my study to Cambridge University Press for publication. His comments and suggestions have contributed considerably to the improvement of the manuscript. Senior Publishing Assistant Gillian Dadd and Publishing Director Kevin Taylor and their co-workers have patiently guided me through the publication process itself.

Finally, I owe special thanks to my wife, Tone, who took upon herself the sole care of our home and three youngsters, and thus made it possible for me to stay in Cambridge.

ABBREVIATIONS

The text of the New Testament is K. Aland et al., *Novum Testamentum Graece* 27th edition, Stuttgart: Deutsche Bibelgesellschaft 1993. Abbreviations are those used by the American Academy of Religion and Society of Biblical Literature. Quotations of Biblical texts are drawn from the *NRSV*. If not stated otherwise, Graeco-Roman sources are quoted in English from the LCL. Texts from Old Testament Pseudepigrapha are quoted according to the *OTP*. The Philonic works are abbreviated according to the guidelines set out in *Studia Philonica Annual* (1993), p. 256. Text editions from well-known series are not listed in the bibliography, but the series and volume will appear in footnotes. The following abbreviations will be of help to the reader.

ANF	The Ante-Nicene Fathers
BAGD	W. Bauer, W. F. Arndt, F. W. Gingrich, F. Wilbur, F. W. Danker, *Greek–English Lexicon of the New Testament*
BDF	F. Blass, A. Debrunner and R. W. Funk, *A Greek Grammar of the New Testament*
CCL	*Corpus Christianorum Latinorum*
CSEL	*Corpus Scriptorum Ecclesiasticorum Latinorum*
FC	*The Fathers of the Church, A New Translation*
GCS	*Die griechischen christlichen Schriftsteller der erste Jahrhunderte*
JSHRZ	Werner G. Kümmel (ed.), *Jüdische Schriften aus hellenistisch-römischer Zeit*
LCL	Loeb Classical Library
LSJ	Liddell–Scott–Jones, *Greek–English Lexicon*
LXX	The Septuagint
NPNF	Nicene and Post-Nicene Fathers
NRSV	*New Revised Standard Version*
OTP	J. H. Charlesworth (ed.), *The Old Testament Pseudepigrapha*

PG	J. Migne, *Patrologia Graeca*
PL	J. Migne, *Patrologia Latina*
SC	*Sources Chrétiennes*
s.v.	sub voce
SVF	H. von Arnim (ed.), *Stoicorum Veterum Fragmenta*
TDNT	G. Kittel, G. Friedrich (eds.), *Theological Dictionary of the New Testament*

PART 1

Prolegomena

To present-day readers, the stomach is a matter of much concern. It serves as a source of shame as well as pride; it is a part of the human body that is often made fun of. Modern cultures, particularly in the West, have developed means to cultivate this part of the body: corsets, exercises to develop a washboard stomach, fashions in which the navel is carefully, but deliberately revealed etc. It is hardly surprising that in a culture in which the body is given such an important role, the stomach receives attention as well. Does Paul in any way address a culture in which the stomach is similarly high on the agenda? To answer this question is the aim of this investigation.

The Pauline tradition quotes an old saying about Cretans which is worth mentioning here: '... they are γαστέρες' (Tit. 1:12).[1] This plural of γαστήρ claims that the entire personality of Cretans is their stomachs. The Cretans are not considered to *have* bellies; they *are* bellies. The term has obviously picked up figurative elements. Hence most Bible translations render the text 'gluttons',[2] which means that the stomach sets the agenda for the life of the Cretans. In this text, then, the belly has become a codeword that might have both physical and figurative implications. The undisputed Pauline letters mention twice *in expressis verbis* people 'whose god is their belly' (Phil. 3:19), and who 'serve their stomach' (Rom. 16:18); in short they address the question of belly-worship. This investigation is especially interested in these enigmatic texts. Are they to be understood along the same lines as Tit. 1:12, and if so how are they placed within Paul's theology and instruction on bodily matters? Since

---

[1] The same saying claims, as well, that they are liars, wild beasts and lazy. For the literary sources of this proverb see Reggie M. Kidd, 'Titus as Apologia', pp. 188–93.

[2] See e.g. Daniel C. Arrichea, Howard A. Hatton, *Paul's Letters to Timothy and Titus*, pp. 276–7. Cf. Johannes P. Louw, Eugene A. Nida, *Lexicon* Vol. 1, p. 251: 'a glutton is often spoken of idiomatically, for example "a large belly" or "a person who is only a stomach" or "a professional eater"'. In the songs which the shepherds taught Hesiod while he was shepherding, they call themselves γαστέρες. The LCL translator renders this 'mere bellies' (*Theogony* 26).

a monograph on this aspect of the Pauline epistles is still awaiting its author, this investigation fills a gap in New Testament scholarship.

In order to answer the question of how Paul addresses a culture in which the belly holds a key position on the agenda, his ancient world must be addressed first. In antiquity the human body was subject to various ideas and perspectives. To physicians the body was the object of scientific investigation. For those whose concern was the moral and decent life, the body with all its needs and desires naturally came into focus. But the body was also – then as now – something to poke fun at. Bodily characteristics easily became targets of criticism, satire and polemics. These three ways of making the body an object all have their correspondences in the Graeco-Roman world.

Ancient medical doctors worked hard to explain how the body worked, and also to describe how to cure its afflictions.

Moral philosophers addressed the imperative to bring the body under control by mastering its desires, lest they turn into lust and greed. This became a favourite topic among philosophers whose concern was a proper lifestyle. They considered food to play a key role for bodily desires in general. Aristotle states this very briefly within a discussion on mating: ἐν πλησμονῇ γὰρ Κύπρις (*Problems* 896a).[3] This saying is quoted approvingly by other ancient writers. Since Cypris is another name for Aphrodite, the sentence might be rendered in this way: 'For sexual appetite accompanies satiety' (LCL).

In her recent study on fasting and sexuality in Early Christianity, Teresa M. Shaw draws attention to the so-called Minnesota experiment conducted in 1944–45.[4] This experiment demonstrated that daily calorific intake level plays a significant role in the sexual drive. Prolonged food deprivation causes a weakening or even disappearance of sexual activity. Shaw claims that this physical nexus between food and sexual desire sheds light on the teaching of the Patristic Fathers on fasting and abstaining from sex. It is beyond the scope of the present investigation to enter this discussion, but it is evident that the Minnesota experiment has put its finger on the key role played by food in matters of desire in general. This present-day experiment has an interesting correspondence in ancient moral philosophy: the question of how to master the desires focused on matters of food and sex. Eating and copulating were commonly given pride of place among the desires which were in need of control.

---

[3] For similar dicta where gluttony and sex are seen in tandem, see Bruce W. Winter, *After Paul Left Corinth*, pp. 84–5.

[4] See Teresa M. Shaw, *Burden of the Flesh*, pp. 124–8, with further references.

Physiognomists developed theories about correspondences between bodily appearances and inner qualities. The surface of the body was seen as an index of the soul. Bodily characteristics were thus explained as signs. In some instances, these theories naturally became means of fighting adversaries.

In the title of this book, 'belly' refers to the focus of interest while 'body' indicates the Pauline framework in which the belly-dicta probably belong.

1

INTRODUCTION, PREVIOUS SOLUTIONS, METHOD AND PAULINE CONTEXT

1.0 Introduction

The commonest terms for stomach in ancient writings (κοιλία and γαστήρ)[1] occur in the following texts in the undisputed Pauline epistles: 1 Thess. 5:13; Gal. 1:15; Phil. 3:19; 1 Cor. 6:13; Rom. 16:18. The first instance refers to pregnancy. Gal. 1:15 is a related text. Κοιλία means 'womb', and refers to the point where life begins according to Biblical thought (cf. Jer. 1:15; *Jub.* 21:8; *Lib. Ant.* 9:2.5; 22:3). Paul's reference to his mother's womb is embedded in a *topos* of vocation, aimed at justifying his divine call.[2] A rather different meaning appears in Paul's dicta on the stomach-devotees in Phil. 3:19: 'Their end is destruction; their god is the belly; and their glory is in their shame; their minds are set on earthly things' and Rom. 16:18: 'For such people do not serve our Lord Christ, but their own appetites . . .' In the last instance, *NRSV* renders κοιλία as 'appetite'. The two references are either polemical or a warning against people who are devoted to their belly. In other words, they belong to a different rhetoric. This study claims that they are similar to the Greek saying of Tit. 1:12, about the Cretans whose entire personality is their stomachs.

It is the aim of the present study to substantiate there being a rhetoric of the belly in Paul's letters, and also to see how it works. Since for obvious reasons 1 Cor. 6:13 has nothing to do with either pregnancy or vocation, it will be investigated as part of Paul's rhetoric of the belly. Belly-servitude, or having the belly as god, seems on an intuitive reading to be related to gluttony and greed, appetite or selfishness. A spontaneous reading will always be subject to discussion. I here refer to what most of my friends, relatives and colleagues were thinking of when I mentioned the topic of belly-devotion to them.

---

[1] For other terms, see chap. 3.0.

[2] Karl Olav Sandnes, *Paul – One of the Prophets?* and Roy E. Ciampa, *Galatians*, pp. 111–14; 332–3.

But this spontaneous reading is far from confirmed in the scholarly literature. There is no consensus either on what Paul is thinking of when he mentions 'belly-worship' nor about the historical reference of his terminology. Gordon D. Fee says that 'all in all, we must again beg a degree of ignorance in this matter'.[3] So saying is a true act of honesty. On the other hand, a scholarly admission of ignorance triggers curiosity, and thus represents a challenge. This study is the result of this curiosity.

In Phil. 3:19 and Rom. 16:18, the references to the belly are synonymous with living a life contrary to the gospel. Some people act and live as though they were driven by their bellies.[4] The stomach is the driving force or higher power in their life. But what does this actually mean, and why does Paul describe a lifestyle opposed to Christian behaviour in this way? How would his addressees understand this? What is the proper background for an adequate reading of the texts? The aim of this study is to answer these and related questions, and thus to elucidate the meaning and reference of the belly-texts. A major task will be to see how these dicta work within the literary and theological setting of Paul's letters.

An investigation into Paul's belly-dicta might to some appear as narrow and limited; after all Paul does not speak frequently about the stomach. If, however, the relevant texts are placed within the broader framework of how Paul conceived of the human body, the belly-texts will gain in interest. It is the conviction of the present writer that the belly-dicta are not simply rhetorical devices aimed at vilifying opponents. They are significant sources for how Paul instructed his recent converts, and attest his thought about bodily needs. This conviction roots belly-worship firmly in Pauline theology as well as in ancient moral exhortation. To argue this is the aim of this study.

1.1 Bible translations

Since Paul's references to the belly are often seen as marginal, mere rhetoric or random phenomena in his letters, they have not been at the centre of the Pauline debate. An in-depth monograph on the topic is still to be written. This is, of course, not to say that scholars have not grappled with

---

[3] Gordon D. Fee, *Philippians*, p. 372; similarly in Markus Bockmuehl, *Philippians*, p. 231 and Barclay M. Newman, Eugene A. Nida, *Romans*, p. 296; Thomas R. Schreiner, *Romans*, p. 803.

[4] It is surprising that Silvia Schroer and Thomas Staubli, *Körpersymbolik*, mention neither Rom. 16:18 nor Phil. 3:19. Anthony Byatt, *Metaphors*, has a chapter on the human body and clothing (chap. 6), but the stomach is left unmentioned. Jerome H. Neyrey, *Paul*, pays attention to various parts of the body, but leaves out the stomach; see e.g. his index of topics p. 261 s.v. 'body'.

these texts. Relevant material is found in commentaries, related articles
as well as dictionaries; not to mention Bible translations. However, in
the light of the vast literature on most New Testament topics, the two
stomach-dicta of Paul represent a neglected field of study. The aim of this
section is to point out the diverse opinions about Paul's aims in warning
his readers not to be servants of the stomach. This will, hopefully, prove
the necessity of an investigation into this problem and these texts. I here
restrict myself to mapping the terrain. The real involvement and argument
will take place in the exegetical chapters themselves. We start with some
examples from the Bible translations.

NEB 1961
Phil. 3:19: 'They are heading for destruction, appetite is their
    god'
Rom. 16:18: 'Avoid them, for such people are servants not of
    Christ our Lord, but of their own appetites'

The New Jerusalem Bible 1985
Phil. 3:19: 'They are destined to be lost; their god is the
    stomach'[5]
Rom. 16:18: 'People of that sort are servants not of our Lord
    Christ, but of their greed'

The Holy Bible Knox Version
Phil. 3:19: 'Perdition is the end that awaits them, their hungry
    bellies are the god they worship'
Rom. 16:18: 'Such men are not servants of Christ our Lord; their
    hungry bellies are their masters'

The New American Bible
Phil. 3:19: 'Such as these will end in disaster. Their god is their
    belly'
Rom. 16:18: 'Such men serve, not Christ our Lord, but their own
    bellies'

The Amplified Bible
Phil. 3:19: 'They are doomed and their fate is eternal misery
    [perdition]; their god is their stomach [their appetites, their
    sensuality]'
Rom. 16:18: 'For such persons do not serve our Lord Christ but
    their own appetites and base desires'

---

[5] In a footnote this translation says that 'the dietary laws loomed large in the Jewish
practice of religion'.

This list of Bible translations is limited to the particular part of the verses where κοιλία appears. Our investigation will, of course, have to deal with the texts in context. The translations exhibit uncertainty on how to render these texts; in particular this is evident in the instances where the translations are accompanied by notes and even parentheses. The uncertainty on how to translate κοιλία in these texts is seen, for instance, in Hans Conzelmann's commentary on 1 Corinthians. He says it refers to the 'organ of digestion, or – probably – of sex'.[6] This is typical of the situation among scholars and Bible translators.

1.2 The scholarly debate

The uncertainty which is visible in the Bible translations is carried over into the scholarly debate as well, or *vice versa*. Even if we are talking about two Pauline passages, Phil. 3:19 and Rom. 16:18, it is justified – at this stage in our presentation – to look at the two together. Although we see them together here, it remains necessary in the exegetical part to treat them separately, since it is the aim of this study to elicit how Paul makes use of a common idiom in a particular literary and theological context. For the time being, it is, however, helpful to give an account of different views held on the two texts. This presentation is accompanied by some comments which lead to the next section on methodological considerations.

Observance of Jewish dietary laws

The references to the belly are very concrete; they address the question of Jewish food laws. Paul says that believers who continue to observe the dietary laws are devoted to their bellies. Probably he has in mind Jewish-Christian opponents. According to Helmut Koester, the people under attack are 'Law-perfectionists of Jewish origin'.[7] Paul is attacking 'Torah-centric Jewish Christians' in a way which resembles the Galatian conflict.[8] This view is often supported by reference to commentators of

---

[6] Hans Conzelmann, *Corinthians*, p. 110 n. 16.

[7] Helmut Koester, 'Polemic', p. 326.

[8] See also Ben Witherington III, *Friendship*, p. 29: '...a euphemistic way to refer to the fact that the opponents are ruled by and tout Jewish food laws and a concern for circumcision (see Phil. 3:2–3) (cf. pp. 89–90)'. Similarly Johannes Behm, 'κοιλία', p. 788; Karl P. Donfried, I. Howard Marshall, *Theology of the Shorter Pauline Letters*, p. 124. Gerald F. Hawthorne, *Philippians*, p. 166. Johannes P. Louw, Eugene A. Nida, *Lexicon* Vol. 2, p. 292 says on Rom. 16:18 that 'it is also possible that *koilia* in Rom. 16:18 refers to Jewish dietary laws and regulations'.

the ancient church who supposedly, in general, took the phrase as a piece of polemic against food laws.[9]

Comments

The phrases 'serving the belly' or 'having the stomach as god' are interpreted primarily on the basis of Pauline polemics against Judaizers. The phrase itself is not given the attention it deserves. Extra-Pauline analogies are therefore of minor interest to these scholars. Furthermore, we need to ask to what extent the predicate of 'having the belly as god', or 'serving the stomach' are to be taken as a descriptive of the opponents. Is it likely that Paul would denounce the Jewish food laws in this strong way, equating them with idolatry?

Flesh

In these texts 'the stomach' is a circuitous way of referring to 'the flesh'. Phil. 3 and Rom. 16 are two related examples of a lifestyle associated with 'flesh'. According to Moisés Silva '... this term is a strong expression roughly equivalent to *sarx* (flesh). If so, the reference is not to a specific kind of misconduct – whether licentiousness or legalism – but to a frame of mind that is opposed to the *pneuma* (Spirit) and that may manifest itself in a variety of ways'.[10] Gal. 5:19–21 lists the works of the flesh, among which are sexual immorality, jealousy, drunkenness etc. Belly-worship belongs within this framework of Pauline theology.[11]

Comments

Interpreting the belly-phrases in the light of the role played by the flesh in Paul's theology is certainly relevant, and there is a lot to recommend this perspective, but this view is none the less unable to catch all the cultural associations with which these dicta are so replete. The rhetorical strategy of Romans may be related to the contrast Spirit versus flesh in Galatians. But this contrast is not very prominent in the strategy of Philippians. Since analogous references are found in ancient literature, Paul's texts

---

[9] References in Johannes Behm, 'κοιλία', p. 788 n. 14. This will be discussed separately in chap. 11.

[10] Moisés Silva, *Philippians*, p. 210. For Phil. 3:19, see Joachim Gnilka, *Philipperbrief*, pp. 205–6; Peter O'Brien, *Philippians*, p. 456; Ralph P. Martin, *Philippians*, p. 144. For Romans 16:18, see Ernst Käsemann, *Römer*, p. 398; Heinrich Schlier, *Römerbrief*, p. 448; C. E. B. Cranfield, *Romans* Vol. 2 , p. 800; James D. G. Dunn, *Romans 9–16*, p. 903.

[11] Gordon D. Fee, *Philippians*, p. 372 takes 'stomach' in Phil. 3 to refer to 'bodily desires of all kind', which brings him close to this category of interpretation although on p. 371 n. 36 he says that the flesh-interpretation 'lacks linguistic and textual support'.

should be seen in the light of that material. This gives the belly-phrases a different ring. Understanding these terms only in the light of Paul's theology runs the risk of losing the allusive element in his language. We can only be alerted to the allusiveness of Paul's language if we see the texts in the light of the broader material available in antiquity. It is my conviction that Paul's texts on the belly communicate on a wider basis, which is not sufficiently described by mere reference to his own theology.

Sex or genitals

The stomach is a euphemism for the sexual organ, similar to the use of σκεῦος in 1 Thess. 4:4.[12] This view has been advocated in a special way by Chris Mearns. He says that 'both κοιλία and αἰσχύνη are euphemisms for the circumcised male organ',[13] and as such a hostile reference to circumcision. Mearns' interpretation is thus not far from the food laws interpretation mentioned above. He considers Gal. 6:12–17, about those who 'look good in the flesh', to be the closest parallel to both Phil. 3 and Rom. 16. The belly may, therefore, be replaced by the flesh and more especially circumcision. Mearns holds that this meaning of κοιλία is widely attested in the LXX.[14]

Comments

Here the rhetorical function of κοιλία is dismissed. In Paul's two relevant texts, the stomach belongs to a polemical rhetorical strategy. Furthermore, the LXX references are entirely different in nature. As rightly pointed out by Gordon D. Fee,[15] the Old Testament material refers to 'the fruit of the loins'. In 2 Sam 7:12 LXX, κοιλία is connected to the family. In 2 Sam 16:11 LXX, it refers to David's son, who has come forth from his own κοιλία; his life or loins. In other words, the Old Testament texts invoked by Mearns belong within the rhetoric of 'where life begins', and are irrelevant to the Pauline texts in question. Mearns may, however, still be right in bringing sexual aspects into the picture, although this has to be done on different terms.

Gluttony or greed

In Paul's references to serving or worshipping the belly, stomach is a metonym for unbridled sensuality, with the emphasis on gluttony or

---

[12] For σκεῦος as the male organ, see Torleiv Elgvin, 'Vessel'.

[13] Chris Mearns, 'Opponents at Philippi', p. 198.   14 Ibid. pp. 198–200.

[15] Gordon D. Fee, *Philippians*, p. 371 n. 36.

greed.[16] This is certainly the most straightforward reading of these texts, but even so, this interpretation can be supported in various ways. It can be substantiated by means of similar expressions in ancient Graeco-Roman material, or it can be seen as a typically Jewish idiom.[17]

Comments

Compared with the other interpretations, this derives strength from being so uncomplicated. It concurs with a major concern in the Pauline literature; but is that sufficient fully to explain the rhetoric of the texts in question? The question of a Graeco-Roman background or a Jewish idiom is very much the same as how Paul's addressees perceived these short remarks of the apostle. Finding the proper background is crucial, owing to the brevity of Paul's belly-dicta. These are so brief that we must depend on analogical expressions in interpreting them. This investigation will argue that the Graeco-Roman material is of the utmost importance.

Avoiding martyrdom

According to Ernst Lohmeyer, Paul's Epistle to the Philippians prepares his addressees for martyrdom. When he urges them to imitate himself, this involves willingness to face death. Phil. 3:17–18 speaks of a contrast with respect to the cross of Jesus Christ; hence both verses speak in terms of walking. The martyrs and those prepared for martyrdom have taken upon themselves the cross, while the belly-devotees seek to escape it. They therefore have their belly as their god.[18] Lohmeyer says that Phil. 3:19 refers to those who seek to escape martyrdom, since they are also called 'enemies of the cross'.

Comments

Lohmeyer's thesis does not relate to the term κοιλία as such, but he sees the term as a metaphor for a selfish life, governed by the wish to safeguard oneself above anything else. Although Lohmeyer is not in touch with the term itself, nor its cultural allusiveness, he may still be not far from the rhetorical strategy in which the term is embedded in

---

[16] See e.g. Martin Dibelius, *Philipper*, p. 71; Robert Jewett, 'Conflicting Movements', pp. 379–82.
[17] This is claimed by Brian Rosner, who has kindly given me a copy of his presentation of the two relevant Pauline texts in his forthcoming study on greed in the New Testament.
[18] Ernst Lohmeyer, *Philipper*, pp. 152–6.

Philippians. His interpretation raises the question to what extent the stomach has become a metaphor. But what, then, is it a metaphor for?

This survey of previous research demonstrates that attempts have been made to place the belly-dicta within a context of wider Pauline themes, such as his opposition to Jewish dietary laws or circumcision, his theology of the flesh, his concept of imitating Christ in terms of suffering. In this way the contributions have taken some important steps towards rooting belly-worship in Paul's theology. The problem is, however, that although belly-worship needs to be seen in a wider Pauline perspective, it cannot be seen merely in a Pauline context. This misses the aspects of contemporary culture which, in my view, are inherent in what he says about belly-worship. This investigation will demonstrate that Paul did not coin this phrase; he made use of a commonly held view on the stomach. To elucidate that background is, therefore, necessary to seeing how it enters his own theology. The cultural background inherent in major Pauline themes has been neglected by scholars. I therefore consider it vital to understand this background in order to place it correctly in Paul's theology on the body.

It is the thesis of this study that Paul is using a traditional idiom, a *topos* or a literary commonplace attested in ancient Graeco-Roman sources, and appropriated in Jewish sources as well. It is wise to make an independent investigation of this before moving into how the idiom of 'serving the belly' works in Paul's letters; otherwise we will easily miss in what way his remarks on the belly made sense to his ancient readers. Paul draws heavily on concepts that were firmly established in the Graeco-Roman world. To substantiate this is the task of Part 2 in this study.

1.3   Methodological considerations

Paul's few references on belly-worship are in brief and coded language. It is, therefore, difficult to extract meaning directly from them. The brevity of his language makes them more difficult to interpret. The scarcity of information in the texts themselves, is, of course, the reason that they appear so enigmatic to the scholars. The only way to overcome this, is to view the Pauline texts in the light of contemporary texts providing similar dicta. In the scholarly literature some references from ancient texts are mentioned, usually contained in parentheses in most commentaries. These are, however, not elaborated on, nor is the extensiveness of this material worked out. Thus, rooting Paul's texts in Graeco-Roman material is nothing new. The new thing is to do this in a more determined and elaborated way than before. This justifies the relatively extensive presentation of background material in this study.

Since Paul is not alone in antiquity in speaking of the stomach in a negative way, we must therefore ask to what the belly refers elsewhere. Are we dealing with a kind of *topos*, a common way of describing a certain lifestyle and attitude? Abraham J. Malherbe defines *topoi* as subjects appearing with some regularity.[19] This may refer to subjects of common interest and treatment, such as περὶ οἰκονομίας or περὶ φιλίας, proverbs or maxims,[20] short teachings as well as common examples and figures of speech.[21] It is the conviction of the present writer that 'having the stomach as god' belongs within the category of commonplaces in antiquity. To substantiate this is, of course, the aim of Part 2 in this study.

What is the benefit or use of labelling Paul's belly-sayings a *topos*? In the words of Malherbe:

> This approach, which moves beyond the listing of 'parallels', and uses *topoi* to construct a real world in which people lived, points in the direction of future research . . . The elimination or modification by the New Testament writers of standard parts of a *topos* would be especially significant.[22]

Paul embarks on a communication with his readers; a dialogue with silent elements – especially to us who are not familiar with the culture in which such commonplaces worked. Looking for analogous sayings in the ancient sources enables us to see how Paul's contemporaries might have read his belly-dicta; we need to define the knowledge of the *topos* which may exist among his addressees. This gives us access to what sense Paul's dicta made to his readers. Seeing 'having the belly as god' as a *topos* brings to our awareness the communicative competence of Paul's ancient readers. To a modern reader the stomach or the belly may give a different set of ideas. Investigation of the ancient material will provide historical guidance for understanding the belly-dicta.

The investigation will then proceed to study how this material has been appropriated in a Jewish setting. Emphasis is given to Philo as well as 3 and 4 Maccabees. By giving the Alexandrian Jew, Philo, a prominent place in our discussion we hope to bridge the gap between the

---

[19]   Abraham J. Malherbe, 'Hellenistic Moralists', pp. 320–5.

[20]   For example 'having all things in common'; see Karl Olav Sandnes, *A New Family*, pp. 139–41.

[21]   For example the philosopher as a physican; see Abraham J. Malherbe, *Moral Exhortation*, pp. 26, 43–4, 49, 52, 64, 70.

[22]   Abraham J. Malherbe, 'Hellenistic Moralists', p. 325.

Graeco-Roman material and Paul; for in Philo the Graeco-Roman material on the stomach has undergone a biblical filtering. Philo provides a lot of relevant material, but this has hardly been noticed. Thus we are paving the way for a new reading of the relevant Pauline passages. Finally, our exegesis of the Pauline texts will be tested by turning to the early interpreters of these texts; i.e. the Patristic evidence will be investigated to see how the belly-phrases were perceived in generations that were close to Paul both in time and culture. This is necessary since Patristic literature has played a significant role in shaping the debate on the two Pauline texts in question, particularly among advocates of the food law interpretation (see 1.2).

It would, however, be illegitimate to transfer all possible meanings or potential inherent in the *topos* to any text; i.e to the relevant Pauline texts. James Barr has coined the term 'illegitimate totality transfer', which he defines as 'the error that arises, when the "meaning" of a word (understood as the total series of relations in which it is used in the literature) is read into a particular case'.[23] The warning issued by Barr is relevant indeed to this study. The material on the belly found in ancient sources cannot be transferred all at once and without further ado to the Pauline passages. Emphasis has to be given to how Paul modifies the *topos*; how it is moulded into his theology and instruction.

The Pauline texts to be investigated are, of course, Phil. 3:19 and Rom. 16:18 in their immediate contexts. These are the two instances where Paul addresses those whose belly is their god, or those who have committed themselves to the stomach. To be added are, however, some related texts, such as 1 Cor. 6:13: 'Food is meant for the stomach and the stomach for food.' This enigmatic verse is usually seen as a Corinthian slogan; therefore many translations render the verse as a quotation – as does the *NRSV*, which is quoted here. Paul's quotations from the Old Testament in 1 Cor. 10:7 ('The people sat down to eat and drink, and they rose up to play') as well as in 1 Cor. 15:32 ('Let us eat and drink, for tomorrow we die') may also have some bearing on our topic. The interpretation of the two belly-dicta in Paul's letters as well as the background material provided in this investigation suggests a renewed look at these Corinthian texts.

Since worshipping the belly is obviously negative to Paul, the impression arises that he is referring to opponents. The scholarly literature fully demonstrates that these texts have been seen as part of a polemic in which Paul is targeting his opponents. No doubt there is a lot to

---

[23] James Barr, *Semantics*, p. 218.

recommend such a conclusion. Paul might be blackening opponents, but he is surely making more out of these dicta than mere polemics. The belly-references enter his own instruction, and thus become not only part of a rhetorical strategy, but a theological conviction as well. By speaking of a rhetorical strategy in which Paul's belly-dicta are embedded, our study focuses on how this maxim is used in its literary setting; i.e. focus is rather on pragmatic textual observations than on gleaning information about opponents.[24] Having done so, we proceed to the question of how the references to belly-worship work within Pauline theology.

This contradicts a commonly held view, namely that accusing opponents of moral depravity was a rhetorical device to undermine their authority. It was nothing but a 'stereotyped technique of vilification'.[25] Scholars arguing this case are certainly right in pointing out that the rhetoric of vilification is by no means an objective description of opponents. But they still assume the presence of opponents, and read Paul's text as mirroring a conflict with opponents. Their emphasis on opponents easily leads them to dismiss the way Paul is deploying this rhetoric. This study argues that the rhetoric of the belly has entered his own instruction and forms a significant component of his conception of proper Christian lifestyle. It becomes a building block of his theology, albeit a small one. If focus is on Paul rather than his assumed opponents, the interpretation of this rhetoric has to move beyond the point of labelling it a technique of moral derogation.

1.4   Belly and body – the Pauline context of the study

It is the conviction of the present investigation that, although belly-worship in Paul's letters is rightly seen as a commonplace of ancient moral philosophy, sometimes even as rhetoric with which to vilify opponents, it is still deeply embedded in his theology of the human body. We will now give some thought, therefore, to how Paul conceived of the believer's body. This is hardly a topic *per se* in his letters, but his basic convictions can still be gleaned from his epistles. What he says about the stomach works within a set of presuppositions about the body. Our investigation into the belly-dicta will proceed letter by letter. In order to provide a Pauline context for the investigation, the study of the individual belly-texts will be followed by attempts to sketch a body-theology in

---

[24] A warning not to take polemic in antiquity at face value has been issued by Luke T. Johnson, 'Conventions of Ancient Polemic'.

[25] Andrie du Toit, 'Vilification', pp. 408–9; Lauri Thurén, 'Hey Jude!', pp. 457–9.

these letters individually, within which the references to the belly are at home. The present introductory presentation of Paul's body-theology is, however, of a general kind, thus providing a Pauline context or framework for the investigation. In this presentation I limit myself to the letters whose authenticity is not disputed.

As a Jew and former Pharisee, Paul was certainly not indifferent to bodily questions. His Jewish heritage, with its focus on clean and unclean, the purity laws, implied a strong concern for bodily boundaries. This concern was, of course, strengthened by circumcision and dietary laws, both of which were intimately connected to how Jewish traditions conceived of the human body. Since these regulations were also markers of Jewish identity *vis-à-vis* Gentiles,[26] the body was equally a sign of identity. In his theology, Paul is very much concerned with reassessing these bodily signs, to the extent of abandoning them. Thus his view on the body becomes a matter of significance, since it developed from the very heart of his theology; i.e. how to define the identity of Christian believers.[27] Paul's concern for the holiness of the body of believers can be discerned from his first letter and throughout: 'May the God of peace himself sanctify (ἁγιάσαι) you entirely; and may your spirit and soul and body be kept sound and blameless (τὸ πνεῦμα καὶ ἡ ψυχὴ καὶ τὸ σῶμα ἀμέμπτως) at the coming of our Lord Jesus Christ' (1 Thess. 5:23, cf. 3:13).

Paul had received disturbing news about his recent converts in Corinth. The reports described a rejection of traditional moral discipline that expressed itself in illicit sexual practices (1 Cor. 5–6), in participation in temple meals (1 Cor. 8 and 10), in discrimination at the Lord's Table (1 Cor. 11), and in questioning the belief in a future resurrection (1 Cor. 15). These issues all raised the question of how Christian faith affected bodily practices. In this situation, therefore, Paul's argument centres around the question of the body for the first time, as well as most extensively, in his letters.[28] Paul not only portrays the Corinthian church as God's temple, but makes the believers individually the dwelling of His Spirit. They are the temple of God since His Spirit dwells in them; i.e. in their σῶμα (1 Cor. 3:16–17; 6:19–20; 2 Cor. 6:16, cf. Rom. 8:29). Paul thereby puts the emphasis on their unity, the lordship of God as well as their holiness; by implication the believers are urged to avoid practices which can destroy

---

[26] See e.g. James D. G. Dunn, 'New Perspective'.

[27] Peter Brown, *Body and Society*, pp. 45–6 similarly starts his presentation of Paul's view on the body with his grappling with the question of how to define God's people.

[28] Thus Robert Jewett, *Paul's Anthropological Terms*, pp. 254–5. See also chap. 10.5 of this study.

the temple of God.[29] Destroying God's holy dwelling implies the danger of polluting the sacred. This pollution takes place through the lifestyle in which Corinthian believers participated. Since Paul feared pollution, he was concerned about maintaining the boundaries of his converts. He urges them to keep away from Christian brothers who commit *porneia*, incest or other vices characteristic of their pagan past (1 Cor. 5:1–13, cf. 2 Cor. 6:14–16).

Furthermore, the notion of the body as a temple brings to mind sacrifices, which in Paul's case means a worship which involves σῶμα, i.e. '... to present your bodies as a living sacrifice, holy and acceptable to God, which is your spiritual worship (παραστῆσαι τὰ σώματα ὑμῶν θυσίαν ζῶσαν ἁγίαν εὐάρεστον τῷ θεῷ, τὴν λογικὴν λατρείαν ὑμῶν)' (Rom. 12:1). Although Paul here extends the meaning of sacrifice in a figurative way, his reference to σῶμα is unmistakable: bodies are to be sacrificed; the body with all its practices is to be dedicated to God on a daily basis. As an offering to God, the believer's body is placed entirely under God's control and at his disposal, 'so that it could no longer be used for normal purposes'.[30] Conceiving of the body in sacrificial terms implies that it will be used up in service, just as offerings are consumed in the temples. Many scholars claim that in Rom. 12:1, as well as in related texts such as Phil. 1:20, σῶμα denotes the whole being of Paul, not a part of him; it is thus a simple anthropological term.[31] This interpretation can surely be supported by reference to Paul's emphasis on a total commitment, but it nevertheless tends to neglect the physical involvement in Paul's sayings on σῶμα.[32] Paul has in mind the bodily consequences of faith, i.e. the physical embodiment of the true worship mentioned in Rom. 12:1–2. This is suggested by his distinction between body and mind.[33] The apostle often refers to the deterioration of his body due to the sufferings which his ministry brings upon him (2 Cor. 4:7–12; Phil. 2:17).

---

[29] James D. G. Dunn, *Romans 1–8*, p. 420: 'Paul perhaps chooses the verb (οἰκέω) here to mark off the lordship which should characterize the Christian.'

[30] Robert Jewett, *Paul's Anthropological Terms*, p. 301; cf. James D. G. Dunn, *Theology of Paul*, pp. 543–8.

[31] This has been argued by e.g. Eduard Schweizer, 'σῶμα', pp. 1065–6; Rudolf Bultmann, *New Testament Theology*, pp. 192–203; also recently Douglas J. Moo, *Romans*, pp. 750–1. In his critical assessment of this holistic interpretation, Robert H. Gundry, *Sōma*, pp. 3–8 describes the scholarly debate: '... it has become orthodoxy among NT theologians to say that in Pauline literature, and perhaps elsewhere as well, *sōma* frequently and characteristically refers to the whole person rather than especially, or exclusively, to the body' (p. 5).

[32] This has been forcefully argued by Robert H. Gundry, *Sōma*; see also T. J. Deidun, *New Covenant Morality*, p. 98.

[33] Thus also Robert H. Gundry, *Sōma*, pp. 34–6.

'Paul brings here [in Rom. 12:1] to a climax that peculiar insistence upon the somatic character of redemption in Rom. 6–8',[34] to which we will return soon.

Paul's view on the body is closely connected with the major pattern of transition in his theology: before versus now or after (Gal. 1:23; 1 Cor. 6:9–11; cf. Eph. 2:11–13).[35] The believers have turned their backs to their pagan past. Their former life Paul characterizes in the list of vices; e.g. 1 Cor. 6:9–11 where emphasis is given to illicit sexual activities, idolatry, greed, and other misdeeds. These sins are all mentioned in texts structured according to the pattern of past–now; such was their former life, such are they now. Paul's instructions in 1 Thess. 4:3–8 are for example dependent upon the transition which has taken place in the life of the believers. This transition has bodily consequences; emphasis is given to questions of sex. Believers have a lifestyle separating them from their pagan past. Their sanctification is to the forefront here; they have been set apart from the Gentiles, and a relapse into that past lifestyle pollutes their holiness. Hence, Paul is concerned about their purity, which implies boundaries in terms of a lifestyle setting them apart from paganism.[36] Believers who do not accept these boundaries bring, as we saw, defilement and pollution upon themselves and the Christian fellowship, but furthermore, they confuse their identity.

In Rom. 1:18–32 bodily sins are seen as examples of the idolatry that characterizes pagan life. Pagans exchange God the Maker for his creatures. From this develop various idolatrous ways of living in which the body is dishonoured. Thus the body can be involved in idolatry. A key-word is the bodily ἐπιθυμία which here has an obvious negative sense (Rom. 1:24, cf. 1.27); it refers to the desire for something forbidden, and is closely associated with the flesh (σάρξ).[37] The former life of his converts Paul can describe as κατὰ σάρκα (Rom. 8:4–5; 2 Cor. 10:2, cf. Gal. 6:7–8) which in Gal. 5:16–21 appears as enslavement to vices, among which a number can be associated with desires deriving from the belly.[38] Pagans and Christians can thus, according to Paul, be distinguished by

[34] Robert Jewett, *Paul's Anthropological Terms*, p. 302.
[35] Cf. Philo on conversion; chap. 7.9 in this study; Eph. 2:3; 4:22; Tit. 3:3 in which passions and the uncontrolled desires of the body are something which the believers have left behind. Worth mentioning is here also Rom. 7:24 where Paul speaks of redemption from τὸ σῶμα τοῦ θανάτου as opposed to Rom. 12:1 where σῶμα has become the centre of Christian worship.
[36] This is emphasised by Dale B. Martin, *Corinthian Body*, see e.g. pp. 163–4, 168–71, 197.
[37] James D. G. Dunn, *Theology of Paul*, pp. 120–1.
[38] This will be substantiated fully throughout this study.

their attitudes to their bodies. This has to do with the fundamental distinction in his theology between Flesh and Spirit. Dale B. Martin calls it Paul's apocalyptic dualism.[39] Paul's thoughts about the human body derive from the concept of the flesh as constantly waging war against the divinely given Spirit, which means the believers' participation in Christ's glorified body. The believers have passed from the enslavement of sin and the desires of the body to obedience and righteousness:

> Therefore, do not let sin exercise dominion in your mortal bodies, to make you obey their passions. No longer present your members to sin as instruments of wickedness, but present yourselves to God as those who have been brought from death to life, and present your members to God as instruments of righteousness. For sin will have no dominion over you since you are not under the law, but under grace. (Rom. 6:12–14)

Baptism releases from any obligation to the flesh (cf. Rom. 8:12). These texts from Romans address the question of the body from the perspective of 'who is in control'. This is clearly seen in the verbs applied here: βασιλεύειν, ὑπακούειν, κυριεύειν, ὑπὸ . . . εἶναι, ὀφειλήτης εἶναι. Obviously, to Paul the body with its members was in need of control; it was either ministering to righteousness or obeying the desires. What Paul here says about the body is entirely dependent upon his distinction between law and grace. In Romans this implies that Paul is not preoccupied with the flesh solely as the source of desire or evil sensuality; the logic of Rom. 6 is directed at Jewish piety as well, in which the body is offered hope if maintained in accordance with customs laid down in the Law. But the Law has, according to Paul, no power over the passions deriving from the body (cf. Rom. 8:3). The power of desires surpasses that of the Law. Hence, the Law and commandments cannot fight the bodily desires. Although the Law points out what desire is, it is unable to change the fact that ἐπιθυμία is a fundamental aspect of human life.[40] Sin has taken advantage of the Law and produces desires in all human beings. Such is Paul's argument in Rom. 7:5, 7–13, which also brings to mind the human condition of despair in Rom. 1:18–3:20. This situation in which the human body finds itself is, therefore, not adequately dealt with by merely calling for control and self-mastery. To Paul passions and mastery are only dealt with by being crucified with Christ; this is what Rom. 6 is all about. Christ

[39] See e.g. Dale B. Martin, *Corinthian Body*, e.g. pp. 172, 176.
[40] This is vividly depicted in Rom. 7:14–25; see Stanley K. Stowers, *Romans*, pp. 260–4; Karl Olav Sandnes, *Tidens Fylde*, pp. 196–7.

is not an example of self-mastery to the believers; they can only master their bodies thanks to their participation in his death and resurrection.[41] The same logic is found in Gal. 5:24. 'And those who belong to Christ have crucified the flesh with its παθήμασιν and ἐπιθυμίαις.'

In Rom. 13:11–14, however, the flesh appears in a *paraenetic* section. The flesh belongs to the deeds of darkness, which are exemplified in terms of revelling, drunkenness, debauchery, licentiousness, quarrelling, and jealousy (v. 13). These are terms which Paul elsewhere refers to the pagan past of his readers; but here he still considers it possible for believers to be committed to the flesh: '. . . and make no provision for the flesh, to gratify its desires (καὶ τῆς σαρκὸς πρόνοιαν μὴ ποιεῖσθε εἰς ἐπιθυμίας)' (v. 14). Christians risk caring for the body in a way which arouses fleshly desires. The body can be treated as both a brothel and a temple. This is the reason why mastery of passions was still of relevance to Christians. According to Gal. 5:16–17, the spiritual life involves opposition to the desires of the flesh; the believer is caught in a continuous struggle between Flesh and Spirit. Paul was aware that his gospel, with its abandonment of physical circumcision as well as the purity laws, could be seen as inviting desires. He therefore warns against using the freedom as an opportunity for self-indulgence (εἰς ἀφορμὴν τῇ σαρκί) (Gal. 5:13). In a situation which aroused ἐπιθυμίαι of various kinds (1 Cor. 8–10),[42] Paul speaks of himself as an example worthy of imitation (1 Cor. 9:24–7; 11:1). His ministry is depicted in terms of athletes, a well-known model of self-control.[43] When his example is applied to the questions of desire which Paul addresses in 1 Cor. 8–10, it becomes an example of fighting desires related to eating; i.e. participation at meals in the temple, eating food purchased in the market, and accepting invitations: 'I punish my body and enslave it (ὑπωπιάζω μου τὸ σῶμα καὶ δουλαγωγῶ)' (1 Cor. 9:27).[44]

The body was located at the centre of Paul's thoughts about the future. In Rom. 8 he describes how the entire creation is longing for freedom, which implies longing for 'the redemption of our bodies (ἀπεκδεχόμενοι, τὴν ἀπολύτρωσιν τοῦ σώματος ἡμῶν)' (Rom. 8:21–23).[45] This hope for the body will one day come true; the indwelling of the Spirit guarantees this (2 Cor. 1:22; 5:5). The indwelling Spirit meant a participation in the body of Christ. This is the bottom line in Paul's argument in 1 Cor. 6: 12–20: 'The man's body is therefore an appendage of Christ's body'.[46]

---

[41] So also Stanley K. Stowers, *Romans*, pp. 255–8.   [42] See later in this study.
[43] More on this later in this study.   [44] More on this in chap. 10.4 of this study.
[45] For a recent discussion of this passage, see J. Ramsey Michaels, 'Redemption of Our Body'.
[46] Dale B. Martin, *Corinthian Body*, p. 176.

The believers share in the Spirit which is characteristic of Christ's resurrected body: 'If the Spirit of him who raises Jesus from the dead dwells in you, he who raised Christ from the dead will give life to your mortal bodies also through his Spirit that dwells in you' (Rom. 8:11). This is Paul's apocalyptic dualism. The Christian body is in a transition, a process of being conformed to Christ's glorious body: 'He will transform the body of our humiliation that it may be conformed to the body of his glory, by the power that also enables him to make all things subject to himself' (Phil. 3:21; cf. 1 Cor. 15:49; Rom. 6:5; 8:29). It is probably worth noting that this verse is found in the immediate context of Paul's most obvious dictum about belly-worship. Furthermore, the immediate context speaks also of sharing Christ's suffering and thus becoming like him in his death, as well as sharing in his resurrection (Phil. 3:10–11).

Paul speaks of this process in terms of a transformation so as to become fully like Christ's glorious body. This transformation is already under way in terms of an inner renewal and outward decay (2 Cor. 3:18; 4:16; Gal. 4:19; Rom. 12:2). Paul addresses this most directly in 2 Cor. 4:16–5:5.[47] The inner renewal represents the first step towards being transformed into the resurrection body. The body shares in the glorious body of Christ, but this implies a decay of the body as well, i.e. experiences of suffering and impending death (e.g. 2 Cor. 4:10–11, 16–17; Rom. 8:10–13 and Phil. 3:10). Sharing in Christ's glorious body cannot be separated from sharing in his sufferings. The decay of the body in terms of suffering was to Paul a necessary preparation for the future glorious body. His own experiences due to his apostolic ministry were a constant reminder of this. He considered his apostolic sufferings applicable to all believers: 'For if we have been united with him in a death like his, we will certainly be united with him in a resurrection like his' (Rom. 6:5). Although in Rom. 6 Paul does not mention suffering as such, since death with Christ here primarily applies to the power of sin, there can hardly be any doubt that he considered being crucified with Christ a reference to daily experiences of agony, suffering, and opposition. This is implied in his emphasis on taking Christ as an example (e.g. 1 Cor. 11:1, Phil. 2:4–11). Crucifixion and death thus marked continuous bodily experiences to the believers in their process of being transformed. Inner renewal and outward decay of the body were thus two sides of being united with Christ.

The apocalyptic dualism in Paul's body-theology implies that a process of heavenly origin is making its way through the earthly body, thus

---

[47] For a discussion of this text, see James D. G. Dunn, *Theology of Paul*, pp. 489–90 with references.

making the body an arena for a cosmic struggle. The end and goal of this process is the resurrection of the body, as depicted in 1 Cor. 15. This process of transformation brings an end to the earthly body, replacing it with a different kind of bodily existence; i.e. heavenly bodies. From his analogies in 1 Cor. 15:36–41, Paul deduces that bodies are appropriate to the world in which they belong. The nature of the resurrected body is, therefore, defined in terms of heavenly embodiments (1 Cor. 15:48–50). The resurrected body does not consist of the perishable σάρξ or σῶμα, but of a body appropriate to the world of the Spirit.[48] Paul thus thinks of the body in terms both of an earthly identity that is perishable, and a heavenly identity that is inner and spiritual, and thus less visible, but which will transform the whole body to become like Christ's glorious body.

In short, then, what is Paul's view of the body? Owing to theological controversies in which he became embroiled about the identity of his converts, the body ranked high on Paul's theological agenda. It is by no means a matter of indifference. Matters of body and lifestyle distinguished believers from their past pagan life. Thus the body became a sign of distinction to Paul. Most characteristically he employs this in speaking of the body as the dwelling of the Spirit. From this concept most of his sayings relevant to the body can be derived. In conceiving of the Christians' body as God's temple, Paul reminds them of God's lordship and presence in their life. They share in Christ's glorious body, which will be enjoyed in full at the resurrection and which provides an appropriate heavenly body. In their present life, believers are preparing themselves for this full transformation. This preparation takes place in service and ministry, which in the end consumes the body; thus suffering and impending death serve the process of transformation. In this process there is a constant danger of polluting the holy body by returning to the lifestyle of the past and by caring for the body in a way which stimulates defiling desires to take control. Paul seems to be more concerned to stress the dangers lurking in the needs of the body, particularly sex,[49] than to

---

[48] For the resurrected body see Eduard Schweizer, 'σῶμα', pp. 1060–2; Edvin Larsson, *Christus als Vorbild*, pp. 3037–323; Dale B. Martin, *Corinthian Body*, pp. 123–9.

[49] Dale B. Martin, 'Paul without Passion', argues that the apostle nowhere mentions a positive kind of desire as being fulfilled in marriage. Martin claims that Paul urged married couples to have sexual intercourse 'in the absence of sexual passion and desire' (p. 202). Marriage was to Paul a tool or means of guarding against desire (p. 207). That Paul urges Christian men to find wives not in the passion of desire (1 Thess. 4:5) does not necessarily mean that sex should be practised without any affection when married (cf. Martin's *Corinthian Body*, pp. 206, 209). According to 1 Cor. 7:5 sex in marriage is seen as a cure for desire. But how can it be so, if it is practised devoid of any affection? Somehow

repeat his Jewish theology of creation.[50] The question of food and hence the stomach do not receive that much attention. But as we will see later in this study, sex and food are not to be entirely separated.

It is my conviction that Paul's dicta on belly-worship are not sufficiently accounted for by labelling them a rhetoric of vilification. I expect them somehow to be related to Paul's thoughts on the believer's body. This expectation is, of course, in need of substantiation. As we now proceed, and particularly when we address the Pauline texts, we will constantly keep this broader framework in mind: Do belly-worship and body in any way relate?

Paul considered and even accepted (not very enthusiastically though) that the power of sexual love, which easily slid into temptation of dangerous desire, met some satisfaction in marital sex. Martin's argument leaves Paul's logic void on this point. Marriage is to Paul clearly a subsidiary option, but it brings a satisfaction which makes adultery appear unnecessary. In this way it is a prophylaxis against adultery. I think Peter Brown, *Body and Society*, p. 55 is correct in saying 'By this essentially negative, even alarmist, strategy, Paul left a fatal legacy to future ages.' Eph. 5 as well as the Pastoral Epistles, which both belong in a wider Pauline tradition, would, of course, balance this picture of 1 Cor. 7.

[50] Exceptions are e.g. Phil. 4:11–12, where both want and abundance are seen as blessings of God, and 1 Cor. 10:26, 30.

PART 2

The Graeco-Roman belly

It has already been claimed that to 'have the belly as god', or to be 'enslaved to the stomach' *et cetera* are commonplaces of ancient literature. This implies that Paul's readers are likely to have recognized his dicta in Phil. 3:19 and Rom. 16:18, as well as some other texts, as familiar. It remains to substantiate this claim, and to see how this *topos* was used. From the very outset we should expect various nuances to appear in the material. Parts 2 and 3 will thus lay bare the contemporary reader competence available, and hence also the competence of Paul's readers. The material presented in the following chapters enables us to read the Pauline texts with a new awareness, and thus in Part 4 to see more clearly how the Pauline belly-dicta are embedded in his rhetorical strategy in their immediate context as well as in his body-theology.

In many texts, of course, the stomach refers in a strict physical sense to the need for nutrition. It has a quite physical meaning, one fills the stomach in order to maintain life. The concern of Part 2 is texts where this vital necessity appears in a negative light, as a codeword for a lifestyle and an attitude to be criticised. The aim is to provide a sufficient basis for the study to continue into the Pauline texts, but in order to prove the existence of a *topos* about the belly, it is necessary to cover a wide range of material.

To avoid making this a study of greed in general, we will restrict ourselves to how ancient writers perceived the stomach, and in particular will look for analogies to the phrases 'having the belly as god', 'being devoted to the stomach' and the like. This cannot mean, however, that the belly can be isolated from body ideology in antiquity. To this we therefore turn first.

2

THE BELLY AS A SIGN – ANCIENT PHYSIOGNOMICS

2.0   Introduction

In most languages the human body or parts of it can be referred to symbolically as well. The body becomes a vehicle for describing attitudes, characters and lifestyle. Furthermore, body language is to a great extent dependent upon the culture. Behind the use of the human body or parts of it as shorthand for various kinds of character lies the conviction that some sort of correspondence exists between body and character. We have already seen (chap. 1.4) that Paul considered bodily matters as a boundary marker, thus creating signs of identity for believers *vis-à-vis* paganism. This leads us to consider ancient theories about the sign-nature of the body. In the Graeco-Roman world it was the task of ancient physiognomics to point out and to describe the correlation between the bodily appearance and the inner character of a person.

Physiognomics was a quasi-science devoted to working out methods and signs indicative of the relationship between physique and character.[1] According to Elizabeth C. Evans, this ancient science 'enjoyed a far greater popularity among Greek and Roman writers, especially those of later Greek society and Roman Empire, than has generally been supposed. As a quasi-science, it always bore a close relationship to the science of medicine; as an art, to the practice of rhetoric. It has also an obvious kinship with the field of ancient portraiture.'[2] A systematic treatment of such material is found in the technical handbooks, of which the

---

[1] For a presentation of ancient physiognomics, see Elizabeth C. Evans, *Physiognomics* and Maud W. Gleason, *Making Men*, pp. 29–54; cf. also Dale B. Martin, *Corinthian Body*, pp. 15–21.

[2] Elizabeth C. Evans, *Physiognomics*, p. 5. Evans demonstrates the appearance of physiognomic consciousness in writers such as Plato, Aristotle, Cicero, and Seneca. Physiognomic material is found in philosophical treatises, drama, rhetorical handbooks and practice, biographies and epic literature. See also Tamsyn S. Barton, *Power and Knowledge*, pp. 95–132. Even the Qumran texts base spiritual judgements on physical appearance (4Q 186 and 4Q 561); see Philip S. Alexander, 'Physiognomy'.

Pseudo-Aristotelian *Physiognomonica*[3] (third century BC) and the work of Polemon Rhetor of Laodicea, *De Physiognomonica*[4] (second century AD), are the most relevant to the time investigated in this study.[5]

The Pseudo-Aristotelian treatise starts by pointing out the basic conviction of this science:

> Dispositions (διάνοιαι) follow bodily characteristics and are not in themselves unaffected by bodily impulses. This is obvious in the case of drunkenness and illness; for it is evident that dispositions are changed considerably by bodily affections (ὑπὸ τῶν τοῦ σώματος παθημάτων). Conversely, that the body suffers sympathetically with affections of the soul is evident in love, fear, grief and pleasure (τὰς ἡδονάς). But it is especially in the creations of nature that one can see how body and soul interact with each other, so that each is mainly responsible for the other's affections.   (*Physiognomonica* 805a1–11)[6]

The text goes on to say that a disposition of the soul is always followed by a given form (σῶμα). This can most clearly be judged in animals. In them the close connection between dispositions or characters and the physical appearance is revealed.[7] The task of physiognomics is to work out this index between character and body, i.e. to point out and to judge the signs (τὰ σημεῖα) of the body (e.g. *Physiognomonica* 805b31; 807a1; 810a14).

This clearly shows how closely related the science of physiognomics is to rhetoric. For Pseudo-Aristotle, it is possible to judge men's character from their outward appearance:[8] 'It is possible to judge men's character from their physical appearance, if one grants that body and soul change together in all natural affections . . . and also that there is one sign (ἓν ἑνὸς σημεῖον) of one affection, and that we can recognize the affection and sign

---

[3] This is very likely a combination of two treatises, since the discussion starts anew in chap. 4.

[4] For a text edition, see Richard Foerster, *Scriptores Physiognomici Graeci et Latini*. A translation is not available. Some texts from this edition will be translated in this book.

[5] In Galen's medical treatises, this science is demonstrated in full. He makes a sustained effort to study the relationship between character and physique.

[6] Cf. Aristotle's *Nic. Eth.* 1123b1–7; 1128a8–13, and also Sextus Empiricus (2nd cent. AD), *Pyrrhonism* 1:85: 'Seeing, then, that men vary so much in body – to content ourselves with but a few instances of the many collected by the Dogmatics – men probably also differ from one another in respect of the soul itself; for the body is a kind of expression (τύπος) of the soul, as in fact is proved by the science of physiognomy.'

[7] The nature of the animals holds a key position in this literature; see e.g. Plato, *Phaedo* 81e–82a; Aristotle, *Analytica Priora* 70b15–32; *Historia Animalium* 488b12–17; Sextus Empiricus, *Pyrrhonism* 1:64–8.

[8] For signs as a key notion in rhetoric, see Aristotle, *Rhet.* 1357a–b; 1402b.

proper to each class of creatures, we shall be able to judge character from physical appearance' (*Analytica Priora* 70b7–14). The kinship between physiognomics and rhetoric will be further elaborated below.

On the basis of typical signs, this Pseudo-Aristotelian piece of physiognomic literature describes and values human characteristics. The method is empirical, drawing on sources such as 'movements, shapes and colours, and from habits as appearing in the face, from the growth of hair, from the smoothness of the skin, from voice, from the condition of the flesh, from parts of the body, and from the general character of the body' (*Physiognomonica* 806a28–34).[9]

The science of ancient physiognomics was, as we have touched upon, closely related to rhetoric. It is hardly surprising that a description of a person's outward appearance can serve the purposes of both panegyric and slander.[10] An obvious illustration of the kinship between physiognomics and rhetoric is the vast amount of statues from this period. The statues of antiquity very often carry a political message. They are symbols of power and are thus means of propaganda or rhetoric in a wider sense.[11] Both theory (handbooks) and practice (speeches or biographies) prove the significance physiognomics and rhetoric have for one another.[12] The handbooks develop a terminology for the rhetorical significance of appearance (*ekphrasis, eikonismos, charakterismos*), and this is put into practice in speeches[13] as well as in biographies.

A well-known example of the last category is Suetonius' *De Vita Caesarum* (*Lives of the Caesars*). Suetonius frequently describes the outward appearance of the emperors. A clear example of this is the description of Gaius Caligula:

> He was very tall and extremely pale, with an unshaped body, but very thin neck and legs. His eyes and temples were hollow, his forehead broad and grim, his hairs thin and entirely gone on the top of his head, though his body was hairy. Because of

---

[9] For the detailed working out of these indices and the application of the signs, see *Physiognomonica* 806b7–808b11 and 810a14–814b10.

[10] It is worth quoting what Tamsyn S. Barton, *Power and Knowledge* says about Polemon: 'Looking at Polemo's treatise in its political context illuminates the real point of the work. The examples are not just anecdotes casually thrown in to spice up a dull theoretical treatise; from a political point of view they are what the work is written for. In physiognomics he found a new resource for attacking rivals and enemies' (p. 113).

[11] See Niels Hannestad, *Roman Art*; Paul Zanker, *Power of Images*.

[12] See Elizabeth C. Evans, *Physiognomics*, pp. 39–46 who also gives a number of examples.

[13] See Dio Chrysostom, *Orat.* 33:52–6 who uses the method of physiognomics himself, and who also depicts an expert *in actu*.

this to look upon him from a higher place as he passed by, or for any other reason whatever to mention a goat,[14] was treated as a capital offence. While his face was naturally forbidding and ugly, he purposely made it even more savage, practising all kinds of terrible and fearsome expressions before a mirror. He was sound neither of body nor mind.   (*Caligula* 50)

This description marks a contrast to how Suetonius presents Gaius' father, Germanicus, who 'possessed all the highest qualities of body and mind' (*Caligula* 3).[15] There is hardly any doubt that Suetonius' description of Caligula serves not only the purpose of entertainment, but also to add to the negative view of this emperor, substantiating the overall negative picture by reference to his bodily details.

2.1   The stomach as a sign

Does ancient physiognomy teach us anything on how the stomach was viewed? Was the belly a sign typical of a particular character in this literature? Towards the end of Pseudo-Aristotle's *Physiognomica* it is stated that some parts of the body yield a more precise impression of a person's character: 'The most favourable part for examination is the region round the eyes,[16] forehead, head and face; secondly, the region of the breast and shoulders, and lastly that of the legs and feet; the parts about the belly are of least importance' (*Physiognomonica* 814b1–10). This does not mean, however, that the stomach is of no interest in this literature. The characteristics of a brave man are listed in *Physiognomonica* 807a31–807b4. Among these are mentioned a flat belly (κοιλία πλατεῖα).[17] Of interest is also the way the distance between the navel and the chest is valued. If the distance surpasses the one between the chest and the neck, this is a sign of being gluttonous (βοροί) and insensitive (ἀναίσθητοι), owing to

---

[14] It is typical of physiognomic theory that an animal is mentioned here. Elizabeth C. Evans, *Physiognomics*, pp. 53–6 has worked out in detail how the description of Caligula's body corresponds to the nature of the panther in Pseudo-Aristotle, *Physiognomonica*, 809b37–810a14.

[15] Cf. also Suetonius' descriptions of e.g. Augustus (*Aug.* 79); Tiberius (*Tib.* 68); Claudius (*Claud.* 8.31–3); Nero (*Nero* 51).

[16] More than one-third of the Pseudo-Aristotelian manual concerns the eyes. The primary role of the eyes is witnessed also in Polemon's writings, see Elizabeth C. Evans, *Physiognomics*, p. 12. By far the longest paragraph in the so-called *Anonymous Latin Physiognomy* is devoted to the eyes; for a text edition with French translation, see Jacques André, *Physiognomonie*, pp. 66–85 (§§20–41).

[17] Cf. *Physiognomonica* 807b14 about the man of easy disposition who is not very fat. The ideal is moderation in every respect; Pseudo-Aristotle, *Physiognomonica* 813b30–5.

the size of the organ designed for receiving the food (*Physiognomonica* 810b16, 23). The logic is that if the size of the stomach surpasses what is natural according to its assigned task, it is a sign of gluttony.

In Polemon's treatise on this subject, it becomes evident what a dangerous weapon this science was.[18] He claims that physiognomics cannot rely entirely on the signs, but has to account also for the overall impression left by the body in general; this he calls *epipreia*.[19] Knowledge of this is a paranormal insight, which means that divination becomes an element in this science. Characters such as gentleness or gluttony leave their physical marks. In his treatise, Polemon enumerates the bodily signs by which the spiritual situation of a person can be judged. Let me present some examples, which have some bearing on the stomach in particular:[20]

> Polemon Chap. 14, Vol. 1, p. 210
> On physiognomy and the signs of the stomach:
> The thinness and leanness of the stomach are marks of a healthy mind, greatness in spirit as well as zeal. Excessive slenderness and thinness of the stomach indicate a timid and distorted mind as well as gluttony. A big and fleshy belly, and especially if it is soft and extending downwards, indicates that the lively sexual appetite has been damaged by drunkenness. If it really has a lot of flesh and is solid, leading a vicious life, it is a sign of imitation, dishonest conduct, cunning and no understanding.
>
> Latin text: *De physiognomonia et signis ventris*
> *Tenuitas et exilitas ventris mentis sanitatem et magnitudinem animi et studii notant. Nimia ventris gracilitas et tenuitas timiditatem pravam mentem et gulositatem indicant. Magnitudo et multa caro ventris praesertim cum ei mollities et demissio est,*

[18] For Polemon, see Maud W. Gleason, *Making Men*, pp. 29–54. The textual basis for his treatise is discussed on pp. 30–3; cf. also her 'Semiotics of Gender', p. 413. In the bitter quarrel with Favorinus of Arles, Polemon made use of his insight into this ancient theory. In fighting his opponent, Polemon gives a rather negative description of the eyes and the physical weaknesses of Favorinus. Physiognomy becomes a tool of suspicion; see Elizabeth C. Evans, *Physiognomics*, p. 12 for references about this quarrel. Gleason, *Making Men*, pp. 46–8, 55–81 provides many examples of how Polemon depicts his opponent. For gender-characterization and physiognomy, see Maud W. Gleason, 'Semiotics of Gender'. *The Anonymous Latin Physiognomy* §§3–8 addresses this question in particular.

[19] See Pseudo-Aristotle, *Physiognomonica* 806a28–34 who speaks of the general character of the body. For *epipreia*, see Maud W. Gleason, *Making Men*, pp. 33–6 and Jacques André, *Physiognomonie*, p. 86.

[20] The translations are my own, and are based on the Latin text. The references are to the text edition of Richard Foerster, *Scriptores Physiognomonici Graeci et Latini*.

[animi] mobilis defectum ebrietatem veneris amorem indicant.
Si vero multam carnem habet et robustus est, pravitatem agendi,
simulationem fraudem dolum et nullam intellegentiam indicat.

Chap. 25.7–9, Vol. 1, p. 226
On physiognomy and the sign of the mouth and lips:
... The breadth of the mouth and fleshiness of the lips signify
the desire and ravenous appetite of the belly, and at the same
time an unjust person with no regard for the divine at all.

Latin text: *De physiognomonia et signis oris et labiorum*
Latitudo oris et labii crassities ventris cupidinem et voracitatem
significat, cum simul iniuriosus et valde impius est.

Chap. 35.14–15, Vol. 2, p. 169
On the signs of the voice, breathing and speaking:
The one who has a deep voice, is serving his belly.

Latin text: *Significationes vocis et anhelitus et loquelae*
... qui vocem habet gravem, sui ventris serviens est.

Chap. 40, Vol. 2, p. 171
Signs of the ribs:
The strength of the ribs and a lot of flesh on them declare stu-
pidity. A thin body is a sign of real cunning. A large stomach
shows excess of craving. Thinness of the ribs as well as their
fineness are signs of feebleness of heart.

Latin text: *Significationes costarum*
Costarum fortitudo et super ipsas carnium multitudo stolidi-
tatem declarat. Corporis subtilitas multam significat astutiam.
Ventris magnitudo libidinis declarat nimietatem. Costarum gra-
cilitas atque earundem subtilitas cordis innuit debilitatem.

In his text edition, Richard Foerster has also·included the codex of the so-
called Pseudo-Polemon. Chap. 16 is on the signs of the stomach (Vol. 2,
p. 156): 'A thin stomach indicates a good intellect; a large belly indicates
spending a lot of time at the table.[21] The narrowness and slenderness of
the ribs indicate feebleness of heart'.

[21] *Concubitus* means either the act of lying together (sex), sleeping or dining; see *Oxford Latin Dictionary* s.v.

Latin text: *De signis ventris*
Tenuitas ventris bonitatem intellectus indicat; magnitudo ventris multum concubitum indicat. Angustia et tenuitas costarum debilitatem cordis indicant.

A Greek paraphrase of Polemon's work is available by the hand of Adamantius the Sophist, composed no later than the first part of the fourth century AD:[22]

Adamantius §14, Vol. 1, pp. 361–2
Hollow bellies signify strength of soul and greatness of mind, but the very slim and flat signify cowardice, bad disposition and gluttony. Large and fleshy bellies, if they are soft or hanging down, indicate obtuseness and drunkenness; if they [the stomachs] consist of hard flesh, gluttony and wickedness.

Greek text: Γαστέρες λαγαραὶ εὐρωστίαν ψυχῆς καὶ μεγαλο-φροσύνην σημαίνουσιν, αἱ δὲ ἰσχναὶ πάνυ καὶ κεναὶ δειλίαν καὶ κακοήθειαν καὶ γαστριμαργίαν σημαίνουσι. γαστέρες μεγάλαι σαρκώδεις, εἰ μὲν μαλθακαὶ εἶεν καὶ ἐκκρεμεῖς, ἀναισθησίαν, οἰνο-φλυγίαν, εἰ δὲ σκληραῖς σαρξὶ συμπεπηγυῖαι, γαστριμαργίαν καὶ πανουργίαν ἐμφαίνουσιν.

Adamantius §44, Vol. 1, pp. 408–10
The form of manhood is straight and with a complete even form, sides and limbs of the body entirely powerful; bones large, hair rough, abdomen broad and flat, shoulders strong, shoulder-blades widely separated, chest and back robust, hip-joint strong, legs fleshy, around the ankles strength, feet well-jointed, complexion bright, look melting, fierce, eyes not large, not at all wide open, and definitely not twinkling, eyebrows not strained, forehead neither smooth nor rough, a firmer voice, powerful, and strong, spirit steadfast. Such is the courageous and strong person.

Greek text: Εἶδος οὖν ἀνδρείου ὄρθιον τὸ πᾶν σχῆμα, πλευ-ραὶ καὶ ἄρθρα τοῦ σώματος πάντα ἐρρωμένα, ὀστέα μεγάλα, κόμη σκληρά, κοιλία πλατεῖα καὶ κοίλη, ὦμοι καρτεροί, ὠμο-πλάται εὐρεῖαι διεστηκυῖαι, στέρνα ῥωμαλέα καὶ μετάφρενα, ἰσχίον σκληρόν, σκέλη σαρκώδη, περὶ τοῖς σφυροῖς καρτερία, πόδες ἀρθρώδεις, χρῶμα ὀξύτερον, βλέμμα ὑγρὸν γοργόν, οὐ

---

[22] See Maud W. Gleason, *Making Men*, p. 31. The text is available in Richard Foerster, *Scriptores Physiognomonici Graeci et Latini*. The translations are my own.

μεγάλοι ὀφθαλμοὶ οὐδὲ πάνυ ἀναπεπετασμένοι οὐ μὴν οὐδὲ
μύοντες, ὀφρύες οὐ τεταμέναι, μέτωπον οὔτε λεῖον οὔτε τραχύ,
φωνὴ ἀπηνεστέρα ἰσχυρὰ μεγάλη, πνεῦμα εὐσταθές. Τοιοῦτος
μὲν ὁ εὔψυχος καὶ ἰσχυρός.

Polemon and Adamantius are combining lists of vices and virtues with
their descriptions of the body, claiming that the one is dependent upon the
other. Physical descriptions and moral judgements are woven together in
a way that makes the body an index of moral qualities. As for the stomach,
its various size and shapes are signs of a strong and intelligent mind or
gluttony and wickedness. This theory of the stomach is witnessed also in
the *Anonymous Latin Physiognomy* §64:[23]

> A huge belly with flesh piled up, flabby and hanging out, indi-
> cates a person with no intelligence, a drunkard and a man of no
> restraint, devoted to luxury and sexual appetite. If there is flesh
> overabundantly, but still firm, it tells of a man who is malevolent
> and skilled in harmful things. If a stomach is very hollow and
> empty as well, this is a sign of a fearful, mean and insatiable
> man. A stomach somewhat soft and flat demonstrates the virtue
> and nobility of the mind.[24]

> *Venter cum est magnus et congestis carnibus, si quidem mol-*
> *libus et pendentibus, sine sensu hominem et vinolentum atque*
> *intemperantem, deditum luxuriae ac ueneri indicat. Si nimia*
> *caro, verum solida sit, malivolum hominem et malorum artificem*
> *declarat. Venter si nimio recessu est tamquam inanis, timidum,*
> *malignum et voracem indicat. Venter aliquanto mollior atque*
> *impressior virtutem animi et magnificentiam monstrat.*

In the words of Dale B. Martin, 'the surface of the body is an expression
of the forces and movements inside the body, that is the soul'.[25] This is
the insight claimed by physiognomics. This insight was widely respected
in antiquity, by philosophers, doctors, people who were practising divination, rhetoricians, and the common people.

[23] This writing was probably composed in the fourth century AD, but transmits traditions
far older than that. For this text in Latin and French, see Jacques André, *Physiognomonie*,
p. 100.
[24] André mentions Pliny's *Nat. Hist.* 11:200 where the length of the entrails indicates a
greedy stomach; cf. Aristotle's *Parts of Animals* 675b. Pliny says that the human entrails are
of extreme length. Moral philosophers would probably add that this proves the significance
of bringing the stomach under control.
[25] Dale B. Martin, *Corinthian Body*, p. 18.

The belly was not considered one of the most significant bodily signs, but this material still demonstrates that it played an important role in physiognomic theory. This ideology of the stomach is applied in e.g. the way Suetonius presents the *Life of Nero Caesar*. Suetonius seems to divide his presentation into four main parts:

(I)   Chaps. 1–7: Nero's descendants and family background; chaps. 6–7 his birth, childhood and youth

(II)   Chaps. 8–19: his reign, seen from the perspective of his positive achievements

(III)   Chaps. 20–50: his reign, seen from the perspective of his many misdeeds. Finally, his cowardly death

(IV)   Chaps. 51–7: afterword: Nero's character

The author himself hints at this disposition in *Nero* 19:3, saying that he has in the preceding part of this work collected Nero's acts that are worth praising, and that he will now proceed to his shameful and criminal deeds. The wickedness of the emperor, his extravagance, his costly banquets and his childish self-centredness are well known. His misbehaviour corresponded to the external surface of his body. By means of typical signs drawn from the science of physiognomics, Suetonius depicts Nero's life in conformity with his outer appearance.

Among the most prominent signs in this biography is the emperor's voice, which was weak and sensitive (*Nero* 20:1; 25:3),[26] and his eyes, which became horrifying during his death (*Nero* 49:4). In chap. 51 the physiognomic description of Nero appears, more or less in full: 'He was about the average height, his body marked with spots and malodorous, his hair light blond, his features regular rather than attractive, his eyes blue and somewhat weak, his neck over-thick, his belly prominent (*venter projectus*), and his legs very slender.'[27] This description is heavily loaded

---

[26] The voice is one of the signs that really matter in physiognomics, see e.g. Pseudo-Aristotle, *Physiognomica* 806a32. Acording to 806b27–28, the high and slack voice means cowardice. That a certain flexibility in interpreting the bodily signs existed is seen from e.g. 807b33–36, where a weak voice is seen as indicative of an orderly man (κόσμιος).

[27] Chap. 51 continues 'His health was good, for though indulging in every kind of riotous excess, he was ill but three times in all during fourteen years of his reign, and even then not enough to give up wine or any of his usual habits. He was utterly shameless in the care of his person and in his dress, always having his hair arranged in tiers or curls, and during the trip to Greece also letting it grow long and hang down behind; and he often appeared in public in a dinner-gown, with a handkerchief bound about his neck, ungirt and unshod.' The LCL translator makes two remarks; a dinner-gown was worn at dinner mostly during Saturnalia, and by women at other times; 'unshod' probably means 'in slippers'.

with bodily signs of Nero's character:

- the body in general[28]
- his hair[29]
- his eyes[30]
- his neck[31]
- his stomach
- his legs[32]
- his effeminacy[33]

This description of Nero can easily be associated with the description of the coward (μαλακός) in Pseudo-Aristotle's *Physiognomonica* 807b5–13, who has the following signs:

- soft hair
- a body of sedentary habit, not energetic
- calves of the legs broad above
- pallor about the face
- eyes weak and blinking
- the extremities of the body weak
- small legs and long thin hands
- thighs small and weak
- the figure is constrained in movement
- not eager but supine and nervous
- the expression on the face is liable to rapid change and is cowed[34]

This means that the reference to Nero's protruding belly is not a detail of minor importance. It appears within a context so replete with physiognomic signs that this adds significance also to the role of Nero's belly in this text. The physiognomic signs are not that forthcoming in the reports on Vitellius' and Domitian's lives. But the mentioning of their bellies[35] may serve a similar purpose.

[28] See on *epipreia* above.
[29] For hair as a sign, see e.g. Pseudo-Aristotle, *Physiognomonica* 806a31; 806b7–25; 808a23–4.
[30] See Josef Mesk, 'Polemons Physiognomik', pp. 54–8.
[31] See e.g. Polemon's chap. 23, Vol. 1, pp. 218–22.
[32] Pseudo-Aristotle, *Physiognomonica* 807b1, 7; 814b7.
[33] See e.g. Polemon's chap. 61, Vol. 1, pp. 276–7.
[34] In Suetonius' report of Nero's death (chaps. 45–50), the emperor appears as a coward, rapidly changing his plans and showing a nervous attitude.
[35] Vitellius is said to have been a glutton with a face marked by hard drinking, and with a huge belly (*venter obesus*) (*Vitellius* 17:2). For his excessive eating and drinking, see

It is worth noting Suetonius' habit of reporting on the outward appearance of the emperors towards the end of his biographies. This can be argued by recalling the important role assigned to omens and signs in his description of the *Lives of the Caesars*,[36] especially at the beginning and end of the biographies. It is in line with this well-known tendency of his literature to extract some meaning also from his mentioning of the bodily nature of the emperors.[37]

2.2   Summary

Ancient physiognomics claimed that the nature or character of the human soul could be measured by the outward appearance of a person. The sources demonstrate this both in theory, i.e. handbooks, and in practice, i.e. texts which show how theories were carried out. Within this theory the body is considered an index of the depths of human character. This goes for the stomach as well. A protruding belly is often a sign of gluttony, extravagance in various ways, and an unhealthy mind. This provides a basis for approaching Paul with the following question: To what extent is the belly a sign in his texts on the stomach? Nothing suggests that Paul considered the outward appearance or form of the belly, nor the rest of the body, to be signs of spiritual significance. But in some way the stomach was to him a codeword too, revealing an identity which endangered true faith in Christ. For what was it then a codeword – and in what way did the stomach jeopardize Christian faith? This chapter has demonstrated that ancient physiognomics were theories of bodily signs bridging spirituality and body. Although Paul shows no traces of putting these theories into practice, his body-theology subscribes to a correlation between body and spiritual qualities.

the commentaries on chap. 13 in his biography; e.g. David Schotter, *Suetonius*, pp. 180–2. Domitian is said to have had a protruding belly as well (*obesitas ventris*) (*Domitian* 18).

[36] Tamsyn S. Barton, *Power and Knowledge*, sees physiognomics in ancient times in such a perspective; see pp. 95–113 in particular. An expert in physiognomy was considered to have supernatural insight.

[37] Andrew Wallace-Hadrill, *Suetonius*, pp. 189–97 rightly points out the physiognomic tendency in Suetonius to be in line with the role of omens, dreams etc.: 'The learned scholar Suetonius belongs very much in the company of such men. The dry lists of characteristics in physiognomists such as Polemon offer the closest stylistic parallel to Suetonius' descriptions of physical appearance' (p. 197). Suetonius himself describes a physiognomist (*metoposcopus*) in action. This 'facereader' examined Britannicus and declared that he would never become emperor, but that Titus – who was present – would rule (*Titus* 2). Teresa M. Shaw, *Burden of the Flesh*, pp. 39–40, 52 mentions some other examples of physiognomic practice.

3

THE BELLY IN ANCIENT MORAL PHILOSOPHY

3.0 Introduction

As we have already stated, the difficulty in this project is that the Pauline texts under consideration are very brief. The stomach appears almost as a catchword with which Paul assumes his readers to be familiar. The exegesis of both Phil. 3:19 and Rom. 16:18, therefore, calls for a context beyond the epistles themselves as well as the Pauline universe of which they are a part. It is the aim of this chapter to provide that context in ancient moral philosophy. In other words, emphasis will be given to ethical and not medical texts. Besides, it is the specific aim of this chapter to search for analogies with Paul's dicta about 'having the belly as god', or 'serving the stomach'. This project will not be undertaken in a narrow lexical sense; i.e. looking only for a particular terminology. In order to see how the *topos* of 'belly' works in ancient sources, we have to relate it to attitudes towards food and consumption in general.

The questions which this chapter aims to answer are the following:

- Do ancient writers refer to the belly with a frequency and in a way that justifies speaking of a commonplace?
- If so, to what does the *topos* of belly refer to?
- Does the stomach in some texts take on a figurative meaning, or become a codeword for something more than eating?
- Does the ancient material suggest a social context to which texts about the power of the belly refer?

In addressing these questions, the ground will hopefully be prepared for a re-reading of the two enigmatic Pauline passages. As will be demonstrated below, the material on the belly is firmly rooted in philosophical discussions on how to master the desires, and how to define the supreme good. These are, indeed, big issues in ancient philosophy. In order not to get lost in the vast amount of material on these topics, the presentation will be guided by the main Greek terms for stomach occurring in this material.

Already here we can make an observation worth noting. The number of words for 'stomach', and related words such as 'glutton', 'gluttony', 'gourmandize' etc., is in itself an impressive fact. The Greek terms appearing most frequently are the following: ἀβροδίαιτος, ἀδηφαγία, ἀπληστία, γαστήρ, γαστρίαργος, γαστρίζεσθαι, γαστριμαργία, γάστρις, γαστρισμός, γάστρων, δειπνομανής, ἐμφορεῖν, ἦτρον, κνισολοιχός, κοιλία, λαιμαργία, λιχνεία, μαργός, νηδύς, ὀλβιογάστωρ, ὀψοφαγία, ὀψοφάγος, παμφάγος, πολυφαγεῖν, πολυφάγος, στομάχος, τρώκτης, ὑπογαστρίζεσθαι.

It is amazing to find so many terms for more or less the same thing; i.e. belly, gluttony, gourmandizing. This represents an important aspect of the culture in which Paul was writing; it was a culture preoccupied with food and eating. The preoccupation with food in Graeco-Roman culture will be substantially attested throughout this study. For now we can refer to the role played by food and gourmandizers in ancient comedies and satire, which often provide a peephole into a culture.[1]

This chapter will also substantiate a claim, namely that the two Pauline passages are not primarily reflecting a Jewish idiom.[2] This is not to deny that relevant Jewish material is at hand. Although the Wisdom text from Cairo Geniza provides a close analogy,[3] it is in the Graeco-Roman sources that phrases similar to 'serving the belly' or 'having the belly as god' are most extensively witnessed. The New Testament passage closest to Phil. 3:19 and Rom. 16:18 is found within the Pauline letter-collection itself, namely Tit. 1:12.[4] The Cretans are described as γαστέρες, This is explicitly identified as a *Greek* saying, obviously a common saying with

---

[1] See e.g. Emily Gowers, *Loaded Table*, pp. 109–219. One might object that the preoccupation with food provides an entrée primarily to the life of the elite, and therefore represents a social stratum with which Paul was not very much involved. There is some truth in that. None the less, recent studies into the social setting and stratification of the Pauline house-churches have pointed out that they were socially more heavily stratified than assumed by the Deissmann tradition; see e.g. Abraham J. Malherbe, *Social Aspects*; Wayne A. Meeks, 'Social Context'; Gerd Theissen, *Social Setting*, pp. 69–119. The attempt to revive the Deissmann theory by e.g. Justin J. Meggit, *Paul, Poverty and Servitude*, is not convincing, since it ignores the existence of at least some elitist elements in Corinth. Anyway, Paul might well draw his *topoi* and rhetoric from sources related to the elite independently of his own social setting as well as his converts.

[2] *Pace* Brian Rosner, according to his forthcoming study on greed in the New Testament.

[3] See chap. 6.7 in this study.

[4] See the prologue to Part 1 above. It is surprising that the commentaries hardly mention Tit. 1:12 as relevant for the understanding of Phil. 3:19 and Rom. 16:18. An exception is Stanley K. Stowers, *Romans*, pp. 49–50. Regardless of how one views the question of authorship, Tit. 1:12 is highly relevant here. Ceslas Spicq, *Pastorales*, pp. 608–11 identifies this as a saying of Epimenides of Cnossos (6th cent. BC). Spicq also mentions Phil. 3:19.

which the author assumes his readers to be familiar. Recognition of this opens a door into the Graeco-Roman material.

In *Strom.* 1:14/59.1–4, Clement of Alexandria demonstrates that Paul assigned some truth to Greek philosophers by quoting from some of them.[5] His first example is the quotation from Epimenides the Cretan in Tit. 1:12. Furthermore, Clement continues his list of examples by turning to 1 Cor. 15:32 ('let us eat and drink, for tomorrow we die'). He calls it a tragic iambic line. Clement does not reflect that this text has obvious links to Isa. 22:13 as well. He takes it as an example of Paul's way of appropriating Greek sayings. In the light of the material to be laid out in the following chapters, it will prove quite natural that Tit. 1:12 and 1 Cor. 15:32 are mentioned in tandem. In other words, it is natural to concentrate our search for analogies with Paul's belly-dicta in Graeco-Roman sources.

3.1 Euripides (born probably in the 480s BC)[6]

In his writing on the Cyclops, Euripides retells one of the most famous episodes of the *Odyssey*, namely Odysseus' encounter with Polyphemus, the one-eyed giant.[7] Polyphemus feasts on men; i.e. the Cyclops has consumed all visitors. With the help of Dionysus' drink, the wine, however, Odysseus succeeds in overcoming this enemy. In the end he manages to put out the Cyclops' sole eye.

The passion for consuming, eating as well as drinking, with which this literature is so replete, adds significance to it for our study. The Cyclops frequently refers to filling up his stomach (*Cyclops* 220–1, 505–6 (γαστήρ); 239–49, 303–4 (νηδύς) cf. 409, 415–17). Odysseus, on his part, urges the Cyclops to give up this greedy appetite of his (πάρες τὸ μάργον σῆς γνάθου), and choose to be godly (εὐσεβές) instead (310). The carnivorous appetite of the Cyclops Odysseus considered impious; it is incompatible with Zeus's piety. This is, of course, related to the Cyclops' eating the flesh of the shipwrecked sailors on his island. In his response to Odysseus, however, Polyphemus relates his impiety, not only to his eating men, but also to his being compelled by the belly or appetite (316–45). Polyphemus speaks of a worship which is an alternative to

---

[5] For the Greek text see *GCS* (Clemens Alexandrinus Vol. 2).

[6] Information on the lifetime of the philosophers is taken from Simon Hornblower, Anthony Spawforth, *Oxford Classical Dictionary*.

[7] For an introduction to satyr-plays in general, and the *Cyclops* in particular, see Richard Seaford, *Euripides' Cyclops*, pp. 1–60.

temples, gods and Zeus in particular. It is a worship marked by wealth (πλοῦτος) (316) and the appetite. Emphasis is given to the appetite:

> When Zeus sends his rain from above, taking my water-tight shelter in this cave and dining on roasted calf or some wild animal, I put on a feast for my upturned belly (δαινύμενος ἑστιως τι γαστέρ᾽ ὑπτίαν), then drinking dry a whole storage vat of milk, I drum on it, making a din to rival Zeus's thunder. And when the north wind out of Thrace pours snow on us, I wrap my body in the skins of beasts, pile up a great blazing fire, and pay heed to the snow. The earth brings forth grass willy-nilly to feed my flock. These I sacrifice to no one but myself – never to the gods – and to my belly, the greatest of divinities (οὔτινι θύω πλὴν ἐμοί, θεοῖσι δ᾽ οὔ, καὶ τῇ μεγίστῃ, γαστρὶ τῇδε, δαιμόνων). To guzzle and eat day by day and to give oneself no pain – this is Zeus in the eyes of men of sense. As for those who have passed laws and complicated men's lives, they can go hang. For my part, I shall not forgo giving pleasure to my heart – by eating you.
>
> (*Cyclops* 323–41)

Some significant observations can be gleaned from this saying. In the first place, the belly is directly named a god, indeed the greatest.[8] Polyphemus describes his appetite in religious terms; instead of bringing sacrifices to the gods, he pleases his belly. In praising his stomach, The Cyclops makes use of hymnic language traditionally applied to glorify Zeus (cf. *Homeric Hymn* 23; Aeschylus, *Choephori* 244; Athenaeus, *Deipn.* 6:248f; Cleanthes' *Hymn to Zeus* in *SVF* 1, no. 537, pp. 121–3).[9] Drinking and eating are replacing Zeus. The belly is a god demanding sacrifices, which consist of eating and drinking. The statement of the Cyclops on the belly is a challenge to the position of Zeus. The mention of Zeus's thunderbolt makes this evident. In the second place, pleasing the belly is tantamount to satisfying one's own needs. Sacrificing to the belly or oneself is, therefore, one and the same action. *Cyclops* 345–6

8 Polyphemus opposes to Zeus not only the worship of his belly; he considers wealth as well to be divine (θεός) (*Cyclops* 316). For similar sentiments on money, see references in Richard Seaford, *Euripides' Cyclops*, p. 164.
9 See also A.F. Garvie, *Aeschylus Choephori*, p. 105. As Richard Seaford, *Euripides' Cyclops*, p. 168 points out, 'τῇ μηγίστηι gives a humorous ambiguity, seeming as it does to qualify γαστρί'. Love had its gods in Eros and Aphrodite. They are praised in terms which recall Polyphemus' praise to his belly; see Athenaeus, *Deipn.* 13:599f: 'Eros is a mighty and most powerful divinity, as is also Aphrodite (μέγαν εἶναι δαίμονα καὶ δυνατώτατον τὸν Ἔρωτα... καὶ τὴν Ἀφροδίτην)' cf. Plato's *Symp.* 178a; 180b; 189c. The Cyclops applies this language to his belly or himself.

speaks of a god (θεός) who dwells within the cave, referring either to the belly or Polyphemus himself. The grammar suggests a reference to himself, but it does not make very much difference; judging from this literature, the two are more or less synonymous. This relationship between belly-worship and selfishness is a fact we will come across many times during this investigation.

In the third place, we have in this text a saying analogous to Paul's text on those whose god is their belly. The Cyclops is speaking of Zeus and the many gods of the Greek pantheon, of course. For a Jewish or Christian reader of Euripides, the language used to denounce Zeus could well recall biblical traditions on idolatry.

The creed-like manifesto of the Cyclops is quoted by Plutarch (*Mor.* 435b) who takes it as a statement which annihilates traditional piety, replacing it with oneself and the stomach. It is worth noticing that Plutarch mentions the Epicureans' contempt for religious oracles in the wider context of his quoting from Euripides here (*Mor.* 434d–e). His quotation from Euripides, therefore serves as an example of an Epicurean attitude (more on this in chap. 4).

3.2   Plato (c. 429–347 BC)

In Plato's *Phaedrus* 237a–242a, Socrates makes an inspired speech about desires and love in particular. He states that in human beings are found both desire for pleasure (ἐπιθυμία ἡδονῶν) as well as a drive which strives for the best (τὸ ἄριστον). These two principles may live peacefully together, but sometimes one of them has the upper hand. The rule of reason is called self-control (σωφροσύνη).[10] When desires prevail, however, their rule is called excess (ὕβρις). This has many names, of which Socrates gives two examples, namely gluttony (γαστριμαργία)[11] and drinking. What Socrates says about gluttony is, of course, just one example. For this study, however, it is of particular interest to notice that gluttony is found within a context full of verbs and nouns denoting power and rule, or being ruled by the passions: ἄρχειν (*Phaedrus* 238a, e; 241a); κρατεῖν (238a, c); τυραννεύειν (238b); ἄγειν (238b); δυναστεύειν

---

[10] According to Alexander Nehamas, Paul Woodruff, *Plato, Phaedrus*, p. 17 this is the appropriate translation of σωφροσύνη.

[11] For a list of the passions, according to Andronicus, see *SVF* Vol. 3, no. 397, pp. 96–7. His list concludes with the three items of gluttony, drinking and sexual appetite. As for gluttony he says: Γαστριμαργία δὲ ἐπιθυμία ἄμετρος σιτίων, 'desire for food beyond measure'.

(238b); δουλεύειν (238e); κύριος (239c); ἀναγκάζειν (239c).[12] This language of being overcome makes it perfectly clear that men are liable to be ruled by the passions, to be enslaved to pleasure, or to be compelled by the stomach.[13] In the dialogue *Protagoras* (353a–356c), Socrates speaks of being overcome by pleasure (ἡδονῆς ἡττᾶσθαι). This verb (Attic for ἡσσᾶσθαι) means to be overpowered.[14] Socrates' most prominent example is people who are 'overpowered by the pleasantness of food or drink and sexual acts (ὑπὸ σίτων καὶ ποτῶν καὶ ἀφροδισίων κρατούμενοι)' (*Protagoras* 353c). Eating, drinking and sex are catchwords for a lifestyle opposed by the philosopher.[15] Those who are overcome by these desires keep on obeying them, even though they know them to be bad; i.e. addictive behaviour, as we say now.

In more philosophical terms the issue of desires or passions is raised in *Phaedo* as well. Socrates makes the claim that the relationship between soul and body is defined by which one is ruling the other. This is a question whether the divine (soul) or the mortal shall rule (*Phaedo* 80a–b). Faced with death, Socrates is comforted by his soul being released from his body, i.e. the mortal and earthly (γεῶδες) (*Phaedo* 80c–81c). There exist, however, souls that are so dependent upon the earthly that they are imprisoned in a body. At this point Cebes interrupts Socrates and asks him to elaborate on this, and he does so by saying: '... those who have indulged in gluttony (γαστριμαργία) and violence and drunkenness' (*Phaedo* 81e). In his answer, Socrates expresses the notion of metempsychosis; the idea of the souls being born in animal bodies (cf. *Timaeus* 91d–92a).[16]

The philosophical perspective on Plato's doctrine of desires emerges in full in *Timaeus*. To have a proper understanding of what Plato says about desires, including the belly, we must turn to this work. Plato does not provide close analogies to Paul's belly-dicta, but his philosophy of desires and passions is of relevance. This is so primarily because he considers the desires to represent the earthly and non-divine part of human life. This view is, on the surface at least, similar to that of Paul, who speaks of having the belly as god as characteristic of an earthly life, as opposed to the heavenly home of the believers (Phil. 3:19).

---

[12] Cf. also *Republic* 573e; 575a.

[13] In Homer the demanding belly is a term for hunger, a force which drives Odysseus (*Odyssey* 6:133; cf. 18:2).

[14] It carries a sense of being defeated; see LSJ s.v.

[15] We will meet these three frequently in our investigation, as manifestations of what it means to be devoted to the belly.

[16] This further attests the important and widely-attested connection between desires and animals in ancient thought; see David T. Runia, *Philo of Alexandria and the Timaeus of Plato*, pp. 309–10.

Timaeus is a fascinating coming-together of anatomy and philosophy. Since philosophy prevails, Plato can be said to depict a philosophical body. He explains that the human head holds the most prominent place in the body, because it represents the soul or divine. The body is a mere vehicle for the head, which rules the rest. The body is designed to carry the head, its most divine part (*Timaeus* 44d; 69c; 87e). The different parts of the body are valued according to how they relate to the divine, i.e. the soul or head. As for the stomach, it is located at a distance, and serves the body by feeding it (*Timaeus* 70d–71a).[17] The body is a sign of the two principles (human versus divine / earthly versus heavenly) in human beings: 'All the bones, that possesses most soul, he enclosed in least flesh, but the bones which contained least soul with most and most dense flesh' (*Timaeus* 74e, cf. 75c). The soul raises the individual towards heaven like a tree, and is a reminder of the heavenly kinship (*Timaeus* 90a). One can easily imagine how this philosopher would conceive of a distended stomach. What the ancient physiognomics stated in a more practical way, Plato seems to argue in a more philosophical mode. Plato's philosophical body is held together by a harmony or balance between human and divine, earthly and heavenly. The nature of the desires is always to have more (see e.g. *Timaeus* 90b); they seek to dominate (κρατεῖν) (91c). By their very nature, the desires of the body thus endanger the balance.[18] The means of keeping balance and harmony is, therefore, moderation, not any kind of excess (*Timaeus* 72e–73a; 86b–c).

Plato thus urges human beings to fight excess of any kind, including that of food, in order to keep and strengthen the kinship with the divine. Although we have presented the ethical section of *Timaeus*, the focus of the dialogue is not on ethical guidance, but what we might call a philosophy of identity. That Plato speaks of food, belly and gluttony in the light of identity becomes evident in his *Republic* 519b. Philosophical training from childhood is here seen as a means of controlling gluttony (λιχνεία).[19] Otherwise gluttony will 'turn downwards the vision of the soul (τὴν τῆς ψυχῆς ὄψιν)'.[20] The person who is in control of his consumption and

---

[17] A. E. Taylor, *A Commentary on Plato's Timaeus*, p. 505 says: 'It is usual to specify as the prominent objects of ἐπιθυμία, σῖτα, ποτά and ἀφροδίσια. The last are purposely not mentioned here because we are dealing with the first generation of men, in whom the distinction of sex has not been made.' Taylor observes that desire is usually defined by a threefold formula of eating, drinking and copulation.

[18] A body out of balance is ill or diseased (*Timaeus* 82a). For this medical theory, see Dale B. Martin, *Corinthian Body*, pp. 146–53. For a presentation of Plato's view on the human soul, see I. M. Crombie, *Plato's Doctrines*, pp. 331–7.

[19] This is a common noun for excessive desire for food; it is used synonymously with γαστριμαργία; see LSJ s.v.

[20] The LCL translator gives further references to the notion of this vision in Plato; p. 138.

is maintaining the vision of what is real and true has experienced a con-version (περιεστρεφέτο). Of course, we should not read the Jewish or Christian concept of 'conversion' into this. But the philosopher is cer-tainly aware of having an identity which obliges him to a certain lifesyle, including how to make use of the stomach.

Plato and Paul are worlds apart. The difference between the two is substantial indeed. They do, however, have a common concern about what they call the belly. Of special interest to this Pauline study is the fact that Plato urges his Academy members to renounce the desires of belly, because their identity is rooted not in the earthly but in the heavenly and divine. Who they are is decisive for how they relate to food. Plato speaks of belly in terms of gluttony, and advises his students by mapping their identity. This forms a bridge to Paul in Phil. 3:19, where he considers 'having the belly as god' to be identical with setting the mind on earthly things. This will be further developed later in this study.

3.3   Xenophon (born around 430 BC)

In his *Memorabilia*, written in memory of Socrates, Xenophon tells the story of when Antiphon came to visit the philosopher (*Mem.* 1:6).[21] An-tiphon claimed that the aim of philosophy was the happy life, the life of εὐδαιμονία. He said that Socrates did not live according to the standards of a happy life. His meat and drink were poor, his clothing was simple, and he refused to accept money for his teaching. Students (μαθηταί) usu-ally imitate their teachers. Socrates had therefore to be seen as a teacher of unhappiness (*Mem.* 1:6.1–3). In his response, the philosopher says that the body is in need of training to get stronger. Since Socrates is practising this, he is able to cope with cold as well as heat, with sore feet etc. In doing so, Socrates enjoys greater pleasures, having the lasting benefit thereof. The alternative to this life of training is to become enslaved to the belly (δουλεύειν γαστρί) or to sleep and incontinence (*Mem.* 1:6.8).[22]

Belly-service is here a symbol of the easy life, seeking the pleasures at hand. Socrates' response urges to a life of toil for the purpose of lasting benefit rather than enjoying the pleasures of the moment. In other words, it

---

[21] This dialogue continues the topic of self-control (ἐγκράτεια) from the preceding chapter (*Mem.* 1:5.1 and 4). Xenophon considers Antiphon to be an example of a person who is a slave to his pleasures (ταῖς ἡδοναῖς δουλεύων) (*Mem.* 1:5.5). That chap. 6 continues the topic from chap. 5 is argued also by Olof Gigon, *Kommentar zum ersten Buch von Xenophons Memorabilien*, pp. 151–7.

[22] In his books on Cyrus' schooling (παιδεία), Xenophon describes the curriculum. One of the aims is to teach the boys self-control (σωφροσύνη), which includes ἐγκράτειαν γαστρὸς καὶ ποτοῦ, self-restraint in eating and drinking (*Cyropaideia* 1:2.8).

is the question of setting one's mind on what will last, not on immediate satisfaction. 'Being enslaved to the belly' is a key-term for a lifestyle seeking instant gratification.

Book 2 of the *Memorabilia* is in many ways a following-up of the conversation with Antiphon. Socrates exhorts his listeners to practise self-control (ἐγκράτεια) towards desires; i.e. in matters of eating, drinking, sexual indulgence, sleeping and endurance of cold, heat and toil. This forms the introductory words of Xenophon to a conversation between Socrates and Aristippus (*Mem.* 2:1.1–2). They agree to take food as point of departure for their dialogue, as a test case, so to say:[23] How should a person who will become a ruler be educated in food matters? The philosopher argues that in order to be fitted to rule, one has to practise self-control (ἐγκράτεια) in all such matters. A person is not fitted to rule if he is not in control of the pleasures, such as food, drinking, sex, climate, and sleep (*Mem.* 2:1.2–9). Aristippus responds by saying that he does not put himself in the ranks of those who wish to govern the city. Xenophon explains Aristippus' declining to compete for eminence in the city's ruling class in terms view of his self-indulgence. In other words, being enslaved to the stomach is a sign of a selfish attitude that leads to neglect of the needs of the community. The belly-slave contributes only to himself, not to the city. Enslavement to the stomach is here seen in a political perspective; it corresponds to selfishness, which neglects the good of the city.

A reference to Book 1 is here necessary. In *Mem.* 1:5.1–6, Xenophon repeats what Socrates said about ἐγκράτεια as the foundation of a virtuous life. The text presents the opposite of this, namely enslavement to bodily desires as well as to money. Socrates focuses on the damaging effect such persons have on public life and duties:

> My friends, if we were at war and wanted to save ourselves and conquer the enemy, should we choose one whom we knew to be the slave of the belly or of wine, or lust,[24] or sleep (ἥττω γαστρὸς ἢ οἴνου ἢ ἀφροδισίων ἢ ὕπνου)? How could we expect that such a one would either save us or defeat the enemy?
>
> (*Mem.* 1:5.1)

---

[23] Olof Gigon, *Kommentar zum zweiten Buch von Xenophons Memorabilien*, p. 17 says that the expression used by Xenophon here, τῇ γαστρὶ χαρίζεσθαι is quite powerful language. It refers to the call of the pleasures to be satisfied: 'For in the same body along with the soul are planted the pleasures (ἡδοναί) which call to her: "Abandon prudence (μὴ σωφρονεῖν), and make haste to gratify us and the body (ἑαυταῖς τε καὶ τῷ σώματι χαρίζεσθαι)"' (*Mem.* 1:2.23).

[24] I.e. sexual appetite; cf. §4.

The concept of enslavement to the pleasures is spelled out many times in this passage. The Attic adjective ἥττων is, however, better translated as 'weaker' or 'inferior'.[25] In other words, a leader of the people must be stronger than his belly. Socrates sees this as a crucial requirement also for people who are appointed to educate children or to protect the goods of the city. A person unable to rule the belly becomes here a symbol of selfishness and hence, a person who is not worthy to be entrusted with any public duties.

Within his discussion on self-control, Xenophon tells the story of Heracles' passing from boyhood to maturity, the age of being self-governed (*Mem.* 2:1.21–33). Heracles was considering with himself which way to choose, the ὁδός of virtue (ἀρετή) or that of vice (κακία). Then two women appeared to him. Xenophon describes the two according to common physiognomic theory, saying that the woman adorned with purity, modest eyes, a sober figure dressed in white, was Virtue. Vice, however, was fleshy (εἰς πολυσαρκίαν) and soft; cosmetics had been applied to the face to heighten its colours. Her eyes were brazen, and she was dressed in a way revealing her feminine charm. The outward appearances of the two women clearly indicate their inward characters (cf. physiognomics).

Vice addresses Heracles, inviting him to embark on the most pleasant and easy way: 'You shall taste all the sweets of life; and hardship you shall never know' (*Mem.* 2:1.23). Vice speaks in terms of tasting (γεύεσθαι), which is significant for the way she presents herself to Heracles. His mind will not be set[26] on war and worries, but on 'what choice food or drink you can find, what sight or sound will delight you, what touch or perfume, what tender love can give you most joy, what bed the softest slumbers; and how to come by all these pleasures with least trouble' (*Mem.* 2:1.24). She promises a life without any toil, profiting from the works of others (2:1.25). Eating and drinking are thus important terms in the self-presentation of Vice.

Virtue presents another way of living, leading to herself. The gods have ordained a way of virtue which includes toil and effort (πόνος καὶ ἐπιμέλεια): 'If you desire the love of friends, you must do good to your friends; if you covet honour from a city, you must aid that city; if you are fain to win the admiration of all Hellas for virtue, you must strive to do good for Hellas' (*Mem.* 2:1.28). We recognize here the political

[25] See LSJ s.v.
[26] Xenophon uses the verbs φροντίζειν and σκοπεῖν, which recall key terms in Philippians (Phil. 1:7; 2:2, 4, 5; 3:15, 17; 4:2, 10).

aspect involved in the question of mastering the desires (see above). The difference between virtue and vice is determined by the attitude taken to food and drink. We noted this on the part of Vice's self-presentation, and it is true for Virtue as well. She blames Vice for filling herself before desiring food and drink, eating without being hungry, drinking before being thirsty, finding cooks for herself, eating for pleasures' sake, drinking costly wines and having costly furniture (*Mem.* 2:1.30). People living like this will develop weak and weary bodies. The attitude to food thus marks the difference between vice and virtue. Those walking on the road of virtue will eat and drink with moderation, according to their needs, and live a healthy life (*Mem.* 2:1.33). Bodily appearance and the attitude to food therefore correspond to each other. Xenophon does not mention the belly in this particular passage. But we can easily infer from his previous dialogues in *Memorabilia* that the belly marks the dividing line between vice and virtue. The distinction between vice and virtue is defined in terms of gluttony or moderation, and a political aspect, or how to be a citizen, appears as well.

3.4 Aristotle (384–322 BC)

In his ethical treatises, *Nicomachean* and *Eudemian Ethics*, Aristotle discusses pleasures and desires. From his presentation it is clear that eating, drinking and sex are seen as a 'trinity';[27] they frequently appear together (*Nic. Eth.* 1118a31, cf. 1118b18; *Eud. Eth.* 1221b10–27). These desires are natural, they are shared and enjoyed by all people. Some, however, are controlled by these desires. These are οἱ ἀκρατεῖς (the uncontrolled), who have neither self-control (ἐγκράτεια) nor temperance (σωφροσύνη) (*Eud. Eth.* 1231a16–26):[28]

> In the case of the natural desires, then, a few men err, in one way only, that of excess in quantity; for to eat or drink to repletion of ordinary food and drink is to exceed what is natural in amount, since the natural desire is only to satisfy one's wants. Hence people who over-eat are called 'mad-bellies' (γαστρίμαργοι),

[27] This expression is taken from Alan Booth, 'Reclining', p. 105 who speaks of the 'intimate and unholy trinity' of eating, drinking and sexual indulgence associated with banquets in antiquity.

[28] In his discussion on σωφροσύνη and ἐγκράτεια in *Problems*, Book 28 (949a–950a), Aristotle takes thirst, hunger and sexual desire as his points of departure. In his *Vices and Virtues* 1250a7–12; 1250b7–15, he attempts to make a distinction between the two Greek virtues. This distinction is, however, a very slight one since both are concerned with how to rule ἐπιθυμίαι.

meaning that they fill that organ beyond the right measure; it is persons of especially slavish nature (ἀνδραποδώδεις)[29] that are liable to this form of excess.   (*Nic. Eth.* 1118b16–21)

Aristotle calls such a person ὀψοφάγος; i.e. a person who consumes delicacies, a gourmet (*Nic. Eth.* 1118a33–34; *Eud. Eth.* 1231a16; *Problems* 950a3–5).

The philosopher devotes large sections of his *Nicomachean Ethics*, to the question of pleasure (ἡδονή) (*Nic. Eth.* 1152b–1154b and 1172a19–1181b). Although the belly is not mentioned in particular, his discussion provides the framework for how he views gluttony. Pleasure is presented as the opposite of ἐγκράτεια, and in need of being controlled, i.e. to be enjoyed only moderately. Towards the end of his presentation it is obvious that Aristotle considers this a key issue of politics, i.e. how to preserve the πολιτεία (*Nic. Eth.* 1180b28–1181b cf. 1152b1–4). He speaks of those who are enslaved by the pleasures (δουλεύειν ταῖς ἡδοναῖς) (*Nic. Eth.* 1172a30–34), or who are eagerly pursuing them, living as they do, by passion (πάθει γὰρ ζῶντες τὰς οἰκείας ἡδονὰς διώκουσι) (*Nic. Eth.* 1179b11–15 cf. 1179b26–28 and 1180a10–14). As for the bodily pleasures (περὶ δὲ τῶν σωματικῶν) which need to be restrained, he mentions in particular food, wine and sex (*Nic. Eth.* 1154a8–9). Aristotle clearly treats the role of the stomach within the framework of a philosophical discussion on desires and how to master them. The passions, including the belly, can take control and men are then being enslaved by desires which should rather be enjoyed only moderately.

3.5   Dio Chrysostom (AD c. 40/50–110)

In his Discourse 32, Dio addresses the Alexandrian population attempting to persuade the inhabitants to change their ways. He reminds them that Troy was taken captive by a single horse. Alexandria, however, is about to be taken captive by many 'horses'. He says that the slaughter, burning as well as the leading of women into captivity represent, however, only a final stage of a long siege of cities: 'For I assert that men have been taken captive (ἐαλώκεναι) not by pirates only or by persons, but also by a courtesan or gluttony (ὑπὸ ... ἑταίρας καὶ γαστρός) or by any other low desire' (*Orat.* 32:90). These desires represent the many horses by which Alexandria is about to be besieged. The notion of being besieged by sex and stomachs is very prominent in this text, in the verb ἀλίσκεσθαι[30] as

---

[29] See LSJ s.v. and cf. *Eud. Eth.* 1215b35.   [30] See LSJ s.v.

well as in the noun αἰχμάλωτοι appearing some lines further down in
Dio's speech. Dio says that the desires mentioned here are ruinous to
σωτηρία, whereby he thinks of the well-being of the city.

Dio speaks similarly in his Discourse 80 *On Freedom*. There are
many prisons and bonds, by which men have made themselves prisoners. Among the many bonds, γαστήρ is given special emphasis (*Orat.*
80:7–10).[31] The fetters of the stomach mean a δουλεία worse than any
other, since there is hardly any prospect of being released; they only
grow stronger and become more numerous. Dio Chrysostom considers
behaviour at banquets a good indication of how people master their desires. The whole of life can therefore be described in terms of a banquet
(*Orat.* 30:30–44). Dio thus indicates that enslavement of the belly at banquets in particular is not merely a philosophical question, but relates to
social life.

3.6   Musonius Rufus (AD 30 – AD 101/102)

This Stoic philosopher lived in Rome in the second half of the first century
AD. Notes from his lectures were taken by his pupils, who published
them around AD 110.[32] The texts of interest for this project are found
primarily in his two fragments *On Food* (18a–b, pp. 112–21).[33] These
fragments have to be interpreted in the light of the practical nature of
Musonius' philosophy. Practical exercises were the most important part
of philosophical training, since philosophy is defined as 'knowing how
to live' (*Fragm.* 3, *That Women Too Should Study Philosophy*). The aim
of philosophical training is to 'exercise restraint in other pleasures, not
to be a slave of desire (μὴ δουλεύειν ἐπιθυμίαις)' (*Fragm.* 3, p. 40.17–
19), which means self-control (σωφροσύνη), i.e. disciplining the desires
(*Fragm.* 7, p. 56.27, *That One Should Disdain Hardships*).

From this Musonius proceeds to urge a moderate life – not necessarily
ascetic – in food, clothing, housing and furnishing. All these fragments

---

[31]   G. Mussies, *Dio Chrysostom and the New Testament*, p. 192 mentions *Orat.* 55:21 as
a parallel to Phil. 3:19. Dio here tells us about Antinous who spent a lavish life in eating,
drinking and love. 'This man ought to die from a blow through the belly', says Dio. The
belly is here obviously an abbreviated idiom summarizing how Antinous lived. For Rom.
16:18 Mussies does not mention any parallels. The life of Antinous is described by the
threefold formula eating, drinking and sex, in which the stomach has a prominent place.
This is the so-called 'unholy trinity' mentioned above, which is in many instances what
belly-enslavement is really about.

[32]   For an introduction to his life, see A. C. van Geytenbach, *Musonius Rufus*, pp. 3–21.
The translation and text edition which I have used is Cora E. Lutz, *Musonius Rufus*.

[33]   A. C. van Geytenbach, *Musonius Rufus*, pp. 96–111 gives a commentary on the two
fragments.

are related in their effort to reject luxury (*Fragm.* 18a + b–20). They provide advice for how to lead a good and healthy life. This is his perspective on eating and drinking as well.[34] According to *Fragm.* 18a, p. 112.5–7, Musonius believed the beginning and foundation of temperance (σωφρονεῖν) was to exercise control (ἐγκράτεια) over eating and drinking. This sounds like a reversal of Epicurus' maxims (see below), but he does not seem to be involved in polemics here.[35] Musonius observes that people are preoccupied with food, and that this interest has increased. He considers tempting cookery books[36] to be indicative of a time replete with λιχνεία and ὀψοφαγία, luxurious and excessive eating (cf. 18a, p. 114.1–15; 18b, p. 118.30–4). Some are like pregnant women who are obsessed with eating. Musonius' comments are not very sophisticated; his main point is that excessive eating ruins the health.

This concern is continued in *Fragm.* 18b which is a refutation of γαστριμαργία and ὀψοφαγία,[37] voracity and gourmandizing. Consuming for the sake of pleasure, not for nourishment, is detrimental to health, and perverting as well. For pleasure in prepared food (ἐπιθυμία τῆς ἐν ὄψῳ ἡδονῆς) transforms human beings into devouring and unreasoning animals (18b, p. 116.11–22). The glutton acts like a greedy animal.

It is worth enquiring somewhat into this animal analogy. What does Musonius mean by that? The clue is found in *Fragm.* 18a, p. 112.22–5, to the effect that since man of all creatures is the nearest kin to the gods, his food should resemble that of the gods. For Musonius this probably meant vegetarianism. Be this as it may; of real importance for our study is to notice that food and behaviour at table are revealing of the character of a person, his identity and kinship. Gluttony reveals kinship with animals; moderation with the divine. Musonius' pupil, Epictetus, often mentions eating behaviour as a sign of divine kinship (Epictetus, *Diss.* 1:13.1;[38] 2:8.12; 4:8.20; cf. 1:4.20). This means that comparing the glutton with animals describes him as being of an earthly nature, denying his divine kinship.

Moderation in eating is essential in achieving self-control since, according to Musonius, the pleasures of the belly are the hardest to fight.

[34] For the practical nature of Musonius' philosophy, see ibid., pp. 40–50.

[35] Ibid., p. 98 argues that it is a maxim commonly found in treatises advocating sobriety.

[36] Literally he speaks of 'flattering the gullet' (κολακεύειν τὴν κατάποσιν).

[37] An ὀψοφάγος is a person who takes no or just a little bread, eats only the relish, and thus allows sustenance to develop into greed and pleasure. Ancient sources depict the ὀψοφάγος as a person who kept fish for himself, grabbed it selfishly and swallowed it whole. James Davidson, *Courtesans and Fishcakes*, p. 146, says that 'the best way to recognize an *opsophagos* is not in the quantity of his consumption . . . but above all in the intensity and immediacy of his desire'; see also pp. 22–6, 144–7.

[38] I.e. eating ἐγκρατῶς καὶ κοσμίως.

Temptation to gluttony is a challenge facing men on a continuous basis, due to the simple fact that they usually eat twice a day. Food, therefore, provides the occasion for a number of vices. Musonius gives some examples; i.e. eating too much, hasty consumption, wallowing in the food, consuming sweet but unhealthy food, reserving a special fare or amount for oneself, different from the guests. Controlling the stomach, therefore, means to be free of many vices. 'Indeed the throat was designed to be a passage for food, not an organ of pleasure, and the stomach was made for the same purpose as the root was created in plants' (*Fragm.* 18b, 118.5–11). For just as the root nourishes the plant by taking food from without, so the stomach nourishes the living being from the food and drink which are taken into it. Hence, simple workers, slaves, poor people who do not rely on expensive foodstuffs are stronger and healthier.

Towards the end of *Fragm.* 20, pp. 124–7 (*On Furnishing*), the concerns of the philosopher in the preceding paragraphs are summed up. Musonius adds a new perspective; the stomach is seen from a political angle. It was not luxury which brought Sparta into being. A person who is used to lavishness is liable to be unjust. It is the nature of such persons to demand ever more. At the end of the day these demands cannot be satisfied by just methods. Furthermore, such persons are hesitant to share the burdens of the city, friends and relatives. The love of luxury will not allow him to suffer for the community. A luxurious man – exemplified in the various topics treated in the preceding fragments – does not undertake burdens or suffer for his *polis*, since this would mean to abandon τρυφή, a life that takes pride in pleasure. The last part of this *Fragment* 20 (p. 126.14–31) emphasizes that people who take pride in excess are liable to neglect the community. Love of luxury does not allow deprivation for the good of the city, relatives and friends. A person who loves luxury is bound to fail in his duties. This is the political perspective on the question of mastering the desires that we have come across many times already, and which also reminds us that Paul in Phil. 3:20 speaks of a heavenly citizenship.

3.7 Epictetus (mid first century to second century AD)

This philosopher[39] was a devout and pious man. His commitment to the gods, and Zeus in particular, can be seen throughout his discourses. His religious commitment is expressed in his *Diss.* 1:16 on God's providence. God is indeed worthy all praise from human beings. This praise is due

---

[39] For an introduction to Epictetus' life and work, see the LCL translation of W. A. Oldfather, Vol. 1, pp. vii–xxx and Robert F. Dobbin, *Epictetus*, pp. xi–xxiii.

not to great matters, but to the fact that 'milk is produced from grass, and cheese from milk, and that wool grows from skin' (*Diss.* 1:16.8). Zeus is praised for having created all things. Hence, people should praise him while digging, ploughing and eating: 'Great is God, that He hath furnished us these instruments wherewith we shall till the earth. Great is God, that He hath given us hands, and power to swallow,[40] and a belly (κοιλία), and power to grow unconsciously, and to breathe while asleep' (*Diss.* 1:16.17). In a way which recalls the Jewish or Christian theology of creation, Epictetus speaks of natural revelation and everyday life as a continuous worship. The human stomach is seen in this perspective; it is a means of God's providence. It must therefore be used accordingly.

Some, however, live in a way which make them 'mere bellies, entrails, and genitals (ὡς κοιλίαι, ὡς ἔντερα, ὡς αἰδοῖα)' (*Diss.* 1:9.26).[41] The philosopher speaks of those who are enslaved to their appetite and sexual desire.[42] This is a lifestyle which Epictetus elsewhere describes as to 'eat and drink and copulate and defecate and snore' (*Diss.* 2:20.10).[43] In this saying, we recognize a threefold formula which we have already pointed out, namely that of eating, drinking and sex. This saying of Epictetus is directed against the Epicureans. The text clearly echoes some of the sayings attributed to Epicurus and his disciples. Epictetus is targeting Epicurean maxims as well as significant catchwords in common ancient critiques of Epicureanism. Although we will return more fully to this in the next chapter, one comment is worth making now.

The criticism of Epicurus and his followers is embedded in a political perspective. Epictetus says that they held opinions which were anti-social (ἀκοινώνητα) (*Diss.* 2:20.16). Furthermore, he claims that Epicureans' neglect of the gods has implications for their civic obligations. They are undermining proper citizenship (21–7). The men who were killed at Thermopylae would hardly have suffered this if they praised the teaching of Epicurus. Addressing himself to the Epicureans, Epictetus asks (rhetorically) whether it is possible to imagine people who assign the supreme good to the flesh (σάρξ) (*Diss.* 3:7.3), as able to make a *polis* (3:7.19).

---

[40]   Robert F. Dobbin, *Epictetus*, p. 160 takes κατάποσις as a reference to an organ (gullet) (cf. Musonius Rufus, *Fragm.* 18a, p. 114.4), not to the faculty of swallowing.

[41]   Cf. Tit. 1:12.

[42]   Robert F. Dobbin, *Epictetus*, p. 127 says that Epictetus' view of the belly goes back to Hesiod's *Theogony* 26, where the Muses are singing of shepherds who are mere bellies; this text is referred to in the prologue to Part 1 in this study.

[43]   Cf. Jesus' parable on the rich fool saying: '. . . relax, eat, drink be merry' (Luke 12:19). Douglas S. Sharp, *Epictetus and the New Testament* has worked out in detail resemblances between the two. He does not mention this parable of Jesus, nor the Pauline texts in question in this study.

They will not perform the duties of a citizen (πολιτευτέον), and their doctrine is subversive of the *polis* and destructive of families (*Diss.* 3:7.21). Although Epictetus does not spell it out, we are justified in summarizing this in the following way: the neglect or even denial of the gods on the part of the Epicureans leads to an earthly and self-loving way of life which is detrimental to the city.

When men lose sight of the stomach as a means of God's providence, they live as though they were nothing but bellies. The belly becomes an instrument for pleasure and pleasing oneself; those who are enslaved by it live like worms. In *Diss.* 2:9.4 this is the lifestyle of sheep, living without any thought beyond satisfying the immediate needs. People living 'for the sake of the belly, or of our sex-organs (ὅταν τῆς γαστρὸς ἔνεκα, ὅταν τῶν αἰδοίων)' resemble sheep, whose only concern is for eating and reproduction. The belly and the genitals represent an animal-like force. They cause people to drift away, led by their passions. Such a lifestyle seriously endangers the divine kinship of human beings.

This divine kinship (συγγένεια) of human beings is a favourite topic of Epictetus' philosophy. One of his discourses is devoted entirely to this subject (*Diss.* 1:9; see e.g. 1:9.3–12 and 2:8.11–23). The true sign of the divine seed in human beings is their reason (cf. Plato). God is their maker and father; hence they are sons of God. This gives to the philosopher and any man who realizes his true kinship, a sense of a calling: 'Men, wait upon God. When He shall give the signal and set you free from this service, then shall you depart to Him; but for the present endure to abide in this place, where He has stationed you' (*Diss.* 1:9.16).[44]

Even though human beings enjoy this kinship, they find themselves in fetters, i.e. the body and its demands (*Diss.* 1:9.11–13, cf. 3:18.1–4). Therefore, the philosopher is caught in a struggle not to live as though life is sufficiently described in terms such as belly or sexual organs (*Diss.* 1:9.26). The stomach should be used as a means of God's providence, not for self-pleasure. To satisfy the belly according to this standard, and not as an instrument for self-indulgence, is the ἀγών of men of reason. Thus the stomach is a symbol of a lifestyle which is bound to earth, and which therefore needs to be controlled. It is incompatible with the divine kinship of any human being to act as if nothing but a belly. As we have seen, e.g. in Plato, the divine kinship and heavenly identity must be incorporated in a lifestyle where the desires of the stomach are mastered.

---

[44] For Epictetus' sense of being called by God, see e.g. *Diss.* 3:1.19, 24, 36–7; 3:21. 11–24; 3:22.23, 45–9, 53, 56. For a commentary on the texts about Epictetus' calling, see Margarethe Billerbeck, *Epiktet vom Kynismus*.

Hence, the true philosopher is not known by his lectures, but by – among other things – how he eats and drinks (*Diss.* 3:21.1–10). Epictetus is not necessarily urging an ascetic life. The philosopher's testimony carries no weight, he says, if it is accompanied by a pale and weak body (*Diss.* 3:22.86–9). Epictetus thus urges a moderate mode of living, just like his teacher Musonius Rufus.

To this philosopher being sons of God means entering the arena to fight the passions, among which the belly is a significant symbol. It is, therefore, quite natural that Epictetus frequently describes the philosopher as an athlete.[45] The athlete represents a lifestyle contrary to those who are enslaved by the belly. Together with the genitals the stomach is a symbol of a lifestyle with no aims beyond pleasing and reproducing oneself. In contrast, athletes exemplify a way of living marked by hard practice in order to reach the goal set for human beings.[46] This becomes an example of how the philosopher has to conduct his life in fighting the desires (*Diss.* 3:15; 3:25.1–5, cf. 1:4.20–1; 2:18.27–9). The opposite poles of stomachs and athletes will be important to our further study, since the two appear in Phil. 3 as well.

3.8   Plutarch (AD c. 50 – c. 120)

In many of his treatises Plutarch adresses the question of mastering the desires. His treatises deal with day-to-day affairs, since it is his belief 'that it is precisely these details that influence character, that is, the health of the soul'.[47] Plutarch uses a metaphor to explain the dangers of desires. A ship cannot sail safely and reach its destination if it is overloaded. This example is particularly used in his treatise on *Advice about Keeping Well* (*De Tuenda Sanitate Praecepta*). He develops this metaphor as a strategy for avoiding excess in food and drinking in particular (*Mor.* 123e–f; 128b; 128f). A ship loaded with too much cargo can easily be a description of eating and drinking excessively. Mastering the stomach thus becomes a key question in fighting the pleasures. To Plutarch this was by no means a mere philosophical statement. The texts just mentioned are all concerned with decent and moderate behaviour at banquets.

---

[45] See Victor C. Pfitzner, *Paul and the Agon Motif*, pp. 28–35.

[46] Dio Chrysostom is also very fond of depicting the philosopher as the real athlete. In *Orat.* 8:11–14 he depicts Diogenes' arrival for the contest in Isthmia. Diogenes claims that he is fighting the real enemies, those of hardships which cannot be fought by those who fill themselves by eating all day long. This is another piece of evidence that the athlete and gourmandizer form two opposite poles in the rhetoric of many ancient philosophers. The two will appear frequently in this book.

[47] Teresa M. Shaw, *The Burden of the Flesh*, p. 43.

In three of his treatises (*Beasts are Rational*; *The Eating of Flesh I and II*), Plutarch addresses the question of eating animals. He expouses an ascetic vegetarianism. Animals are in no way inferior to human beings; on the contrary, they surpass men in virtue.[48] One piece of evidence is how the two species relate to the desires, eating and drinking in particular. Consumption of food is natural and essential for surviving. While animals, however, consume according to the dictates of natural nourishment, men tend to live for pleasure and to eat and drink to excess.

> But man in his pleasure is led astray by gluttony (λαιμαργία) to everything edible; he tries and tastes everything as if he had not yet come to recognize what is suitable and proper for him; alone of all creatures he is omnivorous (παμφάγον).[49]   (*Mor.* 991c)

Plutarch calls to witness the loaded tables where nothing seems to have escaped the menu (*Mor.* 991d). Plutarch's description of men's inability to cope with the desires located in the belly is combined in the context with excess in sex too (*Mor.* 990d–991a).

In *The Eating of Flesh I*, the animals themselves complain that men eat not only out of necessity (ἀνάγκη), but out of arrogance (ὕβρις) (*Mor.* 994e). Plutarch quotes Cato, who says that some men are like bellies which have no ears (γαστέρας ὦτα μὴ ἐχούσας) (*Mor.* 996d). This is a variation of a saying quoted in Tit. 1:12; the glutton is nothing but a belly. Plutarch urges his readers to excise their gluttony (γαστριμαργία) and lust to kill animals. Men do this 'not so much by our belly that drives us to the pollution of slaughter; it is itself polluted by our incontinence (ἀκρασία)' (*Mor.* 996d–e). Plutarch's main point in these treatises is that men's ability or inability to master themselves can be measured by looking at their food-habits.[50] He turns the logic about gluttony and animal-like behaviour upside down; the animals are suffering because of men's devouring appetite. Owing to their behaviour, men are the real animals.

One final passage in Plutarch should be touched on briefly since it adds a point to the discussions on the role of the belly-centred, and is often overlooked. In his essay *On Flattery*, Plutarch draws the distinction between a friend and a flatterer. Peter Marshall has nicely presented the material in this essay. He says that according to Plutarch, the flatterer

[48] David E. Aune, '*De Esu Carnium*', pp. 301–16 presents these two treatises. Aune mentions Phil. 3:19 and Rom. 16:18 in passing; see pp. 313 and 315.
[49] LSJ s.v. renders this as 'all-devouring, voracious'.
[50] Bruce W. Winter, 'Gluttony', pp. 82–3 refers to Plutarch's three treatises on eating habits to attest the nature of Gentile banquets in Corinth in Paul's time; cf. chap. 5 in this study.

is a friend of many, he is a servile person, and marked by inconstancy; in short he is a coward and 'everything he does is for his own gain'.[51] Marshall does not mention, however, that Plutarch quotes an old saying about the flatterer; namely that 'his body is all belly (γαστὴρ ὅλον τὸ σῶμα)' (Mor. 54b),[52] which is, of course, a variant of the saying about gluttons who are nothing but bellies.

The belly is here used in a figurative sense. Nothing in the context suggests that food, gluttony or desires are involved. The stomach is used as a symbol without direct reference to food or gluttony. It is the lack of trustworthiness in a flatterer that justifies speaking of him as nothing but a belly. A flatterer is not to be trusted since he is always seeking what pleases himself. The κόλαξ is a greedy scrounger. This is, of course, the reason that he is so often presented as being addicted to his stomach. The common translation 'flatterer' might here be misleading. Hard times distinguish a friend from a flatterer: 'Yet this is the sort of thing that flatterers do, who apply their frankness to those parts that feel no hurt or pain' (Mor. 60b, cf. 49d; 55e; 64e–f). That the belly becomes a symbol of a selfish attitude is evident also in Mor. 61e–f. Plutarch says that there are some sorts of food which are useless; they only excite the passions and arouse the appetite (κοιλία). He continues to draw a comparison to the flatterer; such are the words of flatterers as well. The self-pleasing nature of the belly is here used to illustrate the conduct of flatterers; they seek their own satisfaction. Gluttony is extended figuratively to mean selfishness. Plutarch's polemic against flattery concurs with the political perspective on the belly-topos; the point of convergence is selfishness or selfish gain which leads to neglect of the fellowship. We notice here a relationship between the belly-topos and selfish living which will be developed later on in this study.

3.9   Athenaeus (flourished c. AD 200)

Deipnosophistae, or The Sophists at Dinner, was composed by Athenaeus, a native of Naucratis in Egypt, who lived in Rome at the

---

[51] See Peter Marshall, Enmity in Corinth, p. 310; see his pp. 70–90.

[52] The rest of the saying proves that it is a saying about greed: πανταχῇ βλέπων ὀφθαλμός, ἕρπον τοῖς ὀδοῦσι θηρίον; 'it's an eye that looks all ways, and a beast that walks upon its teeth'. Plutarch adds that this is a proper description of a parasite, 'one of the saucepan friends and friends post-prandial'. This addition is attributed to Eupolis, probably from his lost writing Flatterers; see Theodorus Koch, Comicorum Atticorum Fragmenta, Vol. 1, Fragm. 346, p. 349 or John Maxwell Edmonds, Fragments of Attic Comedy, Vol. 1, pp. 428–9. The first part of the saying, quoted partly in our text and partly in this note, is found in an anonymous comedy-writer; see Edmonds, Vol. 3A, Fragm. 392A, pp. 418–19.

transition between the second and third century AD Since the book is 'a veritable encyclopedia of sympotic literature',[53] it is a valuable source on food-customs, menus and recipes as well as the agenda of ancient *symposia*. The banquet is constantly interrupted by games or discussions on a number of subjects, by which the guests test and tease each other. The subjects discussed most extensively are those of fish, courtesans, gluttons and drinking-cups.

In the beginning of the book, Athenaeus initiates the topic of gluttony versus moderation, a topic running throughout this literature: 'For in drinking and eating we all take some pleasure; but it needs not rich feasts to quell hunger' (*Deipn.* 1:3f). The dialogues frequently mention persons – past and present – who were enslaved by their pleasures (δοῦλος . . . τῶν ἡδονῶν) (*Deipn.* 10:436b; 12:531c). In practice, this is a reference to indulgence in eating and drinking as well as sex (*Deipn.* 12:530f; 13:556d). A prominent belly was considered a sign of a luxurious and indulgent life (*Deipn.* 2:44f; 12:549d–550f). The lifestyle of the glutton is captured in this slogan 'There is nothing nicer than the belly . . . You will have only what you eat and drink' (*Deipn.* 8:336f). Epicurus, the philosopher, is seen as paving the way for this life of pleasures. He flattered his disciples for the sake of the belly and the pleasures of the flesh (*Deipn.* 7:279f). Epicurus was the father of a philosophy claiming that the beginning and root of all good was to satisfy the stomach (*Deipn.* 7:279a–280c). To this we will return more fully in the next chapter.

During the banquet there is a constant exchange between eating and dialogue. The Cynic guest Cynulcus urges his tablemates to eat rather than talk. Ulpian, one of the fellow guests, takes note of this and says: 'We have filled our bellies full, and it is high time that we do the talking; I urge Cynics to be still, since they have foddered themselves without stint. But perhaps you will like to gnaw to pieces the bones of the jaw and the head; there is no objection to their enjoying that kind of food, being Dogs . . . ' (*Deipn.* 3:96f). The following makes it evident that the main reason for Ulpian's depiction of the Cynics as gluttons is their inability to participate in the philosophical discourse according to Ulpian. Cynulcus and the Cynics behave in a way similar to the girls playing instruments and dancing for the amusement of the guests, and thus interrupt the conversation of wise men. Cynulcus is, of course, outraged by this comment. He cries out: 'You glutton (γάστρων),[54] whose god is your belly (κοιλιοδαίμων),

[53] Alessandra Lukinovich, '*Deipnosophistae* of Athenaeus' p. 266. For an introduction, see also Andrew Dalby, *Siren Feasts*, pp. 168–79.
[54] LSJ s.v. has 'pot-belly'; cf. *Deipn.* 3:125b.

and with no wit for anything else!' (*Deipn.* 3:97c). Cynulcus is involved
in polemics, and claims that his opponent has the belly as god, and with
no understanding for any thing other than filling it up. To have the belly as
god is here seen in the light of a polemic which reminds us of Tit. 1:12 and
similar dicta. The outburst is hardly based on Ulpian's eating, but on the
inability to participate in discourse and history he attributes to Cynulcus.
He returns the charge, and claims 'You're another'! Cynulcus blames him
for playing games with words and, not participating in real dialogue. It is
obvious that this text is speaking figuratively of the dancing flute-girls.[55]
It is, therefore, possible that gluttony and κοιλιοδαίμων have a similar
figurative extension as well.

But why is Cynulcus using this particular metaphor? After all, the
flute-girls, although used in a figurative sense, are not mere metaphors,
but refer to the common agenda of a banquet (see chap. 5). It is hardly just
a matter of giving each other a bad name. The context suggests that being
belly-minded might be an appropriate way of expressing shortsighted-
ness; i.e. to be unable to conceive of horizons beyond the present pleasures. The belly is here referred to in a way which implies a metaphorical
extension of the physiological role of the stomach. It calls into question the ability of belly-minded people to reflect beyond physical needs.
This means that there is a close connection between the physical and
metaphorical use of the belly.

Ulpian once again turns to his fellow guests. He wants them to join in a
word game. They should not eat and drink with an eye only to satisfying
their belly (διὰ τὴν γαστέρα), 'like the persons whom we name parasites
and flatterers'[56] (*Deipn.* 6:228d). This comment triggers a long section
(largely from 6:236d till 6:262a), where flattery is frequently mentioned.[57]
The relationship between κοιλία and the flatterer (κόλαξ and cognates)
is spelled out in a rather strange way in *Deipn.* 6:262a: 'This is the proper
use of the word *kolax* [flatterer], for *kolon* means food; . . . further *koilia*
[hollow, belly] is the receptable for food' (cf. *Deipn.* 6:254c,e and 260a–
261b, where eating is seen as typical of flatterers). Another word-play –
although not introduced as such explicitly – goes very much along the
same lines. The flatterer is a worm (σκώληξ) eating up things until he has
emptied it all (*Deipn.* 6:254c).[58]

---

[55] The LCL text edition makes this clear by rendering 'you are like flute-girls'. This is
a somewhat free rendering of the text, but nevertheless to the point.

[56] The Greek terms παράσιτοι and κόλακες merged into one; see references in Peter
Marshall, *Enmity in Corinth*, p. 73 n. 20; cf. *Deipn.* 6:248c.

[57] Peter Marshall, *Enmity in Corinth*, p. 72 calls it a review of 'Who's who of flatterers
in Antiquity'.

[58] This is a quotation about flatterers by Anaxilas; see LSJ s.v.

Why are the flatterers and belly associated in this literature? The flatterers were keen on dinners; they loved to sit at the table without paying for it. This is a recurrent theme in Athenaeus' presentation.[59] Athenaeus was fond of word-plays, and he makes one which is, in fact, an answer to our question. He tells us of a flatterer living with an old lady, exploiting her, so that he has his belly filled every day (*Deipn.* 6:246b–c). Athenaeus here speaks of ἐν γαστρὶ λαμβάνειν, which means to conceive. The old woman is not able to give birth any more, but the flatterer had a full belly on a daily basis. This material adds to the picture of flatterers as friends or citizens who are not to be trusted. They are seeking only the easy life and their own ends. Athenaeus found the belly to be a proper metaphor for a scrounger.

3.10   Summary

Ancient Graeco-Roman moral philosophy mentions the stomach frequently in the context of the discussion on how to master desires and passions. The belly is a key topic of these discussions. It becomes a catchword for a lifestyle controlled by the desires, and is thus to be considered a *topos*. Mastery of the pleasures deriving from the belly is seen as crucial for controlling the passions in general. The pleasures of the belly were excessive eating and drinking, which also stirred up sexual appetite. Hence, the three often appear together, and belong together, as we will elaborate later.[60] The belly is a code-word for gluttony. Within this ancient philosophical discussion, mastery of passions is seen in terms of moderation or control. Some, however, take a more radical attitude, and speak of extinguishing them completely. Most texts, however, speak of moderation in terms of using the desires according to Nature; i.e. for nourishment and procreation, not in luxury. A danger is always present even in this natural use of the desires. It is the mandate of the wise man, i.e. the rational man, to fight this danger from within, as an athlete fights his opponents. The example of athletes plays a significant role within these moral philosophical discussions; by their training or preparation for the contest, they represent an attitude with which the belly is frequently contrasted.

With the *topos* of the belly is associated a cluster of ideas: (1) The stomach is powerful. It may empower human beings and take control. (2) People are then enslaved to it, and are serving it. This service can even be described in religious terms, as worship. (3) People who are

---

[59] See e.g. *Deipn.* 6:239a–c; 240d–e; 243b, d; 244b, d; 248c.
[60] More on this in chap. 5.

serving the belly have given up their divine destination or the divine element laid down in them. Belly-worship is mundane indeed; it reveals an earthly nature opposed to the divine. (4) The earthly nature of the pleasures of the belly is clearly seen in the animals who have no concern beyond filling their bellies and reproducing themselves. Hence, gluttony is often depicted as animal-like. As a codeword 'belly' is associated with moral philosophy questions of far-reaching significance in antiquity.

Have we found a figurative sense of the stomach as well? The glutton is in some texts a symbol of a person fully controlled by the pleasures. Gluttons are considered to be nothing but bellies. But this is not yet a figurative sense of the belly. Belly-devotion is, however, contrasted with the athlete's self-discipline, referring to a self-centred attitude aiming at pleasing oneself and avoiding costs of any kind. An example of this is the flatterer, as well as the negligence of public affairs by the belly-servant. A selfish person does not contribute to the common good of the city. In these examples the belly becomes a metaphor. The meaning of this metaphor is closely connected to the stomach as an organ for digestion. The physiological denotation of the stomach is extended figuratively to mean a self-pleasing person devoted to his own ends.

The discussions of mastering the desires, and the appetites in particular, in some texts have a relevance to a social context, namely lavish banquets which were the scene of indulgence in food, drinking and sex.[61] This summary is, of course, a kind of fiction, because we are putting together a wide range of material. From a methodological point of view, we cannot assume all aspects to be present in every text. What we have presented is an overall picture which will help us read the Pauline texts, and to see from them what aspects of this picture are relevant to reading Paul's letters.

Have we found any analogies to Paul's phraseology of 'having the belly as god' or 'serving the stomach'? We have found numerous examples both of the concept of serving or worshipping the stomach, as well as being enslaved to it, or the belly as ruling a person. As for analogies to Paul's phraseology, the following observations are worth noting.[62] We have found that the belly is a ruling power and thus that men might be enslaved to it. Submitting to the belly can be expressed in terms both of enslavement and obedience, or service and worship. This is witnessed

---

[61] More on this in chap. 5.

[62] Marvin R. Vincent, *Philippians*, p. 117 mentions Alciphron's *Letters* 2.4 (according to Loeb *Epist.* 4:19.15) (γαστριμαντεύεσθαι) as an analogy as well. This is misleading. The context makes it evident that this verb refers to the practice of divination, which is another matter.

in the appearance of δουλεύειν and cognates related to a dative form of γαστήρ or κοιλία, from Xenophon on. Biblical traditions on idolatry can, therefore, easily be fitted into the ancient moral philosophy discussions. Furthermore, eating is revealing of identity, be it earthly or heavenly. These observations form a significant bridge to Paul's body-theology (chap. 1.4), and thus this ancient material on the stomach provides an approach to Paul's view on the human body. However, the material also demonstrates that the belly can appear as a symbol of selfishness, relatively independently of food and eating. This means that a body-theology cannot necessarily be assumed in the belly dicta; this connection must be demonstrated.

The most direct analogies to Paul's belly-worship are the following:

- The creed-like declaration of the Cyclops in Euripides, who calls the stomach 'the greatest of divinities', to which sacrifices are offered.
- Among the fragments of the Attic comic writers, a work is attributed to Eupolis. It is called Κόλακες (Flatterers), and in the text edition of Theodorus Kock (*Fragm.* nos. 172–3, p. 306)[63] the word κοιλιοδαίμων is witnessed, although there is no context available. Although the context is missing, the fact that it appears in a writing on flatterers is telling. Furthermore, the text does mention κοιλιοδαίμων next to a noun which means 'a frying-pan sniffer (ταγηνοκνισοθήρᾳ)'.[64] It is, in fact, confirmed by Athenaeus, who quotes this saying from Eupolis (*Deipn.* 3:100b).
- Athenaeus, *Deipn.* 3:97c, where one of the guests is called κοιλιοδαίμων.
- Diodorus Siculus was writing in Rome during the last years of the Republic. In his Book 8 (fragments) he gives a description of the Sybarites (18–19). This description starts out in this way: 'they are slaves to their belly and lovers of luxury (γαστρίδουλοί εἰσι καὶ τρυφηταί[65]). Some scholars dismiss the ancient material on the belly, by saying that in the majority

---

[63] See Theodorus Kock, *Comicorum Atticorum Fragmenta*, Vol. 1, p. 306. For this text see also John Maxwell Edmonds, *Fragments of Attic Comedy*, Vol. 1, pp. 378–9. He mentions Suidas, a Byzantine lexicon, which renders the term: φαγεῖν ζῶν, a person who lives to eat. See also LSJ s.v.

[64] See LSJ s.v. Edmonds renders it 'huntsmen always hot on the scent of the frying-pan!'

[65] LSJ s.v. has here 'voluptuary'. Athenaeus, *Deipn.* 1:7a speaks of Apicius, an exceedingly rich voluptuary. As indicative of his wealth, 'he lavished countless sums on his belly'.

of the texts, γαστήρ is used rather than the κοιλία employed by Paul.[66] Although this observation is generally correct, the material is by no means consistent enough to justify its dismissal. The majority of texts speak of γαστήρ, but far from all of the evidence, as is demonstrated above. The findings in this chapter provide a framework for an adequate reading of Paul's belly-texts.

[66] E.g. Paul Ewald, *Philipper*, pp. 205–7; so also Wolfgang Schenk, *Philipperbriefe*, p. 287.

4

ANCIENT CRITIQUE OF EPICUREANISM

4.0   Epicurus – the popularity and reputation of a doctrine

We have seen that that the belly-*topos* worked within the ancient discussions on mastery of pleasures. The belly was a catchword for a life
controlled by pleasures. The discussion on mastering the passions was
closely linked to the question of the highest good (τὸ ἀγαθόν, τὸ ἄριστον,
summum bonum) and happy life. This is the focus of lengthy discussions
among the moral philosophers, and in particular between Stoics and Epicureans. In brief, the Stoics claimed that virtue was the highest good, and
a reliable guide to a happy life. Epicurus and his followers claimed that
this role was played by pleasure and living without pain.[1] Since we have
already seen that Epicurus' philosophy is a rather important element of
the discussion on mastering the desires, it is natural now to turn to the
impact of his philosophy.

Epicurus was born on the island of Samos in the eastern Aegean in 341
BC. He established his school in Athens (306 BC), the so-called 'Garden
Philosophy', which might be taken to denote the master's emphasis on a
pleasant life as well as a secluded life. Epicurus died about 270 BC. In his
last will and testament, the philosopher entrusts his property to his friends,
so as to preserve the life of the Garden (Diogenes Laertius, *Philosophers*
10:16–22). Very little of Epicurus' writings is extant. Diogenes Laertius
devotes Book 10 in his *Lives of the Eminent Philosophers* to Epicurus.
His writings are listed, and Diogenes gives an excerpt of his teaching by
presenting three of his main letters.[2] From these letters emerge the main
doctrines and maxims of the Epicurean school. Since we are concerned

---

[1] For a comparison between the two philosophical schools, see J. C. B. Gosling and
C. C. W. Taylor, *The Greeks on Pleasure*, pp. 397–427.
[2] A collection of Epicurean texts, gathered from remains and quotations of the master
and his disciples, is now available in an English translation: John Gaskin, *The Epicurean
Philosophers*. For the Greek text see Hermann Usener, *Epicurea*, and Cyril Bailey, *Epicurus*.

mainly with the impact of the ethical teaching[3] of Epicureanism, we will mention some of the most relevant maxims.

Diogenes collected forty principal doctrines of the master (Diogenes Laertius, *Philosophers* 10:138–54).[4] The following are of special relevance for this study:

(2)   'Death is nothing to us; for the body, when it has been resolved into its elements, has no feeling, and that which has no feeling is nothing to us.'

(3)   'The magnitude of pleasure (ὅρος τοῦ μεγέθους ἡδονῶν) reaches its limit in the removal of all pain. When pleasure is present, so long as it is uninterrupted, there is no pain either of body or of mind or of both together.'

(5)   'It is impossible to live a pleasant life without living wisely and well and justly, and it is impossible to live wisely without living pleasantly. Whenever any one of these is lacking, when, for instance the man is not able to live wisely, though he lives well and justly, it is impossible for him to live a pleasant life.'

(8)   'No pleasure is in itself evil, but the things which produce certain pleasures entail annoyances many times greater than the pleasures themselves.'

(10)   'If the objects which are productive of pleasures to profligate persons really freed them from fears of the mind – the fears, I mean, inspired by celestial and atmospheric phenomena, the fear of death, the fear of pain; if, further, they taught them to limit their desires (τὸ πέρας τῶν ἐπιθυμιῶν), we should never have any fault to find with such persons, for they would then be filled with pleasures overflowing on all sides and would be exempt from all pain, whether of body or of mind, that is, from all evil.'

To be added to these are two of the so-called Vatican fragments culled from various lost works of Epicurus:[5] 'The flesh cries (σαρκὸς φωνή) out to be saved from hunger, thirst and cold. For if a man possess this safety and hope to possess it, he might rival even Zeus in happiness' (33). 'It is not the stomach that is insatiable, as is generally said, but the false opinion that the stomach needs an unlimited amount to fill it' (59). Finally, a fragment left by Epicurus on the happy life is worth quoting:

---

[3] For a critique of Epicurus' theology, see e.g. Jerome H. Neyrey, 'Polemic in 2 Peter', pp. 407–12.

[4] See also John Gaskin, *Epicurean Philosophers*, pp. 5–11.

[5] These were discovered in the Vatican 1888; see John Gaskin, *Epicurean Philosophers*, pp. 47–53.

'The beginning and the root of all good is the pleasure of the stomach (ἀρχὴ καὶ ῥίζα παντὸς ἀγαθοῦ ἡ τῆς γαστρὸς ἡδονή); even wisdom and culture must be referred to this' (*Fragm.* 409).[6]

From these maxims and quotations we see that Epicurus himself claimed that seeking pleasure and avoiding pain were the means by which a happy life could be attained. It is, however, quite clear from his doctrines, as well as from Diogenes' presentation, that the philosopher did not himself advocate a life of indulgence. He spells this out in a letter to his pupil Menoeceus. His doctrine of ἡδονή as the aim (τέλος) of life has a primary reference to the absence of pain and trouble of soul. It is not the pleasures sought in drinking, sex and the luxurious table: 'it is sober reasoning (λογισμός), searching out the grounds of every choice and avoidance, and banishing those beliefs through which the greatest tumults take possession of the soul. Of all this the beginning and the greatest good is prudence (φρόνησις)' (Diogenes Laertius, *Philosophers* 10:131–2).

A pleasant life is thus inseparable from virtue. In this letter Epicurus is complaining that his philosophy was misunderstood, either through ignorance, prejudice or wilful misrepresentation. It is worth noticing that what Epicurus is denying as the aim of his philosophy is, in fact, the common agenda of the banquets: drinking, revelling, sex with boys or women, fish or other delicacies (132).[7] This is an attempt by his philosophical school to distance itself from what became a widespread view, namely that the proper place to put into practice Epicurus' philosophy was the extravagant banquets. It is indeed possible to imagine that a selective reading of the master could employ some of his maxims to justify a self-satisfying life, centred on the demands of the belly.

The teaching of Epicurus did spread. Cicero, who disliked this doctrine, admits that it was a popular philosophy in Rome in his time. The teaching of this school was not unknown even to persons of moderate learning, he says (*Tusc. Disp.* 2:7–8, cf. 1:77). Cicero remarks, probably out of irritation or resignation: 'Here is a famous philosopher whose influence has spread not only over Greece and Italy but throughout all barbarian lands as well . . . wins the approval and applause of the multitude' (*Fin.* 2:49). He makes a similar statement in *Tusc. Disp.* 4:6–7. The crowd has flocked to this teaching and preferred it to other doctrines. This is due

---

[6] See John Gaskin, *Epicurean Philosophers*, p. 61 and Hermann Usener, *Epicurea*, p. 278. For a full account of Epicurean fragments quoted in Greek literature with a commentary, see Cyril Bailey, *Epicurus*, pp. 388–400. Bailey makes references to Usener's text pp. 92–119. This particular fragment (no. 409) Bailey has as no. 59 (pp. 134–5) among ethical fragments.
[7] For the agenda of banquets, see next chapter.

to the simplicity of this teaching, its seductive message or possibly the absence of any better teaching. The Epicurean maxims have, according to Cicero, taken Italy by storm (*Italiam totam occupaverunt*).[8]

There is a lot of material to support Cicero's remark that Epicurean teaching on pleasure was seductive. This philosophy was therefore embraced and taken advantage of in antiquity. For the purpose of our investigation it is of no importance that this was contrary to the master's own ideas. Diogenes Laertius touches upon this, saying that bad rumours about Epicurus' life derived from Timocrates, who left the school. The rumours took as their point of departure the following dictum of Epicurus: 'I know not how to conceive the good apart from the pleasures of taste, sexual pleasures, the pleasures of sound and the pleasures of beautiful form' (Diogenes Laertius, *Philosophers* 10:6). Timocrates claimed in a book, according to Diogenes, that Epicurus vomited twice a day from eating too much, that he spent a whole *mina* daily on his table, that he was hardly able to rise from his chair, and that he was entertained by *hetairai* or courtesans (Diogenes Laertius, *Philosophers* 10:6–7). Be this as it may, Seneca says that many used his philosophy – for bad motives – as a justification for vice (*Mor. Epist.* 21:9).

In the comedy *The Runaways* by Lucian of Samosata, Philosophy is complaining to Zeus about so-called philosophers who act like 'dogs' only in the negative way; i.e. barking, gluttony, thieving, womanizing, flattering and hanging round the tables (*Fug.* 16.18). Lucian speaks of their *symposia* as putting Epicurus' philosophy into practice:

> they claim to hate toadying (κολακεία), when as far as that goes they are able to outdo Gnathonides and Struthias[9] ... To all of them pleasure is nominally an odious thing and Epicurus a foeman; but in practice they do everything for the sake of it.
> (*Fug.* 19)

The way Lucian speaks of banquets as Epicurus' philosophy *in actu*, although perverted, is of great interest for our study, since the banquets link moral philosophical teaching on the stomach to an aspect of daily life (see chap. 5).

---

[8] Seneca, *Mor. Epist.* 79:15 mentions Epicurus as an example of a philosopher who did not receive proper recognition during his life-time. This sharply contrasts with the admiration he is given today, says Seneca, 'not only by the more cultured, but also by the ignorant rabble' (cf. *Mor. Epist.* 8:7–8; 21:9). Seneca considers Epicurus' doctrine common property, although he himself by no means approves of it (see below).

[9] Well-known gluttonous parasites in antiquity.

The way Epicurus' philosophy was embraced paved the way for an indulgent life which made Epicureanism an oft-despised doctrine in antiquity. In his polemic against Epicurus, Plutarch says that he is concerned with the reputation of this sect, not the truth about it (*Mor.* 1100d). Our concern in the following will also be with the reputation, because I consider this to provide an important access to Paul's dicta on the belly.[10]

4.1 Cicero

In his *Tusculan Disputations*, Cicero's (106–43 BC) polemic against, and even contempt for, Epicurus' philosophy comes clearly through.[11] The books of his school are not worth reading, he says. They do not comply with standards required of philosophical treatises (*Tusc. Disp.* 2:7–8). This strategy of neglect, however, does not prevent Cicero from writing quite a lot on the questions raised by this doctrine.[12]

Epicurus expresses himself in terms worthy of a philosopher in claiming that a pleasant life is impossible unless accompanied by virtue. But this Cicero considers incompatible with claiming pleasure as the highest good. Epicurus is simply not precise in what he says (*Tusc. Disp.* 3:49). His understanding of pleasure as the supreme good implies assigning all good to the body; a philosophy which is welcomed by the inexperienced (*imperiti*). He is therefore followed by a multitude (*Tusc. Disp.* 5:73). Epicurus has a heart like that of animals, following their instincts (*Tusc. Disp.* 5:73). He is *homo voluptarius*, a man of pleasure (*Tusc. Disp.* 2:18). The Epicureans cannot call pleasure the highest good and at the same time claim that only the virtuous man enjoys a happy life. Cicero argues that this is contradictory: they cannot have it both ways.

The proverbial figure of Sardanapalus

To make his point on Epicureanism quite clear, Cicero mentions Sardanapalus. We will pause in our presentation and turn to this figure, and

[10] For a presentation focusing on the 'truth' about this philosophy rather than its reputation, see Howard Jones, *The Epicurean Tradition*, pp. 21–62; Martha C. Nussbaum, *The Therapy of Desire*, pp. 102–39; Phillip Mitsis, *Epicurus' Ethical Theory*, pp. 11–58. See also Wolfgang Schmid, 'Epikur' and Michael Erler, 'Epikuros' with references to recent literature.

[11] For a general presentation of Cicero's antagonism towards Epicurus and his followers, see Howard Jones, *Epicurean Tradition*, pp. 69–80.

[12] And contrary to his claim that the writings of Epicureanism are not worth reading, he has, in fact, read some of their writings, which e.g. *Tusc. Disp.* 3:41–3 makes evident.

then, with a better understanding of the implications of Cicero's mention of him, we will return to his critique of Epicureanism. Sardanapalus is associated with the wealthy king of Assyria, Assurbanipal. Probably various persons and traditions have merged into the proverbial figure of a king named Sardanapalus.[13] He became a well-known archetype of a gluttonous person enjoying luxury and sex. He was a stock figure for what kind of life pleasure led to. Special attention was given to an inscription on his tomb.[14] The inscription varies somewhat according to the sources. According to Cicero it was written: 'This I have, what I have eaten and on what my sexual appetite has satiated itself. These many things remain but all other riches are left behind' (*Tusc. Disp.* 5:101).[15] Cicero actually quotes Aristotle saying that this was an inscription proper to an ox, not a king.[16]

Strabo the Geographer tells about a visit to the tomb of this king from Assyria, and the inscription found there: 'Eat, drink, be merry (ἔσθιε, πῖνε, παῖζε),[17] because all things else are not worthy this' (Strabo, *Geography* 14:5.9). Strabo then mentions another inscription, which he claims is known everywhere; it is the Greek version of Cicero's saying above. Plutarch has a slightly different version of the tomb-inscription: 'These are still mine – what I ate, and my wanton love-frolics (ἔφαγον καὶ ἐφύβρισα)' (*Mor.* 330f); true words of a φιλήδονος, as he puts it.[18]

Dio Chrysostom does not mention the funeral monument of Sardanapalus, but he is certainly familiar with it. Within a context addressing the pleasures of food, drink and copulation (*Orat.* 77/78:28–9), he introduces this proverbial figure. People who devote themselves to eating to satiety

[13] Pauly-Wissowa, *Real-Encyclopädie* II, 1, pp. 2436–75.   [14] Ibid., pp. 2441–2.

[15] My own translation. The Latin goes like this: *Haec habeo quae edi quaeque exsaturata libido hausit; at illa iacent multa et praeclara relicta.* LCL's translation goes like this: 'All I have eaten and wantoned and pleasures of love I have tasted, These I possess but have left all else of my riches behind.'

[16] *Eud. Eth.* 1216a1–2; cf. *Eud. Eth.* 1216a16–20, where Sardanapalus is mentioned as an example of the life of enjoyment (ὁ ἀπολαυστικὸς βίος).

[17] One can hardly avoid thinking of Paul's dicta in 1 Cor. 10:7 and 15:32; see chap. 10 of this study.

[18] Plutarch makes a reference to this tomb-inscription in *Mor.* 336d–e as well. According to this text, the inscription said: ἔσθιε, πῖνε, ἀφροδισίαζε. τἆλλα δ᾽ οὐδέν ('Eat, drink, and sport with love; all else is naught'). Plutarch's comment is bitingly ironic; the inscription tells that there is no difference between the life and death of Sardanapalus. Athenaeus, *Deipn.* 8:336a–b mentions this inscription as well. In 8:336f, he quotes from a play where a slave says: 'Let's drink, and drink our fill, My Sicon, Sicon! Let's have a good time while we may still keep life in our bodies. Whoop it up, Manes! There is nothing nicer than the belly. That is your father, and again, your only mother. Ethics, embassies, army tactics – fine pretences that sound hollow, like dreams. Fate will snuff you out at the appointed time. You will have only what you eat and drink. All the rest is dust – Pericles, Codrus, Cimon.' This is presented as a saying in the spirit of Sardanapalus, and in opposition to philosophy.

or to sex regard Sardanapalus as a person to be envied: 'He spent his life in feasting and in playing the wanton with eunuchs and women' (29). Ironically, Chrysostom says that he envied the happiness of goats[19] and asses.[20] The beast-like character of Sardanapalus' way of life is emphasized; e.g. in the term Chrysostom applies for copulating (ὀχεύειν), which is usually found to describe animals' sexual acts.[21]

Athenaeus, as well, tells the story of Sardanapalus (*Deipn.* 12:529d–530c). This introduces a longer section on various persons who were devoted to luxury and sex. Their devotion to pleasure is depicted in terms of lavish banquets in the presence of flute-girls and courtesans. According to this text, a stone column was found on his tomb, saying the following: '...I drank, I ate, I loved (ἔπιον, ἔφαγον, ἠφροδισίασα), for that I knew the time to be short which mortals live...' (*Deipn.* 12:529f–530a).[22] Athenaeus' information concurs with Plutarch's description of a stone statue at Sardanapalus' tomb. This statue shows Sardanapalus snapping his fingers above his head – a sign of mockery: everything is naught except enjoying pleasures (*Deipn.* 12:529d, cf. Plutarch, *Mor.* 336e).

Athenaeus also mentions writers who loved pleasure while alive, since death was nothingness, a shade in the world below. He refers to the comic poet Amphis, who says that the person who is not taking pleasure in his life while still alive, is a fool. Amphis gives the following advice: 'Drink! Play! (πῖνε, παῖζε). Life is mortal, short is our time on earth. Death is deathless, once one is dead' (*Deipn.* 8:336c).[23] A man named Bacchidas lived a life like Sardanapalus. He left an inscription on his tomb as well: 'Drink, eat, indulge in all things the heart's desire. For lo! I stand here a stone to represent Bacchidas' (*Deipn.* 8:336c).

The proverbial character of Sardanapalus is seen in the way Juvenal mentions him and assumes his readers to be familar with his reputation (*Sat.* 10:360–2). Juvenal says that the deities should be approached in prayer in order to receive *mens sana in corpore sano* (356). This implies the ability to endure hard work and toil, as did Heracles. Juvenal considers him the opposite pole to Sardanapalus. These things are better than 'the loves and the banquets and the downy cushions of Sardanapalus (*venere et*

---

[19] As for goats, see chap. 2 on Gaius Caligula.

[20] Jews as well as Christians were accused of worshipping an ass (Tacitus, *Hist.* 5:4; Josephus, *Ag. Ap.* 2:79–81; Minucius Felix, *Octavius* 8–9). In the text of Minucius, this allegation has an obvious sexual reference; see also Mary Beard, John North, Simon Price, *Religions of Rome*, p. 282.

[21] See LSJ s.v.

[22] The inscription on the tomb is rendered somewhat differently in *Deipn.* 12:530b: ἔσθιε, πῖνε, παῖζε, which is remarkably similar to 1 Cor. 10:7.

[23] This is a logic which runs in tandem with the one Paul is targeting in 1 Cor. 15:32.

cenis et pluma Sardanapalli' (10.362). Even Philo mentions this famous king of greed within a discussion on γαστριμαργία (*Spec.* 4:122). To Philo, Sardanapalus is an example of a lifestyle which the Jewish food laws were aimed at preventing.

By mentioning the proverbial figure of Sardanapalus,[24] Cicero leaves no doubt as to his view on Epicurus' philosophy: it paves the way for φιληδονία, which involves excess in eating, drinking and sex.

In his *De Finibus*, Cicero provides a more advanced and philosophical refutation of Epicurus' doctrine. Book 1 claims to be an accurate and true presentation of Epicureanism, the doctrine 'which to most men is best known of any' (*Fin.* 1:13). The presentation is conducted by one of Epicurus' followers, Torquatus, although Cicero continuously interrupts. The whole presentation centres on pleasure and how to define it. Book 2, then, provides Cicero's refutation, which for us is the more interesting. Cicero argues that Epicurus' teaching on pleasure is imprecise and liable to be misunderstood, especially by the sensualists (*Fin.* 2:20–2, cf. 2:6, 12, 18–19). The maxims of Epicurus on food, drink and the delights of sound are bound to be misunderstood (*Fin.* 2:7). Cicero finds it impossible to say that pleasure is the supreme good and still claim that desires should be kept within bounds.

To prove his point, he draws once again on a stock image related to the inscriptions on the tomb of Sardanapalus. He speaks of banquets where participants were vomiting, being carried home, and still the next day continuing to immerse themselves in food and pleasure. Part of this stock image, which to Cicero is related to Epicureanism, includes sexual performance as well (*Fin.* 2.23). Defining pleasures as the highest good leads to this kind of life. Hence, reason (*ratio*) must define what is the real good, namely virtue (*Fin.* 2:36–7).

Cicero adds a political aspect as well, which is not surprising from what we have seen about the belly-*topos* in the preceding chapter. He considers the doctrine of Epicurus as detrimental to civic duty. In politics, a philosophy that avoids pain and seeks pleasure does not work for the common good of the city. Men's conduct must be ruled by duty (*officium*) or virtue, not pleasure (*Fin.* 2:58–60).[25] Epicureanism is an enterprise

[24] For further references to Sardanapalus, see John E. B. Mayor, *Satires of Juvenal*, pp. 177–9 and Abraham J. Malherbe, 'Beasts at Ephesus', pp. 76–7.

[25] In his discussion on duties (*De Officiis*), Cicero, without directly adressing Epicureans, argues that men consist of body and spirit (*corpus, animus*), to which belong respectively the appetite or passions and reason. It is essential that reason commands and appetite obeys. This is a characteristic of human beings as opposed to animals with 'no thought except for sensual pleasure (*nihil . . . nisi voluptatem*)'. Moderation marks 'the superiority and dignity

in selfishness (*facere sua causa*), says Cicero (*Fin.* 2:60–3). This is the
reason that Epicureans cannot appeal to great names in the history of wars
and politics. Cicero raises serious doubt about Epicureanism as enhancing
good citizenship. We note that when Cicero is most fiercely attacking
Epicureanism, he uses stock images which are related to excessive eating,
drinking and sex. In brief, Epicureans measure whether life was happy or
not by the standards of the belly (*omnia quae ad beatam vitam pertineant
ventre metiri*) (*De Natura Deorum* 1:113). Cicero quotes Metrodorus,
one of Epicurus' closest pupils to this effect. Metrodorus claimed the
stomach to be the standard by which happiness was to be measured. This
he claimed not once, but repeatedly, says Cicero. In other words, Cicero
considers this dictum on the belly as a typical catchword of Epicurean
doctrine.

As a moral philosopher believing in the Stoic doctrine of virtue as
the supreme good, Cicero refutes the Epicureans who honour pleasure
as the highest good. In his speech *Against Piso* (*In Pisonem*), however,
he is targeting Epicureanism not primarily on philosophical terms, but
in a polemical context aimed at having the Senate convict Piso for his
administration during his governorship of Macedonia.

Piso is adressed as 'the present Epicurus' (*In Pisonem* 17, 24, 37, 39,
40, 41, 59, 62, 84, 85, 92) who is constantly banqueting: 'who in those
days ever saw you sober?' (*In Pisonem* 22). He is said to have danced
naked at a party (*convivium*), and it is hardly known what occupied Piso
most of the time, drinking, vomiting or discharging himself of what he
digested (*In Pisonem* 22). He spent his time in the taverns and brothels
with eating and drinking (*in cibo et vino*), which, according to Cicero,
is the happy life Epicurus' philosophy claims (*In Pisonem* 42); and this
is the life of the worst doctrine of philosophy (*In Pisonem* 59)! In this
context, the phrase *in cibo et vino* obviously includes sex as well, owing
to the fact that brothels are mentioned. Piso preferred the pleasures of
the belly (*abdominis voluptates*) to those of the eyes and ear (*In Pisonem*
66). Here the stomach sums up the indulgent life of Piso.

Cicero blames Epicurus' philosophy for the regrettable life of Piso.
He reminds his audience that Epicurean philosophy prefers *voluptas* to
anything else, adding that whether this reputation of Epicurus is correct
or not, is of no concern here (*In Pisonem* 68). Be that as it may, he
says, the Epicurean view is dangerous to put before a man like Piso. His

of our nature (*in natura excellentia et dignitas*)' (*Off.* 1:100–6). When pleasure exceeds
its natural limits, this has bodily consequences; it affects face, feature, voice, motions and
attitudes (*Off.* 1:102). Cicero here applies physiognomic theories to describe how pleasure
affects the body, and how the body is a sign of true human identity.

desires were stimulated by this teaching. He thought to have found 'not a professor of ethics but a master of the art of lust (*auctor libidinis*), and insisted on the literal meaning of Epicurus' words, allowing no discussion on the real intent of his sayings' (*In Pisonem* 69). Piso's life can briefly be summarized in simple poems on lust, sexual immorality, varied dinners and banquets, and adultery: *omnis hominis libidines, omnia stupra, omnia cenarum conviviorumque genera, adulteria* (*In Pisonem* 70); in short, eating, drinking and sex. Cicero goes on to present numerous examples of the greed and avarice (*avaritia*) of Piso. Piso was running his provinces with an eye to exploiting them (*In Pisonem* 85–91).

Throughout his fierce attack on Piso, Cicero argues that he shunned public banquets and games. This was a sign of lack of interest in public affairs. Instead, Piso took refuge in closed banquets – in the pleasures of the belly (*In Pisonem* 66). Cicero here summarizes his critique of Piso's lifestyle in the pleasures of his belly, and he brings up a common point in the criticism of Epicureanism: having devoted himself to the pleasures of the belly, Piso is a self-pleasing citizen.[26] This political aspect is developed in Cicero's *Pro Sestio*, in which §§20–5 are about Piso and his fellow-consul Gabinicus (58 BC). Cicero speaks of the state in the metaphor of a ship whose captains are worn out by drunkenness, gluttony, and adultery. As for Piso, he is contrasted with the good citizens (*omnes boni*). Without inquiring into what Epicurus actually meant by claiming pleasure as *summum bonum*,[27] Piso swallowed his teaching entirely. He adopted Epicureanism's view that wise men did everything for their own sake (*omnia sua causa facere*), and did not engage in public affairs. A life of tranquillity, full of pleasures, was to be preferred to politics. Cicero makes much of the self-sacrifice for the state that Epicureans are abandoning: 'danger for the country, receive wounds, welcome death' (*Pro Sestio* 23). This attitude of duty (*officium*) is contrasted to self-interest (*non commodi esse ducendam*). To Cicero, Piso's view of duty was insane.[28] Cicero scorns the lifestyle of this consul and names him *helluo patriae*, a devourer of the fatherland (*Pro Sestio* 26).[29]

[26] For the political aspect of this polemic, see in particular the presentation of Xenophon, Musonius Rufus, Epictetus and Plutarch in chap. 3; see also chap. 5.

[27] Cicero seems throughout to acknowledge the difference between the philosopher himself and those who took advantage of him.

[28] For the political aspect of Cicero's rhetoric, see Paul MacKendrick, *Speeches of Cicero*, pp. 214, 328.

[29] According to *Oxford Latin Dictionary*, *helluo* means 'one who spends immoderately on eating, a squanderer'.

Cicero's criticism of Piso is based on his attendance at closed banquets, his inappropriate lifestyle of excessive eating, drinking and sex and the lack of interest in politics which followed in its wake. The criticism clearly connects Epicureanism and banquets as the arena in which this doctrine was put into practice. But this does not necessarily mean that Cicero gives a true picture of Piso. Paul MacKendrick says that Cicero is using Piso's friendship with the Epicurean philosopher Philodemus as 'a stick to beat him with', and 'that Piso's Epicureanism was more respectable than Cicero pretends'.[30] The Epicurean and erotic poems of Philodemus were taken by Cicero to describe life in Piso's house.[31] This means that Cicero's speech is to be considered a rhetorical device rather than a description of Piso's actual way of living. Two additional remarks have to be made, however. Although his rhetoric hardly conveys a reliable picture of Piso's lifestyle, it is not entirely without a basis. Piso did entertain Philodemus in his house. In other words, the rhetoric takes his friendship with Epicureanism as its point of departure. Furthermore, Cicero's rhetoric reveals a widespread view of Epicureanism, namely that this philosophy was put into practice in full during indulgent banquets (see chap. 5). This works, however, in polemical rhetoric.

4.2   Seneca

Among the critics of Epicurus and Epicureanism, this contemporary of Paul is the most friendly towards the doctrine. We have already seen that Seneca (born between 4 BC and AD 1, died 65 AD) says that Epicurus' philosophy was embraced out of bad motives. This sympathy is seen elsewhere in Seneca's writings as well. In *De Vita Beata* (*On the Happy Life*) 13:1–3, Seneca expresses himself in a way not common to his own Stoic school, and he admits to doing so. Epicurus' teaching is sacred and correct, although sad. He bids us to obey Nature, as do the Stoics, 'but it takes a very little luxury to satisfy Nature!' (*Vit. Beat.* 13:1). Epicurus' philosophy has been taken as sponsoring gluttony and lust (*gula et libido*). The pleasure of these things is not taught by Epicurus, but rather brought to his philosophy by people who want to indulge under cover of philosophical maxims. The maxims of Epicurus provided a means to come out in public and advocate indulgence. His teaching is not to be judged from its many outside adherents who use Epicurus as

---

[30] Paul MacKendrick, *The Speeches of Cicero*, p. 320.

[31] For Philodemus and his poems, see Simon Hornblower and Anthony Spawforth, *Oxford Classical Dictionary*, pp. 1165–66.

justification for their vices of excessive eating and drinking (cf. *Vit. Beat.*
12:3–4). In his 'defence' of Epicurus,[32] however, Seneca bears witness to
the fact that eating and drinking were catchwords for an Epicurean way of
living.

After all, Seneca is a Stoic and holds another view on the happy life. His
essay *De Vita Beata*, dedicated to his brother Gallio, considers what true
happiness is and how it is to be obtained.[33] All men desire a happy life, he
claims. But so many have renounced the way to achieve this aim. Setting
the mind on inner joys, not on pleasure, makes a man happy. 'The day a
man becomes superior to pleasure (*voluptas*), he will also be superior to
pain; but you see in what wretched and baneful bondage he must linger
whom pleasures and pains, those most capricious and tyrannical masters,
shall in turn enslave' (*Vit. Beat.* 4:4).[34] While the wise man looks after
the body for the sake of mind, those who are compelled by the desires,
however, claim that the highest good is located in the bodily pleasures
(*in iliis . . . summum bonum*) (*Vit. Beat.* 7:1).[35]

Vit. Beat. 7:1 introduces a discussion of the Epicurean view of the
happy life. Seneca blames the Epicureans for cultivating virtue for no
other reason than to get some pleasure from it (*Vit. Beat.* 9:1–4). The
Stoic view, however, he explains by a parable. In a field ploughed for
corn, some flowers will always spring up here and there. Although they
are not the purpose of the farmer, they still please. So is the Stoic attitude
to pleasures; there is no reward beyond virtue. The Stoic seeks the good
of a man (*hominis bonum*), not that of his belly (*venter*) – and Seneca
adds ironically: 'the belly of cattle and wild beasts is more roomy!' (*Vit.
Beat.* 9:4).[36] The Epicurean instinct is, with its emphasis on the stomach,
animal-like. *Venter* is here a catchword for an Epicurean way of living,
seeking pleasures for oneself, or measuring life or good by mere food
(*bonum suum cibo*[37] *metientibus*) (*Vit. Beat.* 10:1).

---

[32] For Seneca's admiration of Epicurus, see also his *Mor. Epist.* 92:25, where he refers
to the philosopher saying 'this is the happiest day of my life' in the midst of his sufferings.

[33] See Elizabeth Asmis, 'Seneca's *On the Happy Life*'.

[34] The Latin text speaks in terms of *servitus, serviturus esse, dominia*.

[35] The LCL translator renders the Latin ablative *in iliis* 'in the belly'. C. D. N. Costa,
Seneca, Four Dialogues, p. 19 has 'in the sexual organs' (cf. p. 176). *Oxford Latin Dictionary*
s.v. *ilia* has 'the groin or private parts'.

[36] J. N. Sevenster, *Paul and Seneca*, p. 147 comments on this text without noticing –
either here or elsewhere in his book – the relevance of this to Paul's sayings on the stomach.
Sevenster's study concentrates on theological concepts, such as God, man, the life of the
individual, social relations, eschatology (such is his table of contents). But his approach is
so theological that he misses *topoi* common to the two. Theology may well be expressed in
the way a *topos* is being appropriated. To demonstrate that is the aim of this entire study.

[37] *Cibus* means 'food' or 'nourishment'; see *Oxford Latin Dictionary* s.v.

While the Epicurean embraces pleasure, or does everything for its sake (*voluptatis causa*), Seneca restrains it (*Vit. Beat.* 10:3). Pleasures are never satisfied, they always demand more; following them is, therefore, destructive. Virtue is the reliable guide to a happy life. Persons having virtue as their sign (*signa*) shall still have pleasures (cf. the flower-parable above), but will master them (*domini eius et temperatores erimus*) (*Vit. Beat.* 14:1–2). In eating and drinking, the aim of men of virtue is to satisfy the requests of Nature, not to fill and empty the belly (*non implere alvum et exinanire*[38]) (*Vit. Beat.* 20:5). The critique of the consequences of Epicurus' philosophy revolves around the belly once again.

In *Vit. Beat.* 11:4, Seneca mentions two examples of people obsessed with pleasure:

> Look at Nomentanus and Apicius,[39] digesting, as they say, the blessings of land and sea, and reviewing the creations of every nation arrayed upon their board. See them, too, upon a heap of roses, gloating over their rich cookery, while their ears are delighted by the sound of music, their eyes by spectacles, their palates by savours; soft and soothing stuffs caress with their warmth the length of their bodies, and, that the nostrils may not meanwhile be idle, the room itself, where sacrifice is being made to luxury, reeks with varied perfumes. You will recognize that these are living in the midst of pleasures, and yet it will not be well with them, because what they delight in is not good.

Seneca here provides a vivid picture of two men who are putting into practice (although to an extreme degree) Epicurus' maxim of conceiving the highest good in the pleasures of taste, sex, sound, and beautiful forms (e.g. Diogenes Laertius, *Philosophers* 10:6; cf. Cicero, *De Natura Deorum* 1:112). The two gourmandizers are men who are never satisfied, always asking for more, and who exhibit an almost religious devotion to their stomach; i.e. they are serving their belly (*abdomini servit*) (*Ben.* 7:26.4).[40]

---

[38] *Exinanire* is probably a reference to vomiting; see Lewis, Short, *A Latin Dictionary* s.v., referring to Pliny's *Nat. Hist.*26:36; see from §35 to catch the context.

[39] Two well-known gourmandizers of his time. Seneca mentions Apicius in *Helv.* 10:8–11 as well. For Nomentanus, see Horace, *Sat.* 1:1.102; 1:8.11; 2:1.22.

[40] For, Seneca says, the belly acts like a master. It 'will not listen to advice; it makes demands, it importunes (*venter praecepta non audit, poscit, appellat*)' (*Mor. Epist.* 21:11). This is Seneca's response to the welcoming words uttered by a representative of the Garden Philosophy: 'Stranger, here you will do well to tarry; here our highest good is pleasure. The care-taker of that abode, a kindly host, will be ready for you, he will welcome you with barley-meal and serve you water also in abundance, with these words: "Have you been well

In Seneca's letters a lifestyle governed by the stomach represents the opposite of what wise men must struggle for, namely moderation. Seneca warns against philosophical gourmandizers whose appetite is bigger then their bellies (*Mor. Epist.* 89:22). This he depicts by means of lavish banquets which make the earth an unsafe place for all animals, except when the gluttons are full to bursting and cannot eat more. They are stuffing their bellies[41] (*Mor. Epist.* 119:14). Lucilius, the addressee of these letters, must turn away from this lifestyle and embrace instead the athletic way of living; a figurative reference to the struggle of wise men for moderation (*Mor. Epist.* 15:5; 78:16; 80:1–5; cf. *Tranq.* 3:1; 9:4; *Const.* 9:5; *Ira* 2:14.2).[42]

4.3   Plutarch

Plutarch is aware of the pervasive influence of Epicureanism, and addresses this issue directly in two treatises. He seems to be one of the fiercest critics of Epicurus' philosophy in antiquity. His *Against Colotes* (*Adversus Colotem*) is a response to one of the disciples of the master, and probably reproduces a lecture given by Plutarch. The essay *That Epicurus Actually Makes a Pleasant Life Impossible* is Plutarch's follow-up to this lecture.

Plutarch criticizes the Epicureans' neglect of community and fellowship. He quotes Colotes, who claims that if the laws were taken away, and people were left without the teaching of Socrates, Plato and some others, people would live the life of wild beasts. In other words, Colotes says that stability and peace are due to the laws (*Mor.* 1124d). That this is said by a follower of Epicurus provokes intense protest from Plutarch. The real threat to stability and fellowship is represented by none other than the Epicureans themselves, who think that

> our good is to be found in the belly (περὶ γαστέρα τἀγαθὸν ἡγούμενοι) and the other passages by which pleasure (ἡδονή) makes her entry.   (Mor. 1125a)

entertained?" "This Garden", he says, "does not whet your appetite; it quenches it. Nor does it make you more thirsty with every drink; it slakes the thirst by a natural cure – a cure that demands no fee. This is the 'pleasure' (*voluptas*) in which I have grown old"' (Seneca, *Mor. Epist.* 21:10).

[41] *Farcire ventrem* means 'to fill completely, stuff, pack' or 'to gorge oneself'; see *Oxford Latin Dictionary* s.v. *farcire*. Cf. *Mor. Epist.* 108:15–16; 114:25–7. These letters speak of *gula, venter, voluptas*.

[42] On the imagery of athletes as a contrast to serving the belly, see e.g. our presentation of Epictetus in chap. 3.7, and of 4 Maccabees in chap. 6.

He claimed that it is precisely to counteract this kind of teaching that the laws are necessary, in order to protect fellow-citizens from their appetites. Plutarch extends the Epicurean appetite in a figurative way; Epicureans are liable to consume their neighbours (τοὺς πλησίον κατεσθίωσιν ὑπὸ λαιμαργίας). They and no others represent the wild beast in society (ὁ τῶν θηρίων βίος). Plutarch is here drawing on a saying of Metrodorus, where Epicurus' teaching on pleasures is compared to the natural desires of the animals. Plutarch mocks this doctrine by speaking of it as a roaring originating in the belly (*Mor.* 1125a–b). Plutarch's critique is occasioned by his view of the Epicurean drinking parties (see chap. 5). Epicurus taught his followers to live in seclusion, to withdraw from the public. This is, according to Plutarch, tantamount to removing the lamps from the *symposia*, thus paving the way for all pleasures to be practised freely. Plutarch assumes the presence of prostitutes at these banquets (*Mor.* 1129b).[43]

Plutarch argues that defining pleasure as the supreme good prevents Epicureans' being good and trustworthy citizens, working for the well-being of the community. An Epicurean is, thanks to the doctrine he follows, necessarily ἀπολίτευτον καὶ ἀφιλάνθρωπον (*Mor.* 1098d). His mind is set on how he may gratify the belly properly (ὀρθῶς γαστρὶ χαρίζεσθαι). The Epicureans describe a circle with the belly as its centre, circumscribing the whole area of ἡδονή; in this circle they then live. This is a line of criticism which Plutarch has inherited from, among others, Cicero. Citizenship and belly-devotion are incompatible.[44] Plutarch considers the pleasure-philosophy to be detrimental to responsibility to the fellowship: ' . . . those who say that there is no need to save Greece, but rather to eat and drink so as to gratify the belly (ἀλλ' ἐσθίειν καὶ πίνειν ἀβλαβῶς τῇ γαστρί) without harming it, are bound to suffer in repute and to be regarded as bad men' (*Mor.* 1100d, cf. 1125d). In *Mor.* 1098c the same saying of Metrodorus is quoted in a slightly different form: instead of saving the nation, the Epicureans eat, drink and gratify the stomach. Rather than being leaders of the people, they consider themselves friends of the table. According to these texts, Metrodorus also claims that they have no interest in winning crowns; i.e. in participating in athletic contests and receiving due honour. For Plutarch this is another

---

[43] The secluded life enjoyed by the Epicureans, according to Plutarch, paves the way for pleasure. Withdrawing from public life can be compared to the removal of the light from the banquets, thus letting the flesh (σάρξ) have the darkness and concealment its practices require. The comparison to the removal of the light brings to mind ancient accusations against the Christians (e.g. Minucius Felix, *Octavius* 9:5–6), accusations which were also made against the Bacchic rites; see e.g. Livy, *Ab Urbe Condita* 39.8–18.

[44] See our presentation of Xenophon, Musonius Rufus, Epictetus in particular (chap. 3).

piece of evidence that they are entirely devoted to enjoying the moment. Thus Epicureans have – in their own words – no share in the athletic fight of the true philosophers (*Mor.* 1105c). Plutarch here deploys a set of opposite examples which we have come across frequently in the material, namely athletes versus belly-servants.

Plutarch's claim that Epicureans are not community-friendly is related to two other lines of criticism in his writings. After his lecture against Colotes, he goes, as usual, to the gymnasium to continue the topic there (*Mor.* 1086d). One of the first points he makes is that the body experiences pain as well (*Mor.* 1089f–1091b). If the highest good is to escape all evil this necessarily leads to an indulgent life and avoidance of all pain and suffering. Belly-centredness is, therefore, bound to be selfish, since the supreme good is sought nowhere else than in the stomach (*Mor.* 1098d; 1108c), which always leads to a yearning for more and fancier food as well as fairer girls (*Mor.* 1097d–1099d). Epicurus' philosophy is then best described in the words of his most prominent pupil Metrodorus: 'how to gratify the belly properly' (*Mor.* 1098d; cf. 1099b; 1100d), which refers to food and sex. The saying of Metrodorus represents a development of Epicurus' basic principles, especially *Fragment* 409 mentioned earlier in this chapter.[45]

According to Plutarch, not only are the Epicureans detrimental to the fellowship, neither do they have 'any spark of the divine (ἀνενθουσίασ-τον)' (*Mor.* 1098d). The LCL translator reads this term in the light of the fundamental theological critique voiced in antiquity: the Epicureans were commonly seen as atheists.[46] The Greek word does not necessarily imply this. It may simply mean 'without inspiration', caused by e.g. wine, love or whatever (cf. *Mor.* 346b; 433c; 437e; 751b; 758e). *Mor.* 1102b in Plutarch's essay against Epicureanism, however, favours a reading along the lines suggested by the LCL translator; their lifestyle is a denial of the gods. We might well rephrase this according to what we have

[45] Rolf Westman, *Plutarch gegen Kolotes*, pp. 179 and 208 considers Plutarch's presentation to be unjust to Metrodorus. What Metrodorus probably had in mind was that 'the mind must be serene in order to pursue knowledge; the first condition of a serene mind is an untroubled stomach' (Westman quoting Kathleen Freeman). I am confident that Plutarch (and Cicero as well) would have interrupted here, claiming that then the stomach can hardly be conceived as the highest good, since its serenity is a means rather than an end. Anyway, Westman comments from a historical point of view. Plutarch admits, as we have seen, that his concern is with the reputation and consequences of Epicurus' philosophy; so is ours in this study.

[46] Epictetus makes this a starting point for his critique of the Epicurean lifestyle in his *Diss.* 2:20 (see chap. 3.7 above).

witnessed to be quite substantial in our material: the Epicureans are hyper-earthly.

4.4   Summary

We have seen the pervasiveness of Epicurus' philosophy in the ancient world. His doctrines were simple and enticing far beyond the circle of the philosophers. His maxims were used to justify an indulgent life which was commonly described by catchwords like eating, drinking and copulating. There is hardly any doubt that Epicurus' philosophy was far more sophisticated than this. But it gained a reputation for going down this path. His critics appear to be using very much the same arguments. One of the prominent catchwords for the critique of Epicureanism was its belly-centredness. The ancient moral-philosophical instruction on the dangers coming from the stomach recalled the memories of proverbial gourmandizers, such as Apicius[47] and Nomentanus. The legendary figure of Sardanapalus was the most prominent example, and Cicero used him to hit the Epicureans hard. The critics are not without a basis in the maxims of Epicurus himself or those of his followers. A belly-devoted lifestyle (*abdomini servire*) manifested itself in eating, drinking and copulating, as already mentioned. Furthermore, this doctrine was considered to enhance selfishness and to be detrimental to good citizenship. The lifestyle of Epicureans, as the critics saw it, was a sign of the earthly and non-divine nature of this doctrine.[48]

Finally, we have seen that criticism of Epicureanism extends into a critique of a pleasure-seeking life as it manifested itself in banquets. Epicureanism is hereby gradually being redefined. It becomes a description of hedonism justifying itself with reference to the hunger of σάρξ.[49] This implies that critique of belly-centredness does not necessarily assume the presence of Epicurean philosophers. It has become a vehicle for a hedonistic lifestyle extending far beyond the philosophical guild.[50]

---

[47] Apicius actually got a book of recipes named after him; see Andrew Dalby, *Siren Feasts*, pp. 179–80.

[48] Among the early Church Fathers, Epicurus was seen as the great advocate of detrimental pleasures, and thus became synonymous with heresy. The Fathers drew on the old criticism we have analysed here; see Wolfgang Schmid, 'Epikur', pp. 792–803; Howard Jones, *Epicurean Tradition*, pp. 94–116. See also chap. 11 of this study.

[49] Satisfying this hunger is happiness, according to Epicurus' principles; see *Fragm.* 33 in the Vatican collection.

[50] For a Pauline study it is of relevance to know that Josephus mentions Epicurus as well. He is an early witness to a long-standing Jewish tradition where Epicurus was a

Epicurean philosophy and the critique it met in Antiquity has received little interest in Pauline studies. Some scholars, however, to explain the belly-references in the Pauline Epistles, have drawn attention to these traditions.[51] This study will more intensively argue that critique of Epicureanism is indeed a relevant background for studies of Paul's moral instructions.

stock-figure for impiety. In *Ant.* 19:32 Josephus speaks of a Roman of senatorial rank who was nevertheless an Epicurean. Josephus draws his readers' attention to the fact that political ambitions and an Epicurean life of ease are here found together. Without saying it directly, Josephus is surprised; the two usually do not go together. Josephus' negative attitude towards Epicureanism is clearly seen in *Ant.* 10:277–8. Within an interpretation of prophecies in the Book of Daniel, he criticizes the Epicurean view that the world is run without divine interference (cf. *Ag. Ap.* 2:180).

[51] See our exegesis of Phil. 3:19.

5

BANQUETS – OPPORTUNITIES FOR THE BELLY

5.0   Introduction

We have seen that mastery of the stomach and the critique launched against Epicureans and belly-devotion were not words plucked out of thin air. From the perspective of the critics, those who participated in lavish and indulgent banquets were hooked on eating, drinking, and sex. The banquets were often seen as nurseries of the pleasures. When we come to Philo in the next chapter, this nexus between banquets and the pleasures of the stomach becomes even more explicit. His warnings against being enslaved by the belly have a clear reference to extravagant pagan meals and the lifestyle which accompanied them (e.g. *Contempl.* 48–56).[1] It is the aim of this chapter to demonstrate that the lifestyle associated with the belly-*topos* concurs with the agenda of *symposia*. In other words, we are searching for a historical point of departure for the belly-rhetoric.

This is not to say that all banquets followed the pattern outlined below, but this agenda is so widely attested that it is worth noting. Furthermore, I do not claim that Epicurean philosophy and banquets can be subsumed under the same heading, but the critics of antiquity made this nexus in their polemic. The authenticity of this polemic might, of course, be disputed. Moral philosophers may well exaggerate according to their aim of fighting what they considered to be flagrantly hedonistic parties. But their critique nevertheless is not to be dismissed as mere polemic; to a great extent the main points of their critique recur on vase-paintings depicting the forms of banquets (see below). Finally, we can safely assume that Paul would hardly distance himself from the fundamental viewpoints of moralists on this issue.

The Greek *symposion* had its counterpart in the Roman *cena*, which was 'inescapably weighed down by food'.[2] To be distinguished from the *cena* was the dinner-party, *convivium*, to which women, too, were admitted as

---

[1] See chap. 7.6 in this study.
[2] Emily Gowers, *Loaded Table*, pp. 24–32; quotation on p. 29.

guests. These distinctions will not be emphasized in our investigation, since they did not make very much of a difference to the moralists.

Many of the sources we will draw upon primarily reflect life in the upper stratum of society. Definitions of 'elite' are always negotiable, and we are not obliged to undertake any here. What needs to be pointed out, however, is that sources depicting the life of the social elite are by no means irrelevant to society in general. The sources depict values which extended beyond the stratum of the elite. Furthermore, extravagant meals were also a means of acquiring prestige and position. This often made the banquets or their rumour into a display. This means that the distinctions between elite and under-privileged were meant to be bridged in this particular way of transferring status and values across social boundaries. Seneca's desription of *voluptas* which 'flows around us on every side and seeps through every opening' (*Vit. Beat.* 5:4) may be applicable here. The life of pleasure enjoyed by the elite had its counterparts among the common people as well. Seneca names them: brothels, taverns, baths, and sweat-rooms (*Vit. Beat.* 7:3).

5.1   Parties for pleasure

In classical Greek literature, a *symposion* had two parts, the *deipnon*, which was for eating (dinner-party) and the *potion*, which was the drinking-party proper. From among the banqueters, who were all men, was chosen a *symposiarch* or *basileus*. He was responsible for mixing wine and water, thus keeping a balance between sobriety and drunkenness. The role of this personage suggests that banquets were traditionally exercises in regulating, controlling and balancing the passions. A banquet was 'a disciplined display of individual and collective passions, in search of a norm to regulate the *epithymiae* and social tensions at the same time as it offers them an outlet'.[3] This intended regulation of desires did not always work out; it was, of course, a difficult balance. Accordingly, moralists advised participants to leave the party before becoming intoxicated and thus like chariots without drivers (Isocrates, *Demonicus* 32). Isocrates is here applying a favourite metaphor of Plato on the desires which must be brought under control. Owing to the moral perils associated with banquets, whether *symposia* or *cenae*, attendance was restricted to males from their later teens.[4] Present-day popular thinking on ancient

---

[3] Ezio Pellizer, 'Sympotic Entertainment', p. 183; cf. pp. 178–9.

[4] See Alan Booth, 'Reclining'; Bruce W. Winter, 'Gluttony'. They both refer to the assumption of *toga virilis* (among the Romans) and the donning of the ephebic cloak among the Greeks.

symposia is primarily indebted to Plato's *Symposion*. This has led to a common impression that these were philosophical events with some refreshment. This is a distortion of what banquets were really like.

During both the eating and drinking the participants were reclining at the table. This was considered appropriate since it was a pleasant position, and banquets were times of pleasure.[5] Athenaeus, *Deipn.* 10:428a–c says that reclining is due to the relaxation and enjoyment that takes place when being drunk; in other words, it was considered appropriate for what was going on during the party.

Xenophon tells us in his *Symposion* that after the dinner-party the tables were removed and the drinking-party proper was introduced by a hymn and a libation (*Symp.* 2:1; cf. Plato, *Symp.* 176a). This marked the transition to drinking and entertainment, and this practice is witnessed throughout our Greek sources. The libation and the hymn were usually offered to Dionysus, the god of wine and merriment (Athenaeus, *Deipn.* 15:675b–c). At the libation women were also admitted to the party (see below). The libations and the singing of hymns to the gods posed an obstacle to the participation of Jews as well as Christians. They considered them idolatrous, and, accordingly, the hedonism which was often practised at these events proved to them that the Graeco-Roman banquets were rooted in paganism.[6]

The drinking was accompanied by various kinds of entertainment. These might include philosophical discussions, conversation, music or dance performed by slaves, the so-called flute-girls, whose presence is widely attested, games or contests, beauty-competitions among the girls present, and sex. The question of proper entertainment occupies an important place in the ancient sources on banquets.[7] The host was responsible for providing proper entertainment.[8]

According to our previous presentation of the belly-*topos*, the focus is now on sexual pleasures, which were the expected sequel to a banquet, the so-called 'after-dinner' entertainment (see below). In his *Characters* Theophrastus describes a host who hires flute-girls to be sexually available to the guests (*Characters* 20:10, cf. 11:7). This service is extensively

[5] Plutarch tells about Cato the Younger, who, as a gesture of mourning, refused to recline. He insisted on sitting at the table (*Cato* 56:4; 67:1).

[6] The banquets were therefore often seen as marking the limits of Hellenization. This has been argued by Sandra R. Shimoff, 'Banquets'; see pp. 441–4 in particular.

[7] See e.g. Plato, *Symp.* 176e–177e and in particular Plutarch, *Mor.* 710a–713f, where this question is directly addressed. See also Hans Licht, *Sexual Life*, pp. 161–79 and Christopher P. Jones, 'Dinner Theater'.

[8] Lucian tells us of a *symposion* where the entertainment turned out to be fighting and shedding blood; *Symp.* 1.3.33, 47.

witnessed across the centuries of antiquity. The amorous nature of the banquets is attested in Xenophon's *Symposion*. Dancers performed the dance of Dionysos and Ariadne in a way which so stimulated the sexual appetite of the banqueters, that 'seeing them in each other's embrace and obviously leaving for the bridal couch, those who were unwedded swore that they would take to themselves wives, and those who were already married mounted horse and rode off to their wives that they might enjoy them' (*Symp.* 9:7).

Dio Chrysostom tells of brothel-keepers who travelled around, providing from their stock of women sexual services at dinners and festivals (*Orat.* 77/78:4.28–29 cf. Athenaeus, *Deipn.* 12:532c). The dancers or musicans who performed at banquets were employed for sexual purposes as well.[9] Hence, banquets were standard places for courtship and amorous activities (Plutarch, *Mor.* 760a Ovid, *The Art of Love* 1:229–52, 603–30; Philo, *Contempl.* 50–1, 54). In this work, Ovid suggests to men places appropriate for seducing women, and advises lovers to make use of banquets for sexual adventures.[10] In *Love Affairs*, he gives a very vivid picture of how sexual activities went on under the covers of the couches during a banquet (1:4).

The pattern depicted above does not rely on written sources alone. The vast number of vase-paintings depicting the nature of banquets confirms the picture given by the sources. These paintings are by no means proof of what happened at any given feast. But it was typical enough to be decorating the utensils employed for these occasions.[11] The vase-paintings are surely more than male fantasies; they must be taken into account when we are addressing the question of what might well happen during the banquets.[12]

[9] Flute-girls are standard in many texts on banquets as well as decorating numerous utensils used at these occasions; see e.g. Chester G. Starr, 'Flutegirls'. Starr seems to underestimate the sexual role assigned to these girls in the material.
[10] See Jo-Ann Shelton, *As the Romans Did it*, pp. 51–3, 58, 317. For the banquets as occasions for sexual enjoyment – whether with males or females – see Andrew Dalby, *Siren Feasts*, pp. 16–20; Catharine Edwards, *Politics of Immorality*, pp. 188–89. John C. Yardly, 'Symposium in Roman Elegy' demonstrates how banquets in Roman literature were more or less synonymous with adultery and love affairs; cf. Bruce W. Winter, 'Gluttony', pp. 82–4. The relationship between excess in eating and drinking and sex is also attested in the fact that sexual matters often were expressed in terms of gluttony or food; see Jeffrey Henderson, *Maculate Muse*, pp. 47–48, 51–52, 60–62, 129–130, 142–144; Emily Gowers, *Loaded Table*, p. 200, n. 319.
[11] Pliny, *Nat. Hist.* 14:410 mentions the drinking vessels decorated with scenes of adultery.
[12] For some examples of such vase-paintings, see e.g. Christopher Miles and John J. Norwich, *Love*, p. 92, showing a picture of a cup with a banquet-scene with *hetairai* or

It is therefore quite natural to find that the topic of mastering the passions is often related to the context of banquets. The saying of a Spartan, according to Plato, attests the nexus between feasts and pleasure:

> For our law banished from the land that institution (i.e. *symposia*) which gives the most occasion for men to fall into excessive pleasures and follies of every description; neither in the country nor in the cities controlled by Spartiates is a drinking-club to be seen nor any of the practices which belong to such and foster to the utmost all kinds of pleasure. (*Laws* 1:637a)[13]

We now turn to some texts in order to see that the banquets could easily develop into unrestrained hedonism, such as excessive eating, drinking and sex; in other words, to demonstrate that the agenda of banquets was belly-oriented. Since the previous chapters to some extent have provided relevant material, I will here restrict myself to texts of special relevance, some Latin and some Greek.

5.2 Seneca – the moral philosopher

Among the Latin authors we will focus on Seneca, Juvenal and Horace, namely a moral philosopher and two satirists. In his *Moral Epistle* 95, Seneca praises the 'good old days'. Those days were good because of eating habits and hard work. Present-day living in Rome, however, represents a sharp contrast to the good old days. Seneca says that people now learn to dispute, but not to live (*Mor. Epist.* 95:13). The decline of traditional Roman values is most properly described, according to the philosopher, by reference to the lavish banquets weighed down by food,[14] drinking and *post convivia* (*Mor. Epist.* 95:21, 23–4). *Post convivia* refers to entertainment, usually sexual play,[15] which followed the

---

courtesans. Two naked girls are leaning towards men lying on the couches. One of the men has exposed his genitals. See also Andrew Dalby, *Siren Feasts*, p. 19 showing a cup with a picture of a reveller capturing a female musician after the *symposion*; cf. p. 155; François Lissarrague, *Un Flot d'Images*, has collected some examples of relevant material. On pp. 56–7 he shows two cups shaped and formed like a penis. The one shows a naked girl drinking from a cup where an erect penis is pointing directly at her (p. 57).

[13] The proper context of this declaration is the damaging effect of banquets on the *polis* as well as the individual; i.e. a political perspective.

[14] *Mor. Epist.* 95:25, 27–9 provides information on dishes which recall the famous description of Trimalchio's dinner in Petronius' *Satyricon*. Seneca develops an old Roman concern for their own ancestral values as opposed to those of the enemies they conquered. This concern is clearly voiced in *Ab Urbe Condita* 34:4, where Livy is concerned that Romans are about to be captured by the alien *mores*, such as *avaritia* and *luxuria*.

[15] So also C. D. N. Costa, *Seneca, 17 Letters*, p. 167.

eating and accompanied the drinking. Cicero names the entertainments *quae sequntur* (*Fin.* 2:23). Philo speaks of the amorous activities as ἐπιδειπνίδες (*Contempl.* 54) which are often rendered 'the after-dinners'.[16] This is a common word for a sexual 'meal' or dessert.[17] Since the word is often used with special reference to sex, sexual adventure is spoken of as being part of the menu.[18]

Seneca's description of the decline in traditional *mores* plays special attention to the stomach. The food, so richly bestowed on the table, is all stuffed down *per unam gulam*, one single throat (*Mor. Epist.* 95:19). A host of slaves are present to serve one single belly (*unus venter exercet*) (*Mor. Epist.* 95:24). Seneca's ironic point is the contrast between the size of the human belly and all the efforts made to satisfy it in all possible ways. Things are entirely out of proportion, he says. The stomach is burdened down (*Mor. Epist.* 95:15–16), which has medical as well as physiognomic consequences. *Mor. Epist.* 95:16–18 gives a lengthy physiognomic description of how over-eating and luxury affect the human body. A bodily sign of this defective way of living is 'the belly growing to a paunch (*distentusque venter*) through an ill habit of taking more than it can hold' (*Mor. Epist.* 95:16). A protruding belly is here a sign connected with the lifestyle of *convivia* as well as an outer proof that Roman values are deteroriating.

Contrasting the good old days with banquets of his own time implies a political perspective. People who are gorging, vomiting, eating and drinking, not to quench but to rouse the appetites, are to be judged in a political perspective as well. Their lifestyle concerns the well-being of Rome. Although Seneca does not bring this out in this particular text, it is certainly implicit in this moral epistle.

In his *Moral Epistle* 110:12–20, Seneca speaks of the lavish tables with waiting slaves – all designed to satisfy *cupiditas* (*Mor. Epist.* 110:15). The belly is filled up as though it can hold all that it receives. A vivid picture of this is provided in Seneca's text on the master who loads his belly until it ceases to do the proper work of a stomach, and who is at greater pains to discharge the food than to stuff it down (*Mor. Epist.* 47:2).[19]

In *Mor. Epist.* 110 he says that it takes only some hours to pass through the agenda (*ille ordo*) of banquets. With this in mind, he asks rhetorically:

---

[16] See e.g. Bruce W. Winter, 'Gluttony', p. 84.   [17] See LSJ s.v.

[18] Cf. Pliny's *Epist.* 15 where he gives a menu-list which includes Spanish dancers; see also Martial's *Epigrams* 5:78.

[19] The slaves are expected to mop up the food which is discharged, and to collect the leftovers under the tables (*Mor. Epist.* 47:5–6). They are also at the sexual disposal of the master during the banquet (*Mor. Epist.* 47:8). To Seneca, all this suggests a bad master.

'Has a business filled up (*occupavit*) this whole life of ours, which could not fill up a whole day?' (*Mor. Epist.* 110:16) In this way Seneca puts his finger on the preoccupation with eating and banquets. Excessive eating stirs up the desires. This occupies the whole life of some banqueters. Eating has become the very focus of life. The same issue is addressed in *Mor. Epist.* 60. In a way resembling modern environmental critics, the philosopher claims that the greed of the table is emptying both land and sea.[20] The small stomach of human beings seems insatiable, obsessed with a greed which is found not even among animals. Those who satisfy the belly beyond hunger are obeying the belly (*ventri oboedientes*), and should not be numbered among men (*Mor. Epist.* 60:4). Seneca here quotes from the introductory words of Sallust in his *War with Catiline* (*Bellum Catilinae*) 1:1. The stomach is, according to Sallust, a mark by which to distinguish animals from men. Animals are obedient to the belly (*ventri oboedienta*), while in men mind is ruling (*animi imperio*). Men have mind in common with the gods, while stomach links them to the animals. Hence, the stomach needs to be ruled not obeyed. Seneca applies this philosophical rhetoric of the belly to his description of the Roman dinner-parties.

Seneca's complaint about traditional Roman values being undermined by greed and luxury is voiced also in his *Consolation to Helvia*, chap. 10, in a lengthy description of lavish meals where the stomachs are loaded (*ventrem onerare*) with delicacies of every kind (*Helv.* 10:2–6). To fill the tables, forests and sea are emptied. The body requires shelter, food and drink; i.e. simple living. Satisfaction beyond these needs implies service not of the needs, but the vices (*vitiis, non usibus laboratur*) (*Helv.* 10:2).[21] The luxurious life at table which marked the Roman elite strongly differed from the ideal of this philosopher. The amount of food is entirely out of proportion to the capacity of the belly (*Helv.* 10:5–6). Hence the stomach is not able to retain what is eaten: 'they vomit that they may eat, and they eat that they may vomit, and they do not deign even to digest the feasts for which they ransack the whole world' (*Helv.* 10:3). His complaint about the banquets can be summarized in the phrase *ventri servire* (*Helv.* 10:5), which recalls Paul's vocabulary in Rom. 16:18 (δουλεύουσιν... τῇ ... κοιλίᾳ).

In his lament over contemporary Roman *mores*, Seneca contrasts Apicius with the ancestors of the city (*Helv.* 10:8–11). Apicius was 'a

---

[20] Similarly in Juvenal, *Sat.* 5:24–37, 49, 80–3, 92–102, 114–19, 146.

[21] A similar view is voiced by Cicero in his critique of Epicurus. He depicts Epicureanism in terms of a banquet where the participants are gorging and drinking till they are carried home. Part of this polemic also concerns the sexual activities which accompanied *convivia* (*Fin.* 2:23).

proverbial cognomen of several Roman connoisseurs of luxury, especially in food'.[22] He corrupted youth by introducing new eating habits.
Seneca calls him a professor in the science of cuisine or kitchen (*sci-
entiam popinae professus*). Within the contrast between the lifestyle of
the ancestors and the banquets introduced by Apicius, Seneca weaves
another, more implicit, but significant still: simple cooking serves Rome,
the Capitol and Jupiter much better than a selfish greed which will never
be satisfied (*cupiditati nihil satis est*) (*Helv.* 10:11). Thus Seneca speaks
of lavish banquets in Rome in terms of 'serving the belly', and he sees
them in a political perspective. Excessive customs in food foster citizens
who are selfish and never satisfied.[23]

5.3   Horace and Juvenal – two Roman satirists

Horace, the lyric poet and satirist who wrote during the reign of Augustus,
shows a pervasive interest in food matters, especially in Book 2. He considers gastronomy a rival to the good life, which is secured only by simple
living. Frugal life in the countryside is his ideal, and Ofellus exemplifies
it. To Horace gluttony was primarily found among the urban elite. The
urban banquets are seen in a way which corresponds to what we found
in Seneca. The way *cenae*, *epulae* or *convivia* have developed is seen
in a framework marked by competing cultural values: traditional Roman
mores versus decadence. Food, menu and eating-habits have become an
arena for these competing values. Persons of power and status, such as
Gallonius have introduced a new enjoyment of the table, and young people are quick to adopt the new ways (*Sat.* 2:2.39–52). The new ways,
as manifested in banquets, strongly differ from *vivere parvo* (*Sat.* 2:2.1)
or *contentus parvo* (*Sat.* 2:2.110–11), living simply and being content
with little. A political perspective on this appears when Horace asks
rhetorically, which of the two lifestyles prepares for warfare? Furthermore, to Horace the new style as contrasted with the traditional *mores*

---

[22] Simon Hornblower, Anthony Spawforth, *Oxford Classical Dictionary*, p. 121.

[23] Thus saying, Seneca draws upon a tradition which is attested already in Polybius. In
Hist. 31:25.2–8 he presents Scipio, who surpassed his contemporaries in Rome in terms
of σωφροσύνη. The youth of his time were, according to Polybius, engaged in sex with
boys and prostitutes. They were influenced by the Greek way of living and enjoyed the
entertainments at banquets. Many young people had embarked upon this lifestyle after
Rome subdued Macedonia. In other words, the conquered were about to conquer Rome by
other means. This lifestyle ruins πολιτεία; it will cause the state to fall apart. To Polybius
Scipio represented a different attitude, since he was fighting all his appetites. Polybius
attests the nexus between extravagant meals and sexual interludes. Furthermore, his text attests the political perspective on soft living; public affairs are neglected as a result of banquets
aiming only at self-satisfaction by all means.

has a corresponding contrast in urban life versus living in the country-side. A dinner-party in the countryside closes his *Sat.* 2:2 (118–36). It is marked by frugal eating, hospitality and friendship. The dinner is inten-tionally presented as a contrast to banquets. Horace says that the drinking is overseen by *culpa*[24] only (*culpa potare magistra*). This is probably a reference to *culpa* playing the role of the symposiarch, who in Latin was called *magister bibendi*.

Finally, Horace talks about banquets within a pattern of contrasts which we have come across quite often in this study, namely mind versus body or belly and divine versus earthly. He uses the language of philosophy which we have traced from Plato's *Timaeus*: ' . . . clogged with yesterday's excess the body drags down with itself the mind as well, and fastens to earth a fragment of the divine spirit' (*Sat.* 2:2.77–9).

Horace's concern for the lifestyle associated with banquets (*cenae, epulae*) is voiced in the belly-*topos* in *Sat.* 2:7.102–18.[25] This satire ends with mentioning Horace's Sabine farm, thus making a link to the satire presented above. Horace compares master and slave on the point of gluttony: why is it more ruinous for the slave than the master to obey the stomach's call (*obsequium ventris*)?[26] A gluttonous slave will be driven to steal, and then be beaten. But the gluttonous master has to pay a price as well, in terms of ill-health. Furthermore, if a master sells a piece of land so as to be able to continue a gluttonous life, is not this tantamount to enslavement to the belly (*servile gulae parens habet*) (*Sat.* 2:7.111)? The Latin *parere* means 'to submit', 'to obey' or 'to be subject', here to gluttony.[27]

Juvenal, the satirist writing in Rome at the beginning of the second century AD, in *Sat.* 6 addresses the ways Roman women lived. The old ways of women, marked by simplicity and chastity, have changed owing to luxurious living. The old way of living safeguarded home and city, but now 'luxury, more deadly than any foe, has laid her hand upon us, and avenges a conquered world' (*Sat.* 6:293). Roman *mores* have been corrupted. The political perspective from which Juvenal speaks is obvious. He values *ritus veteres et publica saltem* (*Sat.* 6:335 cf. 11:183–92). Public order

[24] The LCL edition here says 'forfeit', but it is not entirely obvious what Horace here has in mind.

[25] Cf. *Sat.* 2:2.40 and 43 speaking of *gula* and *stomachus*.

[26] Frances Muecke, *Horace*, p. 225 speaks of a semi-personification of the belly and mentions Horace's *Epist.* 1:15.32, where the gluttonous Maenius is said to give gifts to his greedy stomach (*ventri donabat avaro*).

[27] Lewis & Short, *Latin Dictionary*, s.v. *gula* suggests the translation 'belly-god' for this phrase.

and harmony are jeopardized by a lifestyle which agrees with the belly-*topos* as we have unfolded it in this study. This political perspective on the agenda of the belly is voiced in *Sat.* 11 as well. He mentions those 'whose sole reason for living lies in their palate (*in solo vivendi causa palato est*)' (*Sat.* 11:11). This is a way of living where gluttony (*gula*) and the belly (*venter*) bring poverty. The only thing that expands is the stomach (*Sat.* 11:39–40). This is contrasted to the simple food of the good old days (*Sat.* 11:77–119).[28]

The corruption manifested itself, according to Juvenal, in drunkenness (*ebria*) and indulgent meals. He refers to the rites of *Bona Dea* (*Sat.* 6:314). This was a Roman fertility goddess honoured in an annual nocturnal ceremony from which men were excluded:

> Filthy lucre first brought in amongst us foreign ways; wealth enervated and corrupted the ages with foul indulgences. What decency does Venus observe when she is drunken?[29] When she knows not head from tail, eats giant oysters at midnight, pours foaming unguents into her unmixed Falernian and drinks out of perfume-flasks, while the roof spins dizzily round, the table dances, and every light shows double!   (*Sat.* 6:298–305)

This description of the *Bona Dea* cult hardly reflects real knowledge, but is satire based on men's sceptical attitude towards women's rites. Juvenal's satire nevertheless provides us with a common picture of banquets, although he may well be wrong in applying this to the *Bona Dea* festival. A similar picture, though related not primarily to this cult but to ordinary banquets, is found in *Sat.* 6:419–33. Before joining the banquet, the women take hot baths, with the aim of arousing thirst and appetite.[30] Before the proper meal, huge quantities of wine are swallowed and vomited, to create a raging appetite: 'She drinks and vomits like a big snake (*serpens, bibit, et vomit*)' (*Sat.* 6:432). This excessive eating and drinking is accompanied by sexual appetite.[31] The women cry: 'Now we can act! Let in the men!' (*Sat.* 6:329, cf. 314–34). Juvenal hints at the sexual activities of the women at the *Bona Dea* festival in *Sat.* 6:310–14 as well. They go home on horseback (*equitant*), which is a common metaphor

---

[28] For the political perspective on the moral decline, including the role of the belly, see Catharine Edwards, *Politics of Immorality*, pp. 176–8.

[29] *Venus ebria* refers to a lustful woman when she is drunk; see E. Courtney, *Satires of Juvenal*, p. 296.

[30] For this practice, see Pliny, *Nat. Hist.* 14:138–9. For further references see E. Courtney, *Satires of Juvenal*, p. 317.

[31] Perfume had close associations with sexual foreplay; see Emily Gowers, *Loaded Table*, pp. 236–41. Juvenal says that women were drinking from perfume-flasks.

for sexual activity.[32] On their way they leave *urina*. In the light of *Sat.*
11:162–82 this may have sexual connotations as well. *Urina* (170) there
appears within a presentation of the amorous entertainment which took
place at these occasions. Juvenal mentions it in a context of dancing girls,
singing, vomiting and adultery.

5.4   Athenaeus and Alciphron

The presentation will conclude with some evidence from these two relatively late Greek sources, both from the second and third centuries AD
However, the two have preserved material of a much older date. Alciphron
purports to depict Athenian life in the fourth century BC Both writings
stand in the old tradition of comedies in which eating, drinking and sex
played a significant role.[33]

Athenaeus' *Deipnosophistae* is replete with texts on how *symposia*
were places not only for eating and drinking, but also for sexual interludes.
The universal presence of female dancers, courtesans or prostitutes leaves
no doubt as to the sexual function of the *symposion*. Dancing, playing and
beauty competitions were often expected to introduce sexual games. This
is well attested in the section 'Concerning Women' in *Deipn.* 13:55a–
612f. In Book 13 Athenaeus keeps records of names and events related
to *hetairae*, prostitutes or girls who performed at banquets. In the words
of Bruce W. Winter: 'It shows that the real purpose of their presence
at the meal was primarily for the "after-dinner"'.[34] Athenaeus tells that
when the banqueters had taken leave of all sobriety, there then entered
flute-girls wearing tunics which made them look naked (*Deipn.* 4:129a);
on some occasions they performed naked (e.g. 13:608b).

According to *Deipn.* 13:607b–f, a delegation once appeared at a banquet. Skilled in conversing, they devoted themselves to talking, and acted
in a way alien to the occasion: 'people who desire very earnestly to be
sober maintain that ideal up to a certain point in their drinking-parties;
later when the spirit of wine insinuates itself, then they display the entire
picture of indecency (ἀσχημοσύνη)' (*Deipn.* 13:607b–c). When, after
some drinking, dancing girls entered in nothing but loincloths, members
of the delegation could no longer restrain themselves. Among them was
a philosopher. One of the flute-girls wanted to sit next to him, but he did

[32] See E. Courtney, *Satires of Juvenal*, p. 298 with references.
[33] The fragments of Attic comedy shows a particular interest in these matters. The
extant fragments are found in Theodorus Kock, *Comicorum Atticorum Fragmenta* and John
Maxwell Edmonds, *Fragments of Attic Comedy*.
[34] Bruce W. Winter, 'Gluttony', p. 84.

not permit it, and showed himself a stern person. Later on, this flute-girl was put up for sale in a joke auction among the guests, certainly not for musical performances only – all according to custom, says Athenaeus. In the bargaining this particular philosopher was very active and did his best to have the girl, even after the sale was completed. The moral is very simple: the agenda of banquets is designed to tear down mastery of desires.

We have already seen (chap. 3) that Athenaeus' presentation of *symposia* is replete with traditional belly-language. Amorous activities and filling the belly are intimately connected in this literature. Hence, he says: 'For love dwells where plenty is, but among those who are hard up Aphrodite will not stay' (*Deipn.* 1:28f, cf. 6:270c). Love cannot reside in an empty belly (ἐν κενῇ γὰρ γαστρί) since Cypris (Aphrodite) is a cruel goddess to the hungry (πεινῶσιν) (*Deipn.* 6:270b). 'A well-gorged body . . . went hand in hand with sexual licence'.[35]

Among Alciphron's *Letters*, *Epist.* 3:19[36] reports on a *symposion*. The letter begins by stating that there is hardly any difference between common people and those of wealth, birth and wisdom. This is demonstrated with reference to a banquet where philosophers from the Stoic, Peripatetic, Epicurean, Pythagorean, and Cynic schools were present. As the drinking went on, each acted in accordance with his nature. The Stoic fell asleep and snored. The Pythagorean was humming. The Peripatetic demanded abundant eating. The Epicurean took the harp-girl in his arms, looked at her, saying: this is 'tranquillity of the flesh (τὸ τῆς σαρκὸς ἀόχλητον) and consolidation of pleasure (τὴν καταπύκνωσιν τοῦ ἡδομένου)' (*Epist.* 3:19.8). The Cynic had sexual intercourse[37] with one of the singing girls, right before the eyes of all. Although this text bears the marks of irony and an attempt to characterize different philosophical schools, it also provides an interesting glimpse of how a *symposion* might run.

Some of the most vivid descriptions of ancient drinking-bouts are found in the so-called *Letters of Courtesans*. *Epist.* 4:13 tells of a *symposion* of women in the open air, though the presence of men is assumed later in the letter. The party is somewhat informal, without a symposiarch, which causes the quantity of wine consumed to increase. Amorous interludes took place in between drinking and eating, all described in detail (*Epist.* 4:13.13–14, 18). The carousing went on till cockcrow. *Epist.* 4:14 gives

---

[35] Ibid. p. 84. The meals described by Athenaeus are for the elite.
[36] References to Alciphron follow the system adopted by the LCL translator.
[37] See LSJ s.v. ἐνεργεῖν.

another detailed description of a drinking-party. The letter is formed like a report from one πόρνη to a colleague (Bacchis) who did not attend the party: 'What a party we had (why, pray, shouldn't I vex your heart?), replete as it was with many delights! Songs, jests, drinking till cock-crow, perfumes, garlands, sweetmeats' (*Epist.* 4:14.3). Then the letter tells of a beauty-competition between two of the prostitutes, as to who had the lovelier and softer buttocks; possibly this took place as a dance-performance. Myrhina did well. She undressed, keeping on only a silk shift, shaking her loins, waggling her buttocks, as if she were having in-tercourse. Thryallis, however, competed without clothes, as though she participated in an *agôn*. She undulated her buttocks in such a way that she was declared the winner (*Epist.* 4:14.4–6).[38] Hips and breasts were also objects of competition; 'about bellies, however, we had no argument', probably since no one could compete with Philumena's. After a long night the prostitutes returned home drunk, hoping to find new lovers next time: a *symposion* whose date was already fixed and where Bacchis' presence was expected.

There is no mention of the stomach (except for the beauty-competition where this part was left out, since the winner was obvious anyway) to justify a suggestion that the revelling was a manifestation of the power of the belly. This must, however, not lead to hasty conclusions, since the letters generally portray banquets as occasions for the belly to rule. *Epist.* 3:3 voices Artepithymus' lament that he is unable to control (κρατεῖν) his belly. His stomach keeps demanding and compelling him to satisfy its craving for τρυφή (*Epist.* 3:3.2, cf. 3:4.3–6). The word has a meaning other than τροφή, which simply denotes the nourishment the stomach needs for bodily sustenance (*Epist.* 3:25.3). The LCL translator ren-ders τρυφή 'delicacies', which makes it synonymous with the cognate τρύφημα (*Epist.* 1:15.2; 2:6.1; 3:15.21), and which in the plural is ren-dered 'luxuries'; all three instances have reference to food. But in this literature τρυφή has a related, but still slightly different meaning. In *Epist.* 1:16.2 a fisherman who is in love says: '. . . I burn with a passion as hot as that of rich young bloods? And I who once laughed at men whom luxury (ἐκ τρυφῆς) made slaves to passion (πάθει δουλεύοντας) am now wholly possessed by passion itself.' Some sexual connotations appear in this text. Similarly in *Epist.* 2:21 τρυφή refers to the way of living of a

---

[38] Lucian tells us of a banquet held during the annual festival of Saturnalia (*Saturn.* 4) where the ingredients of eating, drinking and sexual games are easily recognized. A prize in one of the contests was to dance naked with a flute-girl, and to carry her three times round the house. Seneca (*Mor. Epist.* 18:1) complains that for many Romans the festival season of Saturnalia lasts throughout the year.

disobedient slave, which is described as participating in banquets; i.e.

- gorging the belly with heavy drink[39]
- the accompaniment of harp and flute
- perfume

In brief, Alciphron knew well that banquets might become opportunities for the stomach to rule and take control. Although this is stated implicitly, it is still there.

Much more explicit on the connection between stomach and the form of banquets is Pseudo-Lucian's *Erôtes* (*Affairs of the Heart*). This writing presents a speech-competition on whether the love of women or boys is best. Callicratidas advocates homosexual love. His argument involves a lengthy presentation of the ways of women. Before eating they prepare themselves by having long baths, he says (*Erôtes* 42). As we saw above, this was a practice aimed at arousing appetites for both food and sex. They then turn to the loaded tables accompanied by coyness[40] towards men. The beds of women are full of femininity; hence any man rising from there needs a bath. Callicratidas is possibly thinking of bodily fluids.[41] The nexus between excessive eating and drinking, in terms of γαστριμαργία, and sexual appetite, is emphasized. They eat until their throats can hold no more. Since the text mentions γαστριμαργία, the author possibly prefers to speak of a stuffed throat, so as not to repeat himself. Callicratidas scorns women and womanhood, and his presentation is indeed polemical. But his polemic confirms a quite common picture of the banquets: gorging led to sexual appetite, and both were expressions of γαστριμαργία.

5.5   Summary

The moral philosophers who wrote on the dangers of the belly were thinking of the activities that went on during banquets. We have, there-fore, presented the views some of them took, as well as some satirists and texts rooted in the comedy tradition. Although the material primarily depicts life among the elite, and does not, of course, apply to any par-ticular banquet, it has significantly shaped moral instruction in antiquity, in particular the *topos* of the rule of the belly. Banquets were occasions for eating and drinking accompanied by sexual interludes. This 'unholy

---

[39] An expression usually associated with eating is here applied to drinking as well.

[40] For ἀκκισμός as prudery or coyness, see *Erôtes* 4; Philostratus, *Love Letters* 35; LSJ s.v.

[41] Cf. on *urina* above.

trinity', as it has been called, is extensively witnessed in literary sources of various kinds as well as on the decoration of utensils employed at these occasions. When vessels of this kind were used at banquets, they certainly encouraged and justified indulgence. For Jewish and Christian writers, banquets of this kind were characteristic of paganism. The lifestyle associated with them was seen as marking the limits of Hellenization. To Roman writers, the form of banquets represented a Greek lifestyle which was detrimental to the state, since it made its participants soft and selfish. Out of the agenda of banquets developed a philosophy of mastering the desires, a polemic and a *topos* of the belly. Paul's belly-dicta developed from this framework as well.

PART 3

The appropriated belly

Although the ancient world cannot be divided into Judaism and Hellenism as two easily separated parts, it is still interesting to see how *topoi* appearing most frequently in Graeco-Roman sources are appropriated into biblical thought. The aim of this chapter is to see how the philosophical discussions on mastery of passions, and the belly in particular, have been enculturated into a Jewish-biblical setting. In other words, we approach Paul by seeking a bridge in this material. This is not to deny that there are texts of interest and relevance in Old Testament and Jewish sources as well. Before proceeding to address the appropriation in particular, we will consider the most relevant analogies in this material.

In the Old Testament, the enemies or the ungodly are described in the metaphor of an 'open mouth' or in terms of devouring. In some texts this refers to deceitful speech (e.g Ps. 10:3–5, 7/LXX 11:3–5 and 9:28), but usually it is a reference to their greedy nature or appetite (Ps. 22:14/LXX 21:14, cf. Ps. 73:4–6/LXX 72:4–6; Prov. 19:28; Job 20:12–15; Micah 3:2–3): their mouth is open to devour, like a wild animal. In a description of the ungodly, he is presented as a devouring enemy, swallowing the righteous as bread (Ps. 53:5 = 14:4/LXX 52:5 = 13:4, cf. 5:10). To the righteous who has put his trust in God, the enemy is a glutton ready to consume them (Ps. 27:2/LXX 26:2). This is a point of convergence between the Old Testament material and Plutarch's critique of Epicureanism in *Mor.* 1124f–1125a, according to which the appetite of the Epicureans is limitless; in the end it will devour the neighbours as well (see chap. 4.3).

Focus in the Old Testament is not so much on the stomach, but on the open and hungry mouth ready to devour. This may be summarized in Lam. 3:46: 'All our enemies have opened their mouths against us'. This metaphor is used also of political enemies (Dan. 7:23; Jer. 51:34/LXX 28:34). The Jeremiah text is of special interest. The metaphor of the devouring enemy is there connected with the 'filled stomach'. In other words, this text bridges the metaphor of the open mouth and the filled stomach: 'King Nebuchadnezar of Babylon has devoured me (κατέφαγέν με), he has crushed me; he has made me an empty vessel, he has swallowed me like a monster; he has filled his belly (κοιλία) with my delicacies, he has spewed me out.'

The metaphor of the devouring enemy is also transferred to death. Death is described as a hungry and greedy monster (Isa. 5:14; Prov. 1:12; Job 24:19; Sir. 51:5). From the belly of Hades (ἐκ κοιλίας ᾅδου), the prophet cries to the Lord for help (Jonah 2:3). He is about to be devoured by death.

Although this material does not provide analogies as close as those we have found in the Graeco-Roman texts, it should by no means be neglected. In the first place, in Rom. 3:10–18 Paul quotes from some of these Old Testament texts, and so demonstrates his familiarity with this way of describing the ungodly man. In the second place, we have some examples in the Graeco-Roman material where the belly-*topos* is expressed in terms of a greedy mouth or throat.[1] In the Old Testament, the greed of the enemies is in terms not of food, luxury and drink, but rather of hatred and evil plans. Although the open mouth and greedy throat are used differently in this material, it still forms an important bridge between Paul's Jewish background and the Graeco-Roman moral philosophy texts, since in both mouth and throat might replace the greedy belly. In other words, it was not difficult for a Jew to appropriate the material on the belly which we have presented in Part 2 of this study.

---

[1] See e.g. Aristotle, *Nic. Eth.* 1118a33–4; *Eud. Eth.*1231a16–17; *Problems* 950a3–5; Musonius Rufus, *Fragm.* 18b5–11, where throat and belly are interchangeable, and both are related to excess in eating; so also in Pseudo-Lucian's *Erôtes* 42.

6

THE BELLY-*TOPOS* IN
JEWISH-HELLENISTIC SOURCES

6.1   Sir. 23:6

Chap. 23 provides a lengthy prayer of the wise man. He prays not to be overcome by gluttony (κοιλίας ὄρεξις) and lust (συνουσιασμός). A more literal rendering of the LXX text would be the longing or yearning of the belly. Thus the belly is seen as a seat of the desires; here obviously in an unfavourable sense. The noun ὄρεξις is often used of sexual passion in particular (*Ant.* 7:169; Rom. 1:27).[1] The verb καταλαμβάνεσθαι has here a hostile reference; the stomach is spoken of as an enemy from which the pious prays to be protected. Alongside the belly, the prayer mentions συνουσιασμός, which in this context refers to the temptation to illegitimate sexual intercourse,[2] an issue which is elaborated from v. 16 on. The righteous considers himself under threat from two great inner powers, that of the belly (gluttony) and sex. The two are mentioned together,[3] and represent the desires from which he asks God to protect him.

6.2   *T. Rub.* 2:1–3:8

In *Testaments of the Twelve Patriarchs*, *T. Rub.* 2:1–3:8 speaks of human beings as created with seven spirits; i.e. the faculties of breathing, seeing, hearing, speaking, tasting, procreating, and, first of all, life itself. Beliar, the chief of the demons, takes these faculties as opportunities to

---

[1] Cf. Sir. 18:30; 4 Macc. 1:33–35 where the sexual reference is only implicit.
[2] See LSJ s.v. Alexander di Lella, *Ben Sira*, p. 318 renders v. 6a in this way: 'Let not the lustful cravings of the flesh take hold of me.'
[3] Chris Mearns, 'Opponents at Philippi', p. 198 argues that κοιλία in this text is an euphemism for the male sexual organ. Although the noun ὄρεξις to which the genitive of stomach is attached might give some allusions to sexual desire, this is primarily expressed in the noun συνουσιασμός. The stomach is rather to be seen as a word for the inner centre of human activities; it is the place where the innermost thoughts and desires are located. The belly becomes a metaphor for the inner man; see e.g. Sir. 19:12; 36:18–19.

deceive; i.e. his seven spirits of deceit (τὸ πνεῦμα τῆς πλάνης). In 3:2, which is probably part of an interpolation, Beliar is said to introduce the spirits of deceit into the natural faculties. The first among these spirits is πορνεία; the second is the 'spirit of insatiability in the stomach (πνεῦμα ἀπληστείας ἐν τῇ γαστρί)' (*T. Rub.* 3:3).[4] The stomach here represents a perversion of the divinely-given faculty of consuming food and drink (2:7).

6.3   3 Macc. 7:10–11

> On receiving this letter, the Jews did not at once haste for their departure, but requested further of the king that those of the Jewish people who had wittingly transgressed against the holy God and his Law should receive the due punishment at their hands, stressing that those who had transgressed the divine commandments for their belly's sake (γαστρὸς ἕνεκεν) would never be well disposed to the king's business either.[5]

3 Maccabees tells the dramatic events in the life of the Jews of Alexandria during the reign of the Egyptian king Ptolemy IV Philopator.[6] As the king was about to enter the temple in Jerusalem and thus cause its defilement, the Jews in the city offered prayers to God not to let him do this. The king fell overpowered to the ground, and had to return to Egypt without having accomplished his wish. This made him furious with the Jews of Alexandria. He issued restrictions on their traditional piety, and even caused many to die. Ptolemy planned to get elephants drunk and to let them kill the Jews in the hippodrome. God sent his angels to protect his people. Thus the king changed his mind and became friendly towards the Jews. In a letter he announced his turnabout and blamed his officials for having wrongly accused the Jews. They, however, took the opportunity to ask for the right to punish the apostates, that is to say those who transgressed the commandments 'for the sake of the belly', as the text quoted above demonstrates.

---

[4] The Greek and Stoic content of this section is well-known, see e.g. R. H. Charles, *Apocrypha and Pseudepigrapha*, Vol. 2, p. 297.

[5] The translation is from H. Anderson, '3 Maccabees', *OTP* 2.

[6] The work was probably composed between the first century BC and the first century AD in Alexandria. For a discussion of the date of composition, provenance and historical value, see Moses Hadas, *Maccabees*, pp. 1–27 and H. Anderson, '3 Maccabees', *OTP* 2, pp. 509–16. Hadas suggests a date during the reign of Gaius Caligula, which is intriguing, owing to the riots in Alexandria during his principate.

The immediate context makes it perfectly clear that the phrase γαστρὸς ἕνεκεν refers to apostasized Jews. 3 Maccabees presents a story – not unlike 2 Macc. 6–7 and 4 Macc. – where the Jews find themselves squeezed between martyrdom and apostasy (3 Macc. 2:31–3). In this situation some Jews abandoned their ancestral belief and customs. What commandments did they transgress, and what practices did they give up? These commandments were obviously crucial for Jewish identity, since breaking them was considered apostasy. 3 Macc. 3:2–10 says that the Jews were considered enemies of the state. This was due to their worship in terms of food laws. Observance of the food laws marked them off from the 'nations' (3 Macc. 3:4.7). It is a well-known fact that dietary laws played a significant role for Jewish identity.[7] Daniel and his friends who refused to eat the king's rations, and asked for their own menu, so as not to be defiled with unclean food, are well-known examples of this piety (Dan. 1). Since Daniel traditions appear in 3 Macc. 6:6–7, his example is the more relevant here. Our text fits this pattern nicely.

The Jews who abandoned their customs for 'the sake of the belly', did *not* observe these laws. Thus the belly has a clear reference to the question of food and eating. The apostasized were tempted or forced by their stomach to eat forbidden food. Such is the logic of this text. In other words, there is no connection between belly-devotion and food laws as such. The emphasis is on the temptations originating in the belly; a lust to consume what is forbidden. But why is the stomach considered the cause of apostasy? This question is more tricky than it first appears. The following observations may provide a clue.

(1) Transgressing the food laws is a sign of gluttony. The apostates were seized by desire for food and partook of a forbidden menu. However, the meaning of 'belly' must be traced also from the context; i.e. the narrative of 3 Maccabees.

(2) The narrative itself does not suggest that the lapsed Jews abandoned the food laws because of gluttony. Although this is assumed in the text, the emphasis on the belly-*topos* lies somewhere else. Eating and feasting are mentioned in the narrative, but on the part of the king (3 Macc. 5:3.16–17.36) and the faithful (3 Macc. 6:32–6; 7:18–20). The author finds it pertinent to mention that gluttony (πότος καὶ λιχνεία) can develop as an abuse even of the feasting of the faithful (3 Macc. 6:36). In other words, on the narrative surface of this literature the apostasized Jews do not appear as involved in gluttony.

---

[7] See e.g. 4 Macc. 4:26; 5:6; *Ep. Arist.* 128–66; 1 Macc. 1:62; Molly Whittaker, *Jews & Christians*, pp. 73–80.

(3) According to 3 Macc. 2:31 the apostates abandoned their Jewish customs, hoping to benefit from being the king's associates. They simply had an eye to personal gain and prestige. They showed themselves to be disloyal, seeking only their own ends. They did not stay firm in times of crisis, and were not willing to pay the costs. They are therefore considered to embody an attitude opposed to those who were willing to die. Quite naturally, then, the Jewish martyrs are mentioned in contrast with the apostates (3 Macc. 7:16). This is the logic of 3 Macc. 7:10–11, claiming that they were liable to be disloyal to the king as well. Transgressors of the dietary laws for their belly's sake were self-pleasing people. The king should therefore not put any trust in them.

(4) The question of how to find a way for Jews to live in a Gentile environment is a key issue of this literature.[8] The possibility of a harmonious relationship with the authorities is mentioned frequently enough to be noted (3 Macc. 3:3,7–9,23–4,26; 6:25–7; 7:1–9,21). This political interest in citizenship forms the immediate context for mentioning those who apostasized for the sake of the belly.

Mastery of desires is hardly an issue in this literature. Although 3 Macc. 7:11 does indeed have some relevance for the question of food laws (see below), the rhetorical effect of this text goes primarily with the question of citizenship: in whom can the king put his trust? The belly-people, who please themselves, are seeking a life without costs. They have demonstrated this in their neglect of the food laws. In other words, the text is very much in line with the idea of belly-devotees as people with no concern for matters of the city or fellowship, a fact attested in chaps. 3–4 in this study. People who are neglecting the food laws devote themselves to the pleasures of the stomach, and they are liable to seek their own interest when the king calls upon their loyalty in times of crisis.

Since New Testament scholars often take Paul's belly-dicta as referring to observance of food laws, it is relevant to make a brief comment on this here. As we have argued, the relationship between the belly and dietary laws in this text by no means favours an identity between the two. On the contrary, 3 Macc. 7:11 militates against such an identification. The belly is here the power which overturns the divinely given food laws. Since this text refers to transgressing the dietary laws, it is hardly a relevant analogy for Paul, who is supposed to be blaming those who *continued* to observe the food laws. From the perspective of this text, it is rather Paul who is a candidate for being called a belly-devotee.

---

[8] See Moses Hadas, *Maccabees*, pp. 24–5.

6.4   4 Maccabees

The usual terms for 'stomach' do not occur in this literature, but the faithful Jews are strongly urged to resist gluttony; fidelity manifests itself in bringing the appetite under control. This emphasis corresponds to the importance given to the question of mastering the desires in this work.[9] In the prologue, the author lists some typical vices to be mastered, among which are γαστριμαργία and ἐπιθυμία (4 Macc. 1:3). Gluttony is seen as a particular manifestation of the passions.[10] In 4 Macc. 2:7 the cognate γαστρίμαργος is mentioned alongside the eater and drinker (μονοφάγος, μέθυσος). Furthermore, that excess in eating occupies a significant role in this literature is evident also from 4 Macc. 1:25–30, where a traditional list of vices is provided. The word λαιμαργία here occurs in the company of other terms for gluttony and eating, such as παντοφαγία and μονοφαγία.

4 Maccabees[11] presents itself as a philosophical treatise on the subject of mastering the desires: 'Highly philosophical is the subject I propose to discuss, namely, whether devout reason (ὁ εὐσεβὴς λογισμός) is absolute master of passions (αὐτοδέσποτός ἐστιν τῶν παθῶν)' (4 Macc. 1:1).[12] This subject is then particularly related to the question of gluttony, which is defined as what to eat (e.g. 1:27–35; 5:3, 6, 14, 20–1, 25–38; 6:18–21; 8:2; 9:1–2). Being enslaved by gluttony is thus related to the transgression of the Jewish food laws, and it is presented within the framework of Hellenistic philosophy.[13] To eat unclean food means subjugation of reason to slavery of the desires.

In a way common to Hellenistic thinkers, the author claims that the man of virtue is enabled to control the passions, and is therefore characterized by virtues such as σωφροσύνη, ἀνδρεία, αὐτάρκεια.[14] The question of self-control is introduced at the very beginning of this treatise, and thus sets the agenda for the whole writing (4 Macc. 1:2–5). From this follows a philosophical-theological theory which is presented in 4 Macc. 1:13–3:18:[15] reason is the absolute master of desires, and the Jewish law is

[9] This is evident from the prologue and the thoroughly Greek character of this book; see David A. de Silva, *4 Maccabees*, pp. 59–75.

[10] Hans-Josef Klauck, *4 Makkabäerbuch*, p. 693 n. 27 rightly speaks of a list of gastronomical vices.

[11] For an introduction, see Moses Hadas, *Maccabees*, pp. 91–141 and David A. de Silva, *4 Maccabees*, pp. 11–50.

[12] The text is quoted according to H. Anderson, '4 Maccabees', *OTP* 2.

[13] For the Hellenistic character of 4 Maccabees, see David C. Aune, 'Mastery of the Passions' and in particular Robert Renehan, 'Fourth Maccabees'.

[14] This is worked out in detail by Stephen D. Moore and Janice Chapel Anderson, '4 Maccabees', pp. 258–9 cf. David A. de Silva, *4 Maccabees*, pp. 80–5.

[15] For the structure of 4 Maccabees, see Stanley K. Stowers, '4 Maccabees'.

the best ally of reason.[16] Gluttony is therefore fought by means of Jewish dietary laws. The food laws are seen in an entirely Greek framework; they represent the healthy life and are the means of preventing gluttony.[17]

The remaining part of this book forms narrative support for the theory; i.e. by the examples of Eleazar, an aged Jewish man, seven young boys and their mother, fighting the demand of King Antiochus Epiphanes that they eat forbidden food.[18] They were able to fight the tyrant as they had fought their appetite by means of their devotion to the dietary laws. A Jewish requirement of ritual cleanliness is here seen in the light of the philosophical *topos* of controlling the appetite.

In accordance with the agenda of self-control, the real and most dangerous enemy was not the king and his threats, but rather their own appetites. They were in danger of being enslaved by their passions, and thus conquered by gluttony:

> Now, therefore, if the seven brothers scorned sufferings even unto death, it must be universally conceded that the pious reason is complete master of the passions. For if being enslaved to the passions (δουλωθέντες) they had eaten unclean food, we would have said that they had been conquered (νενικῆσθαι) by them. However, in this case it did not happen so, but by the reason which is commended by God they prevailed over the passions, and so we cannot but perceive the mind's supremacy over them since they overcame both passion and suffering (ἐπεκράτησαν γὰρ καὶ πάθους καὶ πόνων). How then can we fail to admit, in regard to these men, right reason's victory over the passions, seeing that they did not shrink from the pains of fire?
>
> (4 Macc. 13:1–5)

The author thinks of the stomach as a power from within, which entices a Jew to break the food laws. The implication of this is that the narrative framework harps on an inner struggle in which every pious man finds himself fighting the appetites. Stripped of all its narrative framework and philosophical mapping, it is about abandoning the practices of faith; it is simply the challenge to fight apostasy. The narrative as such focuses on endurance of suffering, not on fighting the appetites. The framework and the narrative taken together strongly indicate that the two are inseparable.

---

[16] See David A. de Silva, *4 Maccabees*, pp. 133–7.

[17] So also in Philo; see chap. 7.6 in this study.

[18] This story in its different aspects is well presented by Stephen D. Moore and Janice Chapel Anderson, '4 Maccabees'.

Here this book thinks in a way which we found widely attested in the Graeco-Roman material. A person who restrains his appetites enables himself to fight suffering and wage war as well. This is, in fact, the political aspect of the belly-*topos*. Hence the appetite for food, which is focused on in the prologue, and endurance of pain, which is at the centre of the narrative, indeed belong together as contrasting poles.

This struggle is depicted in athletic terms, thus continuing our observation on the *topos* of belly and the athlete-image as forming polar opposites within the discussion of mastering the desires. The *agôn* metaphor actually dominates the entire account of martyrdom.[19] At the end of the development of the theory (3:18)[20] as well as the very last verse (18:23),[21] the author depicts the example of the Jewish martyrs in athletic terms. Allusions to the athletes are many throughout this treatise.[22]

In 4 Macc. 17:11–16 this imagery appears in full, within an epitaph of the dead martyrs:

> Truly divine was the contest in which they were engaged. On that day virtue was the umpire and the test to which they were put was a test of endurance. The prize for victory was incorruption in long-lasting life. The first to enter the contest was Eleazar, but the mother of the seven sons competed also, and the brothers as well took part. The tyrant was the adversary and the world and the life of men were the spectators. Piety won the victory and crowned her own contestants. Who did not marvel at the champions of the divine Law; who were not amazed?[23]

This text is replete with athletic terms: ἀγών, ἀθλητής, νῖκος and their cognates. Bringing the appetite under control was seen as an athletic contest demanding abstinence, training, being goal-oriented, and in the end victory. This genuine Hellenistic motif is here appropriated to aid in understanding the struggle of the martyrs with their own appetite. The author works from the assumption that a person who fights passion will also be enabled to stand firm against suffering. This is the fundamental

---

[19] Victor C. Pfitzner, *Paul and the Agon Motif*, pp. 57–64 gives a survey of the athletic imagery in this writing; see also Stephen D. Moore and Janice Chapel Anderson, '4 Maccabees', pp. 259–61.

[20] According to LSJ καταπαλαίω means to 'throw in wrestling'.

[21] ἀθλοφόρος refers to the victor who bears away the price of victory, the στέφανος.

[22] 4 Macc. 3:5,18; 6:10; 9:8,23–4; 11:20–3; 12:13; 13:13–15; 15:29; 16:14, 16; 17:11–16; 18:23.

[23] Moses Hadas, *Maccabees*, p. 234 says that this text is almost like 'a Pindaric ode in effect', honouring the victor in the athletic games.

assumption of the political perspective on the belly-*topos* which we have found throughout the Graeco-Roman material (cf. 3 Macc. above).

If we relate this treatise to Paul's sayings on the belly, it does not support the view that he is addressing Jewish Christians who *continue* to observe the food laws. If Paul really meant that, he is turning this literature upside down. Paul would hardly consider those who are observing the food laws to be conquered by the stomach. Actually, from the perspective of 3 and 4 Macc. this is inconceivable. From the perspective of these two writings it is more likely that Paul's Jewish opponents would turn this accusation against Paul for setting the food laws aside.[24] If they did so, they would be in harmony with both these writings on this particular point. They are likely to have claimed that Paul, by abandoning circumcision and dietary laws, was paving the way for the unruly belly.

6.5   *Aristeas to Philocrates* 140–1

> Hence the leading priests among the Egyptians, conducting many close investigations and with practical experience of affairs, gave us (the Jews) the title 'men of God' (ἀνθρώπους θεοῦ), which is ascribed exclusively to those who worship the true God, and not to those who are concerned with meat and drink and clothes (ἄνθρωποι βρωτῶν καὶ ποτῶν καὶ σκέπης), their whole attitude [to life] being concentrated on these concerns. Such concerns are of no account among the people of our race, but throughout the whole of their lives their main objective is concerned with the sovereignty of God (περὶ δὲ τῆς τοῦ θεοῦ δυναστείας).[25]

Within this story of how a Greek translation of the Old Testament was created there is an emphasis on the philosophical question of mastering the desires. In the king's questions to the Jewish wise men (*Ep. Arist.* 187–294), the question of how to control the passions plays a significant role (e.g. 221–4, 237, 256, 277–8).

The belly-*topos* is not spelled out, but the text quoted above is still relevant. The first thing worth noting is that Aristeas mentions food, drink

---

[24] Texts like 1 Cor. 8:8; 10:25–7; Rom. 14:2–3, 17 could easily provide a basis for accusations along this line.

[25] The text is quoted according to R. J. H. Shut, 'Letter of Aristeas', *OTP* 2. The Greek text is from André Pelletier, *Lettre d'Aristée à Philocrate*. There is no certainty about the date of this work. Most scholars favour the view that it was composed sometime between 150 BC and the first century AD.

and clothing as markers separating Jews from the pagans. The context in which 140–1 is found speaks of how God has set the Jews apart from the nations (e.g. 139, 142). Aristeas considers the attitude to food, drink and clothing as signs indicative of Jewish identity. The nations, or in this text, the Egyptians in particular, are idolaters (*Ep. Arist.* 135–9). It is the nature of idolaters to be concerned with earthly things like what to eat, drink and wear; they have no horizons beyond this. Hence they also miss an orientation towards the divine. This orientation is, however, found among the Jews, whose minds are set not on food etc., but on divine things. Aristeas spells this difference out in a way which brings him close to the idea of belly-devotion; revealing an earthly nature or identity in contrast to a divine. Aristeas draws upon this common idea to explain the differences between Jews and pagans.[26]

Furthermore, in order to uphold this divine orientation, God has provided some tools, among which are the food laws (142): 'So, to prevent our being perverted by contact with others or by mixing with bad influences, he hedged us in on all sides with strict observances connected with meat and drink and touch and hearing and sight, after the manner of the Law'.[27] The aim of the food laws is thus to keep God's people from bad living. The food laws are given as instruments to control concerns with food, drink and clothing. God did not restrict eating out of concern for the animals, but to promote a decent life among his people (144). God has therefore forbidden His people to eat animals whose nature is wild, base and greedy. These are symbols of a way of life which is not compatible with the Jews' status of being divinely elected (146–50, cf. 163–6, 169).

6.6   T. Mos. 7:2–4

This first-century-work, whose precise circumstances are difficult to trace,[28] has a text of relevance for our purpose. In what is probably an attack on Hellenizing priests, it says:

> Then will rule destructive and godless men, who represent themselves as being righteous, but who will (in fact) arouse their inner wrath, for they will be deceitful men, pleasing only themselves

---

[26] Hence the Jews are called 'men of God'. In Philo this is a name for those whose kinship with the divine is seen in their mind and learning, as opposed to those born of the earth who indulge in their pleasures (*Gig.* 60–1).

[27] The Laws, and in particular the food laws, represent a protection against some of the pleasures which are often connected with an Epicurean life-style; see chap. 7.6 in this study.

[28] See J. Priest, 'Testament of Moses', *OTP* 1, pp. 919–26. For the Latin text, see R. H. Charles, *Assumption of Moses*.

> (*sibi placentes*), false in every way imaginable, (such as) loving
> feasts (*amantes convivia*) at any hour of the day – devouring
> (*devoratores*), gluttonous (*gulae*).   (*T. Mos.* 7:2–4)

The background of this attack is the fact that Jews viewed pagan banquets as occasions for licentiousness in eating and drinking (see chap. 5
in this study). This is mentioned in v. 8 as well, which quotes what the
opponents say about their own lifestyle: 'We shall have feasts, even luxurious winings and dinings. Indeed we shall behave as princes.'[29] Their
lifestyle is depicted as impious, but also as avaricious although they claim
to be righteous and to preserve purity. The following chapter speaks of the
punishment which will come upon them. From *T. Mos.* 8:2–3 we deduce
that the texts speak of Jews who have abrogated their circumcision. In
other words, they are living like Gentiles, not considering the implications
of their circumcision and identity. It is the laxity towards Jewish customs
which generates accusations of being a glutton.

6.7   Cairo Geniza Wisdom

A close analogy to the Hellenistic material, as well as to Paul's belly
references, is found in the so-called *Cairo Geniza Wisdom*.[30] Chap. 14
presents, in a way typical of Jewish wisdom-traditions, the contrast between wisdom and folly. It brings to mind a so-called 'two-way teaching'
(see 17:2–8 in particular):

> Das Denken der Weisen geht auf ihr Ende, doch das Denken der
> Dummen ist ihr Bauch (במ) Das Denken der Gerechten (geht)
> von ihrem Schöpfer aus, doch das Denken der Ungerechten sind
> ihre Begierden. Die Seele ist Denken und Leidenschaften und
> Begehren des Höchsten und Niedrigsten.
>
>   (*Geniza Wisdom* 14:6–8)

According to *Geniza Wisd.* 15:1, the foolish have a special concern for
their bodies; hence they are 'slaves of their bellies' (עבד׳ בטנם) (*Geniza
Wisd.* 15:7). The righteous and the ungodly have embraced two different
kinds of worship: the righteous are servants of God, but the godless are
servants of their belly (בטנ) (*Geniza Wisd.* 17:5). The logic and structure

---

[29] The Latin text has: *Habebimus discubitiones et luxuriam, edentes et bibentes, et
potabimus nos, tanquam principes erimus.* Charles renders *potabimus nos* as 'we shall
drink our fill'.

[30] I owe thanks to Dr Brian Rosner for having alerted me to this text.

of this literature (chaps. 14–15;17 in particular) can be presented in the
following way:

The wise	*The foolish*
wisdom	folly
light	darkness
their concern is their future death	their concern is their belly
their minds are set on the Creator and things above	their minds are on their desires and things below
fighting desires	loving desires
worshippers (or servants) of God	worshippers (or servants) of the belly

As pointed out by Brian Rosner,[31] the Hebrew verb עבד recalls the context
of worshipping God and idols in Old Testament traditions. Belly-devotion
is idolatry. It is relevant indeed to consider these references as analogies
to Phil. 3:19 as well as Rom. 16:18.[32]

The date of the text is, however, very uncertain. The text was published in 1989 by Klaus Berger.[33] He argues that it was composed in
Egypt around AD 100.[34] Berger's arguments have been contested by Hans
Peter Rüger, who pleads for a medieval composition.[35] Brian Rosner concludes that 'it would be unwise to appeal to Gen. Wisdom for help in the
interpretation of the Pauline "belly worship"'.[36] He nevertheless seems
to rely very much on this particular piece of evidence in arguing that Paul
in Phil. 3:19 and Rom. 16:18 is referring to an idiom that 'possibly had
currency in Jewish circles'.[37] With reference to the material presented
hitherto in this study, I find it more pertinent to speak of a Greek idiom
or *topos* appropriated in Jewish texts, among which *Geniza Wisdom* is an
outstanding example. But the uncertainty as to its date remains a major
problem. Of particular interest to our study is Philo's frequent mentioning
of the stomach; we therefore give him a chapter of his own.

---

[31] Brian Rosner in his forthcoming study on greed in the New Testament.

[32] See Klaus Berger, *Die Weisheitsschrift aus der Kairo Geniza*, pp. 356, 374; Markus
Bockmuehl, *Philippians*, p. 231.

[33] Klaus Berger, *Die Weisheitsschrift aus der Kairo Geniza.*   [34] Ibid. pp. 76–9.

[35] Hans Peter Rüger, *Die Weisheitsschrift aus der Kairo Geniza*, pp. 1–15.

[36] I here quote from Brian Rosner's forthcoming study on greed in the New Testament,
of which he has kindly given me the relevant extracts.

[37] Ibid.

7

THE BELLY IN PHILO'S WRITINGS

7.0   Introduction

The Alexandrinian Jew, Philo, was a contemporary of Paul. His abundant writings give us access to a significant part of Hellenistic Judaism. Samuel Sandmel says that 'often Philo has been of interest to scholars not for himself but for the light he sheds on presumably more significant matters'.[1] This is also true for this presentation of Philo, but it is still a tribute to the significance Philo's writings have for a proper understanding of the world in which Paul wrote. Philo's writings represent a blending of Platonic philosophy, Stoic ethics and Scriptural interpretation.[2] Although modern reviewers would speak of a synthesis of various traditions, some even competing, Philo himself considered his writings as bringing out in full the true meaning of Scripture. His work was primarily of an exegetical nature.[3] The means by which he fuses various traditions and biblical texts as scriptural interpretation is his well-known allegorical method.[4] The aim of this method is to trace the deeper meaning of the text, which very often turns out to be a philosophical truth.[5] This is very much the case in the question of how Philo perceived the belly. Philo is confident he can trace the hidden meaning since he considers the Scriptures to be

---

[1] For an introduction, see Samuel Sandmel, 'Philo Judaeus', pp. 3–46; quotation from p. 4. For Philo's social and historical setting, see also John M. G. Barclay, *Jews in the Mediterranean Diaspora*, pp. 158–80 and Peder Borgen, *Philo of Alexandria*, pp. 14–26, 30–45. Philo's highly philosophical interpretation of the Scriptures very often has a reference to historical circumstances which Jews in Alexandria faced. This has been pointed out especially by Peder Borgen in his many works on Philo.

[2] For the philosophical background, see Abraham Terian, 'A Critical Introduction to Philo's Dialogues', pp. 277–81.

[3] This is rightly pointed out by Peder Borgen, 'Philo of Alexandria', pp. 150–4. John M. G. Barclay, *Jews in the Mediterranean Diaspora*, tends to miss this point when he says that 'Philo's debt to Plato is just as great, if not greater, than his debt to Moses' (p. 164).

[4] See e.g. *Congr.* 192; *Fug.* 124; *Abr.* 119.

[5] This probably reveals an apologetic purpose in most of his writings. The apologetic works of Josephus have the same tendency, namely to present Judaism and the Mosaic Law as an expression of universal truths (e.g. *Ag. Ap.* 2:154–6, 182–3, 220–4, 256–7, 291–5).

inspired prophecy, containing universal truths about life.[6] The following presentation will contain many examples of Philo's allegorical method.

Views on Philo's significance for New Testament studies, and the Pauline Epistles in particular, are diverse.[7] Philo's extensive use of allegorical methods has been seen as setting him apart from most relevant contemporary Jewish and Christian sources. But the magisterial work of Martin Hengel has taught us not to push the distinction between Hellenistic and Palestinian Judaism.[8] Life and thought in Palestine were profoundly Hellenized. This is not to blur obvious differences between our sources; it is rather a matter of emphasis. As for Philo and Paul, they both read the same OT texts, and both considered them the true Word of God. Both commented upon these texts in a Greek setting and in the corresponding language.[9] The question of how Philo and Paul are related can hardly be dealt with on a general level. It needs to be pursued into studies of specific topics and texts. I intend to do exactly this on the specific question of belly-devotion. Philo's primary importance is none the less that he provides examples of exegetical traditions available for a biblical interpreter such as Paul encountering the Hellenistic philosophical world.

7.1   Anthropology

One of the special features of Philo is that his exegesis and instructions are rooted in a particular anthropology. His view of man forms a starting-point for an adequate understanding of what he says about the stomach. He assumes the Platonic tripartite division of the soul into parts which are rational, high-spirited and lustful.[10] This philosophical definition of the soul has a correspondence in how the human body has been put together. Philo's philosophical-spiritual hierarchy can be deduced from the appearance of the human body. He applies physiognomic theory not

[6] For Philo's allegorical method, see Samuel Sandmel, 'Philo Judaeus', pp. 13–22 and David Instone Brewer, *Techniques and Assumptions in Jewish Exegesis*, pp. 198–212.

[7] For a survey of this question, see Samuel Sandmel, 'Philo Judaeus', pp. 36–46 and his book *Philo*, pp. 148–63.

[8] Martin Hengel, *Judentum und Hellenismus*.

[9] Henry Chadwick, 'St Paul and Philo of Alexandria', says that 'it seems clear that of all non-Christian writers of the first century AD Philo is the one from whom the historian of emergent Christianity has most to learn' (p. 288). This might be somewhat exaggerated. For a more balanced view, see David T. Runia, *Philo in Early Christian Literature*, pp. 63–86.

[10] For Philo's dependence upon Greek philosophy in his anthropology, see David T. Runia, *Philo of Alexandria and the Timaeus of Plato*, pp. 467–75. As pointed out by Runia (pp. 304–5), Philo sometimes reduces or expands the numbers into which the human soul is parted. The basic distinction is between its immortal (divine) and the mortal part of it.

primarily to individuals, but to the human race as such. The tripartite division of the soul is linked with the head, chest, and stomach; sometimes the belly and genitals are mentioned in tandem.

A clear evidence of Philo's view on man is found in *Leg.* 1:63–73. In accordance with his allegorical approach, he sees the four rivers of Paradise as symbols of the four main virtues:[11] prudence (φρόνησις), self-mastery (σωφροσύνη), courage (ἀνδρεία), justice (δικαιοσύνη). Philo raises the question of the order of these virtues. Why are they mentioned in this particular order? His answer to the question is worth quoting in full:

> We must observe, then, that our soul is threefold, and has one part that is the seat of reason (τὸ λογικόν), another that is the seat of high spirit (τὸ θυμικόν), and another that is the seat of desire (τὸ ἐπιθυμητικόν). And we discover that the head is the place and abode of the reasonable part, the breast of the passionate part, the abdomen (τὸ ἦτρον) of the lustful part; and that to each of the parts a virtue proper to it has been attached; prudence (φρόνησις) to the reasonable part, for it belongs to reason to have knowledge of things we ought to do and of the things we ought not; courage (ἀνδρεία) to the passionate part; and self-mastery (σωφροσύνη) to the lustful part. For it is by self-mastery that we heal and cure our desires. As, then, the head is the first and highest part of the living creature, the breast the second, and the abdomen the third, and again of the soul the reasoning faculty is first, the high-spirited second, the lustful third; so too of the virtues, first is prudence, which has its sphere in the first part of the soul which is the domain of reason, and in the first part of the body, namely the head; and second is courage, for it has its seat in high spirits, the second part of the soul, and in the breast, the corresponding part of the body; and third self-mastery, for its sphere of action is the abdomen, which is of course the third part of the body, and the lustful faculty, to which has been assigned the third place in the soul. (*Leg.*1:70–1, cf. 3:114–17; *Spec.* 4:92–4)

Virtues and the structure of the body are therefore to be kept together. This is the reason why Philo quite consistently speaks of the desires as being located in the belly and the parts below it (*Agr.* 38; *Mos.* 2:23; *Gig.* 18).[12] Since man's access to God is through the mind or reason,

---

[11] Similarly in *QG* 1:12 (Gen. 2:10).

[12] 'The belly and the parts below it' appears as a phrase more or less synonymous with

the soul should be made a house of God (e.g. *Cher.* 100–2; *Somn.* 1:49; *Decal.* 134), striving to be attached to God, to have a vision of God, as did Jacob.[13] The soul as the house of the divine in men is in need of external ornaments, namely grammar, geometry, rhetoric; i.e. the curriculum of the schools (*Cher.* 98–107).

The true and genuine philosophy of the soul, however, is laid down in the Torah, which is according to the natural law.[14] This access of the mind to God is, however, in jeopardy owing to the desires located in the belly and the parts below it. The pleasures, desires or lusts reside in the stomach. It is, therefore, at the centre of Philo's concerns to keep the belly under control, to keep it in its place. To Philo 'contemplation of the divine things is closely related to the control of one's passion'.[15] This is the proper context for the place belly-servitude occupies in Philo's writings.

Since some parts of man always remain rooted in material life, food remains necessary and can never, therefore, be dispensed with (*Leg.* 3:147, 151–9). According to *QE* 2:72 (Exod. 25:30), the loaves on the altar are symbols of the necessity of food. It is superfluous luxury Philo is targeting.[16] Nature demands food and drink, but Philo issues warnings against excess and abundance. The power of the belly is a constant danger to the godly man (*QE* 2:39 (Exod. 24:11b)). This calls for moderation and self-control, and Moses therefore opened a way between Spartan austerity and Sybaritic luxury (*Spec.* 4:102).[17] Philo expected people to achieve mastery over pleasure and desire to different degrees. He speaks of a gradual advance (*Leg.* 3:144; *Spec.* 4:124), and of the necessity of training.[18] The contemplative life requires training and preparation through moderation in matters related to the stomach.

---

desires and passions in Philo's writings. This has an obvious analogy to Plato's *Timaeus* 70d–e.

[13] Jacob's vision of God is to Philo the supreme good; e.g. *Praem.* 43–4; *Ebr.* 82–3; *Migr.* 39, 201; *Her.* 51; *Mut.* 81–2; *Fug.* 208, *Somn.* 1:171; 2:177; *Abr.* 57.

[14] The relationship between the school-education (*encyclica*) and the Mosaic Law is elaborated on in Philo's treatise on the *Preliminary Studies* (*De Congressu*); see Harry Austryn Wolfson, *Philo*, pp. 145–54; Peder Borgen, 'Philo of Alexandria', pp. 115–17; John M. G. Barclay, *Jews in the Mediterranean Diaspora*, pp. 170–6.

[15] David C. Aune, 'Mastery of the Passions', p. 133.

[16] Cf. *QG* 2:67 (Gen. 9:20); 4:35 (Gen. 19:3); *QE* 1:14 (Exod. 12:8b).

[17] For further references on moderation as regards the demands of the belly, see David Winston, 'Philo's Ethical Theory', pp. 405–14.

[18] For references on training for virtue, see Victor C. Pfitzner, *Paul and the Agon Motif*, pp. 41–2; Peder Borgen, 'Philo – A Systematic Philosopher or an Eclectic Editor?', pp. 131–2; David C. Aune, 'Mastery of the Passions', pp. 128–34; David Winston, 'Philo's Ethical Theory', pp. 411–13.

Another favourite metaphor of Philo which is related to the training perspective is that of soul husbandry. The soul needs to be cultivated, protected, pruned, and even have parts cut off if necessary (*Plant.* 36–8). The most important thing that needs to be cut off is gluttony (γαστρι-μαργία) (*Agr.* 35–8). Such is the context of Philo's dicta on the need of mastering the passions coming from the belly. Actually, the stomach is both foundation and reservoir of all pleasures. Philo's discussion on the desires of the lower parts of the body, the region of the navel and below, develops out of an allegorical interpretation of certain texts. To these we now turn.

7.2   The 'geography' of the belly

The most important and constant biblical symbol from which Philo proceeds in his writings on the stomach is Egypt and the Israelites' departure thence. Egypt represents the bodily desires from which men must separate themselves (*Migr.* 14–15). Egypt cannot be reconciled with the vision of God (*Migr.* 18).[19] Philo speaks of both Egypt and Pharaoh in this sense. Gen. 47:3 tells the story of Joseph's brothers, who revealed their identity as shepherds to Pharaoh. Since 'shepherd' is a common name for a king,[20] Philo draws a lesson from this episode. The brothers declared the need to rule the passion-loving body, here in the figure of Pharaoh. Like a charioteer, having control of his wild horses, so a man must rule his 'body and the senses and the belly, and the pleasures whose seat is below the belly' (*Sacr.* 49).

In *Post.* 155–9, Philo describes the temptations Israel faced in the wilderness as efforts of the desires of belly and sex to bring the people under their control anew, to bring them back to the life of dissoluteness and licentiousness (ἀσέλγεια καὶ ἀκολασία) in Egypt. But God provided for their needs. The incident recorded in Exod. 15:25 about the bitter water that was sweetened teaches a lesson for God's people, namely to love bitter labour as well. Without saying it explicitly, Philo wants his readers to be able to resist the call of the belly even in times of bitterness. However, not all partook of this food or water. It was reserved for those who turned away from the golden calf,[21] and who enjoyed Moses' burning

---

[19] For Egypt as a symbol of desires, and Exodus as fleeing from them, see *Migr.* 77, 151–2, 154, 160, 202; *Her.* 315–16; *Congr.* 83–4; *Agr.* 88; *Sacr.* 48; *Post.* 96, 155.

[20] This is a favourite metaphor of Philo, which he takes from Plato; see David C. Aune, 'Mastery of the Passions', p. 147 n. 11. See also *Ios.* 1–3, 54, cf. *Agr.* 41.

[21] The calf is an Egyptian animal, and hence refers to this country.

of it (Exod. 32:20). More material on this episode in the desert will be provided later when we come to our exegesis of 1 Cor. 10 (chap. 10).

For natural reasons then, Passover is seen as a feast to celebrate the flight from Egypt and as a reminder to flee from the desires (*Spec.* 2:145–9). Passover is about the purification of the soul, 'crossing from the body and the passions, each of which overwhelms him like a torrent, unless the rushing current be dammed and held back by the principles of virtue' (*Spec.* 2:147, cf. *Leg.* 3:49). During the feast every house has the dignity of a temple, and a banquet is prepared. Philo describes the Passover meal by aid of its opposite, the pagan *symposia* or drinking-bouts. Hence, it is a festival 'not to indulge the belly with wine and viands, but to fulfil with prayers and hymns the custom handed down by their fathers' (*Spec.* 2:148).

Philo's allegorical interpretation of Egypt places the belly-*topos* at the very centre of the Jewish faith. The ethics of mastering the passions become the focus of his interpretation of this fundamental event in Israel's history. The question of serving the belly therefore comes into focus as well. It forms a contrast with having faith in God's providence. Not only the Passover, but Jewish religious practices and customs in general were inaugurated by Moses to help those who had left Egypt, the place of the pleasures. The practices of piety were created to help keep the belly in its place. To Philo, belly-devotion is not mentioned at random or by accident; it belongs to the very centre of what Jewish faith and piety are aimed at fighting. In the following we will develop this further, by looking into some biblical figures, stories and texts used by Philo to explain the power and nature of the belly.

7.3   The serpent crawling on its belly

According to *Opif.* 77–81, God created man with an element of himself, located in the mind. Human beings are therefore his kin (συγγένεια).[22] God provided everything, and prepared everything before humans were created. He prepared the world as a good place to live. But sin entered the world, and Philo describes this as gluttony (γαστριμαργία) and various desires (ἐπιθυμίαι). The only means by which the lost dignity of men can be regained is self-mastery (σωφροσύνη).

How did sin enter the world created by God to be enjoyed by human beings? This question is treated in *De Opificio Mundi* (*On the Creation*).

---

[22] This is a Platonic idea; see David T. Runia, *Philo of Alexandria and the Timaeus of Plato*, p. 272. We have found e.g. Epictetus to be an advocate of this view.

In *Opif.* 156–66, Philo briefly records the Biblical story of the snake's tempting of the woman. He emphasizes the deceptive aim of the serpent as hidden in soft words about the attractive fruit. His own elaboration of the story begins in 157, as usual with an allegorical interpretation: the serpent spoken of is a fit symbol of pleasure (ἡδονῆς εἶναι σύμβολον); for what a serpent does to a man, pleasure does to the soul, as he put it in *Leg.* 3:76. Gen. 3 and the snake are building-blocks of Philo's way of appropriating the belly-*topos*.[23] Philo develops the story in details: the snake or serpent is an apt symbol of pleasures because

- it creeps on the belly (ἐπὶ γαστέρα)
- it feeds on the earth (γῆς). In *Her.* 238, Philo explains what he has in mind here. The earth is the most suitable place for animals of the land, particularly snakes. They cannot raise themselves up, and are bound to make for themselves holes in the earth. Their kinship is therefore with what is below (πρὸς τὰ κάτω συγγένειαν). This recalls one important idea in the cluster associated with the belly-*topos*; servants of the stomach have their mind on earthly things and have lost sight of the divine
- the serpent has venom in its teeth.

These characteristics of the snake are easily drawn from the OT text itself; the building-blocks Philo certainly found in Gen. 3:14–15 LXX:

- ἐπὶ τῇ κοιλίᾳ πορεύσῃ
- γῆν φάγῃ τὰς ἡμέρας τῆς ζωῆς σου

Philo then proceeds to apply and compare this to the pleasure-lover (φιλήδονος):

- he is dragged downwards and can hardly lift his head, being held down by intemperance
- he grovels in the dirt and feeds on that which comes from earth, not heavenly nourishment; i.e. wisdom[24]
- like a poisonous snake, he is searching for a victim, he is looking for a table, hoping to consume its food all alone. 'His aim is not to sate his hunger, but to leave nothing that has been set before him undevoured. Hence we see that no less than the serpent he carries his poison in his teeth' (*Opif.* 158).

---

[23] See also A. Peter Booth, 'The Voice of the Serpent'. For the passions of the belly as snake-like, see *Leg.* 2:72, 84; 3:86; *QG* 1:47 (Gen. 3:14–17); 1:48 (Gen. 3:14–17).

[24] Heavenly bread is usually connected with manna (Exod. 16:4); see e.g. *Leg.* 3:162.

Philo adds that the snake speaks with a human voice, which is a symbol of the fact that it has supporters everywhere. They spread its doctrine[25] all over. This doctrine teaches a lifestyle marked by excessive drunkenness (οἰνοφλυγία), eating (ὀψοφαγία) and greediness (λαιμαργία): 'These, causing the cravings of the belly (τὰς γαστρὸς ἐπιθυμίας) to burst out and fanning them into flame, make the man a glutton (γαστριμαργία), while they also stimulate and stir up the stings of his sexual lusts' (*Opif.* 158). The snake and pleasure-lover have in common their devotion to the belly, and Philo makes much out of this. The point of comparison is the stomach-nature of the two. As for the pleasure-lover, the belly is a symbol of both his gluttony and his excess in sexual matters. It represents a power of selfishness which in the end is destructive, although appearing in a flattering way like the words of the snake.[26] Stripped of all allegorical and biblical associations in Philo's text, the address is to people whose attention and devotion are set on the lavish tables (see chap. 5).

In the same section, Philo uses another story drawn from Gen. 3 to describe the power of pleasure, namely the woman. Pleasure can be symbolized as a beguiling woman or courtesan (*Opif.* 165–6, cf. *Sacr.* 19–33).[27] The snake's success in tempting the woman to eat is to Philo a witness both of the role played by food in temptations, as well as of the tendency of women to be easily deceived. In *QG* 1:33 (Gen. 3:11) the question why the snake first approached the woman is raised. The answer is that she is more accustomed to being deceived than the man.[28] Man's judgement is, like his body, more resistant. Philo develops a whole theology of gender, based on his conviction that the male represents the mind and the female the senses.[29]

An example of the true man is Jacob (ἀληθὴς ἀνήρ) (*Somn.* 1:120–6). The true man, or the man of virtue, is prepared to face hardships of any kind. He lives a life of self-control.[30] True men are superior to temptations of money, pleasure, popularity, food and drink (124). The opposite of the manly person is the effeminate, who attends lavish parties, where

---

[25] Philo speaks of οἱ τολμῶσιν ἀναδιδάσκειν (*Opif.* 160). This might be a reference to Epicureans; so also David Winston, 'Philo's Ethical Theory', p. 408 n. 116.

[26] *Leg.* 3:61, 66 speaks of τὸ ἀπατᾶν as typical of the snake. The context of this saying is an interpretation of Gen. 3. This is an observation which will have some bearing on our reading of Rom. 16:17–20 later in this study (chap. 9).

[27] For the richly adorned woman as representing a tempting pleasure, cf. 1 Tim. 2:9; 1 Pet. 3:3.

[28] But the woman is not bad in herself, as the serpent is (*Leg.* 3:67–8).

[29] See e.g. *Opif.* 153–69; *Leg.* 2:9–15; *Spec.* 1:200.

[30] Philo here uses the Greek terms σωφροσύνη, ἐγκράτεια, καρτερία to describe this manly person (who might equally well be a woman).

unlimited portions of food and drink are consumed. In this way the sexual appetite[31] is aroused as well. The goal of the training for virtue is to become male-like.[32]

Within a presentation of the food laws (see on this below), Philo also speaks of the reptiles which have no feet but wriggle[33] along on their belly. They are unclean for eating (*Spec.* 4:113). From this, we would then expect Philo to mention forbidden food. But his understanding of the snake wriggling on its belly takes him somewhere else. It is a phrase about persons who devote themselves to their bellies (οἱ ἐπὶ κοιλίαις), paying their tributes (δασμός) to the stomach; i.e. strong drink, meat, fish and all kinds of delicacies. The Greek term δασμός is the tribute a subject has to pay to his superior or lord;[34] see e.g. *Ios.* 135: 'Egypt once held the sovereignty over many nations, but now is in slavery [Philo is not writing allegory here, but speaking of historical circumstances]. The Macedonians in their day of success flourished so greatly that they held dominion over all the habitable world, but now they pay to the tax-collectors the yearly tributes (δασμούς) imposed by their masters (κύριοι)' (cf. *Migr.* 204; *Somn.* 2:116, 132; *Abr.* 226). The proper context of paying tribute to the stomach is, then, to have been seized by enemies or ruled by them. In this subtle way of speaking of tributes to the stomach, Philo indicates that it is not just a matter of being devoted to the belly, but of being enslaved by it. These tributes to the stomach fuel or animate the passions.

What Philo says in this text is, in fact, a continuation of the metaphor of 'two ways', which he maps in *Spec.* 4:112: The way of φιλήδονος (the lover of pleasure) and of ἐγκράτεια (self-control). The road leading to pleasure is easy and downhill. One hardly needs to walk, since one is being dragged downwards (ὑπό-). The road leading to self-control is, in contrast, uphill, toilsome, but it brings good; or it is heavenwards

---

[31] The LCL translator renders ὑπὸ γαστέρα (122) 'sensual passions', but it should be taken as sexual desires. So Pierre Savinel, *Philon d'Alexandrie, De Somniis 1–2*, pp. 74–5; cf. the many texts where 'below the stomach' has an obvious sexual reference. Philo often identifies the stomach with sexual appetite (*Leg.* 3:157; *Det.* 113; *Post.* 155; *Mos.*1:160).

[32] For a similar view, see our presentation of 4 Macc. above. For Philo's view of women, see Dorothy Sly, *Philo's Perception of Women* as well as her 'The Plight of Women'.

[33] Philo borrows, probably from Plato, *Timaeus* 92a, a term (ἰλυσπᾶσθαι) referring to the way snakes move. He frequently applies this term to the pleasures; see *Post.* 74; *Agr.* 97; *Her.* 238; *Somn.* 2:105; *Mos.* 1:78, *Decal.* 149; *Spec.* 3:1; 4:91. Without using this particular term, Philo speaks of the movements practised during sexual intercourse, which are to be likened to those of a snake. The biblical text which is the background of this saying is Gen. 3 (*Leg.* 2:71–85).

[34] LSJ s.v.

(εἰς οὐρανὸν ἄγει).[35] Serving the belly or paying tribute to it is here seen as a question of where one belongs, on earth or in heaven. This is the idea of belly-devotion as earthly, which we found also in the Graeco-Roman material. 'Being enslaved by the belly' is a sign of an earthly identity in contrast to the heavenly kinship.

Leg. 3:65–119 is in many ways a parallel to the texts we have now commented upon. The passage deals with the curses of pleasure. The point of departure is Gen. 3:14 and Philo points out the characteristics of the snake, which we observed above. Pleasure moves on the belly (τῇ κοιλίᾳ πορεύεσθαι), Philo says, with a reference to the snake in Gen. 3. This is so because the belly is a 'reservoir (ἀγγεῖον) of all the pleasures' (*Leg.* 3:138). The power of the belly, when out of control, exceeds its size (149). The stomach is the foundation (θεμέλιος) of all passions; it is the mother of evil (145).

From Gen. 3:14 Philo turns to Lev. 11:42 (*Leg.* 3:139) on reptiles as unclean animals. This might look as if Philo is juxtaposing enslavement to the belly and violation of food laws. But as in *Spec.* 4:113 he takes this biblical text as a dictum about the uncleanliness of men who love their pleasures, who are creeping on the belly (ὁ πορευόμενος ἐπὶ κοιλίᾳ), and who walk on four feet; i.e. the four passions (*Leg.* 3:139).[36] He makes a word-play here; ἐπί followed by the accusative does not mean crawling on the belly (as in the quotation from Gen. 3:14 and Lev. 11:42), but creeping after it. In other words, the φιλήδονος is hooked on the belly.[37] The perfect man, however, cleanses the belly. Philo quotes Lev. 9:14 as an example to be followed; i.e. to rob the whole belly of its pleasures (141, 147, 159, cf. *Spec.* 1:206). These two attitudes are illuminated by the figures of Esau and Jacob (*Leg.* 3:88–93). Esau is a slave (δοῦλος) of his belly.

7.4 Esau selling his birthright for the sake of his belly

In *Virt.* 187–227, Philo addresses the question of nobility of birth (περὶ εὐγενείας). The background of this treatise is probably a situation of tension and rivalry between Jews and Gentile inhabitants of Alexandria. Some Jews made claims to superiority on the basis of their ancestry, which

[35] One can hardly avoid thinking of how Matt. 7:13–14/Luke 13:23–4 make use of the same metaphor of the road.

[36] Philo here refers to a treatise of his which is not extant.

[37] Lev. 11:42 on unclean reptiles is interpreted likewise in *Migr.* 64–7. In this text as well, Philo's interpretation brings together Gen. 3:14; Lev. 11:42 and 9:14 (or 8:21) under the heading 'different attitudes to the belly – serving or cleansing it'.

caused counter-claims.[38] Philo lays down that the fundamental criterion
of nobility is a virtuous life, and he substantiates this claim with scriptural
proofs. In *Virt.* 207–210 he approaches this topic through the example of
Jacob and Esau, both born of a noble father. The two nevertheless differed
greatly, both in bodily appearance (σῶμα) and judgement (γνώμη).[39]
While Jacob was obedient, Esau was disobedient, and he is described as
representing what is base and irrational. From our previous presentation
of Philo's anthropology, we know what this means. And Philo is explicit
on the matter: Esau was 'indulgent without restraint in the pleasures of
the belly and the lower-lying parts' (*Virt.* 208). The proof for this is, of
course, that Esau surrendered his birthright to satisfy his hunger (cf. *Sacr.*
17–18.81; *Leg.* 3:191). He lost in the arena of virtue (ἐν ἄθλοις ἀρετῆς)
(*Virt.* 210), and is therefore an example that nobility of birth is of no help
if it is not followed by a virtuous life.

That Jacob and Esau each represent the two ways, of self-control and
love of pleasure (cf. *Spec.* 4:113 above), becomes evident in Philo's exposition of Num. 20:17–20. This text reports Israel's request to the king
of Edom, asking for permission to cross his land by the royal highway.
This was denied them. Edom is, of course, another name for Esau, a fact
which is stated in the Scriptures themselves (Gen. 25:25;[40] 32:3; 36:8).
Philo comments: 'For wisdom is a straight road, and it is when the mind's
course is guided along that road that it reaches the goal which is the recognition and knowledge of God' (*Deus* 143). Every friend of the flesh (πᾶς
ὁ σαρκῶν ἑταῖρος) hates this road, and seeks to corrupt it. Hence Israel,
the people endowed with vision of God, when they were journeying along
this road, were opposed by Edom; i.e. Esau the earthly one (ὁ γήινος),
as his name is interpreted to mean (*Deus* 144). In closing his comments
on this biblical text, Philo says: 'So then the earthly Edom purposes to
bar the heavenly road of virtue, but the divine reason on the other hand
would bar the road of Edom and his associates' (*Deus* 180).

Esau hated his brother and made plans to kill him. This became known
to their mother Rebecca. She urged Jacob to flee and to stay with her
brother Laban for some time (Gen. 27:42–5). Philo has extended this
into a lengthy farewell speech in which Rebecca, i.e. Patience, gives her
advice (*Fug.* 23–43). She points out to Jacob some of the temptations
he will face: commerce, popularity, posts of honour, state business and

---

[38] According to Peder Borgen, *Philo of Alexandria*, p. 173, cf. pp. 48–51.

[39] This is probably a physiognomic statement. As for the stomach, both *Prov.* 2:18 and
QG 2:2 (Gen. 6:14) suggest that a large belly is a sign of ἐπιθυμία.

[40] Gen. 25:25 says that Edom was red when he was born; this is a word-play in Hebrew
on the name of Edom.

the pleasures of belly as well as the parts below it (τῶν γαστρὸς καὶ μετὰ γαστέρα ἡδονῶν) (*Fug.* 35).[41] The temptations of the belly are elaborated on in *Fug.* 31–2. Philo assumes that Jacob attended parties with lavish tables and where wine was flowing freely. Jacob will be in control in such situations; i.e. he will drink in moderation not out of compulsion (ἀνάγκη). He will only be soberly drunken, if we may put it like that, Philo adds.[42] In other words, to the Jews of Alexandria Jacob is an example of a person who controlled his stomach.

The man of intemperance, however, i.e. Esau, will in such situations 'fall upon his belly (πεσὼν ἐπὶ γαστέρα) and open his insatiable appetites before he opens his mouth, cram himself in unseemly fashion, grab at his next neighbour's food, and gobble up everything without a blush; and when he is thoroughly sated with eating, he will as the poets say "drink with a yawning maw",[43] and incur the mocking and ridicule of all who see him' (*Fug.* 31). The phrase ἐπὶ γαστέρα evokes, in the light of our observations made earlier in this chapter, enslavement to the belly as well as Gen. 3:14. Stripped of the belly-rhetoric of Philo, this is a dictum about attending banquets. 'Falling upon the belly' literally means to position oneself at the couch (see chap. 5).

By far the longest section on Esau is found in *QG* 4:160–245,[44] which comments – by means of questions and answers – on the story of the twin brothers Esau and Jacob. We will concentrate on Esau in this presentation. The text continues and confirms the picture we have built up so far. Throughout this long section Philo speaks of Jacob as the heavenly and Esau as the earthly man (*QG* 4:164, 171, 215, 234). Jacob was a man of visions; he saw heavenly things (233, 245).[45] Esau, however, gave full proof of his earthly identity by selling his birthright for pleasure; i.e. to satisfy his belly (225). He did so because 'he made himself a slave to the pleasures of the belly'. The Greek fragment here has δοῦλος γαστρὸς ἡδοναῖς. Esau is thus an example of a person who failed to

---

[41] These are probably temptations Jews faced in their daily life in Alexandria (see chap. 5). Philo is not urging them to flee from them, but to be able to control them; see *Fug.* 31–32, 36.

[42] Philo tells that he often attended banquets such as these (e.g. *Leg.* 3:156). Faced with this temptation, Philo brings reason, and is therefore able to 'win the noble victory of endurance and self-mastery (καρτερίας καὶ σωφροσύνης)'. Philo here gives a glimpse of present-day life in Alexandria and how Jews tried to cope with their environment.

[43] Probably a reference to Homer's *Odyssey* 21:287–94 which refers to a banquet.

[44] Only a few fragments of *QG* and *QE* have survived in Greek. Most of the texts we possess have survived in an Armenian translation. The translation of the LCL edition is based on that text. If the text referred to is one of the Greek fragments, reference will be made to Françoise Petit, *Quaestiones in Genesim et in Exodum, Fragmenta Graeca*.

[45] This is due to Philo's explanation of the name of Israel; see above in this chapter.

display ἐγκράτεια. In 191 Philo speaks of earthly desires[46] as synonymous with the pleasures of the belly.[47]

That Esau was enslaved by his stomach and had an earthly identity is to Philo primarily demonstrated by the selling of his birthright. Furthermore, the nature of Esau is substantiated in two other ways. He appears to be a person of evil and base character. He was envious, jealous, and deceitful (e.g.161, 227, 238). In short, he was not to be trusted. Hence Rebecca took the beautiful robe of Esau and clothed Jacob in it (Gen. 27:15). The deeper meaning of this is that 'the wicked man has another robe and many garments, by which he conceals himself, inasmuch as he cunningly contrives matters of wrongdoing' (*QG* 4:203) (Gen. 27:15).

Furthermore, Esau was hairy (cf. *Migr.* 153; *Leg.* 3:2). This element of the biblical story is important to Philo. He repeatedly draws attention to this, and considers it a sign of Esau's animal-like nature (QG 4:160, 189, 201, 204, 206).[48] The nature of wild animals as an image of gluttony and sexual appetite occurs quite often in Philo's writings.[49] Esau's hairy body provides the opportunity for Philo to make much of this analogy. The material and interpretations Philo puts forward make it perfectly clear that Esau is the model for a man who is ruled by his senses and not his mind (*QG* 4:189, cf. 198). Contrariwise Jacob's nature was different; he was not hairy, but smooth (*Leg.* 2:59; *Migr.* 153). He sacrificed a domestic animal (*QG* 4:198, 200), which is another proof of his good character.

The story about Esau selling his birthright gives Philo an opportunity to bring together this narrative and the belly-*topos*. With this *topos* as starting-point he re-reads the Biblical narrative, and finds that Esau represents not only enslavement to the stomach's desires, but an earthly identity expressing itself in an animal-like way; i.e. following his passions. Philo was probably not alone in reading the story in this way.[50]

---

[46] The LCL translator suggests that the Greek text would say γηίνων ἐπιθυμιῶν.

[47] The LCL translator suggests that the Greek text would say αἱ περὶ τὴν κοιλίαν ἡδοναί. The old Latin version has *terrenis nimirum cupiditatibus quae circa ventrem voluptates sint.* The Latin version is found in Charles Mercier, *Quaestiones et Solutiones in Genesim I–II* and *Quaestiones et Solutiones in Genesim III, IV, V, VI.*

[48] This is an example of logic based on physiognomic theory; cf. *QG* 4:200 (Gen. 27: 8–10) on the description of Isaac's outward appearance.

[49] E.g. *Agr.* 66; *Abr.* 149; *Contempl.* 74; *Spec.* 1:148; 4:94. Philo is probably appropriating a Platonic image of the desires; see David T. Runia, *Philo of Alexandria and the Timaeus of Plato,* p. 310.

[50] The author of Heb. 12:14–17 draws on Esau traditions which are not far removed from Philo's. The relevant OT texts themselves can hardly provide a full explanation of the early Christian exegesis found in the Epistle to the Hebrews. It rests on a tradition to which Philo is the outstanding witness. For references to this tradition, see Herbert Braun, *Hebräer,* pp. 426–7; Hans Friedrich Weiss, *Hebräer,* p. 666. The negative image given of Esau in

7.5   Joseph and the servants of Pharaoh

The story of Joseph is set in Egypt, which in Philo's symbolic world
indicates that it is a story about desires and how to master them. Joseph
faced the temptations of bodily desires in Potiphar's house (*Leg.* 3:239–
42). His wife urged Joseph to have sex with her. In Gen. 39:7, 12 her
request is rendered as a simple 'lie with me' (*NRSV*). Philo extends this
into an argument uttered by ἡδονή itself: 'As clothes are coverings of
the body, so are food and drink of the living being. This is what she
says, "Why do you decline pleasure, without which you cannot live?
See, I seize and carry off part of what goes to produce her, and I declare
that you would be unable to exist without using something productive of
pleasure"' (*Leg.* 3:239–40). These words of Pleasure herself sound like
philosophical reasoning or justification for an easy life. Pleasure justifies
herself; to Philo, however, this becomes philosophical and theological
reasoning for an indulgent life.[51]

What does then the man of self-control (ὁ ἐγκρατής) do when he faces
this appeal to participate in pleasure? He will not be a servant (δουλεύειν)
of pleasure, and therefore flees, as did Joseph (Gen. 39:12). Philo takes
this as a sign of wisdom, since Joseph was young and hardly able to cope
with the life of the Egyptian body (242).

The temptation in Potiphar's house is mentioned again in *Migr.* 19–
21. For natural reasons, the sexual temptation is made explicit, and
Philo quotes the words of Potiphar's wife. Philo's exegesis is based

---

Det. 45; *Sacr.* 135; *Congr.* 61–2 certainly moves beyond the OT sources. The primary
concern of ours has been to see that Philo tells the story from the perspective of Esau's
enslavement to his stomach. Heb. 12:14–17 provides some interesting links to this interpretation of Philo. The simple logic of the warning is that unless the addressees of the letter
abandon a lifestyle like that of Esau, they will not see God (v. 14). Most commentaries miss
the very probable reference to Jacob (cf. John 1:43–51 focusing on being a true Israelite,
i.e. seeing God). The warning is explicit in v. 16b (do not become like Esau who was a
πόρνος and βέβηλος). *NRSV* translates: 'immoral and godless person'. If we take πόρνος
in its proper meaning, as referring to sexual acts, the correspondence between Heb. 12 and
Philo's image of Esau – the belly-devoted – becomes quite explicit. The relative clause
(v. 16b) provides no real reason for the statement in v. 16a, unless v. 16b is interpreted along
the lines presented above. In the OT, Esau is blamed for having despised his birthright, not
for being a glutton and for sexual appetites. The OT texts do not provide sufficient explanation for associating his selling of the birthright with sexual sin; not even Gen. 26:34–5
and 28:6–9 can do this. If we take Heb. 12:14–17 as an example of the Esau traditions
we have seen in Philo – Esau as representing belly-devotion – the text can be read quite
smoothly. Erik Grässer, *Hebräer*, p. 293 says on Heb. 12:16a: *'dann ist er ganz auf das
Irdische gerichtet'*. Such also would be Philo's comment on Esau.

[51] This reasoning probably reflects arguments Jews in Alexandria found enticing when
faced with temptation to join in the pagan meals and the lifestyle associated with them. See
also *Det.* 33, which is quoted in chap. 8.2 in this study.

on the Septuagint's presentation of Potiphar as Pharaoh's chief cook (ἀρχιμάγειρος),[52] which establishes a link to the power of the stomach. Philo therefore sees Joseph surrounded not only by temptations of sex, but of the organ above as well, namely the stomach (*Migr.* 19). He found himself among a lustful woman, a cook, and later also a baker and butler (Gen. 40:1–23). These are all servants of Pharaoh, and hence, symbols of the desires which derive from the stomach.

In his book on dreams, Philo presents the baker and butler and their dreams (*Somn.* 2:155–63, 205–14). They represent the two forms of gluttony (γαστριμαργία), eating and drinking.[53] Both servants of Pharaoh were dreaming while asleep. Thus their dreams illustrate people whose eyes of the soul are closed. A sleeper is unable to stand upright and be awake (cf. *Somn.* 1:121):

> Thus then let us describe the wine-maddened, raving, incurable pest, the man frenzied by strong liquor. But his fellow, himself too a belly-slave,[54] the friend of gross eating (πολυφαγία) and gluttony (λαιμαργία), the dissolute artificier of viands, must be considered in his turn.   (*Somn.* 2:205)

In his dream, the baker saw himself carrying three baskets of wheaten loaves on his head (Gen. 40:16). Philo explains his dream in *Somn.* 2:206–14. His rather lengthy exposition can be summarized in the following way: the baker did not keep the things of the belly in their place. Since he was carrying bread above his head, the ruling part of the soul (cf. Philo's anthropology), this means that he replaced head with belly. He weighed down his soul by eating and his concern for food. Philo makes this explicit by quoting from Gen. 42:36: 'All these things have been upon me', which he takes as a reference to the burdened mind.[55]

The same story is recounted in *Ios.* 151–6. Bread, meat and drink are necessities of life. Three offices have been provided to care for these things: baker, cook and butler. Philo emphasizes that according to the Scriptural traditions all of them were eunuchs, meaning they are unable to beget wisdom, such as temperance (σωφροσύνη), modesty (αἰδώς), self-restraint (ἐγκράτεια), and justice (δικαιοσύνη).[56] The chief cook,

---

[52] So also in *Ebr.* 210, 214; *Ios.* 154.

[53] Πολυποσία (deep-drinking or heavy drinking) is a form of γαστριμαργία (*Somn.* 2:181) of which the butler is an example.

[54] Γάστρων means pot-belly; see LSJ s.v. This is probably an example of a physiognomic reference. A protruding belly is a sign of enslavement to the belly and gluttony.

[55] That Philo takes Jacob's cry in Gen. 42:36 to refer to the mind is hardly surprising in the light of our presentation of Jacob and Esau above.

[56] For Pharaoh's servants as eunuchs, see *Ebr.* 212–13, 220; *Leg.* 3:236.

Potiphar, was not thrown in prison, since preparing food is not necessarily pleasure although it might be an incitement to it. The two other offices represent more properly the power of the belly, and their holders were therefore detained. The baker was even put to death, for he had sinned in a most important and necessary aspect of life, that of bread and food.[57]

In his writing on drunkenness, Philo sees drinking as a powerful example of a person without self-control (*Ebr.* 221–2). Drunkenness also leads to gluttony (γαστριμαργία), which Philo describes as greed, leaving a void in the desires although every vacant place in the body is filled up (206). To elaborate on this, Philo turns to the Joseph narrative. The king of Egypt had three servants, cook, baker and butler. They are servants of the bodily desires and represent the pleasures of the belly (*Ebr.* 208–24). What this means, Philo brings out in a lengthy and vivid description of different dishes and wines prepared by the three offices of the belly (*Ebr.* 217–19). The focus is on the butler, which is in accordance with the topic of interest in this particular treatise. The butler is said to have the belly as king (220); he is ruled by the stomach.

7.6   Jewish customs as means of controlling the stomach

In our presentation of Philo's exposition of Exodus and Passover, we noticed that religious and cultic rituals were interpreted in an ethical way.[58] This is due both to his allegorical approach and to the circumstances in which the Jewish community of Alexandria lived. The Passover was a festival concerned with purification of the soul. A related view on the food laws has been observed as well. Now this ethical interpretation needs to be substantiated and extended into areas of relevance for understanding the role of the belly in Philo's writings.

In Philo's presentation of Jewish religious festivals, he almost consistently interprets them in an ethical way, as furthering a lifestyle of simplicity and self-mastery in contrast to the lifestyle promoted by the pagan festive life. Sometimes he seems to be more keen on telling of this contrast than to inform about the Jewish customs in question. This observation, which will be fully substantiated below, is a clear indication that Philo is speaking in a historical context, and with a particular purpose in mind: the best way to master the desires, openly displayed in pagan festivals, is to embrace the Jewish faith and its practices.

---

[57] The distinction which Philo makes between the chief cook and the baker is based primarily on the fact that the death of the baker is mentioned in the OT.

[58] Cf. our presentation of the *Letter of Aristeas* and 4 Maccabees above.

Within the context of Jewish festivals, Philo says that every day is a festival. Following the decrees of nature makes life a continuous feast (*Spec.* 2:42–5). For the wicked, however, there is not even a short time of real feast, even though he simulates a smile. This is because his tongue, stomach, and genitals are being misused (*Spec.* 2:49–50). As for the stomach, he seeks to fill it beyond measure. For Philo the belly-*topos* belongs to the question of 'how to feast?' The question of mastering the desires was to Philo not merely a topic of moral philosophy. His concern about this is clearly related to challenges Jews faced in the pagan city of Alexandria (see chap. 5).

The pagan feasts are devoted to the pleasures of the belly, while the Jewish festivals aim at a virtuous life. Festal occasions of relaxation often become opportunities for the belly. In briefly commenting upon the feast of *Sheaf*, Philo adds a remark which gives a general reference to all the rites of purification; their purpose is to: '. . . restrict the pleasures of the belly and the parts below it' (*Spec.* 2:163). Excessive eating and drinking also arouse the desires located below the stomach. In fact, the feasts often serve as points of departure for the pleasures of food and sex, the belly and genitals. Philo's concern about the belly has a historical context. He claims that Moses laid down rules for the Jewish festivals in order to deal with similar challenges; these rules were not aiming at enhancing desires, but at providing remission for sins (*Spec.* 1:192–3).

In *Cher.* 84–97, Philo says that since God alone is the summit, end and limit of happiness,[59] all feasts and festivals should have approaching Him as their goal. Philo measures the festivals of the nations by this yardstick. God is both cause of and goal for the festive life, as demonstrated e.g. by the weekly Sabbaths and other feasts. The Gentiles, however, celebrate feasts whose ends are most properly described in a list of vices (*Cher.* 91–3, cf. 94–7):

> At such times music, philosophy, all culture, those truly divine images set in the divinely given soul, are mute. Only the arts which pander and minister pleasure to the belly (τὰς ἡδονὰς γαστρί) and the organs below it are vocal and loud-voiced.
>
> (*Cher.* 93)

Gratifying the belly and the sexual organs are thus descriptions of the pagan festive life. As long as this takes place in private homes, Philo

---

[59] Philo here picks up the ancient philosophical question of the supreme good, which we have seen to be a seedbed of the belly-*topos*.

considers the sin to be less. But, he says, the wickedness deriving from the belly and the organs below it are even being practised in temples and holy places. He claims that temples and cultic life have become places of lust, namely for food and sex (*Cher.* 94). The text might, therefore, have some relevance to the question of sex in temples during pagan festivals.[60] It is not evident to what extent historical information about the temples and sex can be gleaned from a text like this. It is, however, still evidence of how Jews might have conceived of the festivals in the pagan temples.

Worth considering in this context is also Philo's eulogistic account of the Therapeutae and their communal life (*Contempl.* 34–90).[61] He presents their life from the perspective of ἐγκράτεια. They practised strict rules in matters of food laws and drinking. Philo particularly draws attention to their common meals, which he sees as a clear contrast to the pagan *symposia*. The major part of his presentation is, in fact, given to this counter-example. In *Contempl.* 48–56, he provides a rather vivid picture of a common banquet for the elite. His text is rich in details of the furniture, servants, clothing, dishes etc. These are meals for ostentation; things are on display. This goes in particular for the rich menu described in 53–4. The contrast to the way the Therapeutae lived is sumptuous meals, as described e.g. in *Contempl.* 55:

> Then while some tables are taken out emptied by the gluttony of the company who gorge themselves like cormorants, so voraciously that they nibble even at the bones, other tables have their dishes mangled and torn and left half eaten. And when they are quite exhausted, their bellies crammed up to the gullets (τὰς μὲν γαστέρας ἄχρι φαρύγγων πεπληρωμένοι), but their lust still ravenous, impotent for eating (they turn to drinking).[62]

In contrast to a banquet like this, the meals of the Therapeutae appear as devoted to simplicity and virtue. Philo saw the contrast between the Therapeutae and the pagans in terms of eating habits as an example of how Jews and Gentiles were separated in their way of living. The great divider was the belly.

---

[60] See chap. 10, pp. 210–11.

[61] The Therapeutae were devout Jews who led a contemplative life in Egypt.

[62] The text is in disarray. I have rendered the text according to the LCL edition, which is the shorter. For the longer version, see F. Daumas, P. Miquel, *De Vita Contemplativa*, pp. 118–19.

7.7   Fasts and Sabbaths

De Specialibus Legibus Book 2[63] covers laws that can be assigned to
the commandment of the first table, among which are the various feasts
which are seen as special laws related to the Sabbath commandment. To
these special laws belongs also the Jewish fast. Philo's presentation of
the fast (*Spec.* 2:193–203) immediately turns to address an objection by
outsiders:

> What sort of a feast is this in which there are no gatherings to eat
> and drink, no company of entertainers or entertained, no copious
> supply of strong drink nor tables sumptuously furnished, nor a
> generous display of all the accompaniments of a public banquet,
> nor again the merriment and revelry with frolic and drollery, nor
> dancing to the sound of flute and harp and timbrels and cymbals,
> and the other instruments of the debilitated and invertebrate kind
> of music which through the channel of ears awaken the unruly
> lusts?   (*Spec.* 2:193)

Philo here gives a detailed description of the agenda of the *symposia* in
terms of food, entertainment, and sex. The religious practice of fasting
has a special concern with the virtue of ἐγκράτεια; its concern is with
the control of tongue, belly and the organs below it (195). Self-restraint
is to be practised on a daily basis. As an aid to doing so, one particular
day, the fast, has been dedicated to refraining from food and drink. Philo
considers this a valuable training-ground, for 'to one who has learnt to
disregard food and drink which are absolutely necessary, are there any
among the superfluities of life which he can fail to despise, things which
exist to promote not so much preservation and permanence of life as
pleasure with all its powers and mischief?' (195). Abstaining from food
and drink is thus a training-ground for enduring hardship in general. As
we have seen many times, this conviction forms the basic assumption of
a political perspective on the power of the belly.

Philo goes on to say that God deliberately fixed the day of the fast
immediately after the harvest. From this one ought to draw a lesson. Eating
from what has recently been harvested might bring gluttony (ἀπληστία)
(197, cf. *Spec.* 4:99). In this way God teaches 'not to put trust in what
stands ready prepared for us as though it were the source of health and
life' (*Spec.* 2:197). Fasting is, therefore, a creed of trusting in God.

---

[63] For a helpful survey of Philo's writings, see Peder Borgen, *Philo, John and Paul*,
pp. 17–60.

The creed of those who practise Jewish fasting is the following: 'We have gladly received and are storing the boons of nature, yet we do not ascribe our preservation to any corruptible things, but to God the Parent and Father and Saviour of the world and all that is therein, who has the power and the right to nourish and sustain us by means of these or without these' (*Spec.* 2:198). While in the wilderness the Israelites had to rely on their trust in God's providence. God nourished and sustained them (199).

Although this text does not say so, it can clearly be inferred from many other Philo texts that the plea for food on the part of many Israelites meant distrust of God.[64] In brief, how one relates to the desires of the belly is to Philo an expression of trust or distrust in God.

In *Mos.* 2:17–24 Philo claims that the laws of Moses are respected and admired among virtue-loving nations. He is probably overstating his case (17–20). None the less, he substantiates his claim by mentioning the Sabbath and the fast. As for fast, he urges a contrast between it and the festivals of the Greeks, which are focused on sumptuous tables. These feasts enhance 'the insatiable pleasures of the belly (αἱ ἀκόρεστοι γαστρὸς ἡδοναί), and further cause the outburst of the lusts that lie below it (τὰς ὑπογαστρίους ἐπιθυμίας)' (*Mos.* 2:23). Jewish practices, and not least the fast, are – in contrast to the agenda of banquets – a means of keeping the belly under control. Belly-devotion is to Philo, then, not a mere philosophical *topos* rooted in the discussion of mastering the desires. It can be traced to the lavish parties for which the Graeco-Roman world has become so famous.

Even the celebration of Sabbath is a symbol of ἐγκράτεια (*Spec.* 1:174–6). Two sets of six loaves are put on the table. This simplicity serves to keep the body healthy, as opposed to temptations of lavish tables with many dishes, i.e. it is a protection against the lusts of the belly (γασ-τρὸς...ἐπιθυμίαις) which are here an obvious reference to banquets. Philo is, however, well aware that this simple and restrained table will cause ridicule from participants in *symposia*. They seek tables with many dishes, of which they become slaves (δοῦλοι) (176).

The way Jewish religious life is aimed at subduing the pleasures deriving from the belly is clearly to be seen in Philo's comments on the rights of priests to accept income from sacrifices offered in the temple (*Spec.* 1:147–50). Philo interprets the bodily parts of the sacrifices given to the priests allegorically, i.e. in this context with reference to morality. Particular attention is therefore given to the κοιλία, 'for it is the fate of the belly to be the manger of that irrational animal, desire (ἐπιθυμία)'

---

[64] See chap. 10, pp. 203–10.

(149), manifested in οἰνοφλυγία and ὀψοφαγία, and which is contrasted with ἐγκράτεια. Cultic practices prescribed by the Scriptures had, according to Philo, a hidden reference to moral philosophy questions such as mastering the belly. The regulations laid down concerning the priests were intended to keep under control the pleasures of the stomach (τῶν γαστρὸς ἡδονῶν), gluttony and greed, which all easily inflame ἐπιθυμία. The same concern is raised in a question of why the altar in the temple is three cubits high (*QE* 2:100 on Exod. 27:1c). The answer is: the priests can then perform their service and still 'hide their bellies and the things within their bellies, because of that many-headed beast, desire'. The ethical framework in which Philo sees Jewish pious life is indeed prominent in these examples.[65] Since to many Pauline scholars the question of observing the food laws is the proper context of Paul's belly-texts, we now turn to this aspect of Jewish piety.

7.8   Food laws

Philo discusses food laws within the context of the commandment against covetousness (*Spec.* 4:97–131), which is in itself telling. When desire gets hold of the belly, it produces gluttons who are enslaved to wine and food (*Spec.* 4:91). Among the many desires, Moses took the desires of the stomach as the one most in need of restrictions. By limiting the power of the belly, he restrained the senior and leader of the desires. This marked a first step towards self-control (ἐγκράτεια) and humanity (φιλανθρωπία) (*Spec.* 4:96–7, cf. 99,101). The logic is that when the other desires see the stomach having gained self-control, they will take it as an example as well. Similarly, in *Virt.* 134–6, where dietary laws are seen as limiting the enjoyment of the stomach. The food laws were given to put an end to the pleasures of the belly (διὰ γαστρὸς ἀπόλαυσιν). In this way, ruling the belly paves the way for a virtuous life in general.

Philo makes the observation that the food forbidden by Moses is from animals with the finest and fattest meat. He interprets this in accordance

---

[65] Philo's discussion of circumcision is well-known. His writings show that there were some Jews (probably in Alexandria) who emphasized the ethical aspect of circumcision and abandoned the physical rite (*Migr.* 86–93). Philo agrees that circumcision means the excision of pleasures, but he disagrees when they neglect the external observance of the rite (cf. *Spec.* 1:1–11; *QG* 3:46–7 on Gen. 17:10–11). For a discussion on the relevant Philo texts see Peder Borgen, *Philo, John and Paul*, pp. 65–71, 234–7; Alan Mendelson, *Philo's Jewish Identity*, pp. 54–8 and most recently John M. G. Barclay, 'Paul and Philo on Circumcision', pp. 538–43.

with his ethical approach to explaining the food laws.[66] The finest food is forbidden since it represents a special temptation for the pleasures and the taste.[67] The leader of desires, the stomach, might easily be titillated, which is a trap for the taste-buds. Once gluttony is aroused, one is hooked and ἐγκράτεια is out of reach (*Spec.* 4:100–2). The food which is declared clean is from animals with a cloven hoof and which chew the cud (*Spec.* 4:105–98; *Agr.* 142, 145, cf. *Ep. Arist.* 153–5). This is to Philo a symbol of the method of acquiring knowledge; i.e. by memorizing this lesson again and again.

In *Spec.* 1:220–3, Philo comments on the law that nothing of the food from the altar is allowed to be left over till the third day; it must be consumed by fire (Lev. 19:5–6). Even tasting forbidden food is sacrilege. Transgression of this commandment reveals the transgressor as a glutton (γαστρίμαργος). The logic is the same as we have observed in Philo elsewhere, as well as in the *Letter of Aristeas*, 3 and 4 Maccabees. Partaking of unclean food is equivalent to being devoted to the belly. The reason for this is a double one; as mentioned above, violating the food laws is identical with mistrust of God. Furthermore, a Jew neglecting God's clear commandments on food shows himself to be driven by force other than obedience to God. It was natural to Philo, as well as to other Jewish-Hellenistic writers of this time, to connect this power with the stomach.[68]

With texts like this in mind, we must consider whether it is likely that worshipping the belly in Paul's letters really refers to continuous observance of the dietary laws of Moses. If this is what Paul really meant, he is indeed turning the argument and logic upside down. What Philo (as well as other Hellenistic Jews) claimed to be means of controlling the unruly belly, Paul, then, describes as being itself a belly-worship. Given Paul's polemic against the synagogue, this is not entirely impossible, but it is very improbable. A final decision on this matter will have to wait till the exegesis of the relevant Pauline passages.

---

[66] On Philo's ethical interpretation of the food laws, see also S. Stein, 'The Dietary Laws in Rabbinic and Patristic Literature'. Alan Mendelson, *Philo's Jewish Identity*, pp. 67–71 discusses dietary laws in Philo's writings, but leaves out the ethical and philosophical aspect of Philo's presentation.

[67] Philo mentions the pig in particular. This is probably due to the frequent comments made by Greek and Romans on Jewish food customs; see e.g. *Ag. Ap.* 2:137–42; *Legat.* 361; Juvenal, *Sat.* 14:96–106; Molly Whittaker, *Jews & Christians*, pp. 73–80. For meat and wine as increasing the sexual drive, see references in Teresa M. Shaw, *Burden of the Flesh*, pp. 98–100.

[68] Harry Austryn Wolfson, *Philo* Vol. 1, pp. 73–86 speaks of three kinds of apostasy in Alexandrinian Judaism: (1) the weak of the flesh (cf. our presentation), (2) the socially ambitious, (3) the intellectually alienated. Overlapping motives are certain.

7.9   Conversion – the safest way to rule the belly

Since the law of Moses was the superior way to wisdom and virtue,[69] it is quite natural that joining the Jewish fellowship and faith with its customs meant embracing virtue. Furthermore, since Philo frequently sees the sumptuous table with its revelling as typical of pagan life, it is natural that Jewish faith and customs appear as the best way to bring the belly under control. In other words, this paragraph comes as a consequence of what we have already seen to be present in Philo's writings.

By far the longest section on conversion (περὶ μετανοίας) is found in *Virt.* 175–86.[70] Emphasis is on the life and lifestyle the converts leave behind, and the new ones to which they turn. Abraham, leaving his land, home, family and customs, is the outstanding example of a convert. They pass from ignorance to knowledge, from darkness to light etc.

In *Virt.*181–2 the conversion is seen from the perspective of the desires, and those of the belly in particular. A proselyte turns from 'the delights of the belly (τὰς γαστρὸς ἀπολαύσεις)[71] and the organs below it – delights which end in the gravest injuries both to body and soul' (182). Here Philo, in an abbreviated form, is speaking about the pagan feasts. He considers these lavish parties a sign of paganism, and leaving this life therefore becomes typical of a convert. Belly-devotion is a sign of paganism, which means that how one relates to the desires deriving from the belly is indicative of one's identity.

The converts become superior to both the power of money and to pleasures.[72] Philo's ethical perspective on conversion means a practical view on it as well. He underscores this by quoting from Deut. 30:11–14,[73] saying that the life of a convert is not far away; it is close at hand, residing in mouth, heart, and hands; i.e. in words, thoughts, and actions (*Virt.* 183). The life of conversion is not an abstract; it is at hand in how one deals with the requests of the belly. The life of the convert takes its beginning in changing attitudes towards food and the desires of the stomach. In short, the belly is the great divide between Judaism and paganism.

---

[69] As argued e.g. by the allegory of Hagar and Sarah in *Congr.* 22–80; see Alan Mendelson, *Philo's Jewish Identity*, pp. 128–38.

[70] See Karl Olav Sandnes, *A New Family*, pp. 41–6 with references to the literature.

[71] In *Virt.* 134–6, this Greek phrase was used of the lifestyle against which the food laws were given (see above).

[72] Cf. *Praem.* 15–21 which speaks of a turning from covetousness (πλεονεξία) and injustice (ἀδικία) to σωφροσύνη, δικαιοσύνη and the other virtues (15).

[73] For a recent investigation of Philo's use of this text, see Per Jarle Bekken, *The Word is near You*.

7.10   Summary

We have seen that Philo's distrust of pleasure is a major theme in his writings. His huge number of dicta about the belly, the pleasures of the belly and those of the organ below it belong within this perspective. The stomach was a reservoir of all pleasures; the beginning of a vicious life. The *topos* of belly-devotion is firmly rooted in the very centre of his philosophical theology, and it was brought to life by Philo's allegorical exegesis; a vivid and sometimes imaginative appropriation of a Greek *topos* into a biblical framework. We found it embedded in his theology of Exodus and religious festivals and customs. Key figures in the Old Testament, such as the Serpent, Esau and Jacob, Joseph and the servants of Pharaoh were used to explain what belly-worship is about. The outstanding image was the Serpent crawling on its belly. Philo is quite consistent in speaking of the belly as a codeword for gluttony and sexual misbehaviour. This is almost a stereotype in his writings. Philo is convinced that excess in eating and drinking leads to forbidden forms of sexual intercourse.[74]

Philo's dicta on the belly are, however, not easily reconciled into a harmonious whole.[75] On the one hand, his warnings against being enslaved to the belly and its pleasures mean opposition to immoderate pleasure. The desires of the stomach have to be controlled, mastered or tamed. Philo denounces all kinds of luxury, and especially of eating, drinking and sex – with which he is so familiar from the pagan *symposia*. His texts on belly-enslavement express his strong disapproval of contemporary life and morals in Alexandria. Philo's texts on desires and belly-devotion in particular are not mere philosophical sayings. They were highly topical in addressing the way of life surrounding the Jews in that city. A good example of Philo's interpretation of ἐγκράτεια as moderation is *Somn.* 2:48–67. Jacob thought that the beast which had devoured Joseph (Gen. 37:33) was luxury; i.e. in terms of food, drink, clothing, houses, beds, unguents, drinking cups and crowns. The belly is mentioned first since it is so easily tempted (51). And who is not conversant and familiar with these things (63)? Food and drink are meant to be nourishment, not to be taken with a view to indulgence.

On the other hand, the belly takes on a more sinister aspect as well. It is not only a matter of mastering or taking control of the belly, but abandoning it altogether. This is especially so when the belly is connected with the Serpent and Philo's exegesis of Gen. 3:14. The Serpent cannot

---

[74] See e.g. *Abr.* 135; *Spec.* 3:43; *QG* 2:12 (Gen. 7:2–3).
[75] Alan Mendelson, *Philo's Jewish identity*, p. 96 speaks of 'two incompatible views'.

be tamed; it is venomous, dangerous, and needs to be avoided altogether. Belly-worship becomes a marker for identity, whether heavenly or earthly. At the end of the day, belly-devotion is a sign of paganism. Finally, worshipping the stomach is idolatry, and needs to be abandoned. The proper way to deal with the pleasures of the belly is to embrace the Jewish faith and customs.

A possible way to reconcile the two views might be Philo's concept of gradual progress through training. The fact that Philo does not expect everyone to have achieved the same level in mastering the belly allows for some flexibility in his writings on this point. In other words, the two may be reconciled by keeping in mind Philo's philosophical anthropology.[76]

What does the Philo material bring to our Pauline study on the belly? For now this can be answered by recalling our findings on Paul presented so far. Although Paul and Philo differ in anthropology, they do have a common interest in the belly, and they even share some basic convictions. They both represent Jewish appropriations of a Graeco-Roman moral philosophy *topos*. They both saw a life governed by the belly as a mark of paganism, and thus for both men, how one rules the stomach is a question of true divine identity. Philo considered enslavement to the stomach in the light of a twofold teaching about licentiousness and virtue, which was most truly attained in the Law of Moses and in embracing Jewish faith and customs. In a way which is structurally similar, Paul claimed that belly-worship belonged to the past of the believers. They also shared the view that the life and lifestyle of the believers can be described from the perspective of worship. Both of them saw true piety expressed in bodily ways, e.g. in fighting the passions. To Philo, every day was a religious festival and Jewish homes were seen as temples, since believers had to fight passions on an everyday basis. To Paul, living was an act of bodily sacrifice (Rom. 12:1–2), and hence the body was a temple. Both Philo and Paul took this as their point of departure when it came to how to control the belly. In Philo's view, however, Paul is likely to be seen as paving the way for belly-worship since he has done away with the means (Sabbath, food laws, circumcision) of fighting the pleasures deriving from the stomach. The two thus hold opposite views on how to fight these pleasures. Taken together, there is sufficient evidence to say that the Graeco-Roman *topos* of the belly was appropriated by Jewish Hellenism, and therefore that Paul's line is to be seen as a variant of this.

[76] So also David Winston, 'Philo's Ethical Theory', p. 414.

PART 4

Belly-worship and body according to Paul

As we have pointed out, the Pauline texts on 'serving the belly' or those 'whose god is their belly' are very brief, polemical and in coded language. It is, therefore, difficult to ascertain their precise meaning and to glean information from them. Having now completed a presentation which provides access to an assumed cultural competence on the part of Paul's readers, it is time to approach the Pauline material directly. In reading these texts we cannot avoid the background material presented in the previous chapters. In order to read Paul's texts in a culturally adequate way, we need to be guided by this material. The brevity of his sayings demands this. It now remains to see in what way this ancient material is appropriated in Paul's writings, and to which elements he gives emphasis. This means that there must be an interchange between background material, without which the Pauline texts remain enigmatic and obscure, and the Pauline texts themselves.

We have found that belly-worship or enslavement to the stomach is firmly rooted in moral philosophical discussions on mastering the desires. According to Hellenistic-Jewish material, the Law was seen as a superior means of controlling the passions. The Law is given to fight the desires.[1] Paul also has a concern for self-mastery.[2] His letters demonstrate his familiarity with the language and motives associated with mastery of passions. Terms like ἐγκράτεια, πάθος, ἐπιθυμία, ἀνδρίζεσθαι, ἡδονή, αὐτάρκεια and their cognates occur frequently and with great emphasis in the Pauline epistles.[3]

But Paul has developed a way of thinking which in many ways runs contrary to the Hellenistic-Jewish material. What then is his basic teaching

[1] See e.g. Stanley K. Stowers, *Romans*, pp. 58–66, 278; Karl Olav Sandnes, *Tidens Fylde*, pp. 196–8.

[2] Stanley K. Stowers, *Romans* has made this the key to his reading of Romans, which he summarizes on pp. 36–40. Paul is addressing Gentiles 'who have a great concern for moral self-mastery' (p. 36), and who face pious Jews imposing upon them the idea that the Law helps in achieving that.

[3] This general conclusion includes undisputed Pauline letters as well as those whose authenticity has been questioned.

on this issue? Addressing this question means provisionally putting the
belly-dicta in the context of Paul's theological and moral reasoning. As
we saw in chap. 1.4, the Law has no power over the passions. The power
of desires surpasses that of the Law. Human beings have been taken
captive, and the Law is unable to resolve this. Paul cannot, therefore, do
as Philo did and turn to the Law as a means of fighting belly-worship.
In Rom. 3:10–18 the devouring stomach, mouth or throat become telling
metaphors for humanity's despair. According to Paul, the passions and
the devouring belly can only be dealt with by being crucified with Christ.
This is clearly stated in Rom. 6. Enslavement to sin and desires has
been replaced by obedience to righteousness in the believers who have
been baptized and crucified with Christ.[4] The same logic is found in
Gal.5:24 as well: 'And those who belong to Christ have crucified the
flesh with its παθήμασιν and ἐπιθυμίαις'. This means that Paul's view
on desires belongs within the major pattern of transition ('before versus
now') in his theology. Conversion and baptism involve a transition which
has implications for how believers conduct their lives. In accordance with
this conviction, Paul speaks of the 'lustful passion' (ἐν πάθει ἐπιθυμίας)
of sex as typical of Gentiles who do not know God (1 Thess. 4:5). This
means that to Paul how one deals with the desires becomes a mark of
identity – as it was to some contemporary moral philosophers as well.

Despite this perspective on the desires as belonging to the past, we
cannot miss the fact that mastery of passions was important to Paul's
agenda for the daily life of believers. Self-mastery was *still* of relevance
for the Christians.[5] This is seen in Gal. 5:16–17, where spiritual life
involves opposition to the desires of the flesh. The believer is involved in a
continuous struggle between flesh and Spirit, which is all about mastering
the desires. Paul is aware that his message about freedom could be taken
by some as an opportunity for the sinful flesh to abound: 'For you were
called to freedom, brothers and sisters; only do not use your freedom as
an opportunity for self-indulgence (εἰς ἀφορμὴν τῇ σαρκί), but through
love become slaves (δουλεύετε) to one another' (Gal. 5:13).

'Εγκράτεια is therefore seen as a fruit of the Spirit (Gal. 5:23). Furthermore, Paul's injunctions to stand firm are often formulated in the language

---

[4] Stanley K. Stowers, *Romans*, pp. 255–8 rightly points out that Christ is not presented
as an example of self-mastery to be copied by the believers; it is a matter of pure grace
thanks to participation in his death and resurrection.

[5] Paul's catalogues of vices illustrate the contrast between the pagan and the Jewish and
Christian way of life. On the other hand, these catalogues have an admonitory effect as
well; the believers have to keep away from the pagan way of living which they have now
renounced.

of fighting the desires: 'Keep alert, stand firm (στήκετε) in your faith, be courageous (ἀνδρίζεσθε), be strong (κραταιοῦσθε)' (1 Cor. 16:13, cf. Gal. 5:1). In Phil. 1:27 this is expressed in the language of athletic competition, which was a common discourse 'for thinking about the development of self-mastery in the life of the sage'.[6] Paul included himself among athletes exercising self-mastery in all things (1 Cor. 9:24–7). This involved fighting both passions and temptations.[7] In Acts 24:25 Paul's preaching is summarized so as to include ἐγκράτεια as well. The way Acts here summarizes Paul's preaching is substantiated in letters either written by him or assigned to him. In Col. 3:5 the believers are urged to put an end to fornication (πορνεία), impurity, passion (πάθος), evil desire (ἐπιθυμίαν κακήν), and greed (πλεονεξία), which are all idolatry. These vices are said to represent τὰ ἐπὶ τῆς γῆς, i.e. they are earthly, and believers who are subject to them have lost sight of their heavenly identity, which Paul urges them to seek (Col. 3:1: τὰ ἄνω ζητεῖτε).[8] Here traces of the pattern 'desires (of the belly) are earthly' may be discerned.

I do not claim that the Pauline references to desires and self-mastery are all hidden belly-dicta. They do, however, provide a framework which exhibits common ground with moral philosophy traditions of his time, and within which Phil. 3:19 and Rom. 16:18 function. 'Serving the belly' means a relapse into a lifestyle of the past, and is incompatible with being crucified with Christ. The belly represents a lifestyle against which believers must stand firm. Finally, this means that the two belly-dicta explicit in the Pauline letters do not appear at random. They can hardly be polemical pejorative language alone, but belong to a major concern in Paul's apostolic ministry. His polemic against belly-worship forms an introduction to matters of importance in Paul's instruction to his converts. Paul was convinced that the body mattered in defining the identity of believers. The Christians were holy since they had, both individually and as a fellowship, become the dwelling of the Holy Spirit. Furthermore, they shared in Christ's glorious body. Both these convictions demanded serious attention to how to conduct oneself in bodily matters. We now turn to the Pauline dicta on belly-devotion with a view to how they work within his concern about the body of believers.

---

[6] Stanley K. Stowers, *Romans*, p. 9; cf. pp. 48–9.

[7] For Paul and his apostolic hardships seen in a Graeco-Roman perspective, see John T. Fitzgerald, *Cracks in an Earthen Vessel*.

[8] Cf. 1 Tim. 6:9; 2 Tim. 2:2; 3:6; Tit. 2:12.

8

THE LIFESTYLE OF CITIZENS OF THE
HEAVENLY *POLITEUMA* – PHIL. 3:17–21

8.0   Introduction

The aim of this chapter is to see how the belly-*topos* works in this passage, and, of course, within Philippians as well. Although our purpose is to elucidate what it means to 'have the belly as god', this dictum cannot be separated from 'being enemies of Christ's cross', 'glorifying in their shame', and 'having the mind set on earthly things'. We will approach the *topos* from a *pars pro toto* perspective;[1] i.e. as encapsulating the other complaints as well. Actually, the pattern which we have uncovered as related to the belly-*topos* in ancient sources strongly recommends us to keep these things together (see chap. 3.10).

In other words, we will see how Phil. 3:17–21, with special emphasis on vv. 18–19, is embedded in the structure, argument and purpose of the entire letter. Any reading of this passage is linked to major controversial issues in recent scholarship, namely the hiatus in 3:1 and the questions of unity, opponents and genre. These questions have generated an enormous literature over the past few years.[2] The exegesis of vv. 18–19 has, in my view, suffered from an exaggerated interest in identifying 'opponents' lurking behind Paul's words. The text has not, therefore, been sufficiently

---

[1] This needs to be pointed out against attempts to take vv. 18–19 as including a number of separate allegations; see e.g. Robert Jewett, 'Conflicting Movements', p. 382, who emphasizes 'libertinistic behaviour in the areas of food and sex', but who also claims that the so-called heretics 'denied the saving efficacy of the cross'; cf. his *Paul's Anthropological Terms*, p. 22. In my opinion vv. 18–19 do not provide an index of a series of allegations.

[2] For a strong case for the integrity of this letter; see e.g. Duane F. Watson, 'Rhetorical Analysis'; David E. Garland, 'Composition and Unity'; L. Gregory Bloomquist, *Suffering*, pp. 97–118. On the question of integrity, see the recent book of Jeffrey T. Reed, *Discourse Analysis of Philippians*, pp. 124–52. Reed also provides a survey of recent literature. In contrast to rhetorical reconstructions where there is a noticeable emphasis upon finding a controlling theme (or *propositio*) of the letter, Reed's presentation of Philippians as a personal hortatory letter allows for (almost demands) multiple purposes in the letter. Philippians can hardly be fitted into one particular type of ancient letter. It resembles both family- or friendship-letters and administrative (or official) letters; see pp. 154–78, 417–18.

seen in its rhetorical function within Paul's argument.[3] From this also
follows that belly-worship in Phil. 3 has not been related to what Paul
says about the body elsewhere in this letter.

We will trace the meaning of Phil. 3:18–19 by relating it to Paul's
overall argument in his epistle and consider it in the light of our previous
findings on the belly-*topos*. The argument of the letter is the means by
which Paul appropriates the *topos*. Then we will turn to the question of
identifying opponents, if any. This is, however, a question of minor significance in this study.[4] Finally, we will see if dicta on the body elsewhere in
the letter can shed some light on the belly-worship mentioned in Phil. 3:19.

In a footnote, Davorin Peterlin says that it was suggested to him that
the terminology in vv. 18–19 pointed to 'an Epicurean-influenced outlook
which may be called the "Good Life syndrome" adverse to the Christian
outlook'.[5] It must be clear by now that I consider that such a hypothesis
has much to commend it. This suggestion is, however, not entirely new. It
is the special merit of Norman Wentworth de Witt to have pointed out that
Paul's dictum on 'those whose god is the belly' sounds anti-Epicurean.
De Witt argues that in Philippians Paul reveals his ambivalent attitude
to Epicureanism.[6] According to de Witt, Paul is 'addressing himself to

---

[3] On the question of opponents, see e.g. Peter O'Brien, *Philippians*, pp. 26–35; Gordon
D. Fee, *Philippians*, pp. 7–10. More on this later in this chapter.

[4] I agree with Davorin Peterlin, *Philippians*, p. 78 that precise identification of opponents
in chap. 3 is indeed difficult, and that it is not crucial for the understanding of what Paul is
actually saying.

[5] Ibid. p. 81 n. 14. Peterlin does not undertake to follow this suggestion himself, but
notes in passing that it is worthwhile looking into it, and that it would require research into
relevant classical authors.

[6] Norman Wentworth de Witt, *St Paul and Epicurus*, pp. 21–37; he includes a presentation
of other Pauline texts as well. His book has received very little attention, which is not
surprising. The book is strong on suggestions but short on argument and evidence. A
cautious reading of the book is therefore recommended. Paul is himself considered to be a
former Epicurean, which is indeed difficult to imagine, taking into account his indebtedness
to Jewish Pharisaism. But also de Witt has some precedents in suggesting an Epicurean
background for Phil. 3:19. This is so particularly in some older commentaries; see Heinrich
August Wilhelm Meyer, *Philippians*, pp. 182–3; J. B. Lightfoot, *Philippians*, p. 155. This
insight has been neglected in more recent exegesis of the Pauline passages in question in
this study. Paul Ewald, *Philipper*, pp. 205–7 dismisses the ancient material on the belly, by
saying that in the majority of the texts, γαστήρ is used rather than κοιλία; so also Wolfgang
Schenk, *Philipperbriefe*, p. 287. Although this observation is formally correct, the material
is by no means consistent enough to justify its dismissal. The majority of texts speak of
γαστήρ, but far from all of the evidence. Ewald turns to the food laws instead. Among
the recent contributions to Philippians, L. Gregory Bloomquist, *Suffering*, pp. 132–3, 186
mentions Epicureanism as a relevant background against which to understand opponents
in this epistle. Bloomquist supports this claim by mentioning that Epicureans denied the
providence of God, as well as their entirely this-worldly character. He does not connect this
with the appearance of belly in Paul's rhetoric.

communities in which Epicureans are numerous'.[7] Hence, Philippians represents a modification of Epicurean maxims (e.g. Phil. 4:4, 8, 11) as well as a negative stand towards other maxims, exemplified by Phil. 3:2 ('beware of the dogs') and vv. 18–19.

In his presentation, de Witt makes no distinction between the Epicureans themselves and the language Paul has inherited. Paul's use of anti-Epicurean language by no means suggests the existence of Epicureans among his converts; even less that Paul was himself a former Epicurean. We should rather think in terms of a distinction made by Seneca, who speaks of common people embracing this philosophy to justify their indulgent lifestyle. The anti-Epicurean language of Paul is due to his rhetoric and what he saw as hedonistic tendencies, not to the presence of numerous Epicurean philosophers in Philippi.[8]

8.1   'Stand firm' and the rhetoric of examples

As we have mentioned already, Paul addresses a number of concerns in this letter. The introductory thanksgiving (Phil. 1:3–11) however, sets the tone of the letter,[9] introducing major concerns to be followed up later. Although the thanksgiving hints at different concerns, special attention should be given to v. 6: 'I am confident (πεποιθώς) of this, that the one who began a good work among you will bring it to completion (ἐπιτελέσει) by the day of Jesus Christ'. Paul is assured that God will continue His work within them until the day of fulfilment. Since this assurance looks into the future of the addressees, we should see in it a concern as well;[10] they are encouraged to remain firm in their commitment. This hidden plea is confirmed in vv. 9–11, where the assurance has become Paul's prayer (cf. Phil. 2:12–13,16; 3:15). Even Paul himself cannot rely only on the good beginning, but on God's continuous work in him (Phil. 3:12–14). When he urges his readers to imitate him (Phil. 3:17) this means that the assurance of 1:6 is being implied,[11] and thus that the letter has a hortatory aim.

---

[7] Norman Wentworth de Witt, *St Paul and Epicurus*, p. 27.

[8] De Witt's blurring of the distinction between historical references and Paul's rhetoric is apparent when he interprets Paul's saying about 'setting the mind on earthly things' as based on the Epicurean atomic hypothesis (pp. 25–6). Paul's language is derived from Epicurus and the ancient critique of him, but within Philippians this language works within an entirely different framework.

[9] See e.g. Duane F. Watson, 'Rhetorical Analysis', pp. 63–4 with further references.

[10] Cf. Stanley N. Olson, 'Self-Confidence' who argues that expressions of confidence might also serve as a key to the concerns of an author.

[11] In Phil. 1:25 and 2:24 πέποιθα and πεποιθώς express assurance in terms of a firm hope; cf. Rom. 15:14; 2 Cor. 2:3; Phlm. 21; 2 Thess. 3:4.

Is it a particular situation which urges Paul to call for firmness? Recent scholarship[12] puts emphasis on internal as well as external challenges which can be deduced from the epistle itself. Internally, the Christians in Philippi are encouraged to foster unity and concord among themselves.[13] A concern for a tendency to disunity is well- attested in e.g. Phil. 1:27; 2:1–5, 14–16; 4:2. But the letter also gives the impression that the believers are facing suffering and difficulties from the outside,[14] which is suggested by 1:28–30 and the emphasis on suffering (e.g. 1:7; 2:8, 30; 3:10, 18; 4:14). There is no need to urge alternatives here; Paul may be encouraging unity in order that they may stand firm in a situation calling for them to be prepared to suffer as, according to this letter, Paul himself does. To summarize so far, Paul's letter has a deliberative aim, calling for steadfastness in facing challenges both from within and outside.

A common method of proof employed in deliberative rhetoric was *exempla*, hortatory devices. Paul states directly in Phil. 3:17, as well as in 2:5, that he is working with a rhetoric of imitation. 'The others' in 3:17 probably refers to Clement and other co-workers (4:3), and Timothy and Epaphroditus in particular (2:19–30).[15] Since Phil. 3:18–19 is itself structured on a contrasting example[16] (Paul versus those whose god is their belly) within Paul's rhetoric, a brief survey of this ancient mode of instruction paves the way for an adequate understanding of how the belly-*topos* works in Paul's text.

Firstly, we need to acknowledge the role played by examples or models in the ancient world. This is widely attested in rhetorical handbooks, speeches, letters as well as in educational literature.[17] Aristotle claims that 'examples are most suitable for deliberative speakers, for it is by examination of the past that we divine and judge the future' (*Rhet.* 1368a40,

---

[12] For a helpful survey of recent trends in Philippian research see E. A. C. Pretorius, 'New Trends'.

[13] This is argued in particular by Davorin Peterlin, *Philippians*. See also David E. Garland, 'Composition and Unity', pp. 172–3; Ben Witherington III, *Friendship*, pp. 13, 18–20.

[14] This is emphasized by L. Gregory Bloomquist, *Suffering*, pp. 157–8 and Timothy C. Geoffrion, *Rhetorical Purpose*, pp. 70–82. This viewpoint finds support in historical references to conflict with the Roman authorities in the colony; Lukas Bormann, *Philippi*, pp. 217–24; Mikael Tellbe, *Paul Between Synagogue and State*, pp. 210–78.

[15] The role of examples in Philippians is commonly recognized by the scholars; see e.g. Gordon D. Fee, *Philippians*, pp. 11–12; Duane F. Watson, 'Rhetorical Analysis', pp. 67–8; David E. Garland, 'Composition and Unity', pp. 162–3; David A. de Silva, 'Philippians 3:2–21', pp. 33–4, 51–2; Timothy C. Geoffrion, *Rhetorical Purpose*, pp. 125–58.

[16] Peter O'Brien, *Philippians*, pp. 442–67 rightly treats Phil. 3:17–21 under the heading 'true and false models'.

[17] See the study of Benjamin Fiore, *Personal Example*; Øyvind Andersen, *Retorikkens Hage*, pp. 222–34.

cf. 1418a5). In *Rhetorica ad Alexandrum* 8 (1429a21–8), it says that
'examples (παραδείγματα) are actions that have occurred previously
and are similar to, or opposite of, those which we are now discussing'.

The rhetorical handbooks represent nothing but a synthesis of how
mores were transmitted in the ancient Graeco-Roman world. The examples pointed out the way to be followed or avoided.[18] Arguing from
examples, whether for imitation or avoidance, is to present persons who
have embodied the virtues or vices in question.[19] Hence, the rhetoric of
examples focuses on practice rather than theory. Accordingly, the examples should be considered demonstrations rather than proofs. They
demonstrate by bringing to mind the life of people who embody virtue
and vice, as well as their consequences.[20]

This observation has some bearings on our interpretation of Phil. 3:
18–19. As belonging to a rhetoric of examples they are probably addressing practical matters rather than theological positions (see below). The
negative examples or the antithetical models spell out the options. As
for Phil. 3:17–21 Paul wants his readers to stand firm and consider their
options, a transformed and glorious body in the future or a present life
according to the belly, which brings perdition.

In this ancient instruction, examples are culled from various sources,
but some preferences on what models to call upon is attested: 'We must
take examples that are akin to the case and those that are nearest in
time or place to our hearers, and if such are not available, such others as are most important and best known' (*Rhet. Alex.* 32 (1439a1–5).
Speakers are recommended to draw their examples from a stock familiar to the audience; the models are to be τὰ οἰκεῖα, τὰ ἐγγύτατα, τὰ
μέγιστα καὶ γνωριμώτατα.[21] A preference for examples of relevance
to the audience might have some significance for the question of about

[18] Plutarch refers to the instructional value of negative models: 'Now consider the contrary disposition and learn of it by examples' (*Mor.* 821d). It is worth mentioning that the
philosopher has the imperative σκόπει here, rendered 'consider' by the LCL translator. Paul
uses the same verb in Phil. 2:4 and 3:17. This Greek verb is connected to παράδειγμα or
μιμεῖσθαι and cognates in *Mor.* 428e–f and 639e–f. It means to consider, reflect, ponder or
learn from what the examples teach.
[19] Philo expresses the importance of personal examples, saying that they are prior to
the laws; they are embodiments of the virtues which later were laid down in the laws;
Abr. 3–6.276. *Decal.* 1 introduces the presentation of the commandments as a written
continuation of the virtuous life of the ancestors.
[20] We have worked this out with reference to proverbial gourmandizers, such as Sardanapalus in particular; see chap. 3 and 4.1, section on 'The proverbial figure of Sardanapalus',
in particular.
[21] Cf. *Rhet. Her.* 4:1–7; Quintilian, *Inst.* 5:11.1–2, cf. 11:6.38; 12:4.1–2 for various kinds
of examples to be used. The rhetorical handbooks encapsulate the ancient custom of learning
from the example of the father, teacher or ancestors; in other words, what the rhetoricians

whom Paul is talking in vv. 18–19 (see chap. 8.3 below). We have thus made two preliminary observations with a bearing upon the exegesis of Phil. 3:17–21. The rhetoric of examples prepares the ground for matters of conduct rather than theological controversies. Furthermore, if Paul was using examples according to principles prescribed in the rhetorical handbooks, this might indicate that in one way or another vv. 18–19 speak of a lifestyle with which his Philippian converts were somewhat familar.

8.2 'Whose god is the belly'

The following provides an exegesis of the relevant passage with emphasis on what it means to worship the belly in this text and how the belly-*topos* is appropriated in this epistle. The passage will be re-read with a constant view to the material presented hitherto in this study. The difficult question of how vv. 18–19 relate to the beginning of Phil. 3, including the question of the so-called opponents, will be raised towards the end of the presentation. The exegesis might provide some insight of relevance for these long-standing problems in New Testament scholarship.

In Phil. 3:17 Paul urges his converts to take himself as an example, and to reflect upon the examples of those who live accordingly. What is the virtue or lifestyle Paul wants his addressees to imitate? From the simple mentioning of himself in v. 17a, not very much can be deduced. Some information might be gleaned, however, from looking at the immediate context as well as at other examples worthy of imitation in the letter.

The preceding and immediate context speaks of a Paul who is entirely committed to the final victory which is above (ἄνω), striving hard to achieve that goal. Paul is, like the athletes, involved in a contest for victory; this helps him to keep his mind on higher things (Phil. 3:12–16). Paul's thanksgiving and concern in 1:6 here come into focus; 'standing firm until the end'. Perseverance and preparedness are necessary, lest he might not complete the race. He speaks in terms of the traditional *agôn* motif.[22] Christian commitment is expressed as an athletic or military *agôn* in Phil. 1:29–30 as well. His converts have seen (cf. 4:9) in Paul a man prepared for the suffering which accompanied an *agôn* (cf. 3:10). Being prepared to suffer like Christ should be inferred from 3:10–11, as forming

considered to be what is close to the time and place of the audience; see Benjamin Fiore, *Personal Example*, pp. 34–5. In addition to the texts given by him, the following are also illustrative: Xenophon, *Mem.* 1:6.3; Euripides, *Helen* 940–3; Isocrates, *Against the Sophists* 16–18.

[22] Victor C. Pfitzner, *Paul and the Agon Motif*, pp. 139–53.

the nexus between the athletic imagery (vv. 12–16), and vv. 18–19 as its contrast. Actually, Paul comes very close to his saying in 1 Cor. 11:1: 'Be imitators of me as I am of Christ.'[23]

Next to Paul himself, the lifestyle worthy of imitation applies in particular to Timothy and Epaphroditus (Phil. 2:19–30). Timothy is praised for being a servant (δουλεύειν) (v. 22) who is concerned about the Philippians (vv.19–21). He does not seek his own ends, but that of Jesus Christ (v. 21). Epaphroditus committed himself to Paul's ministry and the Philippians in a way which almost caused his death (μέχρι θανάτου) (Phil. 2:30, cf. v. 8). The conceptual and verbal links to the passage about Christ's example in Phil. 2:1–11 suggest that Paul has a rhetorical purpose beyond giving details about his two co-workers. Their example recalls the master-model in this letter, namely that of Christ. Like Christ, the two, as well as Paul himself, have acted out of a concern for the Philippians.[24] Their ministry has embodied the self-renouncing attitude which is characteristic of Jesus in the Christ-hymn (2:5–11). This means that Paul claims that his addressees have seen and been taught a lifestyle (4:9) which has Christ's preparedness to serve, self-renunciation, and willingness to suffer as its generative example. To win the crown of the contest, the Philippians have to live according to this example of Christ which has been embodied by Paul and his co-workers.

The example of Paul, seen in the light of the preceding text (3:12–16), can be summarized in three points. These three points have their counterparts in vv. 18–19, which make up the contrasting examples:

(1)   Their mind is turned ἄνω (cf. 3:21)
(2)   Like athletes they are committed to reaching their goal
(3)   Like Christ they are not self-centred, but prepared for suffering and death
(4)   Their τέλος (3:12)[25] is the crown or resurrection with Christ (3:11, cf. 3:21)

---

[23] The relationship between the two texts has been worked out by Samuel Vollenweider, *Freiheit*, pp. 209–20. Marvin R. Vincent, *Philippians*, p. 116, says that since there is no mention of Christ in the context, a christological model cannot be implied here. This is a misreading of the rhetoric of this epistle. Furthermore, when v. 18 mentions 'enemies of Christ's cross' it can hardly be said that Christ is out of context here.

[24] That Christ is the generative model, which Paul's co-workers as well as himself embody, and the Philippians are urged to imitate, is emphasized also by Stephen E. Fowl, *Story of Christ*, pp. 92–5; Troels Engberg-Pedersen, 'Stoicism in Philippians', pp. 274–7; Peter O'Brien, *Philippians*, pp. 342–4; L. Gregory Bloomquist, *Suffering*, pp. 113–14.

[25] The cognate verb τελειοῦν is used here.

In contrast to this, vv. 18–19 on the belly-worshippers have a strikingly similar structure:

(1)   Their mind is set on τὰ ἐπίγεια
(2)   They are devoted to the belly
(3)   They are 'enemies of Christ's cross'
(4)   Their τέλος is perdition (ἀπώλεια)

Within Paul's rhetoric, then, the image of the athletes' *agôn* represents a counter-image to belly-devotion. Belly-worship means to be fully devoted to the moment, neglecting to be prepared for what comes, and for suffering in particular. This is in accordance with previous findings of this study: athletes and belly-devotion form rhetorical contrasts.[26] While Paul's concern for his converts is that they remain firm till the day of consummation, the enemies of Christ's cross have their end as well; i.e. perdition and death. The two examples are juxtaposed in terms of their end; a victorious crown or perdition. Furthermore, we have seen that an emphasis on conduct is implied. This is strongly suggested also by Phil. 1:30 and 4:9, speaking of the conduct of Paul, which they have heard and seen. Paul has embodied a Christian life among them. He presents himself and the others as examples (Phil. 3:17) now due to the fact (γάρ) that his readers are faced with others who conduct a life according to the belly.

The emphasis on conduct is confirmed in the term περιπατεῖν as well, appearing both in v. 17 and v. 18, thus introducing both example and its counterpart in the same way. This Greek term sees life under the perspective of a journey with special emphasis on how to conduct one's life. This meaning is frequently attested in Paul;[27] the verb requires a

---

[26] See e.g. Epictetus; 4 Maccabees and the role of athletes within the ancient discussion on mastering the desires. The belly-devotees seek an easy life and are concerned about their own ends. In contrast, athletes prepare themselves for the *agôn*, hardship and victory. Furthermore, we have seen that those who were hooked on the belly were not trustworthy citizens. Vice versa, athletic training aims at forming good citizens who are able to bear the hardship necessary to maintaining and defending a city. This political aspect of athletic training is prominent in Lucian of Samosata's treatise on *Anacharsis, or Athletics*. In this piece of literature, Solon explains to the Scythian Anacharsis the advantages of physical training: it prepares for hardship. The activitites of the gymnasium appear ridiculous to Anacharsis, and Solon then turns to the real intent of sport: building and safe-guarding the *polis* (*Anacharsis* 14–15, 20, 24, 30). This is the common *agôn*, in which all good citizens participate, and where the utility of training is obvious. This goes for wartime as well as peace. Shameful things do not appeal to athletes (30). Belly-worship and athletic training thus form contrasting political images. Phil. 3 displays the same antithetical structure, and thus belongs within this perspective (more on this below).

[27] In the undisputed letters, see Rom. 6:4; 8:4; 13:13; 14:15; 1 Cor. 3:3; 7:17; 2 Cor.

moral application, as does the theme of imitation.[28] This is an important step towards understanding v. 19 adequately.[29]

Vv. 18–19 speak about those who are not imitating Paul, but who represent a conduct against which Paul warns his readers. Their presence seems to be strongly felt among the Philippians. Whether πολλοί is a rhetorical exaggeration (as 2:21 probably is), makes little difference; Paul is not talking about a distant or remote challenge, but something visible to his addressees. Their presence has caused Paul's weeping, which suggests that they are insiders, although Paul in his rhetoric speaks of them as conducting a life devoted to another god, namely their own stomach. The phrase 'enemies of the cross' implies some claim to represent Christ, a claim which Paul denies. It is not likely that Paul would speak in such terms about pagan opposition. His painful conclusion is that some who claim to be believers are in fact leading a life which makes them enemies of Christ.[30] What this means precisely, is then laid out in four statements:[31]

(a)   ὧν τέλος ἀπώλεια
(b)   ὧν ὁ θεὸς ἡ κοιλία

4:2; 5:7; 10:2–3; Gal. 5:16; 1 Thess. 2:12; 4:1, 12. The verb has a special emphasis on the moral sense. This is clearly seen in e.g. Gal. 5:16 where 'walking' is Paul's perspective on a list of virtues and vices. Jeffrey T. Reed, *Discourse Analysis of Philippians*, p. 310 mentions περιπατεῖν as part of a semantic chain of various terms for behaviour and conduct in Philippians.

[28] So also Davorin Peterlin, *Philippians*, pp. 80–1; Markus Bockmuehl, *Philippians*, pp. 230–1.

[29] This is emphasized *vis-à-vis* those who interpret vv. 18–19 as speaking about theological controversies; see e.g. Gerald F. Hawthorne, *Philippians*, pp. 166–7: 'They are Jews who have set themselves against Paul's gospel which says that salvation is exclusively through the crucified and resurrected Christ. They are enemy "Number One" of the cross, *the* enemy, to whom the message of the cross is a *skandalon*...their rejection of the crucified Christ' (quotation p. 167). Similarly in Ulrich B. Müller, *Philipper*, pp. 175–6 who reads the passage in the light of the theological controversy in Galatians. In itself the observation on Paul's imitation-rhetoric and his use of περιπατεῖν makes a doctrinal approach like this unlikely. The recent commentary of Nikolaus Walter, Eckhart Reinmuth, Peter Lampe, *Briefe an die Philipper, Thessalonicher, und an Philemon*, p. 85 interprets the belly as a reference to religious satisfaction (*'der satten religiösen Zufriedenheit'*). On p. 90, however, Phil. 3:19 is mentioned alongside 1 Cor. 6:12 on luxurious eating and drinking. The commentary is confusing on this point.

[30] The fact that Paul in Phil. 1:6 gives thanks for the Christians in Philippi does not necessarily imply that there are no Philippian believers among those Paul has in mind in v. 18; cf. our exegesis of 1:6 above; *pace* Peter O'Brien, Philippians, p. 452.

[31] Gerald F. Hawthorne, *Philippians*, p. 162 takes κοιλία and δόξα to be connected by καί; as the two subjects of θεός, rendering the sentence in the following way: 'Their observance of food laws and their glorying in circumcision has become their god.' B + c then make one nominal sentence with two grammatical subjects related to ὁ θεός. Hawthorne's interpretation emphasizes the intimate relationship between belly and shame in Paul's text, but it seems artificial.

(c)   καὶ ἡ δόξα ἐν τῇ αἰσχύνῃ αὐτῶν
(d)   οἱ τὰ ἐπίγεια φρονοῦντες

The statements should not be taken as separate phrases; they are closely related. This is seen by the use of the relative pronouns. Since the second relative clause, according to our investigation, must have been familiar to its readers, it also holds a key position in the unravelling of what vv. 18–19 are all about. Furthermore, (b) and (c) are held together by a single relative pronoun. This means that belly and 'glorying in their shame' must be seen together. Given our exegesis so far, however, being 'enemies of Christ's cross' must refer to an attitude which does not take his life as an example to follow; i.e. they are turning their back on the self-denying life of Jesus which manifested itself in obedience and willingness to suffer and die.

As for 'having the belly as god', three interpretative options are worth considering:

(1)   Continuous observance of food laws by Christians (Judaistic interpretation)

(2)   Appetite; i.e. a libertinistic practice regarding food and sex (the most simple and straightforward interpretation)

(3)   A figurative meaning where κοιλία, usually associated with gluttony, is extended into a metaphor of selfishness.

This means that (3) and (2) are related, the third being a figurative extension of the second.[32] In chaps. 3 and 4 we have provided sufficient evidence that the phrase 'whose god is the belly' has antecedents in Graeco-Roman literature, in precisely the sense embraced by alternatives (2) and (3) mentioned here.

As mentioned earlier in this study, option (1) is widely supported by present-day expositors, claiming also the support of Early Christian exegesis (see chap. 11 in this study). Vv. 18–19 are interpreted as continuing the question of Jewish customs which was introduced in Phil. 3:1–2. Paul speaks polemically against believers who continue to observe Jewish food laws as well as circumcision, saying that 'their glory is in their shame'. There is, however, no external support for this view; nowhere in Graeco-Roman or Jewish sources[33] is the belly a reference to people who are devoted to Jewish customs in general and dietary laws in particular. On

_____

[32] Cf. Jeffrey T. Reed, *Discourse Analysis*, p. 303 who sees κοιλία as embedded in a semantic chain with words speaking of desire, want and wish in this letter.

[33] Chap. 11 will argue that even in Patristic texts such an interpretation is rarely to be found.

the contrary, we noticed in the Jewish appropriation of this *topos* that it was frequently applied to those who *neglected* these customs in obedience to the commands of the pagan king; i.e. its reference was just the opposite of what advocates of alternative (1) claim. By submitting to the demands of the king (e.g. 4 Maccabees) the Jews escaped suffering and death. For obvious reasons, Jews would never consider observance of dietary laws as belly-worship. The non-Pauline material does not lend any support to the claim that belly-service is a question of food laws.

It might, of course, be assumed that Paul has coined or rephrased this language himself. This seems to be a hidden assumption when Phil. 3:17–21 is seen primarily in the light of the Galatian crisis.[34] This assumption can only be maintained by a general reference to Paul's doing away with Jewish customs as identity-markers, in Galatians and Romans in particular. Furthermore, it is unlikely that Paul himself did this, since 'having the belly as god' and related phrases were most likely familiar to his audience. Paul would hardly coin a new meaning for a maxim with whose meaning his readers must have been familiar. At least, this should not be assumed if the text is to be fully understandable within a perspective which Paul has in common with his contemporary sources. The only conclusion to be drawn is, then, that this reading of vv. 18–19 must be abandoned. It remains, however, to explain how these verses relate to the beginning of chap. 3; to this we will return later.

The second option is that Paul is speaking about appetite, in terms of both food and sex.[35] Besides massive support from the external material, this reading is also supported by the immediate context. V. 21 addresses the question of the physical body. The body of the believers will be transformed to conform to Christ's body of glory. Accordingly, the stomach should be taken in its most straightforward sense, i.e. the physical. Paul addresses the question of an improper or indecent way of dealing with the stomach. The rhetoric of Paul's argument – athletes versus belly-worshippers; setting the mind on things above versus having the mind fixed on earthly things; resurrection versus perdition – brings to mind logical structures or a cluster of ideas with which the belly-*topos*, with its constant view of gluttony, has made us familiar to throughout this study.

[34] See e.g. Ulrich B. Müller, *Philipper*, p. 176; cf. Gerald F. Hawthorne, *Philippians*, pp. 166–7.

[35] See e.g. J. B. Lightfoot, *Philippians*, p. 155; Marvin R. Vincent, *Philippians*, p. 117; Robert Jewett, 'Conflicting Movements', pp. 379–82. Even Johannes Behm, 'κοιλία', p. 788, whose influence has contributed strongly to alternative (1) admits that the Graeco-Roman material clearly suggests a reference to 'unbridled sensuality, whether gluttony or sexual licentiousness'. It is the context of Phil. 3 which causes him to dispense with this evidence.

The term θεός (as well as δόξα) evokes the question of loyalty, worship and idolatry. Paul's vocabulary here might be illustrated by Philo's presentation of the so-called disobedient or rebellious son (Deut.21: 18–21). The most serious accusation brought against him is his drunkenness (*Ebr.*15, cf. 27). In *Ebr.* 9–10 the model for this son is – not surprisingly – Esau. Philo interprets Gen. 27:30 about Jacob entering the house and Esau leaving it in a symbolic way; prudence (φρόνησις) and folly cannot dwell together. The folly of the disobedient son is presented in *Ebr.* 20–2: slackness, indolence, luxury, effeminacy, and complete irregularity of life, which means that they are competing in the arena[36] of wine-bibbing and gluttony. The Greek words used are πολυοινία, ἐπ' ἀπληστίᾳ γαστρός, τὸ ἁβροδίαιτον, which all make the connection between the disobedient son and his devotion to his belly evident.[37]

In *Ebr.* 95–6, Philo returns to the disobedient son who adds sin to sin. His whole life is spent in endless drunkenness. Philo says that he makes a god of his body (θεοπλαστεῖν τὸ σῶμα), which he immediately connects with the Golden Calf episode (Exod 32). Philo is here close to Paul's phrase of having the belly as god. Philo speaks of making a god of the body, i.e. a sin which for him is witnessed in the sin of the people in the desert, and which manifests itself in heavy drinking and eating. His description fuses together body-worship, honouring the Egyptian Apis and the Golden Calf episode.[38] The verb θεοπλαστεῖν is used by Philo to describe various idols, such as the gods of Egypt, including the Golden Calf, and Emperor-worship. *Spec.* 1:21–2 represents the traditional OT criticism of idols, claiming that they were made by artists from silver, gold and other dead materials. Θεοπλαστεῖν describes the activity of the sculptors involved. Philo's perspective on this activity is obviously the first two commandments (*Spec.* 1:22, *Her.* 169). Philo thus sees the disobedient son who makes a god of his body; i.e. in gratifying the belly, as an idolater. Motives and language normally associated with how the Old Testament traditionally describes idolatry are here applied to bodily misbehaviour. Paul thinks similarly in Phil. 3:18–19. The stomach has usurped the position which rightly belongs to God alone; hence gluttony is idolatry.

[36] Philo uses this metaphor ironically since the son of prudence in *Ebr.* 21 is said to be persistent in training (ἄσκησις).

[37] As demonstrated by Peder Borgen, 'Yes', pp. 28–9 the son is blamed for attending pagan club-associations (see *Ebr.* 20–1,27,95).

[38] A natural inference is that the Jews who sinned in the wilderness worshipped their belly. Philo does not elaborate on this here, but he does so elsewhere; see our exegesis of 1 Cor. 10:7 (chap. 10 of this study).

Finally, taking v. 19 as speaking of sensuality (alternative (2)) is supported by the appearance of αὐτάρκης in Phil. 4:11. Paul says that he has learnt to be content with whatever he has. This is a phrase rooted in the ancient *topos* of mastering the desires.[39] Paul is not an ascetic; he is familiar with both shortage and abundance; food is mentioned in particular (4:12). Paul interprets this term of moral philosophy in the light of his faith. It is a question of relying on God's providence in all circumstances. The term means 'self-sufficiency', which corresponds well with its role within the topic of mastering the desires. This term alerts us to the philosophical discussion which has followed us throughout our study; i.e. the perspective from vv. 18–19 is here extended into chap. 4 as well. To Paul, however, it is not a matter of self-sufficiency, but of trust in Divine providence.[40] Paul masters his desires since he is confident that God cares and provides. Paul has learnt to go hungry as well as full, thanks to his trust in God. Paul declares that he is familiar even with being satisfied (χορτάζεσθαι). This is a part of Paul's imitation of Christ; note ταπεινοῦσθαι (Phil. 4:12), which recalls a key term in the Christ-poem (Phil. 2:8, cf. v. 3). Phil. 4:6 spells out what it meant to Paul to be αὐτάρκης; i.e. to put trust in God, expressed in prayers and thanksgiving. But in the light of Paul's claim that he knows well to be full, it is unlikely that in vv. 18–19 he is primarily targeting rich tables. He would certainly include the lifestyle which was often associated with loaded tables. But it seems justifiable to consider that Paul is extending the physiological function of the belly in a figurative way; gluttony includes reference to a selfish life (alternative (3) above). This is suggested also by Paul's focus on Christ's self-abnegating example in this epistle, which certainly has implications beyond the question of eating.

We have pointed out that belly-worship, when seen in the light of the entire letter, appears as a sharp contrast to the example given by Christ in his self-sacrificial life (more on this below), to the extent that having the belly as god is seen as a practical denial of Christ's saving cross. Belly-worship in Phil. 3 works, however, within another contrast as well. In this short letter the frequency of θεός is quite high.[41] With the exception of 3:19, where θεός is the belly, this noun elsewhere refers to God, who

[39] See e.g. Plutarch, *Mor.* 13f; 413f and *Mor.* 523d–f, where the context is about love of money, as well as food; see Edward O'Neill, 'De Cupiditate Divitiarum', pp. 311–13, 321, 331; John Ferguson, *Moral Values*, pp. 133–58; Peter O'Brien, *Philippians*, pp. 519–22; Gordon D. Fee, *Philippians*, pp. 431–2.

[40] For Paul's redefinition of the Stoic self-sufficiency, see G. W. Peterman, *Paul's Gift*, pp. 134–42.

[41] Phil. 1:2, 3, 11, 28; 2:6, 9, 11, 13, 15, 27; 3:3, 9, 14, 15, 19; 4:6, 7, 18, 19, 20.

is depicted as Paul's witness, as having initiated the story of Christ, and as providing for the daily needs of the believers. In the light of Paul's emphasis on the Divine as forming both the beginning and end of his message (cf. Phil. 1:6), it appears as nothing less than idolatry to be devoted to the belly instead.

Self-loving citizens

The rhetoric of v. 19 speaks of persons who do not organize their life according to faith in God's providence, but who rather stuff themselves, as though God is not in view at all. A figurative extension of this lifestyle is widely attested in the sources. We have found it in Xenophon, Musonius Rufus, Plutarch, and even 3 Maccabees, reaching back to the words of Euripides' Cyclops, who saw no distinction between worshipping the belly and worshipping oneself. In his criticism of Epicureanism, Cicero puts this very precisely; they are always seeking their own ends (*omnia sua causa facere*) at the expense of the fellowship or city.[42] Epictetus claimed that the soldiers who embraced death at Thermopylae would hardly have done so if they had praised the doctrine of Epicurus (*Diss.* 2:20, 26). In other words, we have seen that servants of the belly were not citizens on whom the fellowship could rely. They did not share the burdens and costs of being a citizen; in this way they resembled the flatterers, who were also commonly seen as gratifying their belly or serving their own ends.

A helpful example of this figurative extension of the belly-*topos* is found in Demosthenes' speech *On the Crown* (*De Corona*).[43] This speech concerns political and military controversies between Demosthenes' party and that of his opponents. The orator of the party opposed to him was Aeschines. For our purpose, the accusation which Demosthenes puts forward against Aeschines and his company is significant: 'They measure their happiness by their belly and their baser parts (τῇ γαστρὶ μετροῦντες καὶ τοῖς αἰσχίστοις τὴν εὐδαιμονίαν)' (*De Corona* 296). Aeschines is blamed for seeking to please his stomach as well as his sexual appetite.

What Demosthenes was aiming at by describing his opponent in the rhetoric of the belly must be judged on the basis of the immediate context (285–305). Nothing indicates that Aeschines is blamed for being a sensualist or a glutton. The context is obviously political; Aeschines

---

[42] See chap. 4.1 of this study.

[43] This work is about στέφανος, which Paul mentions as well in Phil. 4:1 (cf. βραβεῖον in 3:14). The crown in Demosthenes' writing refers to the honour conferred upon leaders who contributed in a special way to the well-being of the city (*De Corona* 83–6).

and his friends have not acted like good citizens; on the contrary they have flung away national prosperity for private and selfish gain (τῆς ἰδίας ἕνεκ' αἰσχροκερδίας τὰ κοινῇ συμφέροντα προῖεντο)' (*De Corona* 295). Demosthenes' rhetoric of the belly implies that Aeschines is an enemy (ἐχθρός) of Athens (286–7, 292). He is not well disposed towards the common good of the citizens (291–2, 298); in short, he is not a citizen of πρόνοια, εὔνοια and προθυμία towards the city (286, 291, 301, 321). Aeschines and his party act like parasites (κόλακες). They are contrasted with the citizens who willingly suffered and died for their country (πά-τρας ἕνεκα), in the words of the epitaph for those did not spare their lives (289). As in traditional criticism of Epicureanism, Aeschines is said to measure his happiness by his belly. This is clearly a figurative ex-tension of the greedy stomach: Aeschines was a man seeking his own ends, who escaped the unpleasant demands of the fellowship.[44] Demos-thenes uses a rhetorical device against Aeschines which concurs with the words of Socrates according to Xenophon, about the need for pub-lic servants to be stronger than the belly (Xenophon's *Mem.* 1:5.1–6). Aeschines was weaker than the demands of his belly. In his *Praise of the Native Land* (*Patriae Laudatio*), Lucian of Samosata applies a sim-ilar rhetoric of the belly when addressing the question of proper or true citizenship (γνησίοι πολῖται). True citizens are contrasted with aliens who have been brought up elsewhere. The newcomers expect to be pro-vided for rather than to serve their country, 'measuring happiness by their appetites (μέτρον εὐδαιμονίας τὰς τῆς γαστρὸς ἡδονὰς τιθέμενοι)' (*Patr. Laud.* 10).

The way a figurative extension of the belly-*topos* is connected with the question of being a proper citizen, is, of course, significant for the exegesis of Phil. 3:19. The following v. 20 is explicitly a saying about citizenship (πολίτευμα). The heavenly *politeuma* is introduced as a contrast to the belly-worshippers; notice the emphatic position of ἡμῶν γάρ.[45] This links up with 'we' in v. 17, Paul and his followers. The citizens of the heavenly *politeuma* have their minds turned upwards to the coming Christ. Paul here follows a figurative extension of the Epicurean lifestyle which is widely attested; gluttony paves the way for self-love. Worshippers of the belly are not citizens to be trusted in hard times.

---

[44] According to Plutarch, Cato once said to a fat ambassador of Rome: 'Where can such a body be of service to the state (τῇ πόλει . . . χρήσιμον), when everything between its gullet and its groin is devoted to the belly (ὑπὸ τῆς γαστρὸς κατέχεται)?' (*Marcus Cato* 9:5). This is clearly a political application of the belly-*topos*.

[45] 'We' here works in the same way as in Phil. 3:3; it is seen in contrast with another group of people, although the contrasts are not the same in 3:3 and 3:20.

There is a hidden agenda in Paul's use of the belly-*topos* here. Believers who seek only their own ends, and who are unprepared to undertake a self-abnegating life according to the pattern set by Christ, have neglected their heavenly citizenship. What is true for the earthly city, goes for the heavenly *politeuma* as well; belly-devotion is a neglect of the duties of a citizen and is incompatible with true citizenship. This interpretation of vv. 18–19 corresponds to belly-devotion as indicative of an earthly identity. Furthermore, it corresponds to the picture of Christ in the hymn (Phil. 2:8: ἐταπείνωσεν ἑαυτόν) and the admonitions which Paul deduces from this example: 2:4: μὴ τὰ ἑαυτῶν ἕκαστος σκοποῦντες and 2:21: οἱ πάντες γὰρ ἑαυτῶν ζητοῦσιν, οὐ τὰ 'Ιησοῦ Χριστοῦ. This is very close to Cicero's *omnia sua causa facere*. Since they are not prepared for a self-sacrificial life, even to death, they are not members of the heavenly *politeuma*. In Phil. 3:17–21, Paul summons the Christians to see themselves as members of the heavenly *politeuma*, to stay firm and to live accordingly (cf. Phil. 1:27 πολιτεύεσθε).[46] Paul warns his readers against self-love, which makes them unfit both for a life according to the cross of Christ,[47] and for the final restoration of the body (v. 21).

The Greek term which most naturally covers this interpretation of belly-worship is φιλαυτία and cognates. I have argued, on the basis of both external and internal observations, that in Phil. 3:18–19 belly-worship is best explained in terms of a figurative extension of gluttony; i.e. self-love. This interpretation nicely fits the widely acknowledged emphasis on friendship (φιλία) in this epistle. Christ's self-renouncing example is depicted by Paul in terms commonly associated with friendship.[48] The egoistic orientation Paul is warning against is friendship towards oneself only.

In Aristotle's ethical treatises, φιλαυτία appears in discussions on friendship. Being a friend of oneself alone is a reproach, and it refers to people who 'assign to themselves the larger share of money, honours,

[46] See Pheme Perkins, 'Heavenly *Politeuma*', pp. 98–104. An interpretation along the lines presented above goes well with a historical reconstruction regarding the question of Roman citizenship as a major issue in Philippi; see Peter Pilhofer, *Philippi*, pp. 122–34.
[47] On this point my interpretation concurs with that of Ernst Lohmeyer, *Philipper* (e.g. pp. 152–6). Brian J. Dodd, *Personal Example*, pp. 176–80 argues that Paul warns against proponents of a triumphalism avoiding all suffering and cost. This remains, however, only loosely connected to his exegesis of Phil. 3:19, since Dodd sees this verse as a continuation of the confidence in the flesh expressed in Phil. 3:3–4. Dodd's exegesis of Phil. 3:19 is, in my view, ambiguous and confusing.
[48] See L. Michael White, 'A Paradigm of Friendship'; Stanley K. Stowers, 'Friends and Enemies' and John T. Fitzgerald, 'Philippians'. Part 2 in John T. Fitzgerald, *Friendship* (pp. 83–160) is all about the significance of friendship terms in Philippians. For the Christ hymn as patterned on the ideal of friendship, see Karl Olav Sandnes, *A New Family*, pp. 86–91, 152.

and bodily pleasures (ἡδοναῖς ταῖς σωματικαῖς)' (*Nic. Eth.* 1168b). Some lines further down Aristotle sums up the nature of such people; they are men who indulge in their desires (χαρίζονται ταῖς ἐπιθυμίαις). Hence this term appears as the opposite of self-restraint (ἐγκράτεια) (*Nic. Eth.* 1169a), a theme adjacent to belly-worship.⁴⁹ In *Magna Moralia* 1212a, φίλαυτος is described in a way which reminds us very much of Cicero's description of the Epicurean belly-devotees, being in fact a Greek rendering of *omnia sua causa facere*: ὁ αὑτοῦ ἕνεκεν πάντα πράττων.⁵⁰ He is a person devoted to his own profit (συμφέρον) and his pleasures (καθ' ἡδονήν) (*Magna Moralia* 1212b).⁵¹

Turning to Philo, we find that φιλαυτία and cognates are used about people who cannot master their desires, and those of the stomach in particular. Within a context about gluttony and the uncontrolled belly (*Spec.* 4:113–27), Philo comments upon the sin which was committed at the so-called 'Monuments of Lust' (μνήματα τῆς ἐπιθυμίας) (Num. 11)⁵². From this episode Philo draws the lesson that self-love should be discarded: 'Let no one indulge his own lust (μηδεὶς τῇ ἐπιθυμίᾳ τῇ αὑτοῦ χαριζέσθω)' (*Spec.* 4:131). There are other examples as well where φιλαυτία is related to the uncontrolled belly. In *Sacr.* 19–33, Philo speaks of φιλήδονος, and characterizes him by a number of nouns, among which self-love is one. The lover of oneself, who is also a pleasure-lover, seeks only the pleasures of the belly and the body (33). For Philo the attitude of self-love is illustrated by biblical figures, such as Cain and Onan. Cain has a creed (δόγμα) which was about himself; the creed of a φίλαυτος (*Det.* 32).⁵³ In *Det.* 34 Philo lists the kind of persons who represent this 'creed' of the self-lover. The list emphasizes those who revel in eating and drinking, who do not know hard work and pain (πόνος), but only the things which make life sweet. The creed of Cain is spelled out later, in *Det.* 156–7. Part of his doctrine, according to Philo, manifests itself in 'indulging in full in all the pleasures arising from the digestive and other organs (ταῖς γαστρὸς καὶ μετὰ γαστέρα ἡδοναῖς εἰς κόρον χρήσασθαι)'; i.e. a catchword for this attitude is the belly.

⁴⁹ True friendship might be manifested as true self-sacrifice in laying down one's life for the interest of friends and country (*Nic. Eth.* 1169a). Aristotle's presentation of this attitude as the opposite of self-love concurs with our exegesis of Phil. 3:18–19.
⁵⁰ Cf. Epictetus, *Diss.* 1:19.11 who says about φίλαυτος that 'everything he does is for himself (αὑτοῦ ἕνεκα πάντα ποιεῖ)'. This is, according to the philosopher, the nature of an animal.
⁵¹ In his treatise *On Living Unknown*, Plutarch discusses and refutes Epicurus' philosophy of a withdrawal from the public. The selfish attitude of these food-lovers can, according to Plutarch, be seen by those who blow their noses over the food to discourage other banqueters from eating, thus hoping to enjoy the food all alone (*Mor.* 1128b).
⁵² See my exegesis of 1 Cor. 10, where this text is mentioned as well (chap. 10).
⁵³ On Cain see also *Sacr.* 3.52; *Post.* 121.

Onan is depicted as a person of self-love. He was seeking pleasure and profit for himself alone. His act is seen as a neglect of his responsibility towards parents, wife, bringing up children, and house-management, even of public duties such as the interest of the city, laws and the past generations. The refusal of all these duties is due to gluttony and licentiousness (γάστριν καὶ ἀκόλαστον), in which all evil things have their origin (*Post.* 180–1). *Deus* 16–18 runs very much in tandem with this text, but is even more clear on Onan being a person of φιλαυτία, who is devoted to the belly and the organs below it (15).[54] Our exegesis of the belly-lover in Phil. 3:18–19 has brought us to consider the self-lover as a close analogy.[55] A belly-devotee is a stock figure of a person who is seeking his own ends. The affinity between the two has now been demonstrated. A true citizen of heaven follows the example of Christ; the example of self-loving belly-devotees leads to final destruction. The belly-devotees fail to participate in the suffering and will therefore also miss the future glory which the resurrected Christ embodies.[56]

Shameful living

Paul continues to say that belly-devotees have their glory in their shame. He is speaking ironically here. This comes through clearly when this saying is elucidated in the light of v. 21. There δόξα refers to the future body which is transformed according to the glorious body of Christ. Belly-worshippers have their glory as well, albeit located in their shameful living. The interpretation of this phrase in Paul's text depends very much on the whole reading of chap. 3. It is, therefore, no surprise that a number of scholars, in the light of the Jewish 'opposition' in the beginning of the chapter, take αἰσχύνη to refer either to the circumcised male genital[57] or the Jewish law more generally.[58]

---

[54] While Philo in *Gig.* 29–31 deems matters of family and child-rearing as keeping human beings down-looking, they are here a duty which is to be fulfilled. This is an example of the divided statements of Philo as to the proper attitude towards the needs of the human body. The tension is solved by his theory of the tripartite soul; see chap. 7.10 in this study.

[55] Jean-François Collange, *Philippians*, p. 138 reaches a similar conclusion: 'They have their eyes fixed on their own navel; their god is themselves!' But he does not reach this conclusion by drawing on the Epicurean material available in this study.

[56] That Phil. 3:19–21 represents a counter-image of the Christ-hymn in 2:6–11 is emphasized also by Dale B. Martin, *Slavery*, pp. 130–2.

[57] E.g. Gerald F. Hawthorne, *Philippians*, p. 166; Howard C. Kee, 'Shame', p. 142. Such language is, however, completely unprecedented, and is due to a particular reading of vv. 18–19, implying that Paul was denouncing Jewish practices throughout Phil. 3.

[58] Wolfgang Schenk, *Philipperbriefe*, pp. 289–90. Schenk argues from the parallel statement in 2 Cor. 4:2 (ἀπειπάμεθα τὰ κρυπτὰ τῆς αἰσχύνης), which he takes to refer to the Law of Moses, which is at the centre of Paul's discussion in the preceding chapter. But

Our point of departure for interpreting this saying must be that κοιλία and αἰσχύνη are held together by a single relative pronoun. Paul speaks of two sides of a single lifestyle, which means that what is shameful must be seen in the light of our interpretation of having the belly as god. This is significant since it means that the self-love implied in this *topos* is meaningful only against the background of a particular way of living. Self-love is a metaphorical extension of a particular shameful lifestyle. In joining together the stomach and shameful living, Paul brings to mind the shameful lifestyle associated with the belly (see chap. 5). In this way αἰσχύνη raises objections to a purely metaphorical reading of v. 19 and thus strengthens the relationship between interpretations 2 and 3 above. Many scholars have therefore seen it as an allusion to sexual immorality, an interpretation which finds support in Rom. 1:26–7, although the term αἰσχύνη does not appear there. This Greek term has no very precise reference. It is wise to take it as a wider reference to conduct which ought to be regarded as shameful, and which in this context has conduct associated with loaded tables as a particular point of reference. In other words, αἰσχύνη is taken as a term denoting the life at table and after dinner,[59] described earlier in chap. 5 in this study. Paul warns against those boasting about this conduct. He might well be exaggerating, but he is probably familiar with some – even among the believers – who justified such a self-loving conduct.[60]

the most natural reference of this phrase is not the Law, but accusations of proceeding in a veiled way, watering down the word of God. In other words, it refers to accusations that were levelled against Paul; so also Rudolph Bultmann, *Korinther*, pp. 102–3. Furthermore, in 2 Cor. 4:2 αἰσχύνη is related to something that is hidden. There is no such thought in Phil. 3:19; on the contrary, Paul assumes his readers' familiarity with belly-devotion. People who are glorying in their shame can hardly be paralleled with those who are veiling their shame. So the two texts must be kept apart. Interpreting 2 Cor. 4:2 along Schenk's lines creates a sharp contrast to Paul's saying about the δόξα of the Law in 2 Cor. 3:9.

[59] Lilian Portefaix, *Sisters Rejoice*, pp. 135–6, 140 interprets Phil. 3:19 as speaking about people who are devoted to 'banquets and sexual matters in this connection' (p. 140).

[60] Andrew D. Clarke, *Leadership*, pp. 105–7 and Bruce W. Winter, 'Gluttony', pp. 88–9 and *After Paul Left Corinth*, pp. 77–80, 98 refer to Philo's *Det.* 33–4 as an example of how an indulgent lifestyle involving gluttony and self-love was justified: '"Is not the body the soul's house?" Why, then should we not take care of a house that it may not fall into ruins? Are not eyes and ears and the band of the other senses bodyguards and courtiers, as it were, of the soul? Must we not then value allies and friends equally with ourselves? Did nature create pleasures and enjoyments and the delights that meet us all the way through life, for the dead, or for those who have never come into existence, and not for the living? And what is to induce us to forgo the acquisition of wealth and fame and honours and offices and everything else of that sort, things which secure for us a life not merely of safety but of happiness?' (*Det.* 33). This is according to Philo, the δόγμα of the self-loving person. This justification paved the way for a lifestyle claiming that 'all is permissible'. Clarke and Winter apply this in particular to 1 Cor. 6:12, but it might be relevant to understanding

8.3   Opponents?

Scholars often turn to Phil. 3:2–4 with its obvious emphasis on Jewish piety to explain vv. 18–19. This assumed connection is very often the basis for claiming that Paul is thinking of dietary laws in vv. 18–19. It is impossible to approach vv. 18–19 without raising the question of whether Phil. 3 forms a united argument. Obviously, there is a continuity in Paul's argument in this chapter, but how is it to be defined? Phil. 3 plays a significant role in research done on Paul and his opponents. It is now time to address this problem. The question will be discussed with a view to the interpretation of vv. 18–19; no full-scale presentation of the Philippian opposition is intended.[61]

Are Paul and his converts in Philippi faced with a single opponent, depicted both in Phil. 3:2–4 and 18–19, or a two-front opposition? Advocates of a single-front opposition usually see vv. 18–19 as a continuation of Jewish claims mentioned in vv. 2–4, and which Paul also is countering in the following verses. This would then make a coherent interpretation of both ends of this chapter. As claimed by e.g. Wolfgang Schenk, κοιλία then represents an abbreviated expression for σκύβαλα in Phil. 3:8.[62] That the issue of Jewish claims is raised in this part of chap. 3 can hardly be disputed.[63] The question is whether this is to be assumed also for vv. 18–19.[64] As pointed out many times in this study, the Achilles' heel of this 'Jewish' interpretation is that a rhetoric, which Jewish sources have appropriated and turned against lenient observers of Jewish customs – is

---

the claim behind Phil. 3:18–19 as well; so also Robert Jewett, 'Conflicting Movements', pp. 380–1. *Det.* 32–4 is about self-lovers (φίλαυτοι) who justify their riotous lifestyle, with excess, luxury and all the sweets of life; cf. Cain's creed which is mentioned above and on justification of indulgence in chap. 10.3.

[61] See the commentaries; for a most helpful survey see Peter O'Brien, *Philippians*, pp. 26–35.

[62] Wolfgang Schenk, *Philipperbriefe*, pp. 289–90.

[63] A. J. F. Klijn, 'Opponents' speaks of Jews or Jewish missionaries. The majority of scholars, however, speak of a Jewish-Christian opposition. The arguments against Klijn's view put forward by Peter O'Brien, *Philippians*, pp. 28–9, 33–4 are in my view conclusive on this matter. A single-front opposition is also argued by Helmut Koester, 'Polemic', but he claims that this consists of misguided Christians holding a radically spiritualized eschatology akin to early Jewish Christian gnosticism. Walter Schmithals, 'Die Irrlehrer von Rm 16, 17–20' emphasizes a single set of opponents, but they are libertines or pneumatics of a Jewish Gnostic type. Both Koester and Schmithals have contributed helpful insights, but all in all, their interpretations demand too much imagination.

[64] For scholars who take 'belly' to refer to Jewish food laws; see chap. 1.2 in this study. Peter O'Brien, *Philippians*, pp. 33–4 takes κοιλία in v. 19 to be a sharpening of vv. 2–4, or a stronger expression for what is meant by σάρξ there; similarly Moisés Silva, *Philippians*, p. 210 and Wolfgang Schenk, *Philipperbriefe*, p. 288. All this makes a coherent picture of the opposition Paul faced in Philippians.

here supposed to be targeting people who *continue* to observe them faithfully. It is unlikely that Paul has re-phrased the belly-*topos* in such a way that it simply refers to the Laws and the commandments laid down there.

Recognizing then the obvious Jewish character of 3:2–6 and, on the other hand, claiming that vv. 18–19 can only be properly understood when seen against a wider Graeco-Roman background of belly-worship as a catchword for a so-called Epicurean lifestyle, makes a two-front opposition preferable. Paul and his converts would then be faced with Jewish-Christian opposition as well as believers agitating for a selfish sensualist lifestyle.[65]

To have the belly as god, as it appears in Phil. 3:19, might by some be taken as paving the way for a redefinition of a Judaizing one-front opposition. If v. 19 speaks of self-love, one could argue that Jewish claims reflected in 3:2–4 are then in vv. 18–19 presented as manifestations of self-love. This would give a unified reading of Paul as confronting Jewish opposition throughout chap. 3, and it would recall Paul's words about his opponents in Gal. 6:12: 'It is those who want to make a good showing in the flesh that try to compel you to be circumcised . . . ' This would be a purely metaphorical interpretation of v. 19. On the basis of my exegesis I consider this to be a misleading conclusion. In the first place, belly-worship as self-love works best with the Epicurean background. It is against this background of self-pleasing gluttony that we can speak of a figurative extension of the *topos*. In the second place, this interpretation renders αἰσχύνη superfluous. This word can hardly be interpreted purely figuratively. Self-love manifests itself in shameful living, and that was to Paul no pointer to traditional Jewish piety.

Recent considerations of difficulties involved in finding and describing opponents in Paul's texts should make us cautious to do so in Phil. 3.[66] In contrast to most commentaries, the most recent, that of Markus Bockmuehl, does not include an excursus on the opponents. This is indicative of a shift in present-day scholarship. The so-called opponent-texts are seen primarily in the light of Paul's argument and rhetoric. The relevant

---

[65] A two-front oppostion is assumed by a number of scholars (see references in Peter O'Brien, *Philippians*, pp. 31–2), of whom I will mention in particular Robert Jewett, 'Thanksgiving', pp. 44–9 and 'Conflicting Movements', pp. 377, 382–7. Mikael Tellbe, *Paul Between Synagogue and State*, pp. 269–71 argues that in Phil. 3:18–19 Paul is targeting Philippian *collegia* which propagated traditional Roman worship and the outrageous behaviour associated with it. His theory is based on the appearance of political terminology in 3:17–21. It is, in my view, dubious to extract historical details from this. I have argued that a political terminology in this passage appears as a traditional motif associated with the belly-*topos*.

[66] See the works of Klaus Berger, 'Gegner' and John M. G. Barclay, 'Mirror-reading'.

verses in Phil. 3 can be seen from the perspective of Paul instructing with the aid of examples and counter-examples (see above).[67] This approach is promising and might break the deadlock on the question of the Philippian opposition. Phil. 3 provides warnings, and does not necessarily demand the presence of actual opponents. In the words of David A. de Silva, the opponents 'function rhetorically as a foil to the example of Paul'.[68] This can be illustrated in the basic structure of Paul's logic in chap. 3: Judaizers' example (vv. 2–4) versus Paul's example (vv. 5–11) and Paul's example (v. 17) versus the example of belly-worshippers (vv. 18–19).[69]

But what is a rhetorical foil? To consider vv. 2–4 and 18–19 as rhetorical foils is by no means to say that they are accidental examples, chosen at random. Rhetoric does not work if it is of no relevance to the addressees. We have noticed already that examples were usually chosen according to their relevance for the addressees. This suggests that although vv. 2–4 and 18–19 do not imply the presence of opponents, their views are latent as 'underlying tendencies'.[70] The believers are under potential threat from Judaizers as well as from self-loving libertines. The views of these people 'illustrate the incipient dangers of certain tendencies which have taken root among the Philippians without the active influence of "opponents"'.[71] Paul is practising 'protective discipline',[72] passing on the fruits of previous experiences in his ministry. He sees in Philippi tendencies among some believers which bring to mind previous controversies.[73] Some were ready to put the latent tendencies into practice in terms of imposing Jewish customs or to justify selfish indulgence in an easy life.

[67] This perspective on the question of opponents has been emphasized by David E. Garland, 'Composition and Unity', pp. 166–8; David A. de Silva, 'Philippians 3:2–21', pp. 29–32, 51–4 and Markus Bockmuehl, *Philippians*, p. 232: 'Paul's interest in these enemies of the cross is general and rhetorical rather than specific and sustained. They are evidently of no acute importance to Paul, and their sole appearance in this letter serves merely to give sharper definition to the Christ-centred orientation which Paul wants to commend to his readers. It is this concern which governs his argument both before and after the parenthesis of verses 18–19.'

[68] David A. de Silva, 'Philippians 3:2–21', p. 52.

[69] Paul's example in Phil. 4:9 is either a summing up of the example-rhetoric or presents Paul and his co-workers as examples opposed to the two women in 4:2–3.

[70] I take this phrase from Davorin Peterlin, *Philippians*, pp. 90–2 to be a proper description of the situation.

[71] Ibid. pp. 98–9.   [72] Ibid. p. 95.

[73] David A. de Silva, 'Philippians 3:2–21', pp. 31–2 refers to experiences drawn from Galatia and Corinth. The Galatian crisis might then be reflected in the first part of chap. 3, which makes belly-worship in vv. 18–19 a brief summing-up of challenges Paul faced among the Corinthians. The Corinthian correspondence is certainly a much more relevant perspective on vv. 18–19 than the Galatian crisis, which has so often set the agenda for the interpretation of this passage. This means that this study's chap. 10 on 'The Corinthian belly' should be seen as continuing Paul's concern in Phil. 3:18–19.

The presence of some of these tendencies is witnessed in Paul's injunctions (Phil. 1:27; 2:3–4, 21). It is, therefore, not at all necessary to consider vv. 18–19 as speaking of non-believers.[74] On the contrary, the whole passage makes better sense if Paul has in mind that some Christians are walking down the belly-path and are so heading for their final destruction.

Is there any connecting link between the minatory example of the Judaizers and that of the belly-worshippers? In other words, can the two still in some way be held together, beyond the fact that they both work as examples? Is there, after all, a link between circumcision and belly-worship? Our presentation of 3 and 4 Maccabees as well as Philo has demonstrated that Jews with a lenient attitude to circumcision and food laws were seen to be liable to become belly-worshippers; i.e. seeking an easy life among the Gentiles. Circumcision and food laws were means of bringing the unruly belly under control. This means that there was a long-standing view that Jewish customs and belly-worship were connected in this particular way.

With this in mind, we approach the question of how Phil. 3 forms a unity. In Phil. 3:3, Paul claims emphatically that faith in Christ represents the spiritual worship mentioned in the Scriptures: 'For it is we who are the circumcision, who worship in the Spirit of God and boast in Christ Jesus and have no confidence in the flesh.'[75] This argument functions in both examples in this chapter. *Vis-à-vis* the Judaizers it claims to represent the true fulfilment of Jewish piety; *vis-à-vis* the belly-worshippers it claims that faith in Christ – the sole and true circumcision – is an obstacle to the pleasures of the belly. Having left behind a piety based on Jewish customs (Phil. 3:7–9), Paul claims that this is by no means an opportunity for selfish desires to rule. In this way Paul's claim in v. 3 unites the two examples and adds coherence to his argument,[76] and in fact, paves the way for Paul's dictum in vv. 18–19: a spiritual circumcision, or having the heart circumcised, in no way prepares for belly-worship.[77] Paul's logic

[74] *Pace* E. A. Castelli, *Imitating Paul*, pp. 95–7.

[75] An ethical interpretation of circumcision is derived from the OT, and is attested in Philo (*Migr.* 86–93; *Spec.* 1:1–11; *QG* 3:46–7) as well as in Josephus (*Ant.* 20:34–48).

[76] Stanley K. Stowers, *Romans*, pp. 48–9, 68 has made a similar remark on Phil. 3. Both the question of Jewish customs involved in the beginning of the chapter and devotion to the belly can be seen within the framework of self-mastery. It is not necessary, as Stowers does, to assume the presence of Judaizing missionaries in Philippi claiming that observance of circumcision and food laws was the means to control the desires; cf. his 'Friends and Enemies', pp. 115–16.

[77] A similar view is taken by Markus Bockmuehl, *Philippians*, p. 232: 'The logical progression in this chapter, from the rejection of legalistic righteousness to a commendation of trust in Christ and then a warning against licentiousness, is in fact a familiar one in Pauline theology.'

in Phil. 3 in many ways concurs with his reasoning in Galatians. Having fiercely attacked circumcision and obedience to the Law as contrary to faith in Christ, Paul emphasizes that this freedom should not be used as an opportunity for the flesh, but rather as enslavement to serve one another (δουλεύετε ἀλλήλοις) (Gal. 5:13). This is a recurrent pattern in Paul's attitude to Jewish piety.[78]

8.4   Belly-worship and body in Philippians

We have seen that Paul's dicta on those whose god is their belly are embedded in the rhetorical strategy at the centre of this letter; i.e. instructing his converts to follow Christ's example and thus to serve the One True God. Phil. 3:19 is, therefore, not sufficiently accounted for by considering it a polemic directed at opponents. The question which now remains is to see whether belly-worship can in any way be fitted into Paul's body-theology as voiced in this particular letter.

In our investigation, belly-worship appears as a reference to a self-pleasing life in which all costs are avoided. This is a figurative extension of gluttony, a lifestyle which is most vividly seen in lavish banquets where the belly and the desires associated with it set the agenda. Worshipping oneself is, therefore, manifested in what Paul calls shameful living. Belly-worship and ἐν τῇ αἰσχύνῃ αὐτῶν are therefore mentioned in tandem, since having the belly as god takes the form of shameful attendance at banquets. Since the figurative interpretation of belly-worship is thus entirely dependent upon bodily misbehaviour, it is necessary to ask if in this epistle Paul makes other dicta which imply a body-theology and which also throw further light upon his polemic against belly-worship. This is even suggested by the immediate context which speaks of the bodily transformation (Phil. 3:21, cf. v. 10).

As pointed out in chap. 1.4 as well as in our chapter on Philo, Paul's reassessment of circumcision could easily be turned against him; he was paving the way for the desires of the belly. This is echoed in Phil. 3:1–4 where Paul claims to worship God according to a spiritual circumcision. Thus Phil. 3, in its beginning as well as its end, defines Christian identity as involving also the body, keeping it blameless (ἄμεμπτος) (Phil. 3:6). Elsewhere in this letter this word expresses Paul's concern to present a

---

[78] Having criticized Law-observance in a fundamental way, Paul turned to emphasizing the moral implications of his gospel; see John M. G. Barclay, *Obeying the Truth*, e.g. pp. 216–20. His study addresses the question of how Gal. 5:13–6:10 works within the Galatian argument.

blameless or holy[79] congregation on the day of Christ (Phil. 2:15–16, cf. 1:6; 4:1). This means that the body is involved in how Paul conceived of Christian identity in Philippians.

A proper place to start is therefore Phil. 1:20, where Paul states his hope that 'Christ will be exalted (μεγαλυνθήσεται) now as always in my body (ἐν τῷ σώματί μου)'. Paul is awaiting trial, and the outcome is uncertain. In this situation he expresses his conviction that whatever happens, Christ will be glorified through his body. Σῶμα is here most probably more than a circumscription for 'in me'; it refers to the actual physical body.[80] Paul's body thus becomes an instrument of glorifying Christ. Paul's use of μεγαλύνειν is noteworthy; it is the opposite of putting to shame (αἰσχύνεσθαι), which Paul himself makes clear in this text. Furthermore, μεγαλύνειν is rooted in the Old Testament, in contexts of praising or worshipping God.[81] The term is associated with worship.[82] Paul's σῶμα is thus involved in worship; he is confident that this is so whether he lives or dies. When compared to Phil. 3:19, there is a striking similarity which makes the two texts appear as contrasts:

Phil. 1:20	Phil. 3:19
Paul will not be put to shame (αἰσχυνθήσομαι)	Shameful living (ἐν τῇ αἰσχυνῃ αὐτῶν)
Christ is praised (μεγαλυνθήσεται)	Praise or glory (ἡ δόξα)
The body (ἐν τῷ σώματί μου) is an instrument in worshipping Christ	The belly is itself worshipped (ὁ θεὸς ἡ κοιλία)

The body is here a distinctive mark; it is either an instrument in worshipping Christ, or it is itself turned into the object of worship; i.e. the idolatrous body. While in Rom. 12:1–2 the body is involved in

---

[79] This word is closely associated with the concept of holiness in Paul's letters; see e.g. 1 Thess. 2:10; 3:13; 5:23; 2 Cor. 7:1.

[80] In the immediate context ἐπιμένειν [ἐν] τῇ σαρκί (Phil. 1:24) refers to Paul's life in general; σῶμα adds a particular nuance to this. It is the nuance which is frequently expressed when Paul lists his apostolic sufferings (1 Cor 4:11–13; 2 Cor. 4:7–12; Gal. 6:17). These texts certainly address bodily experiences. Similarly Robert Jewett, *Paul's Anthropological Terms*, p. 253; Gordon F. Fee, *Philippians*, p. 137.

[81] See LXX Ps. 33:4–5; 39:17; 56:11; 68:30–1; Mal. 1:5; Sir. 43:31. In the majority of these texts the verb refers to the oppressed who rejoice in God's salvation. Further references are found in most commentaries, see e.g. Joachim Gnilka, *Philipperbrief*, pp. 67–8; Markus Bockmuehl, *Philippians*, p. 85.

[82] Clearly so in Luke 1:46, 50; Acts 10:47; 19:17.

worship, Phil. 1:20 – albeit addressing the body in a similar way – seems to be more related to the possibility of impending death. The idea of Paul's body as involved in a worship which might well lead to death is spelled out explicitly in Phil. 2:17, which speaks of his being 'poured out as a libation over the sacrifice and the offering of your faith'.[83] The immediate context addresses Paul's apostolic labours, pictured in the metaphors of 'running'[84] and 'labour'. It is worth noticing that this brings to mind that in Phil. 3 belly-worshippers and athletes formed contrasts in Paul's argument. In Phil. 2 the metaphor of running emphasizes preparedness for suffering. Paul speaks of the possibility of his labours as bringing his death.[85] Phil. 2:17 is heavily loaded with words of sacrifice or worship.[86]

As for Phil. 3:19 and the question of Paul's body-theology, two observations are worth pondering. Phil. 2:17 continues Paul's saying about exalting Christ through the body (Phil. 1:20). We have noticed that this text formed a contrast to the belly-worshippers in chap. 3. Furthermore, Paul's description of his ministry in Phil. 2:17 develops from a comparison with the running of athletes, a comparison which in chap. 3 formed the contrast to those whose god is their belly. Paul and others were presented as examples to be imitated in their role as athletes. Although the motif of being purposeful and goal-oriented was focused on in chap. 3, while in chap. 2 labour is in focus, still the metaphor of athletes brings Phil. 1:20, 2:17 and 3:17–19 together. This implies that belly-worship in 3:19 is deeply embedded in how Paul in Philippians assumed that Christian identity, ministry and life had bodily consequences. Believers yield their body to God as instruments of worship, to the extent of giving up the body. Paul's body-theology therefore forms a strong contrast to worshipping the belly.

A strong indication that κοιλία in Phil. 3:19 is not without reference to the physical body is found in Phil. 3:21 where σῶμα is explicitly addressed: 'He will transform the body of our humiliation that it may be conformed to the body of his glory...' Most commentaries rightly point out that key terms in this verse echo Paul's description of Christ exalted and humiliated in Phil. 2:6–11 as well as his own situation,

---

[83] Phil. 2:30 speaks of Epaphroditus' risking his life in terms of λειτουργία.

[84] Cf. Phil. 4:1 where Paul speaks of the Philippian congregation as his στέφανος.

[85] I agree with Peter O' Brien, *Philippians*, pp. 303–6 who argues that ἀλλά in Phil. 2:17 has an ascensive force, which means that it introduces v. 17 as the climax of Paul's apostolic labours.

[86] Σπένδεσθαι, θυσία, λειτουργία.

between becoming like Christ in his death and the hope of resurrection in 3:10–11:

Phil 3:21	Phil 2:6–11	Phil 3:10–11
μετασχηματίζειν	σχῆμα (v. 7)	
ταπείνωσις	ταπεινοῦν (v. 8)	
	θάνατος (v. 8)	θάνατος
συμμορφίζεσθαι	μορφή (vv. 6–7)	σύμμορφος
δόξα	δόξα (v. 10)	resurrection from the dead
all things subject	every knee shall bend (v. 10)	

This demonstrates in the immediate literary and rhetorical context of Phil. 3:19 what we have already seen in chap. 1.4: the body of the believers is an appendage of Christ's body, which implies present participation in his sufferings and humiliation and future transformation of the mortal body. Christ is thus the model for how Paul conceives of the body as well as the belly. Belly-worshippers might glory in their shameful living; true believers of Christ, however, trust in the bodily glory to come at the resurrection. Their body will be transformed into a likeness of Christ's glorious body, thus corresponding to the spiritual world of the resurrection. Phil. 3:21 thus fits nicely into what we noticed in chap. 1.4 in e.g. 1 Cor. 15:40–51 and 2 Cor. 5:1–10. Belly-worship involves, as we have seen, a denial of Christ's sufferings and humiliation on the cross; it means enmity to the cross. It also bereaves its practitioners of their share in the glorious body to come. Body and belly thus play important roles in Paul's theology in this letter. Body and bodily behaviour mattered to Paul since participation in Christ was expressed in bodily terms.

8.5   Summary

In Phil. 3:17–21 Paul instructs his converts to live according to their identity as heavenly citizens. Matters of conduct and body are at the centre of his interest, not a refutation of controversial doctrinal views. The key to a proper understanding of this passage and vv. 18–19 in particular is not the presence of opponents, but Paul's rhetoric. His rhetoric is not words taken out of thin air; he is probably speaking not only with previous experiences in mind but also some underlying tendencies in Philippi. He is instructing his readers by examples and contrast-patterns, thus urging them to stand firm till the end of days. Paul is drawing on the stock figure of the glutton or belly-devotee as examples of a self-loving Epicurean lifestyle. In contrast to this he instructs the believers to be prepared for self-renunciation, even to the point of suffering. The protective instruction of Paul in vv. 18–19 is not primarily informing us about conflict and opposition, but relates to to his rhetorical strategy and theology in this epistle. Paul's appropriation of the belly-*topos* draws heavily on a cluster of related ideas:

(1)   Belly-devotees are concerned only with earthly things and the pleasures of the moment. In this way they constitute a contrast to the athletes whose life is oriented to do what their goal and purpose require of them. Athletes thus lead a purposeful life; Paul urges his converts to follow their example.

(2)   Belly-devotion involves shameful living, usually associated with sumptuous meals accompanied by excess in eating, drinking and love-making. A figurative extension of these physiological needs is well attested, and Paul makes use of it here.

(3)   Belly-devotees are not reliable citizens to whom questions of the common good can be entrusted. Always seeking an easy life, they are not prepared for the necessary costs of being a citizen. Epicurean self-love and true citizenship are incompatible.

In short, Paul warns them against wasting their citizenship in selfish conduct, and thus becoming enemies of Christ's cross. Christ's life and death in particular set an agenda wholly different from that of the stomach, and so does also the goal of the believers, namely perfection with him.

Generally speaking, New Testament scholarship has seen Phil. 3:19 either as mere polemical strategy aimed at vilifying opponents, or as a polemic targeting Jewish Christians who continue to observe dietary laws. In the latter case, this polemic is associated with the major Pauline concern about the Law and believers. I have argued that both views fail to do justice to Paul's text as well as the traditions he makes use of here. Phil. 3:19 does, however, relate to a major theological concern in this letter. The belly-*topos* as it appears in Philippians shows affinity with another common *topos* in antiquity, namely that of friendship. The belly-devotees are friends of their pleasures, or of themselves alone. In this way they represent the opposite of the ideal friend, who seeks the interest of the other; an example embodied by Christ and followed by Paul and his named companions. Paul's warning against worshipping the belly in Phil. 3:18–19 functions according to this major concern in this epistle.

Furthermore, Paul's polemic against belly-worship is set within his concern for the body as a shibboleth of identity. How one views the body, and relates to its needs, reveals the true nature of man, be it heavenly

or earthly. Paul's concern to present a holy and blameless congregation
has a bearing upon bodily practices. The body is either an instrument
for glorifying Christ or a means of worshipping oneself. Thus belly-
devotion appears as a contrast with the true worship of Christ. This is
so since worshipping Christ involves the body; Christ's bodily sufferings as well as his glorious body form two aspects with which believers
identify. Accordingly, present labours and future bodily transformation
are important approaches to how Paul views the belly; and both relate to
Christ's body and the participation of believers in it. Paul's apocalyptic
dualism applies to the body, and belly-worship certainly belongs to the
flesh.[87] Believers who are devoted to their stomach consider life to be
exhausted by the present moment, thus denying the future transformation. Thus belly-worshippers do not wage war against selfish desires, and
are accordingly unprepared for the labours which necessarily precede the
future vindication and transformation of the heavenly citizens. How Paul
conceives of the body and belly in Philippians does therefore not develop
primarily from a concern for morality and decency. Although his belly-
dictum takes lifestyle as its point of departure, it is religiously based.
His instruction concerning belly-worship develops from the idea of the
body's participation in Christ's suffering as well as his glorious body.

---

[87] See chap. 1.4.

9

'SERVING THE BELLY' AS KINSHIP WITH SATAN – ROM. 16:17–20

9.0 Introduction

Interrupting a series of greetings Paul inserts[1] a final admonition to Christians in Rome. Verse 17 is a sharp warning formulated in two sentences: (1) to be wary of those who are distorting the transmitted teaching and (2) to keep away from them. In v. 18 Paul supports this warning (γάρ). He first urges a sharp contrast: οὐ . . . ἀλλά; i.e. either Christ or the belly. Serving both of them is not possible. The keyword of the first sentence of v. 18 is δουλεύειν, and ἐξαπατᾶν in the next. Verse 19 expresses Paul's confidence in the Roman Christians, and he adds a final promise (v. 20): God will crush Satan under their feet.

Paul works with contrasts here: Christ versus the belly, good versus bad, God versus Satan. These are contrasts that really matter to the Roman Christians, but some are blurring them in a deceitful way. They do so by softening the distinctions and smoothing them out, they speak a flattering message: they are belly-servants and deceivers. The aim of our exegesis is to trace what Paul means by 'serving the belly' in this particular text, and also how this element works within his final admonition in this letter. We will also ask if Rom. 16:18 can in any way be seen in the light of how Paul views the human body in this epistle.

9.1 Warning against deceivers

In Rom. 16:17, Paul exhorts his readers to be on their guard against people who cause dissension and speak against the received teaching of the Roman church. Before elaborating on this, we must consider a question of

---

[1] There is no external evidence to support the view that this text comes from the hand of someone other than Paul. The blessing of v. 20 seems, however, out of place and is a reference to the problems of the ending of Romans. I consider the arguments for Rom. 16 as an integral part of the Epistle to be conclusive; for a recent presentation of this debate, see Thomas R. Schreiner, *Romans*, pp. 5–10.

method. On the basis of our findings in this study so far, the belly should
be seen as a catchword. It is no dead metaphor. It made sense to Paul's
addressees. This should imply that the *topos* of the belly has to precede
an understanding of this passage.[2] This idiom is not to be ignored, and
it might have some implications for the reading of the entire passage;
it certainly involves more than merely saying that they are *not* serving
Christ. Furthermore, when we approach the passage from the role played
by the belly-*topos* in ancient moral philosophy, it is surprising that most
commentaries speak of opponents in doctrinal terms.[3] The distinction
between teaching or doctrine and ethics should, however, not be over-
emphazised. Paul's ethics are closely integrated with his theology and
cannot be easily separated. In Phil. 3 we saw how Paul's polemic against
belly-worshippers, albeit with a clear reference to conduct, was founded
on theological convictions and concerns. This observation indicates that
to Paul theology and morality must be kept together.[4] The occurrence of
belly-devotion has not been accounted for if the deceivers are depicted
mainly as disputing theological matters. This *topos* has its focus on behavioural matters. Emphasis on conduct does not, of course, prevent its
being supported by some reasoning, in a way similar to e.g. Philo's *Det.*
33–4.[5]

For Paul is not speaking about silent practititoners. The people he has
in mind have voiced their message as well (cf. v. 18), probably a message
justifying their own behaviour. The closest parallel to the transmitted
teaching mentioned in Rom. 16:17 is found in Rom. 6:17; and it should
not escape our attention that behavioural aspects are apparent in that
context as well. Paul urges Roman Christians to turn away from advocates
of a non-Christian lifestyle. He implies that they are insiders, but their
behaviour and deceptive message qualify them as outsiders.

Paul supports his case in Rom. 16:18 by describing the people against
whom he is warning his addressees. His language does not aim at identifying them, but at characterizing them. Centred around δουλεύειν, Paul

[2] There is a tendency in many commentaries to neglect this idiom in the text. This is
seen in e.g. Douglas J. Moo, *Romans*, p. 931: 'In any case, the decisive point is really the
negative one: they are *not* serving our Lord Christ.' A similar trivial reading is seen in Ulrich
Wilckens, *Römer (12–16)*, p. 142.

[3] See e.g. Peter Stuhlmacher, *Romans*, p. 252: '... persons who engage in critical dis-
putes concerning the faith'; Douglas J. Moo, *Romans*, p. 929: '... the doctrinal threats'.
John Ziesler, *Romans*, p. 355 says that 'since Paul is warning against their teaching, it is
improbable that he is here talking about their gluttony'.

[4] In my view this is accounted for not by exaggerating the doctrinal aspect of Paul's
controversies, but by seeing the theological implications of his ethical instruction.

[5] See chap. 8.2 of this study.

draws a contrast; belly-service means abandoning Christ. Being a true servant of Christ is incompatible with being a belly-devotee. It is not possible to have it both ways, as the deceivers seem to think. This contrast lies at the very heart of Paul's argument. Since he goes on to say that they deceive by soft speaking, we can assume that they presented themselves, their way of living and its justification in a manner that claimed conformity with common Christian belief. Paul's sharp contrast (οὐ . . . ἀλλά) is targeting exactly this: they are not what they claim. His strategy is highly congruent with Phil. 3:18–19; belly-worship is enmity with Christ. This means that Paul is here applying an aspect of how the belly-*topos* was appropriated in Hellenistic Judaism; it refers to the life of pagans or apostates.[6]

Expressions like δουλεύειν κοιλίᾳ/γαστρί or κοιλιόδουλος occur quite often in our material. We have found that they refer to a person who has not mastered the desires of the belly, viz. those of food and sex. The appetites are out of control, and are in charge. This finding of ours must not be abandoned in the exegesis of this particular passage. In this text, however, enslavement to the belly is given a particular focus since it concurs with the frequent use of δουλεύειν in this letter. This verb strikes the note of both enslavement and worship. In a Pauline context, emphasis should be given to the latter, although the two are by no means separable. Δουλεύειν is a substantial verb in this epistle. Together with its various cognates it appears 16 times in Romans. Paul introduces himself as a δοῦλος of Christ (Rom. 1:1), and now towards the end of his letter he returns to this concept. There is a density of these terms in Rom. 6:1–20. Through baptism the believer has been incorporated into the death and resurrection of Christ, which means that sin is no longer to be served (Rom. 6:6, 16–17, 20, 22). In this section Paul pictures sin as enslavement, and baptism as liberating to a new life, serving Christ instead (Rom. 6:18; 7:6, 25; 12:11; 14:18).[7] Furthermore, in some of these texts δουλεύειν takes on the meaning of worship (cf. Rom. 8:15). Since Rom. 16:18 recalls the question of servantship, enslavement, and worship addressed in Rom. 6, it is natural to see belly-worship as opposed to participation in Christ, which in Rom. 6 was explained in terms of suffering and future vindication (vv. 3–9). Paul therefore considered belly-worship as a practical denial of being crucified with Christ and united with his resurrection. In

---

[6] Enslavement to the stomach marked the divide between Jews and pagans both in 3 and 4 Maccabees, the *Letter of Aristeas*, *Testament of Moses*, and Philo (see especially *Virt.* 182). For this see chap. 6 in this study.

[7] For the metaphor of good slavery, i.e. being owned by Christ and serving him, see Dale B. Martin, *Slavery*, pp. 60–8.

this way, belly-worship in Rom. 16:18 approaches his dictum in Phil. 3:18–19, where enmity to Christ's cross is juxtaposed.

We noticed above the contrast related to οὐ ... ἀλλά in this text. Once this contrast is linked to δουλεύειν in v. 18:

> δουλεύουσιν
> οὐ τῷ κυρίῳ ἡμῶν Χριστῷ
> ἀλλὰ τῇ ἑαυτῶν κοιλίᾳ

it brings to mind a fundamental biblical pattern; i.e. Israel's constant vacillation between serving God and the idols. In LXX, δουλεύειν is a common term for total commitment to Yahwe, and it also comes to describe the exchange of this true worship for idols.[8] Although Paul here shapes the pattern christologically, it is easily recognizable, not least since Paul makes reference to it elsewhere in Romans. In Rom. 1:25 he speaks of those who exchange the proper worship of God for veneration of the body and created things, and in 9:33 and 10:21 he briefly records the wavering of Israel towards Yahwe. Rom. 10:21 quotes Isa. 65:2 which is a chapter laying out this history of wavering, turning from the Lord to the idols.

The historical books of the Old Testament are very explicit in depicting both Israel's worship and apostasy in terms of δουλεύειν and its cognates.[9] Serving the Lord or the idols appears as synonymous with ἀκούειν, ὀπίσω κυρίου, λατρεύειν, προσκυνεῖν, φοβεῖσθαι. The devotional nature of the term is thus evident in this material. This pattern of vacillation, centred around the question of true versus false worship, is frequently found in Jeremiah as well.[10] The Pauline text that mirrors this pattern most precisely is 1 Thess. 1:9: '... how you turned to God from idols, to serve (δουλεύειν) a living and true God ... ' It is highly significant that in Rom. 16:18 Paul fits the stomach into this pattern, exactly where we (and his primary readers) would expect the idols to appear. Thus the belly is seen as an idol being offered the worship which properly belongs to God alone. The Graeco-Roman *topos* on serving the belly or being enslaved by it is here seen in an OT perspective of true and false worship. The stomach-worship advocated by some of the opponents has replaced Christ. Overtones of idolatry lie heavily upon this text. Being devoted to one's belly is idolatrous living.

---

[8] Karl H. Rengstorf, 'δοῦλος', pp. 265–8.

[9] See in LXX, Exod. 23:33; Deut. 28:64; Judg. 2:7; 10:6, 10, 13, 16; 1 Kgs. 2:24: 12:14; 26:19; 3 Kgs. 9:6; 16:31; 22:54; 4 Kgs. 10:18; 17:41; 21:3: 2 Chr. 7:22; 24:18; 30:8; 33:3, 16, 22; 34:33.

[10] See in LXX, Jer. 2:20; 5:19; 8:2; 11:10; 13:10; 16:11; 22:9; 25:6; 42:15.

9.2 Worshipping the belly – Gen. 3:15, Satan and flattery

Is it, however, possible to take this some steps further, attempting to define what Paul in this particular text means by serving or worshipping the stomach? To some extent this is 'disinformation propaganda'[11] or conventional polemic or a caricature. But general judgements like this tend to ignore the impact of Paul's belly-sayings and their being rooted in his theology. Hence we need to pursue the question beyond such stereotypes. There is no consensus on the meaning of 'worshipping the stomach' among the scholars. The commentaries suggest the following options: (1) observance of food-laws;[12] (2) gluttony or a greedy lifestyle;[13] (3) flesh or selfishness.[14] This investigation has so far found plausible reasons to abandon (1) altogether. Alternatives (2) and (3) are well attested in the material uncovered in this study; but so are other aspects as well. We must turn to the text and the Epistle to the Romans itself to see what aspects Paul makes use of in this particular text.[15]

We are alerted by Paul bringing together in this passage belly-worship, deception in terms of ἐξαπατᾶν, and Satan. This combination brings to mind the theme of Satan disguised as the Serpent in Gen. 3, something which our presentation of Philo in particular unravelled. For Philo the description of the snake was a proof-text in his appropriation of the belly-*topos*. The snake crawling on the belly was his outstanding example of a belly-devotee. Rom. 16:20 – although far from being a quotation – brings to mind the words of judgement on the Serpent (Gen. 3:15).[16] Against this one might object that in Gen. 3:15 nothing is said about *God* trampling

---

[11] So James D. G. Dunn, *Romans 9–16*, p. 903.

[12] Charles K. Barrett, *Romans*, p. 261 says, with reference also to Phil. 3:19, that serving the belly refers 'not to gluttony but by their preoccupation with food laws'; similarly Joseph A. Fitzmyer, *Romans*, p. 746; Mark D. Nanos, *Mystery of Romans*, pp. 216–17, 234.

[13] Walter Schmithals, *Römerbrief*, p. 561; Peter Stuhlmacher, *Romans*, p. 253 says that living for the stomach here means to obtain provisions from the church; cf. the bread-prophets in *Did.* 11–12.

[14] Otto Michel, *Römerbrief*, pp. 480–1 (flesh); C. E. B. Cranfield, *Romans*, Vol. 2, p. 800 (selfishness); Ulrich Wilckens, *Römer 12–16*, p. 142 (selfishness). Thomas R. Schreiner, *Romans*, p. 803 suggests that self-worship is meant. Walter Schmithals, *Römerbrief*, p. 561 says that Wilckens' interpretation of the belly as a reference to selfishness lacks support. Here he is obviously wrong. It is, however, artificial to separate entirely selfishness and libertinism, as Wilckens does. The material presented in our study suggests a close link between the two.

[15] Thus trying to comply with James Barr's advice on the 'fallacy of total transfer'; see chap. 1.3 in this study.

[16] So also C. E. B. Cranfield, *Romans*, Vol. 2, p. 803; Peter Stuhlmacher, *Romans*, p. 253; Otto Michel, *Römerbrief*, p. 482; Douglas J. Moo, *Romans*, p. 932. James D. G. Dunn, *Romans 9–16*, pp. 905, 907. This is not to deny that other biblical texts merge as well; such is Ps. 110:1.

Satan underfoot. However, what Paul actually says is that God will crush Satan under the feet of the Romans. This is exactly how Gen. 3:15 is often talked of in the tradition. The evil forces will be given over (by God) to the faithful to be trampled underfoot (*T. Sim.* 6:6; *T. Levi* 18:12; *T. Zeb.* 9:8; cf. Ps. 91:12, Luke 10:18–20). Before we argue this further, the relationship between the belly-worshippers in Rom. 16:18 and Satan must be settled.[17]

According to 2 Cor. 11:14–15, the false teachers in Corinth were under the influence of Satan; so too in Rom. 16:20. The belly-devotees are disguised servants of Satan. There is hardly any sense in Paul promising his readers that Satan will be crushed, if that has no echo of the peril he has pointed out in the beginning of this passage. We are justified then, in keeping together belly-worship, deception, and Satan. Not only does v. 20 bring to mind Gen. 3, but so does the verb ἐξαπατᾶν. Gen. 3:13 LXX has the cognate verb ἀπατᾶν. In 2 Cor. 11:3, however, Paul obviously renders Gen. 3:13, although in a free way, using ἐξαπατᾶν and mentioning the snake as well. The false apostles in Corinth were disguised servants of Satan; like him they transformed themselves into messengers of light and servants of righteousness. But in fact they were false. This is a relevant analogy and helps in understanding Rom. 16:18. Furthermore, this analogy demonstrates that references to Gen. 3 found in Paul's letters can be re-read with reference to how he viewed his opponents.

With soft words and blessings the belly-servants deceive; that is their way. Paul speaks ironically in v. 18 by using in a negative sense words that are usually associated with goodness (χρηστός) and blessing (εὐλογία). When he speaks like this, it is obvious that Paul is referring to the cunning of the deceivers. These words are in themselves no proof of an echo of Gen. 3, but in the light of the sub-text pattern in 2 Cor. 11, this is a further indication that he is using the image of Satan and the snake to portray opponents in Rome. According to Gen. 3:1, the snake was cunning and clever, and deceived Eve with flattering words.

This biblical portrayal of the snake is further developed and emphasized in the traditions on the Fall as attested in *Life of Adam and Eve* and the *Apocalypse of Moses*. According to *Adam and Eve* 9:1–5, Satan

---

[17] James D.G. Dunn, *Romans*, p. 905 denies any link between the two; cf. C. E. B. Cranfield, *Romans*, Vol. 2, p. 803. According to their understanding, Paul is speaking of the final eschatological triumph over Satan. Otherwise in Peter Stuhlmacher, *Romans*, pp. 253–4; John Ziesler, *Romans*, p. 355 and Thomas R. Schreiner, *Romans*, pp. 803–4 who rightly emphasize that the victory over Satan and the downfall of the opponents should not be separated. Schreiner is explicit about Paul's dependence on Gen. 3:15.

transformed himself (*transfigurans se*)[18] into an angel of light. He pretended to weep with Eve, and thus seduced her with cunning. The *Apocalypse of Moses* tells very much the same story, including the emphasis on the cunning of the snake and Devil. The story of the fall is introduced with the words of Eve herself, saying that she was deceived (ἀπατᾶν) by the enemy (*Apoc. Mos.* 15). The Devil here appears as instructing the serpent on how to proceed in order to deceive Adam and Eve (*Apoc. Mos.* 16): 'Do not fear; only become my vessel, and I will speak a word through your mouth by which you will be able to deceive him (ῥῆμα ἐν ᾧ δυνήσῃ ἐξαπατῆσαι αὐτόν)',[19] using one of the key-verbs which occurred also in Rom. 16:18. Paul's warning proceeds from the conviction that Satan is the present agency in the activity of the belly-worshippers.

Apoc. Mos. 17 says that Satan disguised himself and appeared as an angel praising God; i.e. he claimed to be a true worshipper, but was, in fact, a deceiver – like the belly-worshippers in Rom. 16. The sophisticated cunning of the Devil is clearly stated in *Apoc. Mos.* 19:1, according to which his purpose is to destroy Eve completely. Eve was led to eat the fruit of covetousness: 'For ἐπιθυμία is the origin of every sin' (*Apoc. Mos.* 19:3). This emphasis on pretence, disguise, and soft words as tools of the Devil's deception are important aspects of how the Devil is portrayed in the *Life of Adam and Eve* and *Apocalypse of Moses*. Judging from Philo's exegesis of Gen. 3, it is all the more natural that it was the Serpent crawling on its belly that led men to ἐπιθυμία, for 'the serpent is a symbol for desire' (*QG* 1:47 and 48).

To sum up so far, Paul calls some Christians in Rome belly-worshippers. In his view, they are pretending to be true worshippers of Christ, but in reality they are disguised servants of Satan. They resemble the Serpent. On account of this kinship, Paul calls them belly-devotees. Philo's material on Gen. 3 is of great help in understanding more clearly how Paul is reading Gen. 3 in Rom. 16:17–20. However, in naming his opponents as belly-devotees uttering soft words, he is also very close to calling them flatterers. Many modern Bible-translators actually render the attractive and seductive speech in v. 18 as flattery.[20] We have noticed that the belly-*topos* was quite often associated with flatterers who were seeking pleasure without being willing to pay for it; they wanted to enjoy a

---

[18] The Latin text is found in J.H. Mozley, 'The Vita Adae'.

[19] The Greek text is from Constantinus Tischendorf, *Acta Apostolorum Apocrypha*.

[20] See e.g. Johannes P. Louw, Eugene A. Nida, *Lexicon*, Vol. 1, p. 393 and Barclay M. Newman, Eugene A. Nida, *Romans*, p. 296: '"By their fine words and flattering speech" may be translated as "they use beautiful words and they flatter people"; i.e. in this way they deceive'.

free meal.[21] Actually, Philo, in a comment on Gen. 3:15, says that flatterers are disguised as friends, just like the Serpent (*Leg.* 3:182).[22] Flatterers pretended friendship to have a share in the pleasures of the table, without paying the costs.[23] Plutarch describes the flatterer as a person who deceives by transforming himself into a friend, changing his appearance (σχῆμα) (*Mor.* 51b–c; 52c–f). He is chameleon-like (53d). He is a pretender (53f); his words are sweet (53f–54a). This is how the flatterer catches his victim. The imitation and self-transforming of flatterers are also attested in Athenaeus. The transformation manifests itself in sweet words (*Deipn.* 6:254e). Flatterers are disguised worms (σκώληξ), biting and eating up from the inside. Devouring snakes and flatterers are thus juxtaposed, in a way which brings to mind Philo's exegesis of Gen. 3. Just like Philo, Paul brings together Gen. 3 on Satan, belly-worship and flattery. In doing so, he hopes to deprive these people of any authority among the Roman Christians. The judgement of Satan thus echoes Gen. 3:15 and is certainly not without reference to the situation Roman Christians were facing. An eschatological horizon without reference to the peril in which they found themselves would hardly have been presented by Paul.

9.3   Why call the adversaries belly-worshippers?

I have insisted that belly-worship usually has a reference to behaviour. It is not primarily a phrase about false doctrines, but about misconduct, albeit supported by its doctrinal quasi-justification. So far, however, this claim remains somewhat unsubstantiated with regard to this particular text. Is there any reference to behavioural matters in this text? To put the question in another way: can Rom. 16:17–20 be associated with other texts about misconduct in this epistle, thus indicating why Paul was so upset? Two options are worth considering.

The first is Paul's discussion of menus, what to eat and what to avoid eating, among the Roman Christians (Rom. 14:1–15:13). It would certainly fit the material on the belly-*topos* to argue that Paul has in mind the selfish attitude of the strong in this section. Since so many scholars take belly-devotion as a reference to preoccupation with food laws, it needs to be emphasized here that I am not thinking of food laws as such, but

---

[21] See chap. 3 of this study.

[22] For flatterers are belly-servants, see *Plant.* 105–6 and *Ios.* 61–3.

[23] This use of the flatterer-tradition is more fitting here than the philosopher-flatterer mentioned by Peter Marshall, *Enmity in Corinth*, pp. 311–12. Marshall does not connect flattery and belly-*topos*. But Rom. 16:17–20 is after all about belly-servants. This ought to guide the exegesis of the entire passage.

the selfish attitude of those who did *not* observe the dietary laws, i.e. the 'strong'. They insisted on their menu without taking into account that the faith of the weak might be ruined. It says in Rom. 14:17–18 that serving Christ (δουλεύειν τῷ Χριστῷ) does not consist in eating and drinking; this echoes Rom. 16:18 and would fit nicely into an interpretation in which Rom. 16:17–20 and chaps. 14–15 are seen together. None the less, this is hardly what Paul had in mind in Rom. 16. The sharpness of Paul's words there and the mentioning of Satan are entirely different from the passage on menu.[24]

So we must look elsewhere to find a reference for Paul's polemical dictum in Rom. 16. The other option is Rom. 3:8.[25] A relationship between the two texts is suggested by two significant observations. In the first place, the indirect quotation in 3:8 ('Let us do evil so that good may come') is echoed in Rom. 16:19: 'I want you to be wise in what is good and guileless in what is evil'. Furthermore, Rom. 3:8 anticipates the question in Rom. 6:1 ('Should we continue to sin in order that grace may abound?').[26] This is significant since the following passage in Rom. 6 has a density of δουλεύειν and its cognates (cf. Rom. 16:19), and finally, because Rom. 6:17 is a close parallel to Rom. 16:17 on the transmitted teaching. There is therefore a basis on which to assume that Rom. 3:8 and 16:17–20 are interrelated. In other words, the belly-worshippers of chap. 16 appear in 3:8 as well. The literary context of Rom. 3:8 makes it evident that it is referring to Jewish or Jewish-Christian objectors.[27]

Does it make sense at all to call these people worshippers of the belly? After all, the focus of their objection, according to Rom. 3:8, was that Paul himself appeared as paving the way for sin and evil. To them Paul's gospel provided an opportunity for an indulgent life to develop in its wake. They are more likely to have seen Paul and his gospel as allies of the belly. This is indeed a puzzling question.[28] The results of our exegesis leads

---

[24] This is rightly pointed out by Otto Michel, *Römerbrief*, p. 479 and Douglas J. Moo, *Romans*, p. 929.

[25] That Rom. 16:17–20 picks up Paul's indirect quotation from some adversaries in 3:8 is suggested by a number of scholars; see in particular Peter Stuhlmacher, *Romans*, pp. 252–3. He says that Paul is here concluding his view on the adversaries mentioned in 3:8.

[26] This is indicated in the margin of the Nestle–Aland 27th edition as well.

[27] Peter Stuhlmacher, *Romans*, p. 53; Douglas J. Moo, *Romans*, pp. 194–5 speak of Jewish Christian opponents, while James D. G. Dunn, *Romans 1–8*, p. 143 seems to include both. Anyway, the objection reflected in Rom. 3:8 was voiced among the believers.

[28] For scholars who take serving the belly as a reference to false teachers who attempted to impose dietary regulations on the Christians, this is, of course, not a problem. As pointed out frequently in this study, belly-worship is very unlikely to be a reference to Jewish food regulations. Walter Schmithals, 'Die Irrlehrer von Rm 16, 17–20' rightly points out that belly-service refers to a libertinistic lifestyle. From this insight, however, he draws the

us to say that Paul is really turning the accusation – of paving the way for indulgence – against his Jewish-Christian adversaries in Rome. This is, of course, pejorative rhetoric. But Paul would himself very probably claim that this rhetoric was not out of touch with the usual reference of belly-worship in antiquity.

This language can only work pejoratively if the audience is familiar with it as referring to a discrediting lifestyle. So the question must be pushed further: what echoes was Paul's audience likely to have heard in Paul's naming of his Jewish-Christian adversaries worshippers of the belly? This has to be judged on the basis of the belly-*topos* itself as well as from the Epistle to the Romans. Since Paul's text gives no hint of adversaries who were bent on gluttony or indulgence, the figurative meaning of the belly-*topos* is worth considering. We have found that belly-service was associated with selfishness and self-gain; an attitude of neglecting the fellowship for the sake of pleasing oneself. As our investigation has demonstrated, this figurative extension of 'serving the stomach' is drawn from the concrete reference of the loaded table and its vices: people whose mind is set on satisfying the appetites easily become self-pleasing. Paul's text should not be isolated from this material. But do Jewish-Christian opponents fit into this picture?

An attitude that blames the gospel for being an opportunity to sin is liable to fall into its own trap. After all, a life in opposition to Christ and his gospel, be it pagan or Jewish, would, according to Paul, necessarily develop into service of the desires (ὑπακούειν ταῖς ἐπιθυμίαις) (Rom. 6:12). Enslavement to sin as the alternative to faith and baptism is very much alive in Rom. 6:1–20 (see in particular vv. 6, 12, 14, 17, 19), where Paul is addressing the objection of his adversaries in Rom. 3:8. Hence, people who were opposing and ridiculing his gospel were liable to turn to a lifestyle of the belly.

To Paul, enslavement to sin, as he depicts it in Rom. 6:1–20, was no mere theological statement, but a lifestyle he exemplified in a list of vices, among which Rom. 13:13–14 is worth mentioning here. Paul speaks of the necessity 'not to make any provision for the flesh, to gratify its desires (ἐπιθυμίαι)', which means to keep away, not only from quarrelling and jealousy, but also from κῶμος, μέθη, κοίτη, ἀσέλγεια.[29] In short, these

conclusion that a reference to Judaizers is excluded. In my investigation we will see in full later that polemic against Jews and Judaizers might well be expressed in the libertinistic terms of the belly (chap. 11). Schmithals' emphasis on the libertinistic reference of belly-devotion is surely correct, but his claim that this refers to Gnostics is unwarranted.

[29] For these terms, see the lexicons and also Douglas J. Moo, *Romans*, p. 825; cf. also 1 Pet. 4:1–3.

terms refer to gluttony, drinking and sexual orgies. This is the way of
life to which opponents of the gospel are likely to turn. Paul includes
his Jewish-Christian adversaries in this scenario since he considers crucifixion with Christ as the only means of fighting desires. The power of
desires surpasses even the holy and good Law, as well as Jewish piety.
Thus runs his argument in Rom. 7:7–13.[30]

9.4   'Serving the belly' and body in Romans

In Rom. 16:18, Paul mentions the belly in a simple piece of rhetoric aimed
primarily at vilifying his opponents. In this text, he applies belly-worship
primarily to argue that his opponents were servants of Satan, rather than
to address them as gluttons. But this polemic can only work if it brings
to mind a lifestyle associated with the belly, one which was commonly
held to be shameful. Paul's rhetoric derives its pejorative force from a
lifestyle where the agenda is set by desires of the belly. It is therefore
meaningful to see if belly-worship, as it appears here, is related to major
Pauline concerns about the body voiced elsewhere in this epistle.

Rom. 16:17–20 picks up the topics with which Paul introduced this very
letter. While his opponents are said to serve (δουλεύειν) their belly rather
than Christ, Paul is himself Christ's servant (δοῦλος Χριστοῦ 'Ιησοῦ)
(Rom. 1:1). Furthermore, the introductory thanksgiving presents Paul as
worshipping (λατρεύειν) God, who according to Rom. 3:30 (cf. 16:27)
is the One God. This verb of worship appears again in his description
of false worship in Rom. 1:25, in which the body is involved as well. In
a context (Rom. 1:18–32) where Paul, using terms of traditional Jewish
polemic, addresses the question of pagan worship as idolatry, he says:
'Therefore God gave them up in the lusts of their hearts (ἐν ταῖς ἐπιθυμίας
τῶν καρδιῶν αὐτῶν) to impurity, to the degrading of their bodies (τοῦ
ἀτιμάζεσθαι τὰ σώματα αὐτῶν) among themselves' (Rom. 1:24). This
saying is embedded in a context listing vices which are characteristic of
paganism. Idolatry means according to Rom. 1:25 exchanging the truth of
God for a lie and worshipping created things rather than God, the Creator
of all.

Paul speaks from the Jewish conviction that idolatry manifested itself in
immoral behaviour, particularly in illicit sex: 'Idolatry leads to shameless
and abominable immorality, which is itself an instance of worshipping the

---

[30] See the prologue to Part 4. In chap. 11, we will see that allegations of gluttony are
turned against the Jews quite often.

creature instead of the creator'.[31] In the wake of idolatry followed bodily misbehaviour which Jews, and Paul too, considered a conduct appropriate to pagans who did not revere the One True God. In this argument, idolatry perverts the functions of the body. Philo depicts this in terms that are quite similar to Paul's (*Spec.* 2:46–51; *Abr.* 135). It is worth noticing that in both these Philo texts illicit sex, gluttony, belly, and body figure prominently. In *Leg.* 3:138–9, Philo speaks of the belly as the reservoir of all the pleasures: 'For when the belly has been filled, cravings after the other pleasures also become vehement . . .'[32] The opposite of this way of life is to submit to God (παραχώρησιν τῷ θεῷ) (*Leg.* 3:137). The cognate verb παραχωρεῖν frequently refers to yielding to God in terms of worship or praise.[33] Paul does not say in Rom. 1 that the body is itself venerated, but there is sufficient evidence that e.g. Philo considered that idolatry necessarily developed into making a god of the body itself,[34] and in Phil. 3:19 and Rom. 16:18 Paul does so himself. When Paul, therefore, in these two texts directly addresses veneration of the body or belly, he is not being innovative, even though he moves beyond what is explicitly stated in Rom. 1. But it seems to be well within the horizon of the logic he applies there.

Dishonouring the body in Rom. 1:24 (cf. v. 26 πάθη ἀτιμίας) is, accordingly, not primarily a reference to the question of decency and social respectability. How Paul here views the body is dictated by his theological perspective on idolatry versus true worship. In Rom. 1:24 this perspective is voiced in his description of pagans who dishonour the body in terms of uncleanliness (ἀκαθαρσία). This term has here not lost its cultic connotations in favour of a moral sense;[35] Paul redefines cult in terms of conduct. Separating cult and ethics is alien to Paul's way of thinking. We have throughout in this study seen how the questions of true worship and the lifestyle of the belly coalesce in Paul's letters.[36] The fact that ἀκαθαρσία appears next to terms of sexual immorality in the list of vices can hardly be taken as evidence that Paul is separating cult from ethics. On the contrary, Paul conceived of cult in terms of conduct and lifestyle in terms of

[31] Markus Bockmuehl, *Jewish Law*, pp. 129–30 mentions this as a typical element of Jewish logic on pagan idolatry.

[32] Philo here speaks of τῆς γαστρὸς ὀρέξεις which brings to mind Paul's way of addressing homosexual lust in Rom. 1:27.

[33] See e.g. *Leg.* 1:82; 2:95; *Sacr.* 136; *Somn.* 2:25.

[34] In chap. 8.2 we demonstrated this with reference to *Ebr.* 95–6, according to which the disobedient son devoted to heavy drinking was said to have made a god of his body.

[35] Against e.g. James D. G. Dunn, *Romans 1–8*, p. 62.

[36] See also T. J. Deidun, *New Covenant Morality*, pp. 89–100 who argues this convincingly with reference to sexual morality.

worship. Accordingly, he considered the immoral life of pagans to represent a threat to the body of the believers, a threat of defilement. This brings to mind the notion of the believers as God's temple and dwelling of the Spirit which clearly brings out the cultic aspect in Paul's logic (chap. 1.4). The distinction between uncleanliness and cleanliness corresponds to the transition-pattern 'before – now' in Paul's way of instructing his converts. It is in this light we must understand what 'dishonouring the bodies' implies. It would be misleading to claim that Paul on this basis indicts the body as such. What he is condemning is a body in control. From this follows that a body in charge, as well as an unruly belly, belongs to the believers' past.

That Paul does not take out an indictment against the body as such is clear from texts in Romans where an alternative worship or service is attributed to the body. This brings us to Rom. 6:12–14, 19 and 12:1–2 which we introduced in chap. 1.4. These texts speak about a bodily worship in which believers are involved, and which arises from their participation in Christ's death and resurrection. This sets a new agenda for their bodies. Instead of being enslaved by sin they have become God's true agents. The cultic perspective of their new life is most clearly voiced in Rom. 12:1,but it is there in Rom. 6 as well. V. 19 speaks from the same perspective as we found in Rom. 1:24; now in terms of ἀκαθαρσία versus ἁγιασμός (cf. v. 22). But still Paul emphasizes that the body is mortal and weak; a fact which makes it meaningless to worship the body itself. This implies, of course, that the body belongs to this world and age, and that it is vulnerable to sin. This vulnerability causes Paul to call upon his addressees to live according to their participation in Christ. By implication this means that, although belly-worship in Rom. 16 as well as in Phil. 3 belongs to the Devil and the believers' past, a relapse into the power of the belly is still possible, but fatal. Paul elsewhere addresses Christian life in terms of an ἀγών,[37] which in his Epistle to the Romans is depicted as a struggle between Spirit and Flesh.

Paul is clearly speaking of a total self-commitment to God (παρασ-τήσατε ἑαυτοὺς τῷ θεῷ) (Rom. 6:13); a commitment with bodily consequences. Hence he speaks of both σῶμα and μέλη in this context. The bodily emphasis has two implications in Rom. 6 and 12. In the first place, it involves service to God that brings suffering and bodily decay, as well as the hope of final vindication and resurrection like Christ.[38] In the

---

[37] See e.g. 1 Cor. 9:24–7 and Phil. 3:12–16, just to mention two texts which are deeply embedded in Paul's texts on the power of the belly; see chaps. 8.2 and 10.4.
[38] See chap. 1.4.

second place, Paul urges his readers to keep away from sins which affect the body. He has in view a practical ethical agenda beyond the more
general statements in Rom. 6 and 12. This is attested in the metaphor of
'walking'[39] in Rom. 6:4, and in 6:12 which speaks of obedience to desires, thus bringing to mind the complex of texts mentioned in our study.
Finally this is witnessed in Rom. 6:6, strongly recalling Gal. 5:24, which
brings to a close a list of deeds in which ἐγκράτεια figures prominently.

Our sketching of body-theology in Romans leads us finally to
chap. 8. Here Paul is envisaging the body from his apocalyptic dualistic perspective.[40] The body of the believers has been liberated from the
power of sin and the flesh (Rom. 8:2, cf. 6:6; 7:24), and is now in the
process of being transformed according to the Spirit who dwells in their
body. Although spiritually liberated, Christians are still awaiting a final
liberation of the body: ἡ ἀπολύτρωσις τοῦ σώματος (Rom. 8:23).[41] That
the body is to be finally freed is the theme of vv. 18–30 in this chapter.
The body will be transformed by the Spirit according to Christ's image
(Rom. 8:29 cf. v. 17), and thus made appropriate for the coming age.
The participation in Christ will then become full, i.e. believers will share
fully in Christ's glorious body. Terms such as δόξα, ἐλπίς, τὸ πνεῦμα
loom large in this passage. On the other hand, the conditions which characterize the present experiences of the body are captured in terms such
as τὰ παθήματα τοῦ νῦν καιροῦ, ἡ δουλεία τῆς φθορᾶς, ἀσθένεια. The
present world is thus described in terms of suffering, death and destruction as well as weakness. Paul does not speak of a liberation *from* the
body as such,[42] but from all that associates it with the present world; i.e.
its bondage of death and destruction. Being freed from this, the body is
enabled to participate in the reality of the resurrection.

For the present life this hope implies that believers are expected to
mortify αἱ πράξεις τοῦ σώματος (Rom. 8:13). The negative connotation
of putting to death the deeds of the body is here equivalent to Paul's dicta
on σάρξ elsewhere.[43] Paul has in mind a lifestyle of total dependence
on the present world: '"The deeds of the body" therefore are the actions
which express undue dependence on satisfying merely human appetites

[39] For the concreteness of περιπατεῖν see references to Phil. 3:17 in chap. 8.2; see also
Karin Finsterbusch, *Thora als Lebensweisung*, pp.113–20.

[40] For this term see chap. 1.4.

[41] Paul's repeated emphasis on physical embodiment in this passage makes it, in my
view, less likely that σῶμα is here used only in the sense of 'self'.

[42] So also Robert Jewett, *Paul's Anthropological Terms*, pp. 290–9.

[43] This is probably the reason that some manuscripts and old translations have suggested
a correction here; τῆς σαρκός to replace τοῦ σώματος.

and ambitions.'[44] Certainly, 'belly-worship' as we have found it in our material belongs here. Paul urges his readers to a continous effort to mortify bodily desires which are associated with this-worldly selfishness. In other words, the belly, although not directly mentioned, is seen in an agonistic perspective. The believers must stand up to the rule of the belly.

This admonition is due to the major concern of chap. 8: since believers participate in the Spirit, they are presently undergoing a bodily transformation[45] that will be completed in the future. The agenda of the stomach addresses the mortal, weak and decaying part of the body. Devoting oneself to this necessarily means going back to past bondage. The belly, whether it denotes enslavement to fleshly desires or self-devotion, is therefore inappropriate for Christians. Hence, Paul views the body in the light of 'who are the Christians' and 'what will become of them'. Their participation in the Spirit and Christ's glorious body, although on a preliminary scale, has alienated them from belly-worship; or vice versa, devoting oneself to the stomach alienates one from present and future participation in Christ.

9.5   Summary

Paul issues a warning against deceivers whom he considers to be belly-worshippers, not the servants of Christ they claim to be. His aim is not to identify these people, but to explain their ways, and thus also to instruct his readers themselves on how to live. Paul's opponents are enslaved to their belly in terms of worshipping it, and they speak flattering words. Paul is confident that God will crush Satan under the feet of the faithful, which is an obvious reference to the future fate of the deceivers. We found that in this text Paul draws on traditions available in Philo's exegesis of Gen. 3; the Serpent crawling on the belly. Belly-devotion is, therefore, primarily a reference to their kinship with Satan. In Rom. 16:18 belly-worship is about to become a pejorative term for an apostasized life. No reference to food matters or an indulgent life is forthcoming in this passage.

The warning is, however, issued against those who are responsible for the objection voiced in Rom. 3:8, probably Jewish Christians. They ridicule Paul's gospel for paving the way for sin. Paul turns this against them, and says that in deceiving the believers, they demonstrate their kinship with Satan, and owing to this kinship they are liable to please themselves or their belly. People who turn away from Paul's gospel in this emphatic way are bound to fall for the desires of the belly. The apostle

---

[44] Thus James D. G. Dunn, *Romans 1–8*, p. 449.   [45] More on this in chap. 1.4.

wants his readers to conceive of the adversaries who are leading the believers astray in this perspective.

Since the polemic in Rom. 16:18 is fully understandable against the background of the shameful life associated with 'the loaded table' in antiquity, our presentation proceeded to texts on the human body in this letter. We are thus interested in a Pauline context from which this polemic of the belly arose. From Romans 1 on we noted a concern for not dishonouring the body in a way which was associated with pagan idolatry. Worshipping oneself and the needs of the body is the beginning of replacing the One true God for idols. This gives his moral instruction a profound basis within Paul's notion of true cult. The body becomes either an object of worship, i.e. self-devotion, or an instrument for ministering to God.

Out of participation in Christ comes a bodily commitment which brings death and decay, but which also shares in the future redemption. Paul does not speak of being freed from the body, but envisages a body liberated from the this-worldly powers of death and weakness, to which belong also the desires of the belly. Thus the body is made appropriate to the reality of the resurrection. How Paul conceives of the body in Romans is thus deeply embedded in how he thought about the identity of Christians. Our findings on how belly-worship in Rom. 16:18 is placed within this epistle very much concur with observations made on how Phil. 3:19 is placed within Philippians. From this it seems safe to conclude that Paul's polemic of the belly is not exhausted by labelling it conventional polemic. Paul is drawing heavily on a well-known *topos*, but the bedrock of his belly-dicta is his own theology.

10

THE CORINTHIAN BELLY

10.0   Introduction

Paul's correspondence with the Corinthians is well known for its unravelling of misconduct among his converts. The apostle considers his recent
converts to be in need of instruction on matters such as sexual misbehaviour, lawsuits among the believers, marriage, food sacrificed to idols,
seemly behaviour in the church, spiritual gifts and the future hope of resurrection. Four passages in 1 Corinthians show a special concern for food
and matters related to it: 6:13–20; 8:1–11:1; 11:17–34; 15:29–34. It is
essential to note this emphasis on food matters in order to understand the
Corinthian situation.[1] It is, therefore, quite natural that this letter should
be read anew in the light of the material on the belly-*topos* as presented
hitherto in this study. Furthermore, we have observed that both 1 Cor. 10:7
and 15:32, although they are Old Testament quotations, have predecessors in traditions about proverbial gourmandizers and pleasure-seekers
such as Sardanapalus. This was rooted in the critique of Epicurean hedonism. This observation stimulates a re-reading of these passages in their
Pauline context.

The chapter starts with a presentation of 1 Cor. 15:32 in its immediate
context. It will be argued that the text provides an Epicurean framework
which makes it meaningful to look for analogical ways of expressing
belly-worship in the Corinthian texts. At end of the chapter our findings
will be viewed in the light of Pauline texts on the body elsewhere in this
epistle.

10.1   1 Cor. 15:32: Epicurean lifestyle versus faith in resurrection

Within the context of Paul's arguments for Christ being raised from the
dead and its consequences for Christian belief, in 1 Cor. 15:29–34 he puts

---

[1] This is pointed out by Jerome H. Neyrey, *Paul*, p. 114 as well.

forward some purely human arguments as well.[2] The logic of the section can be grasped from the sentences introduced by εἰ and followed by τί which introduce a case (v. 29,32a, cf. 32b); εἰ is conditional, introducing the belief in the raising of the dead as a basic assumption. On the basis of the firm belief in the resurrection there follows a rhetorical question introduced by τί.[3] The way Paul is conducting his apostolic ministry is a testimony to his faith in the resurrection of the dead, and this extends to practices found among the Corinthians as well:

– the practice of baptizing an behalf of the dead[4]
– facing dangers on a daily basis, even to the point of death
– fighting wild beasts in Ephesus[5]

The questions are rhetorical: why are we doing these things, if the dead will nevertheless not be raised? These arguments are pieces of a message which is not entirely transparent to present-day readers of Paul's text, but we can assume they were known to his Corinthian audience. Although the precise reference of these sayings remains hidden to us, their function in Paul's argument is evident. Paul presents practices as well as hardships well-known to himself and his readers, and which would make no sense if the belief in the resurrection was false.

In the list of cases put forward in Paul's argument, I deliberately left out v. 32b: 'If the dead are not raised, "Let us eat and drink, for tomorrow we die."' The first part of this sentence puts it in company with the others (vv. 29–32a). The hortatory subjunctives (φάγωμεν καὶ πίωμεν), however, take the argument in a somewhat different direction, or rather, one step further. They work like ironical imperatives. The hortatory perspective introduced in v. 32b is substantiated in vv. 33–4, which are clear warnings and admonitions to the Corinthians. Hence vv. 32b–34 suggest that there are some close links between the issue of belief in the resurrection and the behaviour of the believers. This means that towards the end of this section Paul turns his arguments *for* the resurrection into a logic *based*

---

[2] Gordon D. Fee, *Corinthians*, p. 760 speaks of '*ad hominem* arguments for resurrection'.

[3] The interrogative τί followed by καί (v. 29) should be rendered 'why at all, still. . .'; see BDF §442.14.

[4] This much-debated question is of no relevance for our study. Paul is probably referring to a practice of believers baptizing on behalf of family or church members who passed away before they were baptized. Paul seems not to have any objections to this; at least he does not voice any. But no certainty is attainable on this difficult question. For a survey of the exegetical options as well as references to further literature, see Gordon D. Fee, *Corinthians*, pp. 762–7.

[5] I take ὄφελος to refer beyond immediate gain, and thus to extend to the future of the resurrection.

on this faith: to believe in the resurrection of the dead has implications for lifestyle; or, vice versa, how they live can be a practical denial of this faith.

The lifestyle indicated by the verbatim quotation in 1 Cor. 15:32 of Isa. 22:13 LXX is an example of a practical denial of belief in the resurrection of the dead. Although Paul quotes from an Old Testament text, this background seems to be of no significance here. The context is closer to that of pleasure and Epicureanism. This context, hinted at, is also found in Wisd. 2:5–9, which depicts the reasoning of the sensualist: since death is coming for us, let us join in the pleasures of youth (see more below).

In his article on θηριομαχεῖν (fighting beasts) (v. 32a), Abraham J. Malherbe has presented material providing access to v. 32b as well.[6] He argues that Paul's fighting beasts in Ephesus should be taken in a figurative sense.[7] In ancient philosophy human pleasures and passions are widely presented as beasts against which men have to fight. This concurs with observations done throughout this study. Esau, for instance, became to Philo the model of a belly-devotee, because he was hairy like a beast or animal.[8] The terminology of the arena became a widespread way of describing the wise man struggling with desires and passions, as has been demonstrated in many places in our study.

Malherbe's point can be illustrated by a brief presentation of Dio Chrysostom's *Discourse* 8 on virtue (περὶ ἀρετῆς). This treatise takes the Isthmian Games outside Corinth as its point of departure. Dio gives a vivid description of the life surrounding the games. Someone approaches Diogenes, asking if he is there to watch the games as well. The philosopher then makes a surprising claim; that he is participating in the games of true hardships, the *agôn* that really matters. The pleasures are antagonists much greater than those fought in the arena (*Orat.* 8:20). They have to be fought like beasts (θηρία) (*Orat.* 8:21), and they are like deadly snakes (*Orat.* 8:25, cf. 8:36); reminding us for instance of Philo's exegesis of Gen. 3.[9] In non-metaphorical language, the enemies Diogenes has to fight are sight, sound, smell, taste, touch, food, drink and sex. We here recognize the unholy trinity (food, drinking, sex) which we have found to be associated with the belly-*topos* in ancient philosophy.[10] This language

---

[6] Abraham J. Malherbe, 'Beasts at Ephesus'.

[7] The arguments against a literal reading are compelling. Paul's Roman citizenship militates against him fighting in the arena. It is furthermore unlikely that Paul would survive an incident like this. There are no other sources indicating this, nor in Paul's many lists of his apostolic tribulations.

[8] See chap. 7.4 of this study.   [9] See chap. 7.3 of this study.

[10] Further references in Abraham J. Malherbe, 'Beasts at Ephesus', pp. 74–5. His material concurs with observations made throughout this study.

of fighting pleasures forms the background against which 1 Cor. 15:32 should be read.

This material has, however, to be integrated with Paul's life and letters. He probably had some particular circumstances in mind. A general reference to fighting pleasures hardly fits the line of thought in 1 Cor. 15:29–34. Texts such as 1 Cor. 16:9 about the many adversaries in Ephesus and 2 Cor. 1:8–11 about the deadly peril Paul faced when he was there may be hints of historical experiences behind the figurative language of Paul fighting beasts.[11] The incidents were obviously of a nature which made Paul speak of them in terms of an *agôn*.

The language of fighting hedonism (although Paul might here use it for fighting adversaries who represent tempting pleasures to him) is, therefore, a significant part of Paul's argument in 1 Cor. 15:32a. From this it follows quite naturally that he addresses the question of eating and drinking, which we have seen throughout this study to be a formula in ancient writings for a dissolute life, with special emphasis on the issue of the unruly pleasures of the belly. We have seen that many ancient writers mentioned this in their critique of Epicureanism.[12] Later in this study (chap. 11) we will see that 1 Cor. 15:32 was commonly seen as depicting the lifestyle of Epicureanism among writers in the Primitive Church. If there is no resurrection, the Corinthians and Paul may as well join in the life of the banquets, the common venues for excessive[13] eating and drinking.

The quotation in v. 32 must, however, be considered together with v. 33, which is also commonly seen as a citation, namely from Fragment 218 in the lost writing *Thais* of the comic poet Menander.[14] This fragment – even in its wording – corresponds exactly to Paul's. No doubt, this gives to Paul's citation of Isa. 22:13 a Greek 'touch', and thus provides a key to seeing the perspective from which 1 Cor. 15:32 was likely to be understood by Paul's readers. It is really not surprising that to many among Paul's earliest expositors (see chap. 11), this was an Epicurean-sounding

---

[11] There is only scanty information on Paul's ministry at Ephesus, so we can hardly be more specific than this.

[12] W. M. L. de Wette, *Korinther*, p. 136 mentions in passing that Epicureanism is relevant for understanding 1 Cor. 15:32, but does not elaborate on this; see also Abraham J. Malherbe, 'Beasts at Ephesus', p. 76 n. 44. Gordon D. Fee, *Corinthians*, p. 772 says that Paul's citation of Isa. 22:13 reflects contemporary anti-Epicurean sentiments. Graham Tomlin, 'Christians and Epicureans', pp. 58–9 considers 1 Cor. 15:32 as reflecting a Corinthian slogan shaped by the Epicurean mentality and its denial of any afterlife; cf. Abraham J. Malherbe, 'Beasts at Ephesus', p. 77; Dale Martin, *Corinthian Body*, pp. 275–76 n. 79.

[13] As we have seen throughout this study, when eating and drinking are mentioned together in a negative or ironic context (as here), the reference is to excess in both, often including sex as well.

[14] See Theodorus Kock, *Comicorum Atticorum Fragmenta* Vol. 3, p. 62. See also John Maxwell Edmonds, *Fragments of Attic Comedy* Vol. 3b, pp. 626–7.

creed. Furthermore, Paul quotes in v. 33 from an outstanding figure of the comedy tradition,[15] which is a genre well-known for its emphasis on questions of eating and sex. Paul here shows a familiarity with a well-known ancient writing derived from circles with an attested interest in describing and poking fun at the agenda of belly.

There is, however, a question whether so much can be made of this. Menander's dictum may have become a commonplace, and Paul's quotation does not necessarily involve familiarity with Menander's writing as such. Similar passages are often encountered in ancient literature,[16] urging seizure of pleasure since life is short. Thucydides' *Peloponnesian War* 2:53 relates how during the period of the great plague the Athenians embarked upon a life of frantic enjoyment since death was likely at any time. In Euripides' *Alcestis* 780–9, Heracles says that when men learn of their debt to death, not knowing if they will live tomorrow (τὴν αὔριον μέλλουσαν εἰ βιώσεται) (784), they live from day to day, following this advice: make merry, drink (εὔφραινε σαυτόν, πῖνε 788).[17] In the midst of his extravagant dinner, when a special dish is being served, Trimalchio says:

> Alas for us poor mortals, all that poor man is is nothing. So we shall all be, after the world below takes us away. Let us live then while it can go well with us (*ergo vivamus, dum licet esse bene*).
> (Petronius, *Satyricon* 34)

All this means that Paul's familiarity with the comedy of Menander cannot be assumed. What he does know, however, and very well, is a morality of instant gratification based on the fragility of life: since death is approaching anyway, let us enjoy the moment in full; i.e. eat and drink and enjoy ourselves in all possible ways. It is the maxims and the logic of Sardanapalus again. Not surprisingly, this reasoning provided opportunities for living according to the belly. To Paul's ancient readers, 1 Cor. 15:32 is thus very likely a critique of the morality associated with the loaded table. According to Paul, this morality and its call for immediate satisfaction militates against the faith in the resurrection. To believers, the future is *not* uncertain.

[15] See Simon Hornblower, Anthony Spawforth, *Oxford Classical Dictionary*, pp. 956–7. Bruce W. Winter, *After Paul Left Corinth*, pp. 98–9 assumes Paul's familiarity with Menander.

[16] See e.g. Archibald Robertson, Alfred Plummer, *Corinthians*, p. 363. To the list mentioned there, Philo's *Det.* 38 should be added; it is quite close to Paul's saying in 1 Cor. 15:33.

[17] Euripides' saying brings to mind Sardanapalus; see chap. 4.1, section on 'The proverbial figure of Sardanapalus'. Cf. also Herodotus, *Hist.* 2:78 and Horace, *Odes* 2:3. In short, this is the morality of *gaudeamus igitur, iuvenes dum sumus*.

It is worth noticing the literary and theological setting in which Paul voices this critique. 1 Cor. 15:29 proceeds from the conviction that Christ was raised from the dead, thus guaranteeing the future salvation of his followers (v. 23). Although in somewhat different terms, Paul here speaks of the believers' participation in Christ's resurrected body.[18] Vv. 29–32a claim the certainty of this belief as well as some practical consequences. From this follows the moral instruction given in vv. 32b–34. The passage is immediately followed by the question of with what kind of body (ποίῳ δὲ σώματι) the dead will be raised. This makes evident that Paul's critique of belly-worship is here rooted in his belief that life must be led in a way which is appropriate to the future destiny of the body. Believers are therefore expected to live with a view towards the resurrection of the body. Their morality must differ. The resurrection makes the difference between the moral standards of the converts and those who are indulging in the *symposia*. A life without the hope of resurrection is marked by eating and drinking, characteristics of earthly existence.[19] Faith in the future resurrection of the body makes the difference; true believers make use of their stomach according to this firm hope. Paul's argument on eating and drinking is thus deeply embedded in his theology of identity, which is here expressed in terms of the future hope. Heavenly identity (Phil. 3:20) or resurrection-faith is assessed by food and drinking habits. This brings us, in fact, very close to the findings in our exegesis of Phil. 3, which the following list of similarities demonstrates:

Phil. 3:17–21	1 Cor. 15:29–34
Paul as an example: fighting for the crown	Paul fighting wild beasts
citizens of heaven/ resurrection-hope (v. 21)	resurrection of the dead
versus	versus
whose god is their belly	'let us eat and drink'
setting the mind on earthly things	practical denial of the resurrection
glory in their shame	ruin good morals (v. 33) / it is shameful (πρὸς ἐντροπὴν ὑμῖν λαλῶ)
their end is destruction	death

---

[18] See chap. 1.4.

[19] Paul's argument has a narrative unfolding in the parable of the rich fool in Luke 12:19: 'Relax, eat, drink, be merry'. This is the attitude of a man whose mind is set only on earthly things.

The pattern of Paul's thought, his logic, is very much the same in both instances: having faith in resurrection, the believer fights the earthly pleasures of the belly and the shameful behaviour associated with them, the end of which is final death. Paul's indirect admonition in 1 Cor. 15:32b is, then, part of a theological reasoning very similar to the basic argument in phil. 3:17–21. This is significant because it provides a basis on which to speak of 'the Corinthian belly' emerging in these texts, although Paul is here not using the same phrase as in phil. 3:19. In both passages worshipping the stomach by joining in an indulgent life is incompatible with faith in the resurrection.

In vv. 33–4 the hidden plea of v. 32b is brought out in full, although in quite general terms. Paul may be referring to people who are advocating an Epicurean denial of the resurrection,[20] but his primary concern in vv. 32–4 is with behavioural misconduct related to unbelief or false belief. The verb ἐκνήφειν (v. 34) has become a common word in Christian instruction about being prepared for the eschaton (e.g. 1 Thess. 5:6–8), but in this context it has very likely kept its meaning 'to sober up', since v. 32b speaks of drinking.[21]

Since the reasoning of 1 Cor. 15:32 is so deeply embedded in Paul's theological convictions, and since the text must be included among the belly-dicta on account of the pattern shared with Phil. 3 and the belly-*topos*, it is worthwhile looking for other texts in 1 Corinthians where the belly-*topos* might appear as well. To this we now turn.

10.2 1 Cor. 11:17–34: the Lord's Supper or stuffing one's own stomach?

In Paul's text on the Lord's Supper the question of proper food-behaviour is at the centre of his interest. His quotation of the words of institution is embedded in a context addressing division and groups in the church. There is a division between haves and have-nots, and this division is maintained and even reinforced when they gather for the Lord's Supper. This takes the form of different menus for the two groups,[22] a practice which, according to Musonius Rufus, is tantamount to gluttony and other

---

[20] So e.g. Gordon D. Fee, *Corinthians*, pp. 773–4; Graham Tomlin, 'Christians and Epicureans', pp. 59–62.

[21] For references, see Gordon D. Fee, *Corinthians*, p. 775 and Hans Conzelmann, *1 Corinthians*, p. 279. Actually, the relationship to being drunk (μεθύειν) is expressed in 1 Thess. 5:6–8 as well.

[22] For examples of this practice in antiquity, see Gerd Theissen, *Social Setting*, pp. 155–8; Karl Olav Sandnes, *A New Family*, pp. 156–8; Ben Witherington III, *Conflict*, p. 242. Excavations of private houses in Corinth, especially among the élite, have added

vices connected with excessive eating (*Fragm.* 18b/116.32–118.8). It is the opposite of self-control (σωφροσύνη). Similarly, Plutarch in his *Table Talk* says that at a meal where the diners are each enjoying his or her own dishes (τὸ ἴδιον), the fellowship suffers, and it is an example of greed for what is common (πλεονεξία περὶ τὸ κοινόν) (*Mor.* 644b–c). Paul's text can, therefore, safely be seen as addressing behaviour associated with gluttony among his converts.

The Pauline text is usually interpreted in the light of various reconstructions of the situation. According to the most common reconstruction, the 'haves' were commencing their own meal before the others arrived. Hence Paul urges them to wait for one another (1 Cor. 11:34).[23] Bruce W. Winter has suggested an alternative reconstruction. He argues that προλαμβάνειν in v. 21 has no temporal reference, but simply means 'to eat or devour', and that ἐκδέχεσθαι in v. 33 is a term for hospitality, meaning to 'receive in one's house'.[24] Winter puts his finger on the Achilles' heel of the common reconstruction: 'How much sense does it make to argue, that by waiting for one another you overcome the difficulty of the have-nots being hungry if, as Paul reports in v. 21, each is taking his own dinner?'[25]

Be this as it may in this study, the problem raised in the text is that some members, most probably among the elite, are using the Lord's Supper as an opportunity to gorge. In his instruction Paul takes verbs from both parts of the banquets, eating and drinking, and uses them in their extreme form; i.e. to be hungry or to be gorged and drunk (v. 21).[26] The meaning of μεθύειν carries weight in Paul's rhetorical strategy here. It means 'to get drunk' or 'to be intoxicated by wine',[27] and it is associated with the partying and *symposia* of antiquity (e.g. Dio Chrysostom's *Orat.*

knowledge of how the architectural structure was itself a factor contributing to divisions; see e.g. Jerome Murphy O'Connor, *St Paul's Corinth*, pp. 153–61.

[23] This reconstruction forms the basis for most modern Bible translations; see e.g. *NRSV* to 1 Cor. 11:22, keeping to the temporal element in προλαμβάνειν and reading v. 33 in this way: '... when you come together to eat, wait for one another'. See e.g. Peter Lampe, 'Eucharist', pp. 37–41 with references to further literature.

[24] Bruce W. Winter, 'The Lord's Supper at Corinth' and his recent book *After Paul Left Corinth*, pp. 143–52. Winter's reconstruction concurs almost exactly with my own arguments in *A New Family*, pp. 154–61. I was unaware of Winter's article when I wrote that work and argued along the same lines.

[25] Bruce W. Winter, 'The Lord's Supper at Corinth', p. 73. A further obstacle to the common opinion has been pointed out by myself, namely that πεινᾶν 'to hunger' is then used with reference both to the needy (v. 22) and to the wealthy (v. 34) within the same passage; see Karl Olav Sandnes, *A New Family*, p. 156. This is in my view a flaw in the common reconstruction of this text.

[26] So also Gordon D. Fee, *Corinthians*, p. 543.

[27] Paul uses this verb and its cognates in lists of vices (1 Cor. 5:11; 6:10; Rom. 13:13; Gal. 5:21). See BAGD s.v; LSJ s.v.; H. Preisker, 'μέθη', pp. 545–8.

30:33–9). Dio here uses this verb in a parable on the virtues. In this parable 'being drunk' represents Pleasure. The parable vividly picks up the agenda of a *symposion*: excessive eating, drinking, fighting, shouting, sleep, vomiting. This verb is for natural reasons often associated with gorging (Dio's *Orat.* 33:33, cf. 6:36; 9:3, 9).[28] In *Orat.* 70:10 μεθύειν is joined with ὀψοφαγεῖν. Athenaeus' *Deipn.* 2:44f mentions being drunk and having a protruding belly (προγάστωρ) in tandem, while 10:435a–f combines γαστρίζεσθαι and μεθύειν within a context speaking of Philip's banqueting life. In other words, Paul is using a verb which is commonly associated with the intoxication following in the wake of *symposia*.

In evoking the excessive eating and drinking of pagan banquets when addressing the issue of how the Corinthians are celebrating the Lord's Supper, Paul is most probably exaggerating. But he seems to be doing so intentionally, and for rhetorical reasons. He chooses the analogy of banquets quite deliberately. The analogy conveys a simple message: when the Christians in Corinth come together, there is too much emphasis on food and drinking on the part of the 'haves'. The Lord's Table becomes an opportunity for wine-bibbing and gluttony, instead of sharing.

In this rhetoric which aimed at putting things right in Corinth, Paul makes use of a language focused on excessive eating and drinking. In viewing the Christian gatherings as *symposion*-like, Paul is arguing that the 'haves' are bringing shame on the congregation by offending the 'have-nots'. They are acting like Gentiles. The analogy with the banquets is thus at the very heart of Paul's argument. He is aiming at making his converts celebrate the Lord's Supper in accordance with its nature as a partaking of Christ's death. Drawing on the material presented thus far in this study, we can say that some Corinthians were taking the attitude of φιλαυτία (self-love) when food was being enjoyed in the Christian gatherings. This creates a link with Phil. 3. The belly-worshippers were there seen as 'enemies of the cross'. When the Corinthians gathered to commemorate the night Jesus was handed over to die, and to remember his sacrificial death, some devoted themselves to gluttony. They failed to identify with the cross, which is at the centre of the Lord's Supper, and which would imply a quite different attitude to eating and fellowship. Bearing in mind that belly-worship in Phil. 3, Rom. 16 and 1 Cor. 15 was seen as a mark of apostasy, typical of deceivers or outsiders, it is no wonder that Paul's instruction is severe. He has noticed traces of belly-worship in the midst of his converts and their way of celebrating Christ. He considers this unworthy of believers (v. 27).

---

[28] Dio's *Orat.* 9 provides a glimpse of the life in Corinth during the Isthmian Games.

But does Paul actually present them as being devoted to their belly? This is not said directly, but some hints are certainly worth noticing:

- the emphasis on excessive eating and drinking
- the analogy of the *symposia* in Paul's argument
- selfishness on the part of the 'haves'

These observations correspond to some clusters of ideas which we have found constituting the belly-*topos*. Furthermore, these ideas work within a framework addressing the question of right conduct in worship. The question of proper worship occupies a significant role in this part of 1 Corinthians. Paul raised the issue of proper worship versus idolatry emphatically in chaps. 8 and 10. This concern is continued in chap. 11 as well: 1 Cor. 11:2–16 raises the question of right and proper conduct in worship. The appearance of συνέρχεσθαι in our pericope (vv. 17, 18, 20, 34, cf. 1 Cor. 14:26) and ἐπὶ τὸ αὐτό (v. 20) make this evident for this text as well. In other words, it is the question of proper worship which is addressed. Although Paul does not spell out in chap. 11 that the opposite of proper worship is idolatry, his readers would probably have inferred this from the previous chapters of this letter. Instead of celebrating the Lord's Supper, some Corinthians celebrate their own, for the purpose of stuffing themselves. This is not far from saying that when they gather for the Lord's Supper they tend to worship the belly rather than Christ. They are devoted to their own appetite, not to Christ whose death they are commemorating in the meal. Paul's rhetoric aims at this logic, in the hope that the 'haves' will change their ways.

Musonius Rufus considered different menus for guests a sign of gluttony (see above). This view is continued, with explicit reference to 1 Cor. 11:17–34, in early Patristic exegesis. Clement of Alexandria considers it a text about gluttony, and he connects it with the explicit Pauline belly-texts.[29] Similarly, Cyprian mentions 1 Cor. 11:33–4 in tandem with Isa. 22:13 (1 Cor. 15:32) and Exod. 32:6 (1 Cor. 10:7) as examples of the dangers of desire for food.[30] Augustine also mentions 1 Cor. 11:21–2 alongside biblical texts which represent a warning against a way of life associated with those 'whose god is their belly'.[31] From the perspective of Paul's oldest expositors, then, how the Corinthians celebrated the Lord's Supper is firmly rooted among the Pauline belly-texts, which seems to confirm our exegesis. Paul's concern for σῶμα appears in this text as well (1 Cor. 11:29), but its reference is not bodily or individual. His concern

---

[29] See chap. 11.1 of this study.   [30] See chap. 11.3 of this study.
[31] See chap. 11.10 of this study.

is here with the fellowship considered as a body. In v. 29 σῶμα is not mentioned alongside 'blood', which indicates that the reference here is not christological. Furthermore, an ecclesiological reading here corresponds to Paul's concern in this passage for not bringing shame upon fellow believers. Paul's use of σῶμα is probably by intention slippery here (cf. 1 Cor. 10:15–17); but the ecclesiological interpretation should be emphasized.

10.3   1 Cor. 6:12–20: the Christian faith has implications for stomach and sex

In Patristic exegesis (see chap. 11), this text was often associated with the belly-texts of Paul; not surprisingly, since it includes both food and the stomach. We will now view the text with the benefit of the insights gained so far in this investigation. The key question lies in v. 13. How is this enigmatic verse to be understood, and what does it yield for our investigation?

(a)   'Food is meant for the stomach and the stomach for food',
(b)   and God will destroy both one and the other.
(c)   The body is meant not for fornication but for the Lord, and the Lord for the body

In a note, the *NRSV* says that the quotation might be extended even to the word 'other', which makes the whole sentence (a + b) a Corinthian slogan. This discussion of where to put the quotation marks introduces a problem that has vexed New Testament scholarship. There is no consensus on how to interpret this dictum of Paul or the Corinthians; it is open to various interpretations. The main questions in our presentation are the following:

– how to interpret v. 13?
– why does Paul mention food, belly and sex together?
– how does v. 13 work within Paul's argument in this passage?

These questions are, of course, intertwined, and the key to all of them lies with the issue of Corinthian slogans.

The verse is embedded in a context dealing with misconduct among the Corinthians. Paul has received news from Chloe's people (1 Cor. 1:11) or from other co-workers, and he is now trying to put things right. The wider literary context in which this happens is 1 Cor. 5:1–6:20. L. William Countryman seeks to subsume the cases Paul addresses as examples of πλεονεξία or of a greedy inclination, i.e. to have more than others or what rightly belongs to another. The cases of πορνεία (5:1–8), lawsuits (6:1–8), a catalogue of vices (5:9–11; 6:9–11) as well as 6:12–20 on food and sex are all examples of competitive greed.[32] This perspective can be extended to 1 Cor. 7 as well.[33] In 1 Cor. 7:5, 9 Paul strikes the same note, but there in the language of desires.[34] To judge from the context, 1 Cor. 6:12–20 is therefore a text where Paul addresses the question of mastering desires, and sex in particular.[35]

There is general agreement that Paul is in dialogue with catchwords of the Corinthians, both quoting, qualifying and rejecting them. But when is he doing what? This question is crucial to the interpretation of v. 13. But we must still rely on guesswork. Bible translations do this by adding quotation-marks. As for v. 12, most scholars agree that here Paul twice mentions a slogan; 'all things are permitted' (cf. 1 Cor. 10:23) and twice qualifies it, almost to the point of negating it.[36] This means that Paul has twice voiced restrictions to be put on the moral life of his converts: what is permitted has to be beneficial to the fellowship (συμφέρει),[37] and has to be mastered as well.

Verse 13a + b is most naturally taken as continuing the Corinthians' slogans; v. 13c is then Paul's counter-argument, calling into question the

---

[32] L. William Countryman, *Dirt, Greed & Sex*, pp. 104–9.

[33] Brendan Byrne, 'Sinning Against One's Own Body' pp. 614–16 argues that 1 Cor. 6:12–20 should be seen as preparing for chap. 7. Bodily desire is obviously important in Paul's discussion in chap. 7 as well; see e.g. 7:5, 9, 36.

[34] The noun ἀκρασία and the verb ἐγκρατεύεσθαι are firmly rooted in the ancient discussions on pleasure. With Gordon D. Fee, *Corinthians*, p. 289 I take 'burning' to refer to sexual passion. The immediate context is decisive for this reading. Cf. Sir. 23:16 (LXX: 23:17) where sexual passion is described metaphorically as a burning fire. This reference is of special interest since the mention of the burning sexual passion is a continuation of a prayer not to be overcome by the yearning of the stomach (Sir. 23:6).

[35] So also Benjamin Fiore, 'Passion in Paul and Plutarch', pp. 137–8.

[36] See e.g. John Coolidge Hurd Jr, *Origin of 1 Corinthians*, pp. 67–8; Gordon D. Fee, *Corinthians*, pp. 251–2; Bruce W. Winter, 'Gluttony', pp. 80–1. This consensus on the slogans has recently been called into question by Brian J. Dodd, '1 Corinthians 6.12'. He argues that the text should be read without any quotation marks. The 'I' of v. 12 is paradigmatic. Paul portrays himself as a model of self-restraint. The first person singular here reflects his persuasive style rather than slogans he opposes. Dodd's view fails, in my view, to convince, because it does not account for v. 13a + b as running contrary to Paul's basic theological convictions expressed in this text as a whole. Furthermore, Bruce W. Winter, *Welfare*, pp. 166–77; 'Gluttony', pp. 79–81 and *After Paul Left Corinth*, pp. 89–91 has shown that it is likely that 'all things are permitted' is derived from the rights obtained by the elite in Corinth. Winter argues that this is a maxim related to the assumption of the *toga virilis* by male Roman adolescents.

[37] On Paul's argument for what is beneficial, see Karl Olav Sandnes, 'Prophecy', pp. 3–6.

view that matters of sex are morally irrelevant.[38] How one lives in sexual matters is, according to Paul, far from irrelevant. He argues this strongly in vv. 15–20 (cf. 6:9–11). A major difference between the slogans and Paul's position is the question of a future body: is the body to be destroyed or raised by God? Underlying this text is, therefore, a dispute on how to view the body (see below). Sexual misbehaviour is to Paul a sin against the body which is to be raised from the dead. Frequenting prostitutes or *hetairai* is therefore incompatible with

- belief in the resurrection
- being united with Christ as a member of his body
- the Scriptures
- the presence of the Holy Spirit in the believer
- the liberation[39] brought about by Christ's death
- the body which is a means to glorify God

Since Paul in v. 13c continues to put restrictions on the lifestyle of the Corinthians, we must ask how v. 13a + b is to be fitted into his argument which we have just summarized. Is this (v. 13a + b) Paul's own dictum or that of some among his converts in Corinth? Our preliminary conclusion needs to be substantiated.

Let me start by assuming that v. 13a + b is a genuine saying of Paul. This being so, what then are the possible implications for our reading of that part of v. 13? Taken by itself v. 13a + b might reflect a Pauline view of food and stomach in two ways. In the first place, food is not unclean. In Gal. 2–3 Paul has abandoned purity rules as a means of putting things right with God. In some texts this has led him to express himself on food-matters in terms that make it reasonable to say that food is indifferent, of no importance, for Christians (e.g. Rom. 14:2, 17; 1 Cor. 8:8). Food is not a matter of ritual cleanliness, but of nourishment. Food serves the needs of the stomach, and the stomach is for digesting the food. Thus the two are inseparably linked. This is then a piece of Paul's doctrine on justification by faith alone, not by observing Jewish customs, such as food laws.

In the second place, since the stomach is for digesting food, it is not for indulgence or luxury. In other words, v. 13a + b can be seen as urging

[38] This means that δέ in 1 Cor. 6:13c is taken to be an adversative, introducing Paul's first refutation (vv. 13c–14). Gordon D. Fee, *Corinthians*, p. 255 says that 'Paul thus counters their argument with his own theological construct, formulated after the manner of theirs'; similarly Jerome Murphy O'Connor, 'Slogans', p. 394.

[39] In v. 20 Paul returns to the question of freedom which introduced the section. Christian freedom can only be properly understood in the light of Christ's liberating death. In this way Christ's death and mastering the things permitted are kept together.

moderation; keeping the belly in its place, so to say. The attitude towards
the stomach should be in accordance with its role in the body; i.e. it should
be used as the digestive organ, not beyond that. Accordingly, Paul pleads
for a simple lifestyle, not lavish tables. This second point can easily be
illuminated by a widely attested view on moderation in food and sex
in antiquity. Philo says about Moses that he gave to his belly no more
than Nature required as necessary, likewise he used the organs below the
belly only for the sake of begetting children. He set himself apart from
a life of luxury (ἀφροδίαιτος) (*Mos.* 1:28–9, cf. *Praem.* 99; *Virt.* 5–6).
Pseudo-Phocylides 69 urges moderation in eating, drinking, and story-
telling, and a master to provide for his slave 'the tribute he owes to his
stomach' (Pseudo-Phocylides 223).[40] In his treatise on food, Musonius
Rufus says that 'God who made man provided him food and drink for
the sake of preserving his life, not for giving him pleasure (οὐχὶ τοῦ
ἥδεσθαι)' (Musonius Rufus 18b:21–2). This text speaks of a naturally or
divinely given role assigned to the stomach, which involves abstention
from gorging. Similarly, in his *Moral Epistle* 47 (*On Master and Slave*)
Seneca speaks of a master who, in front of his slaves,

> eats more than he can hold, and with monstrous greed loads his
> belly until it is stretched and at length ceases to do the work of
> the belly, so that he is at greater pains to discharge all the food
> than he was to stuff it down.   (*Mor. Epist.* 47:2)

Interpreting v. 13a–b along these lines, Paul would then be urging his
readers to use their stomach according to its proper purpose.[41] This reading can call upon a lot of relevant ancient material, but it is still untenable.
This is so for two main reasons. In the first place, food and stomach are
not matters of real interest in this Pauline text. They serve as a foil or transition to the question which is Paul's real concern: sex with prostitutes or
hetairai.[42] Why does Paul then bring up the question of food? Since this
issue plays no role in the rest of the text, it seems justified to assume that

---

[40] Pseudo-Phocylides was probably composed between 100 BC and AD 100, a Jewish
writing acculturated into Greek culture; see P. W. van der Horst, 'Pseudo-Phocylides', *OTP*
Vol. 2, pp. 565–73; John M. G. Barclay, *Jews in the Mediterranean Diaspora*, pp. 336–46.

[41] This interpretation is a result of my own thinking about 1 Cor. 6:13 in the light of the
ancient material on the belly.

[42] Bruce W. Winter, 'Gluttony', argues convincingly that Paul's concern is not only with
brothels, but with banquets as well: '... the background to 1 Cor. 6:12–20 is banqueting and
that the élitist's self-justification for the notorious conduct by the Corinthian Christians –
"all things are permitted" – concerned what has been termed the "intimate and unholy
trinity" of eating and drinking and sexual immorality' (p. 79).

v. 13 is dependent on arguments put forward by the Corinthians themselves. This means that v. 13 can hardly be fully explained as Pauline.

Next, if v. 13a-b is taken as a Pauline saying on moderation, it still
declares food and stomach as matters of no relevance to the resurrection.
This obviously militates against his emphasis on glorifying God in the
body, and against our exegesis of 1 Cor. 15:32. The future resurrection
carries present moral demands regarding sex, and as this investigation
makes evident throughout, in questions of food and the belly as well.
Finally, we have seen that Paul is inclined to distinguish between the
question of food being clean or unclean and behaviour related to eating as
bringing defilement upon both the individual and the Christian fellowship.

These objections are in my view conclusive, and hence I think – with
many other scholars – that v. 13a-b represents Corinthian slogans, although reformulated here by Paul. Against this conclusion it might be
argued that Paul nowhere comments on or refutes it. He simply takes
it as a point of departure from which to refute the Corinthian claim to
sexual liberation. Paul must, however, have had confidence in his own
letter, allowing him to leave questions here which he will later pick up
and elaborate on (1 Cor. 8–10; 11:17–34; 15:32). In other words, this
objection has to be answered on the basis of the letter as a whole, not
of this particular text alone. In v. 13a–b Paul is then quoting Corinthian
slogans, the results of which are to be seen later on in this letter.

As suggested by Jerome Murphy O'Connor[43] the structure of vv. 12–14
demonstrates that Paul is taking the slogan in v. 13a–b as basis for his
response:

Corinthians	Paul
All things are lawful for me	But not all things are beneficial
All things are lawful for me	But I will not be dominated by anything
Food is meant for the stomach	The body is (meant not for fornication but) for the Lord
and the stomach for food	and the Lord for the body
And God will destroy both one and the other	And God raised . . . and will also raise us by his power

Paul's argument therefore takes Corinthian slogans as their point of departure. From this we infer that some Corinthians argued that since food
and dietary laws were of no importance for defining Christian identity,

---

[43] Jerome Murphy O'Connor, 'Slogans'; see p. 394 in particular. See also Richard B.
Hays, *First Corinthians*, p. 102.

so sex was an indifferent matter as well. In other words, they 'jumped from the notion of Christian freedom with respect to food to freedom with respect to sexual relations'.[44] Verses 13–14 make sense within a line of thought claiming that what one did with the body was morally irrelevant.[45] Some Corinthians claimed that the body did not matter, and bodily activities could therefore affect neither themselves nor the body of believers.[46] The appearance of food and sex in tandem is, therefore, due to the logic of the slogans. And certainly Paul knew all too well that if Christian freedom in food-matters was interpreted to imply freedom to attend all kinds of banquets, sex would naturally follow in its wake.[47]

Paul does not agree with any of the claims (neither on the stomach nor on the genitals or sex) made by some Corinthians. His warning against being dominated is, of course, relevant to the question of what to do with the demands of the belly – although that is not elaborated on in this particular text. The very point in Paul's text is the theological conviction that the body is not temporary, but is to be raised.[48] Hence believers are not free to define for themselves what to do with the body, neither in matters of the stomach nor the genitals. Paul rejects dualistic thinking entirely here. 'For the Corinthians the fact that the body is soon to be done away

---

[44] Brian S. Rosner, *Paul, Scripture and Ethics*, pp. 128–30; quotation on pp. 128–9. So also Gordon D. Fee, *Corinthians*, p. 254 and Graham Tomlin, 'Christians and Epicureans', p. 63. It is worth noticing that 1 Cor. 6:11 speaks in terms of justification. In 6:12 then Paul starts to draw some moral boundaries relevant for his teaching on justification by faith.

[45] Andrew D. Clarke, *Leadership*, pp. 105–7 suggests that Philo's *Det.* 33 is a good example of how some Corinthians might have justified, theologically and philosophically, sensual indulgence: nature had created a need for sex; in other words the body was for sex. For a presentation of that text, see my chapter on Phil. 3 in this study. See also *Leg.* 3:237–40. The way Potiphar's wife argues in order to make Joseph sleep with her is strikingly similar to the reasoning which Paul is refuting in 1 Cor. 6. I consider it likely that some Corinthians were influenced by a reasoning which justified their misconduct, a reasoning which was similar to these Philonic texts, and which could draw upon popular versions of Epicurean philosophy. By some Corinthians, Paul's own initial teaching might have been seen as going down this path, or they seized this opportunity from his teaching.

[46] As pointed out by Dale B. Martin, *Corinthian Body*, p. 71 this does not imply that they were Gnostics who held the body to be evil; they simply considered it irrelevant.

[47] See chap. 5 of this study. Paul's injunctions in 1 Cor. 5–6 have been noted by many scholars as having links with Deuteronomy; see e.g. Benjamin Fiore, 'Passion in Paul and Plutarch', p. 137; Brian S. Rosner, *Paul, Scripture and Ethics*, p. 178. Of particular relevance is the law on not bringing into the temple money earned by a prostitute (Deut. 23:17–18). Philo comments on this law, saying that there are things more unholy than doing this, namely excessive drinking and eating (οἰνοφλυγια, ὀψοφαγία), love of money (φιλαργυρία), love of reputation (φιλοδοξία), love of pleasure (φιληδονία) and a number of other passions. The business of a harlot has to be ended by her age; it is not so with the vices mentioned: 'What length of time can purge away the stains of these?' (*Spec.* 1:280–2). This interpretation of the Deuteronomic law given by Philo reminds us not to separate the vices from each other. Paul might well have spoken of food in a section dealing primarily with sex.

[48] The future tense in v. 14 (ἐξεγερεῖ) is the preferable reading.

with renders bodily action here and now of no moral significance (cf. v. 13a). For Paul, on the other hand, the sphere or ambience of the risen Lord extends "back" into the present existence – so that body is . . . for the Lord and the Lord for the body.'[49]

1 Cor. 6:18–20 adds arguments which are drawn from Paul's theology of the body.[50] Paul sees adultery as 'sinning against the body itself' (1 Cor. 6:18c). As we have seen in Rom. 1:24 this is not primarily a concern with keeping up with standards of moral respectability, but with the body being holy; i.e. the indwelling of the Holy Spirit (1 Cor. 6:19, cf. 3:16). What sinning against the body implies, follows from this perspective. Sin against a temple is normally thought of in terms of pollution; the sacred is being profaned. As God's own property, and as a means of honouring and worshipping God (1 Cor. 6:20, cf. Phil. 1:20), the body is affected by adultery.[51] All this has relevance and a deep impact also on what a believer does with the stomach, according to Paul. Although gluttony and belly-worship are not explicitly mentioned in this text, they remain on its hidden agenda. The slogans Paul is fighting certainly paved the way for a lifestyle which he elsewhere in this epistle considered as belly-worship.

1 Cor. 6:12–20 makes it clear that Paul's critique of a belly-devoted lifestyle is not rooted in dualism. With some of the philosophers we have found this to be the case. In e.g. Epictetus we found a negative attitude to the body itself, an attitude of which his *Encheiridion* 41 is a good example:

> It is a mark of an ungifted man to spend a great deal of time in what concerns his body, as in much exercise, much eating, much drinking, much evacuating of the bowels, much copulating. But these things are to be done in passing; and let your whole attention be devoted to the mind.[52]

Paul's belief in the resurrection, as well as the Spirit as a first instalment of this, makes the difference. His concern about excessive eating and drinking is voiced in ways which bring him close to Epictetus, Plutarch, Philo and other moral philosophers of antiquity, but his concern is motivated

---

[49] This quotation from Brendan Byrne, 'Sinning Against One's Own Body', pp. 611–12 strikes the note in Paul's logic exactly.

[50] Whether v. 18b is a Corinthian slogan to which Paul is responding in v. 18c remains an open question. Brendon Byrne; 'Sinning Against One's Own Body' argues against this view.

[51] Cf. Dale B. Martin, *Corinthian Body*, p. 178: 'The way Paul deals with *porneia* is soaked in the logic of pollution and invasion.'

[52] Cf. Plutarch, *Mor.* 686c–d; Philo, *Gig.* 29–31. In these texts, anthropology and morality merge in a way which recalls physiognomical theories.

not by the mind being of supreme importance, but by the resurrection of the body. The body is for glorifying God; this goes for the genitals and stomach as well.

What then is the recipe provided by Paul concerning passions or desires? The means presented by most philosophers is to let Reason control the passions, i.e., letting the mind regulate their extremes.[53] Philo and 4 Maccabees have appropriated the same logic, although they claim that the life described in the Jewish laws represents the supreme expression of reason and mind. Here Paul really takes his leave of them. The attitude of believers towards sinful passions is not primarily self-imposed mastery or control, but being crucified with Christ: 'And those who belong to Christ Jesus have crucified the flesh with its passions (παθήματα) and desires (ἐπιθυμίαι)' (Gal. 5:24). In the immediate context of 1 Cor. 6:12–20 this is emphasized in 5:7–8: Christ has died as the paschal lamb, initiating a lifelong passover marked by newness of life. We notice that 1 Cor. 7:23 repeats 6:20 (ἠγοράσθητε τιμῆς) with an emphasis that this implies an obligation not to become δοῦλοι of men; it is consistent with Paul's logic to add: nor of anything else. When in this context he brings to mind Christ and Passover, it recalls chap. 7.2, where we found that Philo considered Passover as the main Scriptural text for fighting bodily desires, those of the belly and genitals in particular.

This *theologumenon* leads directly to the well-known dialectic indicative. That is, the believers are expected to conduct themselves according to the identity they are ascribed in Christ; see 1 Cor. 5:7 in particular: 'Clean out the old yeast so that you may be a new batch, as you really are unleavened. For our paschal lamb has been sacrificed.' 1 Cor. 6:11 continues this perspective of renewal, now in terms of the believers having been cleansed and sanctified. Finally, 1 Cor. 6:19–20 develops the same theme of sanctification. The Corinthians have a new identity; God's renewing Spirit is working in them, transforming them. The body is holy since it is the dwelling-place of the Holy Spirit.

Who the Christians are, or what will become of them in the future, has consequences for what to do with the belly and genitals. To Paul therefore living properly with the stomach and genitals is a definitional activity. Such is Paul's strategy *vis-à-vis* the question of passions and desires. This theological substructure of Paul's text represents a confirmation of what we found in phil. 3:18–21 and Rom. 16:17–20. Devoting oneself to the desires of the belly, whether in terms of food or sex, implies a practical

---

[53] Plutarch in his treatise on *Moral Virtue* says that λόγος and prudence (φρόνησις) put limitations upon the passions and thus bring about moderation (*Mor* 443c–d).

denial of Christian faith. Hence belly-worship is identical with enmity to Christ's cross; it is a neglect of the indicative-perspective in Paul's soteriology; i.e. the basic identity of believers. Just as the Corinthian slogans in 1 Cor. 6:13 pave the way for belly-worship, so too Paul's argument in this text paves the way for how Christians should think of their body in general. This is the theological framework within which Paul's dicta on serving the belly rightly belong.

10.4   1 Cor. 10:7 in context: the belly – a tempting force in Corinth as in the wilderness

Introduction

The literary context of 1 Cor. 10:7 does not mention the stomach. But Paul quotes from Exod. 32:6, which emphasizes eating, drinking and playing, with a probable reference to sexual play as well: 'The people sat down to eat and drink, and they rose up to play.'[54] The Greek παίζειν is attested in an amorous meaning in Gen. 26:8 LXX. The context there makes it perfectly clear that it refers to sex, probably intercourse. Xenophon, *Symp.* 9:2 uses this verb to describe the relationship between Ariadne and Dionysus after they got drunk at a banquet. Since the marriage between the two was a popular theme in ancient literature as well as on vase paintings, it is likely that Paul's readers were familiar with the sexual reference of this term. The verb does not always, of course, refer to sexual activities, but Paul's argument in 1 Cor. 8–10 makes it likely that in 1 Cor. 10:7 he does so use it. That is, there is an emphasis on a way of living which recalls the unholy trinity associated with the belly. This emphasis on eating is in accordance with the whole of 1 Cor. 8:1–10:22.[55] It is, therefore, natural to look for the belly-*topos* and to see if it is in any

[54] Charles Perrot, 'Examples', p. 450 n. 10; Wayne A. Meeks, 'Rose Up', p. 70. If this is so, Paul is here very close to the so-called unholy trinity of eating, drinking and sex. For παίζειν as a reference to banqueting indulgence, see e.g. Athenaeus, *Deipn.* 8:336e. This reference is interesting for two reasons. In the first place, the verb is mentioned next to πίνειν, as in 1 Cor. 10:7. Furthermore, the context is about banquets, the lifestyle of Sardanapalus and other proverbial pleasure-lovers. In the traditions on Sardanapalus, παίζειν is exchangeable with ἀφροδισιάζειν, which is indeed relevant, since 1 Cor. 10:7 runs parallel to some versions of the Sardanapalus inscription (ἔσθιε, πῖνε, ἀφροδισίαζε); see chap. 4.1, section on 'The proverbial, figure of Sardanapalus'.

[55] The arguments for partition-theories fail to convince; for a discussion of this see Khiok-Khng Yeo, *Rhetorical Interaction in 1 Corinthians 8 and 10*, pp. 75–83. Yeo argues that 1 Cor. 8:1–13 and 10:1–22 reflect two different rhetorical situations. We therefore have here two different letters. The arguments for unity are, in my view, overwhelming, see e.g. Wolfgang Schrage, *Korinther*, pp. 212–13.

way appropriated in Paul's argument. Scholarship on these chapters has generated an enormous literature on different issues in the Pauline text. My presentation will be limited to what 1 Cor. 10:7 in its context can yield about Paul's way of enculturating a Hellenistic *topos* in his argument. The scholarly debate has focused on the eating of manna in the desert (1 Cor. 10:1,5), while less attention has been paid to the role of Israel's demand for meat in this tradition.[56] For our investigation the people's demand for food and their longing for the flesh-pots in Egypt are of importance.

Line of thought

The question of eating idol-meat runs throughout 1 Cor. 8:1–10:22; in fact, 10:23–11:1 continues the question of eating, but now on a related issue; food from the market and dinner-invitations. The setting is no longer the temples of Corinth, but the market and private homes. The social contexts addressed by Paul are meals in the temples (8:10), tables of the demons (10:21), the market (10:25), and invitations by outsiders (10:27). Gordon D. Fee has argued convincingly that 1 Cor. 8:1–13 and 10:14–22 are addressing the same problem, namely that some Christians had returned to their former practice of attending cultic meals in the temples.[57]

1 Cor. 9:1–23 represents a development of one particular element in Paul's argument in chap. 8, namely the willingness to renounce one's rights for the good of Christian brothers and sisters. 1 Cor. 9:24–7 marks a transition between chaps. 9 and 10.[58] It has repercussions for the previous discussion on willingness to renounce. But the emphasis is on abstaining and training like the athletes for the sake of winning the prize, which prepares for Paul's exhortations in 1 Cor. 10:1–13.[59] This is most clearly seen in the basic logic of both sections (see below): participation of all,

[56] See e.g. Paul Douglas Gardner, *Gifts of God*, pp. 121–33 who gives a review of the wilderness-traditions in Jewish literature. The demand for food is not sufficiently noted in his presentation. This is also the case in Bruce J. Malina, *The Palestinian Manna Tradition*. An exception is here Gary D. Collier, '"That We Might Not Crave Evil"'.

[57] Gordon D. Fee, *Corinthians*, pp. 358–63. He is followed by Derek Newton, *Deity and Diet*, pp. 266–8 and Peter D. Gooch, *Dangerous Food*, pp. 79–94. This implies that Paul's logic in chap. 8 is provisional, and is brought to an end in 10:14–22. This is due to Paul's persuasive strategy; see Gooch pp. 83–84. Fee's position has been contested by e.g. Bruce N. Fisk, 'Eating Meat Offered to Idols'. In my opinion Fisk seems to underestimate the fact that meals in the temples easily, and probably usually, carried a cultic meaning as well. His dichotomy between social and religious meals is thus problematic. Newton has convincingly demonstrated that 'the ancient world knew no such distinction' (p. 389).

[58] So also Wendell Lee Willis, *Idolmeat*, pp. 273–4; Samuel Vollenweider, *Freiheit*, pp. 220–1.

[59] See also Victor C. Pfitzner, *Paul and the Agon Motif*, pp. 82–4; Otto Schwankl, 'Lauft', pp. 188–90.

but success only for some (or one – owing to the athletic imagery in 9:24–7). The second-person plural imperative οὕτως τρέχετε (9:24) anticipates Paul's concern in 10:1–13. The metaphor of running to win the prize is tantamount to the imperatives in 10:12: βλεπέτω μὴ πέσῃ and 10:14: φεύγετε ἀπὸ τῆς εἰδωλολατρίας. The athletic imagery with its focus on ἐγκράτεια, self-control and self-denial (v. 24)[60] as well as enslaving the body (v. 26), thus set the scene for the following passage, 10:1–13.[61] For the purpose of this study this is, of course, not without significance: Paul here presses some well-known 'buttons': the athlete and the struggle to master desires. To an ancient reader it would come as no surprise if the following includes the belly-*topos* as well; the ground seems well prepared for the belly-*topos* to appear. The perspective of mastering the desires is the starting point from which Paul now proceeds to discuss a question of food, namely idol-meat.

Paul's argument in 1 Cor. 10:1–22

Paul is involved in deliberative rhetoric; he is warning his readers to keep away from idol-meat served in the temple-precincts or associated with the activities there, and thus to make them continue in faith.[62] As in his letter to the Philippians, Paul makes use of examples to drive home his point. In 1 Cor. 9:24–7, Paul provides the positive example of the athletes. This brings us close to Phil. 3, where the struggle of athletes for future victory formed the example to be emulated by the converts in a clear contrast to the belly-devotees. Being determined to win the victory, athletes work hard to achieve this, which means that they are willing to abstain from all things jeopardizing their goal. The example of the athletes and that of Paul himself[63] both serve the same purpose; they live according to what the prize requires of them.

In 1 Cor. 10:1–13 Paul turns to his contrasting example. He wants his readers to learn a lesson from how their ancestors failed.[64] The basic

---

[60] Ibid. p. 185 emphasizes the self-discipline of the athletes as an example for the believers.

[61] This connection is also emphasized by Derek Newton, *Deity and Diet*, pp. 323–6.

[62] Judith Gundry Volf, *Paul and Perseverance*, pp. 120–30 makes v. 12 'Beware not to fall' the centre of her presentation of the text.

[63] Take notice of 1st person sing. in 1 Cor. 9:26–7.

[64] Both positive and negative examples are taken from comparisons close to the recipients of the letter. They were all familiar with the Isthmian Games which were held in the vicinity every second year. Their own 'fathers' make up the negative example. It is surprising that Paul speaks of the desert-generation of Jews as ancestors of the believers in this Roman colony in Greece. It is possibly evidence of his theology of justification by faith, more

structure and logic of his argument is seen in the fivefold πάντες: all were under the cloud, all passed through the sea, i.e. all were 'baptized into Moses', all drank and ate the same spiritual food. Although God's presence and blessings in the desert embraced all, He was nevertheless pleased only with some of them: οὐκ ἐν τοῖς πλείοσιν (v. 5) is sharply contrasted to πάντες in vv. 1–5, and followed by τινες αὐτῶν (vv. 7, 8, 9, 10). Both πάντες and τινες refer to the fathers mentioned in v. 1b. Paul reminds the Corinthians about their Jewish ancestors; he wants them to learn a lesson from them.

His argument builds upon a contrast between on the one hand the gifts of God which were conferred upon all and, on the other hand, their complaints. God's gifts were in vain since they consistently turned their back on Him. The fathers were tempted and partook of idolatry and sexual immorality; they tested the Lord and grumbled against Him. Of special interest for this study is the fact that Paul – in accordance with the Exodus traditions – conceives of idolatry, and the Golden Calf story in particular, as caused by their desires and their distrust of God. In the wilderness-traditions, which clearly form the substructure of Paul's argument, their desire means their demand for food. The desire of the fathers prefigured the challenge of idol-meat which the Corinthian Christians were now facing (vv. 6, 11): they both craved the wrong kind of food.

The believers in Corinth and their ancestors find themselves in the same situation, namely that of being tempted.[65] In their fathers the believers are presented with analogies, from whose stories they are expected to revise their practices in the question of participating in temple-meals. To assure his readers of the authority of this analogy, Paul quotes from Exod. 32:6 (1 Cor. 10:7). This verse relates to key elements in the story of the Golden Calf.[66] The introductory ὥστε in 1 Cor. 10:12 suggests its conclusive character. 'The history of Israel was recounted to show that God's people may not sin safely, presuming upon their election.'[67] It is a matter of standing or falling.

The style of 1 Cor. 10:14–22 differs from the first part of the chapter, but the two are held together by διόπερ (v. 14), which draws the issue of

---

fully witnessed in Galatians and Romans. By faith in Christ, the Corinthian believers have become members of God's people. The history of Israel has thus become theirs as well.

[65] Note the fourfold use of πειράζειν and cognates.

[66] Not to forget the close similarity to the material on Sardanapalus; see chap. 4.1, section on 'The proverbial figure of Sardanapalus'.

[67] Wendell Lee Willis, *Idolmeat*, p. 155. I agree with Willis (p. 156) that it is not necessary to think that the Corinthians were over-confident owing to the power of the 'sacraments'. Their confidence is simply grounded in their status as believers.

idol-meat to a conclusion. It is not possible to be a guest both at Christ's table and that of the demons. By conceiving of eating idol-food within the temple as enjoying fellowship with demons,[68] Paul has closed the issue. At the end of the day the discussion is a question of to whom the Corinthians belong, Christ or the demons.

We noted that the end of chap. 9 opened up a perspective from which to read 1 Cor. 10:1–13, namely mastery of desires. This impression is continued in this section itself:

- it is a matter of eating, drinking and sex (v. 7)
- a key word is ἐπιθυμία and cognates (twice in v. 6); this also links Paul's text to Old Testament traditions on Israel's demand for food and distrust of God in the wilderness
- temptation (πειράζειν and cognates appear twice in v. 9 and three times in v. 13)

In other words, Paul's text is replete with elements drawn from the common theme of mastering the desires. That food, drink, and sex are mentioned is, of course, of special significance. These elements of mastering the desires are here steeped in Old Testament texts, among which Exodus and wilderness traditions are prominent. By bringing together well-known elements from ancient mastery discussions and Exodus traditions, Paul is here echoing Philo's perspective on the Exodus narratives. Philo's interpretation is surely more direct and extensive. But having noticed the basic similarity between Paul's and Philo's argument, it is worth pondering this further.

Reading 1 Cor. 10:1–13 in the light of its subtext

Paul's argument has rightly been called a midrash, paraphrasis or exposition of a collection of Old Testament texts.[69] A glance at the margin of

---

[68] While the argument in 1 Cor. 8:4 draws on the tradition of denying the existence of idols, and even ridiculing them (e.g. Isa. 40:19–20; 41:6–7; 44:12–17; Jer. 10:3–5; Wisd 13:10–19; 14:17–21), 1 Cor. 10:19–21 draws on another tradition; evil spirits are working through the idols (Ps. 95:5 LXX: πάντες οἱ θεοὶ τῶν ἐθνῶν δαιμονία; Bar. 4:7; 1 *Enoch* 19:1); for further references on the demon-tradition, see Oskar Skarsaune, *Proof from Prophecy*, pp. 368–9.

[69] See Wayne A. Meeks, 'Rose Up'; Hans Josef Klauck, *Herrenmahl*, pp. 252–3; Khiok-Khng Yeo, *Rhetorical Interaction in 1 Corinthians 8 and 10*, pp. 157–62. Further references are found in the works mentioned here. Gary D. Collier, 'That We Might Not Crave Evil', pp. 63–7 argues that Num. 11 is the main text in Paul's exposition, and that Exod. 32:6 is a midrashic interpretation of that text. Meeks raised the question whether 1 Cor. 10:1–13 was a homily, a self-contained unit of Christian or non-Christian composition; this is not a matter of interest for this study.

the Nestle–Aland 27th edition is itself sufficient to prove that the text is replete with Old Testament references. Underlying the entire structure of the passage is a subtle use of Scripture. Besides a retelling of some key events of the Exodus tradition, Paul brings to mind a number of texts, such as Exod. 13; 14; 16; 17; Num. 11; 14; 16; 17; 21; 25; Ps. 77; 105 (LXX),[70] and he quotes from Exod. 32:6. From these texts a picture of a disobedient people emerges. When faced with challenges they forgot the works of the Lord in the past and complained. The people lost faith in God's providence and guidance in the desert; they relapsed into eating, drinking and sex (1 Cor. 10:7); i.e. the desires of the belly, according to the material we have uncovered in this study. The demand for food and meat in particular are recurrent themes in the story Paul is recalling to his readers. In the Old Testament the demand of the fathers for meat is a symbol of their lack of faith in God. This element in the Exodus narrative forms the sub-text of Paul's injunctions in 1 Cor. 10.

As pointed out by Wayne A. Meeks, Num. 11 is a text built upon a word-play on the Hebrew verb 'to desire',[71] which in LXX is rendered by ἐπιθυμία and cognates. Ps. 105:14 (LXX) has the same verb, and it appears as well in Paul's own text (1 Cor. 10:6). What the Israelites desired was meat (Num. 11:4,13, cf. Exod. 16:3; 17:3; 20:27–9; Num. 16:13–14; 21:5). This means that Paul is not working with a loose analogy between his addressees and their fathers; his words of exhortation have at their centre a correlation which is quite precise, namely the desire for meat. Charles K. Barrett says that 'there is nothing to suggest that complaining was a special failing of the Corinthians'.[72] This is to underestimate the link between the desert generation and the Corinthian problem which Paul elaborates in this chapter, and to overlook how subtly Paul is working with biblical traditions here. The language of complaint is taken from the Old Testament incidents, and does not suggest that the Corinthians were doing the same. But the desire of some of the Corinthians to join the tables in the temples is a passion for forbidden food, just as the Jews were longing for meat, not finding God's providence sufficient. In a text where the author works with common patterns (typology) between the past and the present, the correspondence between the wilderness and the Corinthian situation does not necessarily imply that Corinthian believers were complaining, but it does imply that the two must be seen together.

---

[70] Since Paul's use of the Old Testament is not concerned primarily with particular verses, but with narrative events, I give only the chapters here.

[71] Wayne A. Meeks, 'Rose Up', p. 68 cf. p. 71; Margareth Mitchell, *Reconciliation*, pp. 138–9 n. 439.

[72] Charles K. Barrett, *Corinthians*, p. 226.

The whole tenor of Paul's text evokes the cries for the flesh-pots in Egypt, so widely attested in the Exodus traditions. The underlying Old Testament texts speak of Israel's sin in terms of eating, which is here interpreted in the light of ἐπιθυμία.[73] In particular the demand for food and meat is echoed in Paul's use of γογγύζειν in 1 Cor. 10:10. This verb and its cognates are used in the Septuagint with reference to the lack of confidence in God (e.g. Isa. 30:12; 58:9). The terminology occurs frequently to describe the people's distrust of God during the years in the wilderness (Num. 14:2; 16:11, 41; Deut. 1:27; Josh. 9:18), and it is usually rendered 'to murmur'. The density of this terminology is especially high in texts about demands for food, meat and drink in the desert (Exod 15:24; 16:2–3.7–8; 17:3; Num. 11:1.4; Ps. 105(106):15). In Exod. 16:4 and 17:2 this complaint is seen in terms of testing (πειράζειν). The context of murmuring is apparent in Exod. 16:2–3. The people missed the meat (κρέα) of Egypt (cf. v. 8: κρέα φαγεῖν) and desired to eat bread abundantly (εἰς πλησμονήν). Num. 11:4–5 mentions the whole menu they were longing for, where again κρέα heads the list.[74] Their appetite is introduced in the following way: . . . ἐπεθύμησεν ἐπιθυμίαν.

The Exodus narrative is a story about how the demands of the belly overcame belief in God's providence. Paul reminds his readers that demand for food and falling away might be two sides of the same coin. For this view Paul could easily find Old Testament references. One of the prominent examples is Ps. 78, which provides a review of Israel's history:

> They tested God in their heart by demanding the food they craved.[75] They spoke against God, saying, 'Can God spread a table (τράπεζα) in the wilderness? . . . can he also give bread or provide meat[76] for his people?' (Ps. 78:18–20; LXX:Ps. 77)

Paul is thus in conformity with the Old Testament in arguing that the desire for meat – in Corinth idol-meat – might lead to apostasy. Paul is retelling the Exodus narrative by bringing it to mind, weaving into it hortatory elements. He wants them to draw a lesson from this example taken from Israel's past: 'Flee from the worship of the idols' (1 Cor. 10:14).

---

[73] This is also noted by Gary D. Collier, "That We Might Not Crave Evil", pp. 67–71.

[74] It is worth noticing that Paul in 1 Cor. 8:13, the first steps of the argument to be continued in chap. 10, puts the issue very clearly; it is a matter of φαγεῖν κρέα.

[75] LXX here has αἰτεῖν, but in v. 30, which is a parallel dictum, ἐπιθυμία refers to the demand for food in the desert.

[76] The Hebrew text here has שאר, which means 'meat'; see BDF s.v. LXX has rendered this as a phrase, ἑτοιμάσαι τράπεζαν. In v. 27 LXX renders שאר as σάρξ, which is here the meat of birds.

Paul is fighting apostasy. He does so with the help of Old Testament heritage, emphasizing the seriousness of joining the idols. He describes the
situation related to eating of idol-meat in Corinth in biblical terms, such
as idolatry, temptation, falling away, protesting or testing God, joining the
demons, fornication. Alongside this biblical terminology, Paul speaks of
fighting apostasy in terms of mastering the desires as well. The question
of eating idol-meat is also a matter of self-control, of fighting the desires
(ἐπιθυμία); i.e. eating, drinking and sex. Like athletes (cf. 1 Cor. 9), the
Christians are expected to control the dangerous temptations of the life
associated with meals in the temple. Here Hellenistic moral philosophy
traditions and the Exodus narrative with special emphasis on Exod. 32:6
(1 Cor. 10:7) are merging.

Paul fights apostasy in language quite similar to the theme of 'how to
master the desires'. This is interesting for at least two reasons. In the first
place, partaking of food in the temple precincts was a real temptation
since the very fabric of idolatry was interwoven with the social life of
the city.[77] Paul's reference to self-control and mastering the desire for
meat thus shows us the temptations in Corinth. The Christians faced
temptations closely related to basic human needs, such as food, drink,
sex, and fellowship.

In the second place, by presenting the issue of idol-meat within the
framework of mastering the desires of food and sex, Paul brings the text
close to the belly-*topos*. Is Paul here really warning his converts not to
become devoted to the demands of the belly? Although Paul does not
mention the stomach directly, he draws heavily on the Exodus narrative
in which the demand for food and meat are essential. The following will
argue that this question is to be answered affirmatively. We do this by turning to Philo's appropriation of the belly-*topos* in the Exodus narrative.[78]

Paul's use of the Old Testament in this text reaches its peak in 1 Cor.
10:7 where he quotes from Exod. 32:6,[79] i.e. from the story of the Golden

---

[77] On the social nature of the cultic meals, see Wendel Lee Willis, *Idolmeat*, pp. 47–64;
Peter D. Gooch, *Dangerous Food*, pp. 26–46 mentions weddings, birthdays, funerals, special
occasions of thanksgiving. 'It would not be possible to maintain social relationships with
those outside the Christian circle without a major adjustment and the serious possibility of
misunderstanding and hostility' (p. 46). Meals in antiquity were expressions of friendship;
see Karl Olav Sandnes, 'Omvendelse og gjestevennskap'. Bruce W. Winter, 'Theological
and Ethical Responses', p. 222 n. 48 mentions papyri with examples of invitations to dine
in the temple for various occasions. Meals in Corinthian temples were multi-dimensional
and multi-functional, as demonstrated by Derek Newton, *Deity and Diet*, pp. 226–57.

[78] We have already seen that to Philo, Egypt and Exodus were major symbols of the
bodily desires and the need to abandon them, or at least bring them under control.

[79] In chap. 11 we will see how this text is frequently mentioned in Patristic texts as an

Calf. In Jewish tradition this was the classic instance of idolatry.[80] We will concentrate on Philo's view of the episode of the Golden Calf and the Israelites' demand for food while in the desert. Philo consistently sees the episode of the Golden Calf as a turning away from spiritual things to the material world, and embracing the needs of the body in particular; it is a story about Israel turning from heavenly to earthly needs. The Calf is a symbol of Egypt, which represents the body and bodily needs;[81] he considers the calf an imitation of the Egyptian Apis.[82] According to Philo's logic, the Golden Calf, in fact, represents a temptation to bring the people back to Egypt, to the land of the belly.

With this point of departure, the story is necessarily seen as a narrative of Israel's failure to master their desires. This is clear in the two texts where Philo comments most extensively on the incident of the Golden Calf (*Mos.* 2:159–73 and *Spec.* 3:124–7). Both texts emphasize that this happened because of revelry, and drinking in particular. The people were intoxicated by wine and folly (οἶνος καὶ ἀφροσύνη) (*Mos.* 2:162 cf. *Spec.* 3:125–6).[83] It is, therefore, not surprising that Exod. 32 appears in Philo's treatise on drunkenness (*De Ebrietate*), where the Golden Calf episode is seen as a text about the fight against bodily desires (95–100, 124, 127).

In *Post.* 155, 158–9, 162–3, Philo says that Exod. 32 is about the bodily desires, and the temptations coming from the stomach and the organs below it in particular.[84] Hence, Philo views the Golden Calf episode as a story about what might happen when the stomach and sexual organs are in control. The perspective of fighting the bodily desires is prominent in his comments on the killing of the sinners according to Exod. 32:27–9:

> No? They are cutting away from their own hearts and minds all that is near and dear to the flesh (σάρξ). They hold that it befits those who are to be ministers to the only wise Being, to estrange themselves from all that belongs to the world of creation, and to

example of the belly-worship of the Jews. The textual as well as cultural substructure, which we are here attempting to uncover, is there spelled out in full.

[80] See e.g. Leivy Smolar, Moshe Aberbach, 'Golden Calf'; Scott Hafemann, 'Golden Calf'.

[81] For references see above in chap. 7.2 of this study; see e.g. *Ebr.* 95; *Sacr.* 130.

[82] In a passage dealing with the enslaving power of food and sex, Aristotle mentions the ox in Egypt, which is revered as Apis. This ox has a 'greater abundance of such indulgences than many monarchs' (*Eud. Eth.* 1216a1–2).

[83] *Mos.* 2:162 speaks in a way in which Philo elsewhere addresses the ruling belly; e.g. *Spec.* 4:127.

[84] Cf. *Fug.* 90–2 where the incident is seen as an excision of ἐπιθυμία.

> treat all such as bitter and deadly foes. Therefore, we shall kill
> our 'brother' – not a man, but the soul's brother, the body; that
> is, we shall dissever the passion-loving (φιλοπαθές) and mortal
> element from the virtue-loving and divine.   (*Ebr.* 69–70)

Finally, Philo's emphasis on the drinking on this occasion has repercussions for his presentation of the commandment on adultery (*Spec.*
3:8–82), an obstacle to gluttony (ὀψοφαγία), unlawful sexual relationships and wine-bibbing (οἰνοφλυγία). It is not difficult to recognize here
the unholy trinity of eating, drinking and sex so commonly associated
with the belly-*topos* in antiquity. The commandment not to commit adultery is aimed at putting restraints on those who crave ἐπιθυμία. To Philo,
this powerful desire derived from 'pleasures of the belly and the parts
below it' (*Spec.* 3:43). The relationship between the tempting power of
the belly and the Golden Calf story is further strengthened in the way
Philo presents the demand for food in the desert.

With a reference to Num. 11, Philo gives some comments on the people
demanding food in the wilderness (*Spec.* 4:126–31, cf. *Her.* 79–80). They
acted like γαστρίμαργοι, gluttons. Their belly was uncontrolled. Even
when God provided for them, they grabbed food out of ἐπιθυμία, and acted
out of greed. Hence the place was called 'Monuments of Lust' (*Spec.*
4:130, cf. *Migr.* 155).[85] It is a warning example against self-pleasing
indulgence. Philo is here involved in an exegesis of one of the key texts
underlying the structure of 1 Cor. 10:1–13.

If we are to have an adequate understanding of Philo's exegesis, we
must view it in the light of the perspective in which Philo has embedded
Spec. 4:126–31. This section belongs to his discussion of the particular
laws related to the commandment 'thou shalt not covet (οὐκ ἐπιθυμήσεις)'.
This commandment leads to a long discussion on how to master the
passions, running from 79 to 131.[86] According to Philo Moses had a
special concern for controlling food and drink, or the belly (*Spec.* 4:96–
7), because it is the bodily region from which desire for both food and
sex arise (94). When desire (ἐπιθυμία) takes control of the belly

> it produces gourmands, insatiable, debauched, eagerly pursuing
> a loose and dissolute life, delighting in wine-bibbing and glut-
> tonous feeding, base slaves to strong drink and fish[87] and dainty

[85] The LXX has μνήματα τῆς ἐπιθυμίας (Num. 11:34).

[86] For a survey of how Philo's exposition of the laws is structured, see Peder Borgen,
'Philo of Alexandria – A Systematic Philosopher or an Eclectic Editor?'

[87] On fish as a sign of luxury, see James Davidson, *Courtesans and Fishcakes*, pp. 3–19.

cakes, sneaking like greedy little dogs around banqueting halls
and tables.   (*Spec.* 4:91; cf. §113)

In other words, Moses' commandment not to covet had been given out
of special concern with the issues related to food and drink (97). The aim
of the commandment is to foster self-control (ἐγκράτεια) (*Spec.* 4:99,
101) in these matters.[88] Within this perspective and context it is clear
that Philo's comments on the demand for food in Num. 11[89] are intended
to give some examples of people who were controlled by their belly.
This is stated explicitly in the introductory words of *Spec.* 4:126: 'Moses
censures some of his own day as gluttons (γαστριμάργους) who suppose
that wanton self-indulgence is the height of happiness (ἐν τοῖς μάλιστα
εἶναι ὑπολαμβάνοντας)'. Philo's language brings to mind the ancient
discussion of the highest good. The Jews in the desert are described in
the light of the traditional Epicurean definition of the supreme good. The
Exodus traditions about the people's food-complaint is explained within
the philosophical pattern in which the belly-*topos* works in antiquity.
Philo has entirely appropriated this *topos* into the Exodus narrative on
the demand for food in the desert.

Philo's exegesis of the demand for food in the desert is indeed helpful
to a re-reading of Paul's injunctions in 1 Cor. 10. I am not claiming that
Paul and Philo can be put side by side; the differences between the two
are substantial. On the other hand they are both commenting on the same
biblical texts. Both emphasize the demand for food and meat as signs of
unbelief.[90] Philo gives these texts a name; they are stories about people
unable to control their belly. Paul does not spell out a similar name, but his
argument brings him close to it. After all, both of them are commenting
on the demand for food as the beginning of apostasy within a context of
ἐγκράτεια and ἐπιθυμία. Philo sees the Jews in the wilderness as examples
of an Epicurean lifestyle, while Paul later in this letter (1 Cor. 15:32) (see
above) does the same with reference to Christians whose main concern
is with eating and drinking. Paul's whole argument aims at bringing his
converts to look anew at the question of participating in meals in the
temples, and to do so in the light of the material which is presented here

---

[88] See also *Spec.* 2:195–9 where God providing food in the wilderness is seen as a gift
of God to those who controlled 'the belly and the organs below it'.

[89] Cf. Philo's comments on Exod. 16 where he makes a quotation out of the people's
demand for food. Moses is blamed for he 'tortures our bellies with hunger' (*Mos.* 1:191–5).

[90] The idea that abundance in food might cause the people to forget about God is a
significant part of the Jewish faith; actually, it is laid down as related to the creed (*Shema*)
itself (Deut. 6:10–12).

as the subtext of his argument; a subtext which brings us close to Philo's biblical appropriation of the belly-*topos*.

Sex as well?

So far we have been concerned mainly with the question of food and drink. However, the quotation from Exod. 32:6, as we have seen, is probably a reference to sexual sin as well.[91] Furthermore, this is suggested by 1 Cor. 10:8, where Paul urges the Corinthians not to indulge in sexual immorality (πορνεύειν) as did their fathers in the desert. The question can be put in this way: Does Paul's concern in 1 Cor. 10 go beyond the question of idolatry and include a warning against sexual sin? Some scholars consider this to be a kind of a sidetrack in Paul's argument; his only concern is with the idol-meat served in the temples. The appearance of πορνεία must then be seen in the light of this. Hence it is a traditional biblical metaphor for idolatry. Turning one's back on God is often described in terms of deceiving a beloved (e.g. Hos. 1–3; Ps. 106:39).[92] A metaphorical reading of v. 8 along these lines, however, in my opinion represents a narrowing of Paul's perspective.

In 1 Cor. 5:1–11, Paul speaks of a man living with his father's wife, and some Corinthian believers who were sleeping with prostitutes (1 Cor. 6:12–20). The noun πορνεία is within the extant Corinthian correspondence found in 1 Cor. 5:1; 6:13, 18; 7:2; 2 Cor. 12:21; πόρνη in 1 Cor. 6:15–16; πόρνος in 1 Cor. 5:9–11; 6:9; the verb πορνεύειν in 1 Cor. 6:18. None of these occurrences deal with sex as a metaphor. An interpretation of 1 Cor. 10:8 which is in accordance with this literal sense is to be preferred. This means that fornication and temple-meals are associated in Paul's text. It is, however, more difficult to define this further. Probably Paul is refering to 'sexual play or amusement after the idolfeast'.[93] There

---

[91] As we have seen elsewhere, to Philo the Serpent in Gen. 3 is a symbol of ἐπιθυμία or ἡδονή. In *Leg.* 2:71–85 he explains this by saying that the movements of both are tortuous and variable. As for pleasure, it is occasioned by sight, hearing, taste, smell, touch and sexual intercourse in particular. Movements during intercourse may be likened to a moving snake (*Leg.* 2:74). Philo applies this to his reading of the people being killed by snakes in the wilderness (Num. 21). The only means of fighting the snakes was self-mastery (σωφροσύνη), whose symbol is the serpent raised by Moses at God's bidding.

[92] So e.g. Hans Josef Klauck, *Herrenmahl*, p. 256. Klauck refers to Num. 25:1–5 as well. I consider that reference to be misleading. The sexual relationship mentioned there is quite real; it is not a metaphor for idolatry as such. The real point of Num. 25 is that idolatry paves the way for sexual sin as well (cf. Wisd. 14:22–7), which brings us closer to the issue of 1 Cor. 10.

[93] Ben Witherington III, *Conflict*, p. 221. So also Gordon D. Fee, *Corinthians*, p. 455; Robert Jewett, *Anthropological Terms*, p. 258.

are some texts indicating that temples could become places for sexual sin.[94] This does not necessarily imply temple prostitution,[95] but may be a reference to the common practice that temple banquets included a sexual 'after-dinner' as well.[96] This means that Paul is not necessarily thinking of sacred prostitution here, which also makes it easier to link 1 Cor. 10 to the other references to πορνεία in this letter.[97] In other words, eating, drinking and sex are allied with apostasy in 1 Cor. 10; and it all derives from their craving for food, i.e. to participate in temple-meals.

Why are food and sex allies of apostasy and idolatry? The answer is provided by the Exodus traditions on which Paul is drawing. The demand for food was a practical denial of God's providence.[98] God was not seen as a sufficient provider; this mistrust was the beginning of apostasy. The temptation to participate in temple-meals in Corinth works very much in the same way. This is the lesson which Paul wants his converts to draw from Israel's past.

[94] The most famous being Josephus, *Ant.* 18:65–80 about Paulina, who engaged in sex during the night in the temple, being deceived into believing that she was having intercourse with Anubis. In an encomium for the Roman people, Dionysius of Halicarnassus compares the Greeks, saying that 'they have no Corybantic frenzies, no begging the colour of religion, no bacchanals or secret mysteries, no all-night-vigils of men and women together in the temples, nor any mummery of this kind' (*Rom. Ant.* 2:19.2). This is an indirect witness to the existence of temple-sex among Greeks, very similar to what Josephus relates about Paulina. Within a passage on prostitutes, Athenaeus, *Deipn.* 13:573c–574d, focuses on the role played by prostitutes and courtesans in the cult of Aphrodite in Corinth. They offered petitions in the temples, and, on the festival dedicated to their patron, they revelled and got drunk (μεθύειν). It is questionable, however, whether this practice continued in Paul's time. Wolfgang Schrage, *Korinther*, pp. 399–400 mentions some other references as well, but concludes that there is not sufficient evidence to assume temple-prostitution in Corinth in Paul's time.

[95] Brian S. Rosner, 'Temple Prostitution' has recently argued that temple, or cultic, prostitution was practised in Corinth at Paul's time. His understanding of temple prostitution is, however, too wide. In his article it refers to the well-known link between feasting and sex, with prostitutes who might have been hired for special occasions (see e.g. p. 350). This is not necessarily sacred prostitution. Rosner argues for the existence of sacred prostitution by pointing out that Paul's argument is couched in terms of religious allegiance, as well as the obvious links to idolatry in 1 Cor. 6. This argument is hardly convincing, since Paul is prone to extend the meaning of idolatry to unlawful sex in general. To Paul, illicit sexual relationships might well be called idolatry; this is implicit in his use of the belly-*topos*. Having the belly as god often refers to sexual appetite as well. Being devoted to the sexual appetite can therefore apply to profane sex as well. By themselves therefore terms of religious allegiance cannot justify speaking of temple prostitution.

[96] See chap. 5 of this study.

[97] Cf. Paul Douglas Gardner, *Gifts of God*, p. 151: 'Since instances of πορνεία had already been addressed in the letter, perhaps the application of this material was meant to be wider'.

[98] How one relates to food is indeed a matter of trust or distrust in God; see e.g. *Spec.* 2:193–203. This is also the essence of Paul's understanding of 'sufficiency' in Phil. 4:11–13; see chap. 8.2 of this study.

10.5   Belly and body in 1 Corinthians

In our presentation we have made some significant observations. It is now
a matter of putting them together and seeing from what context Paul's
concern for the desires of the belly emerges in this letter. 1 Corinthians is
the letter in which Paul's theology of the body is most prominent.[99] Inspired by the work of social anthropologists such as Mary Douglas, there
is a growing consensus that body and cosmology belong together. In other
words, the body is perceived according to fundamental preconceptions.[100]
A connection between Paul's dicta on belly-worship and his basic convictions is therefore to be expected.

In this epistle Paul's theology of the body seems to develop from his
firm hope in 'a body, even in heaven'.[101] This is, of course, most clearly
voiced in 1 Cor. 15 in which a dispute emerges over the body and bodily
activities, a dispute which is discernible also in other texts.[102] Paul's
warning against obeying the demands of the belly in 1 Cor. 15:32 is
sandwiched between a discourse on the resurrection and on what kind of
body this will bring. As pointed out by Jerome H. Neyrey, this discourse
is governed by the principle mentioned in v. 50: 'flesh and blood cannot
inherit the kingdom of God'. This implies transformation and change of
the body, into a spiritual, glorious, celestial and resurrected body; i.e. a
body appropriate for coming into God's presence. The transformation is
already under way, owing to the body's participation in Christ's glorious
body.[103] This brings us to a second implication of the principle uttered
by Paul in v. 50. Since flesh has no part in the transformed body, the
resurrection of a transformed body carries moral demands which are
extended into daily life among Paul's converts. Paul's ethical imperatives
on how to make use of the body were based on the resurrection both
of Jesus and the believers. Visiting prostitutes, whether at brothels or
banquets (1 Cor. 6:12–20), eating in an idol's temple (1 Cor. 8–10), and
gluttony at the Lord's table (1 Cor. 11:17–34) – all represent issues which
Paul is rethinking in the light of his perception of the transformed body.

[99] It is not therefore surprising that a renewed focus on the body in Paul's theology has
this particular letter as its starting point; see e.g. Jerome H. Neyrey, *Paul*, pp. 102–46; Dale
B. Martin, *Corinthian Body*.
[100] See Jerome H. Neyrey, *Paul*, pp. 104–14 with references.
[101] This phrase is taken from Jerome H. Neyrey, *Paul*, p. 140.
[102] The question whether Paul is here confronted with a single group in the different
issues is outside our ambit here. In these issues appears, however, a common body ideology
to which Paul responds.
[103] See chap. 1.4.

Moreover, all these texts are imbued with the language of worshipping the desires of the belly.

In 1 Cor. 6:12–20 Paul insists that body matters for how believers lead their lives in questions of food and sex; neither is irrelevant to the individual's freedom to act. We are familiar with the substance of his argument from preceding chapters in this investigation. The body participates in the resurrected Christ (1 Cor. 6:15) and belongs to him exclusively. Furthermore, the body is the dwelling place of the Spirit; this forms a bridge to chap. 15 about the transformed body. Present bodily existence is, therefore, a vehicle not for self-pleasing belly-worship, but for glorifying God. Paul urges his converts to control the body by restraining the activities involved in worshipping the belly. Paul's regulations on bodily activities are clearly envisaged in the athletic metaphor (1 Cor. 9:24–7), which plays a significant role in his attempt to control the belly. In 1 Cor. 6 Paul sees the body of the individual as endangered by impurity or pollution. The holiness of the body, which implies the purity of Christ as well, is violated by an improper lifestyle of the belly.[104]

What underlies this passage in particular is two different ideologies of the body,[105] in short, Paul's restraint or control of the body versus freedom; Paul's concern for the holiness of the body versus the Corinthians' unconcern about its pollution. In other words, Paul considered the improper lifestyle of belly not only to violate rules and ethical ideals, but also to endanger the identity of his converts. To some Corinthians the human body was of no importance. They justified hedonism, epitomized in the belly and sex, by reference both to Paul's abandonment of Jewish purity rules and to an anthropology that Nature's demands did not affect the soul.

In so far as it is expressed at all, in 1 Cor. 11:17–34 Paul's concern for the body appears in terms of division of the fellowship. The bodily problem of individuals is not addressed. It is, however, worth noting that Paul is addressing gluttony within a discourse on proper worship. This continues the perspective of the preceding chapter; craving for food might well develop into bodily idolatry. The body is then a vehicle not for glorifying God, but for pleasing oneself. At the centre of true worship in 1 Cor. 11:17–34 is the celebration of Christ's death. This makes bodily

---

[104] That Paul's body-theology is at the centre of this text, is emphasized also by Bruce N. Fisk, 'ΠΟΡΝΕΥΕΙΝ'.

[105] See Jerome H. Neyrey, *Paul*, 115–19, 125–8. On p. 128 Neyrey lists the main differences.

demands of the stomach, and thus brings to mind Phil. 3, where belly-worship and enmity with Christ's cross were seen as allied.

Dale B. Martin has attempted to explain the conflicting views on the body operating in 1 Corinthians as derived from two different ancient theories of disease aetiology.[106] The 'aetiology of balance' attributes disease to imbalance in the proper hierarchy of the body. This aetiology is found among physicans who prescribe the proper balance characteristic of the natural and healthy body. Health is then defined as a harmonious mixture of bile, phlegm, water, blood, pneuma, heat or cold, dryness or moisture. Some Corinthians took this view of the body as a starting-point for the bodily activities which Paul addresses in this epistle. It makes sense within this theory to speak of the Corinthians' philosophical justification of their hedonism: Nature permits us to obey her demands.

On the other hand, the 'invasion aetiology' conceives of the body as a scene for a cosmic battle between good and evil forces. The body is under constant danger of being invaded by supernatural powers, or of being polluted. This was the popular mentality. According to Martin, 'Paul operates by a logic of invasion, with its anxieties about purity and firm boundaries.'[107] These two aetiologies explain that some among the Corinthains claimed that the body was irrelevant to believers, while Paul argued that bodily activities easily turned into entrances for pollution of the individual, of Christ himself, and of the fellowship.

Martin thus sees Paul as primarily concerned with dangers coming from the outside.[108] How does this fit our findings on the body in 1 Corinthians? The Corinthian texts which I have considered leave the distinction between inside and outside somewhat blurred. When pollution and idolatry come from within, i.e. from ἐπιθυμία or belly, 'invasion' is hardly a proper term. The danger from within arises when the body is not properly controlled. When control is conceived in terms of moderation, as we have seen to be important in Paul's culture, this implies that control is not adequately described as typical of an invasion aetiology. Since control and moderation are not necessarily contrasts, balance and invasion theories might at some point converge. In antiquity a belly that is not under control was perceived as reigning; i.e. the proper hierarchy of the body was destroyed. In my view, this demonstrates that Martin's explanation has not exhausted the material in this epistle. The belly-texts

---

[106] Dale B. Martin, *Corinthian Body*, pp. 139–64, 197. Martin considers that this difference between the groups of Strong and Weak, as he calls them, covers all the issues in dispute among the Corinthians.

[107] Ibid. p. 163.

[108] The motion from the outside is explicitly emphasized; see e.g. p. 178.

open up a more complex picture than that provided by his two disease aetiologies.

10.6 Summary

Within his discussion of faith in the resurrection, Paul also says that this faith might be nullified or ruined by conduct. His illustrative quotation from Isa. 22:13 sounds like an Epicurean slogan: 'Let us eat and drink, for tomorrow we will die' (1 Cor. 15:32). This observation, together with the logical structure recalling Phil. 3, moves us to seek further texts in 1 Corinthians related to Paul's belly-dicta.

From this perspective, the lack of sharing when Corinthian Christians met to celebrate the Lord's Supper is to be considered gluttony on the part of the 'haves'. Paul addresses this situation by bringing to their mind the excessive eating and drinking of the banquets. In doing this, he is exaggerating, but this is nevertheless a key to his strategy in this text: they are worshipping themselves, or their own stomach, rather than Christ. To Paul their gluttony represents a neglect of the sharing implied in Christ's death. In this way gluttony and Christ's death appear as incompatible, as they did in Phil. 3.

In 1 Cor. 6:12–20 Paul enters a dialogue with Corinthian slogans, and claims that the body belongs to the Lord, and will be raised (cf. 1 Cor. 15:32). What to do with the stomach and genitals is, therefore, not a matter of indifference to Paul. This passage revealed a dispute between the apostle and some Corinthians on what value to place upon the present body. The significance of the present bodily conduct was seen in the light of its being destined to be raised from the dead.

Finally, we turned to 1 Cor. 10:7. Paul's use of OT traditions in 1 Cor. 10:1–13 was not a general one. He was working from the assumption that the Corinthian situation and that of the wilderness-generation were correlated in terms of cravings for food and meat in particular. From this viewpoint, the desert-generation and the challenge of the Corinthian believers looked the same. Paul exhorts his converts not to partake in idol-food served in the temples. He urges them to ἐγκράτεια, self-control in the face of this temptation. Their desert ancestors were short on self-control, and their demand for food led to their destruction (Num. 11:34). They thought they were standing, since they had been blessed by God's many gifts. But they fell. This comparison goes to the root of the Corinthian problem in chaps. 8–10: many believers thought they were standing safely, but they were about to fall. Gary D. Collier summarizes this passage in a way with which I agree: 'To insist on one's right to eat idolmeat is to insist on eating from the fountain of ἐπιθυμία, rather than from Christ, the rock. The desire to eat and drink in an idol's temple grows out of a larger problem: a selfish craving which proceeds without concern for the will of God or for others'.[109]

Philo's exposition of the same traditions helped us to give the desert-generation a name: they were belly-devotees. They had – in Philo's words – left the country of the stomach, i.e. Egypt, but they did not trust in God. They were hooked on the belly and became belly-devotees, primarily due to their demand for food and the Golden Calf episode. Although Paul does not mention the power of the stomach directly, 'belly-devotees' is an apt description of his argument. The Graeco-Roman belly-*topos* has been entirely embedded in biblical thinking on apostasy, the obvious bridge being the craving for food. By bringing together idol-food in the Corinthian temples and the demand for more food in the wilderness, Paul explains why belly-worship leads to apostasy. Belly-service is disbelief in God's providence. God provides, in Corinth as he did in the wilderness. From our presentation of the belly-*topos* throughout this study, it is indeed likely that Paul's addressees would recognize his instruction as rooted in a biblical re-reading of the belly-*topos*. Paul is likely to have had in mind the Golden Calf episode and the temptation to eat in temples when he wrote 1 Cor. 15:32 on eating and drinking since death is approaching. As we will see in the next part of this study, Patristic exegesis read both 1 Cor. 10:7 and 15:32 as examples of belly-worship in Epicurean terms. In this the Fathers were not far from what Paul wrote to his converts.

We have seen that 1 Corinthians is the Pauline epistle which deals most extensively with the body. The apostle's view on the body is clearly expressed, to the extent that to some it has become the point of departure for laying out the entire Corinthian situation (Dale B. Martin). Faced with some among his converts who did not pay very much attention to how the body was affected by their faith, their identity as believers, and their holy lifestyle, Paul retorted that the body was by no means irrelevant. The future transformed body had serious repercussions for bodily activities. This is the framework in which 'belly' works in this epistle.

---

[109] Gary D. Collier, "That We Might Not Crave Evil", p. 74.

PART 5

The earliest expositors of Paul

Expositors of the two Pauline belly-dicta in Phil. 3:19 and Rom. 16:18
quite often refer to how these texts were interpreted in the Patristic literature. The article of Johannes Behm in *Kittel's Theological Dictionary*
has been very influential. He concludes his presentation on Paul's use of
κοιλία by claiming that he is probably alluding to the observance of food
laws: he presents this as 'the older view', with reference to Theodore
of Mopsuestia, Ambrosiaster and Pelagius.[1] The references given are,
however, often general, imprecise or with little awareness of the literary
context.[2] Since Patristic texts are often mentioned as decisive evidence
favouring reference to Jewish dietary laws, it is necessary to give a survey
of this material. Owing to the brevity of Paul's dicta on belly-worship,
we have insisted that a culturally adequate reading was urgent. This led
us to present the ancient background quite extensively. This chapter is
written from the conviction that Paul's first interpreters may provide an
approach to his texts, that from a historical and cultural point of view is
highly relevant.

The aim of the coming chapter is to bring our investigation towards an
end by providing an overview of various readings of the Pauline passages
in question. It will become evident that the Church Fathers should not be
referred to in general in this question; their ways of reading the relevant

[1] Johannes Behm, 'κοιλία', p. 788. Behm seems to consider that the Patristic evidence
more or less generally supports his view that Paul's belly-sayings refer to Jewish Christians
who continue to observe the food laws. Behm's article has been very influential. In my
view he is lumping together the Patristic evidence in a very general way. Gordon D. Fee,
Philippians, p. 372 n. 39 says that it is an ancient view that Phil. 3:19 refers to Paul's
sarcasm against those who observe food laws. He mentions in a parenthesis Ambrosiaster,
Hilary, Pelagius, Augustine and Theodoret. Marvin R. Vincent, *Philippians*, p. 117 says
that Theodore of Mopsuestia held this view, although he finds it a fanciful interpretation of
Paul's text; cf. Peter O'Brien, *Philippians*, p. 455 and Gerald F. Hawthorne, *Philippians*,
p. 166; C. E. B. Cranfield, *Romans* Vol. 2, pp. 799–800. Behm's view has in many ways
set the agenda for the interpretation of the relevant Pauline passages; see e.g. Brian Dodd,
Paul's Paradigmatic 'I', p. 176 ' . . . as commentators in the ancient church took this phrase'.

[2] The references may be taken from a catena, as for instance John Anthony Cramer,
Catenea or Karl Staab, *Pauluskommentare*.

passages are simply too different for that. We will draw upon texts up
to the sixth century AD. This is necessary to give a picture of how the
generations closer to Paul were reading his texts. Furthermore, modern
commentaries refer to texts from within this period. We will not embark
on a full-scale presentation of the Patristic evidence, but we aim to move
beyond the 'pick and choose' method found in most commentaries on
this question. The context in which the Church Fathers found Paul's texts
worth quoting or alluding to is very important. Sufficient awareness of
the context is missing in most references to this literature in modern
commentaries. In other words, we aim to move beyond providing so-
called proof-texts.

The Patristic material certainly invites us to walk down many side-
roads. The most intruiging would be the ascetic theology and lifestyle
of this period in the history of the Church.[3] Doing so, will, however,
take us far beyond an investigation of the Pauline passages. But it is
not possible completely to separate asceticism, fasting and the history of
how Paul's belly-dicta were interpreted. The three are gradually being
woven together; which will also be reflected in my presentation. We will
nevertheless attempt to confine ourselves to seeing how writers in the Old
Church worked with the Pauline passages. This means that the question
of body-theology in these ancient Christian texts will not be addressed.
It is not possible to present the texts in groups categorized according to
various interpretations, since there are variations within the individual
authors as well. The relevant Pauline passages may be given different
interpretations even by the same author. This inconsistency suggests that
the authors should be presented one by one.

---

[3] On asceticism in the Old Church in general, see Herbert Musorillo, 'The Problem of
Fasting in the Greek Patristic Writers'; and in particular the most recent monograph of
Teresa M. Shaw, *The Burden of the Flesh*, in which a number of important observations
relevant to our topic have been made; Veronica E. Grimm, *Feasting to Fasting* and most
recently Elizabeth A. Clark, *Reading Renunciation*.

11

THE BELLY-DICTA OF PAUL IN PATRISTIC LITERATURE

11.1   Clement of Alexandria (c. 150 – c. 215)[1]

In his *Stromateis* (*Miscellanies*), Clement sets out texts from the Holy Scriptures and excerpts from Greek philosophy. It has therefore been called a 'patchwork-quilt'[2] in which Clement brings together Hellenistic philosophy and the Christian faith.[3]

In *Strom.* 4:16 the author writes on the martyrs, urging them, as well as other Christians, to endure in love and patience. It is just a little while until they obtain the promised victory. They are being tested like gold in the furnace. Faith in the resurrection makes the difference to believers who face trials like this. But the resurrection also makes a difference to how Christians relate to eating. Clement provides two contrasting examples. The first is about οἱ φιλήδονοι, the lovers of pleasure: they crawl on the belly (ἕρποντος ἐπὶ κοιλίᾳ) (*Strom.* 4:16/100.3).[4] The terminology brings to mind the movements of a snake. Clement confirms this by saying that God gave the name 'brood of vipers' (Matt. 3:7) to these people who are serving their belly and genitals (οἱ γαστρὶ καὶ αἰδοίοις δουλεύοντες). Clement adds that they cut off one another's heads for the sake of worldly pleasures (ἐπιθυμίαι). The reference is vague; it might be a negative description of pagan feasts from the perspective of the snake-analogy. Clement is not quoting any Biblical passage here, but Matt. 3:7 and Rom. 16:18 seem to be in his mind. His use of the belly-*topos* in this text has much in common with Philo's exegesis of Gen. 3.[5]

---

[1] The names of the Patristic expositors are given according to F.L. Cross, E.A. Livingstone, *Oxford Dictionary of the Christian Church*. For an introduction to Clement's life see John Ferguson, *Clement of Alexandria*, pp. 13–43.

[2] John Ferguson, *Clement of Alexandria*, pp. 107–8.

[3] Annewies van den Hoek, *Clement of Alexandria*, pp. 209–30.

[4] The text reference is to *GCS* (Clemens Alexandrinus Vol. 2).

[5] In her study on Clement's dependence on Philo, Annewies van den Hoek, *Clement of Alexandria*, does not take note of this.

The opposite example, on how the perfect Christian lives, gives a full quotation from Phil. 4:11, on Paul's αὐτάρκεια: he knew both to have in abundance and to be in want, to be satisfied and to be in hunger (*Strom.* 4:16/101.1). Clement clearly sees the apostolic 'being content with little' as the opposite of belly-service, which is not far removed from what we have found in Paul himself.[6]

In *Strom.* 2:20 Clement speaks of how the perfect Christian exercises self-restraint (ἐγκράτεια). He quotes from Gal. 6:14 on the believer who in Christ is crucified to the world. Life is, therefore, a cross-bearing endeavour, following in the footsteps of the Saviour (*Strom.* 2:20/104.3). Clement immediately turns to the question of food, and in a way which very much reminds us of Philo's writings. Clement says that the divine law, in aiming at virtue (ἀρετή), laid down laws for eating which are the foundation (θεμέλιος) of all virtue (*Strom.* 2:20/105.1). Clement assumes that the food laws were given as means of self-restraint. The laws forbid partaking of fatty food, such as swine; in this way the desire for delicacies is being subdued. Food which the law for this reason forbids, is reserved for voluptaries:[7] 'If, then, we are to exercise control over the belly, and what is below the belly, it is clear that we have of old heard from the Lord that we are to check lust by law (Εἰ δὴ γαστρὸς καὶ τῶν ὑπὸ γαστέρα κρατητέον, δῆλον ὡς ἄνωθεν παρειλήφαμεν παρὰ τοῦ κυρίου διὰ τοῦ νόμου τὴν ἐπιθυμίαν ἐκκόπτειν)' (*Strom.* 2:20/106.2).[8] Like Philo, Clement regards the food laws as a means of self-restraint.

Clement does not say, however, that Christians are expected to observe the food laws. But his thinking takes as its starting point the aim of the dietary laws, which was to put an end to gluttony. Similarly, Christians should shun pleasures, particularly those of food, which fuel the lusts. In failing to do so, the believer is prone to live a life not differing very much from Sardanapalus, whose life is summarized in the epigram 'I have what I ate – what I enjoyed wantonly; and the pleasures I felt in love. But those many objects of happiness are left, For I too am dust, who ruled great Ninus' (*Strom.* 2:20/118.6).[9] The example of Sardanapalus introduces Epicurus' philosophy of ἡδονή. In urging the Christians to control the pleasures of the belly, Clement is here drawing on ancient traditional critiques of Epicurus.[10]

---

[6] See chap. 8.2 of this study.

[7] ANF Vol. 2 renders the Greek τρυφητής 'epicures'. That this word is related to belly-enslavement is clear from e.g. Diodorus Siculus 8:18 and Athenaeus, *Deipn.* 1:7a.

[8] The translation is taken from ANF Vol. 2.

[9] On Sardanapalus, see chap. 4.1, section on 'The proverbial figure of Sardanapalus'.

[10] See chap. 4. For Clement on luxury and self-control, see Eric Osborn, *Ethical Patterns*, pp. 55–6, 64–5.

At the end of this chapter of *Stromateis*, Clement winds up his presentation. It is essential to control the passions related to βρῶμα, κοίτη, ἄνεσις, τρυφή, which means 'food', 'sex', 'indulgence', and 'luxury'. Self-control is the mild yoke of which Jesus spoke (Matt. 11:30), and which is 'the charioteer driving each of us onward to salvation' (*Strom.* 2:20/126.3). The traditional motif from the philosophy of mastering the pleasures, namely the charioteer controlling the wild horses, is here appropriated by Clement. Controlling the belly, that is, not being enslaved by gluttony as well as sex and luxury, means not drifting away, but moving steadily towards final salvation.

In his writing *Paedagogus* (*The Instructor*), Clement gives instructions on how Christians ought to live. The Instructor or the Tutor is the Divine *Logos*. Book 2, chap. 1 is on how to deal with food-matters.[11] The chapter on food is followed by topics such as drinking, costly vessels, feasts etc. This resembles the way in which Musonius Rufus organized his instructions on food.[12]

Some people live to eat; their whole life is belly (ἡ γαστήρ ἐστιν ὁ βίος) – like the animals (*Paed.* 2:1.1.4).[13] The Divine has instructed men to eat. But the aim is not pleasure or luxury. Food is to be taken in moderation to foster health and strength. The advice given in *Paed.* 2:1.2.1 is very health-related. The instructions for a simple life, and for pleasure as a slippery slope leading towards luxury, are all supported by references to what is healthy (see also 2:1.5.1–2). They very much recall the writings of the Stoic Musonius Rufus.

Clement gives a lengthy description (*Paed.* 2:1.3.1–4.2) of the loaded tables with lavish dishes of all kinds. He depicts in detail the menus of rich people and describes them with common words for gluttony and gourmandizing: γαστρίμαργοι, λαιμαργία, πλεονεξία,[14] παμφάγοι, λιχνεία: 'A man like this seems to me to be all jaws (γνάθος), and nothing else' (*Paed.* 2:1.4.1). Christians, however, seek the heavenly bread and must, therefore, rule the belly (ἄρχειν ἀνάγκη τῆς . . . γαστρός) (2:1.4.2–3). Here he quotes 1 Cor. 6:13, that God will execrate gluttony by destroying the belly. Therefore, the Christian 'feasting' is presented as a counter-culture

[11] Clement here provides important examples of table manners. The aim of this is to distinguish human beings from how animals behave when eating. Table manners are, in other words, a means of imposing self-control on human beings' dealings with food matters; see Blake Leyerle, 'Table Etiquette'.

[12] See chap. 3.6 of this study. For a summary of the practical teaching of Book 2, see John Ferguson, *Clement of Alexandria*, pp. 79–102.

[13] For the Greek text see GCS (Clemens Alexandrinus Vol. 1). Translations are taken from ANF Vol. 2.

[14] This is a general word for greed, and defines gluttony as a special kind of greed; see LSJ s.v.

where one does not seek the highest couches, and to which the poor are invited. Clement is here drawing on synoptic traditions found in Luke 14:8, 10, 12–13, 16.

Clement sees basically two ways to deal with food (*Paed.* 2:1.7.1–5). One is marked by moderation and discipline, in short, αὐτάρκεια (2:1.7.3). The diet is light and easily digested, it is measured in due quantity and is healthy to the body. Clement is not speaking primarily as a health consultant of his time. He does so with the same conviction as did Musonius Rufus: the mind is weighed down by heavy food. And since the righteous man does not live by bread alone (2:1.7.2), the light menu is essential to keep healthy in a spiritual sense.

The other way is marked by gluttony, pleasure, excess. Clement lists first the vices connected with richness in food, and then proceeds to derogating people living like this. He categorizes these into three groups:

(1)   those who have given up reason; i.e. animals
(2)   those who have given up friendship; i.e. flatterers or parasites
(3)   those who have given up life; i.e. gladiators

They all lead a life according to the pleasures of the belly (γαστρὸς ἡδονῆς). They crawl on their bellies,[15] being beasts in human shape like their father. In mentioning their father, Clement has the Devil in mind; belly-worshippers and the Devil are kindred. This conclusion is justified on the basis of the snake-tradition and the belly-*topos* (cf. chaps. 7.3 and 9.2 in this study).

The believers do not serve the belly; they rule and master it (*Paed.* 2:1.9.2).[16] Clement applies the philosophical idea and the terminology of 'mastery of desires'. In *Paed.* 2:1.9.4–12.1, Clement addresses practical matters such as invitations to banquets and so forth. The passage has some similarity with questions on food matters which Paul addresses in 1 Cor. 8–10. Clement describes the banquets in a vivid manner and gives advice on how a Christian can behave decently at these events. His basic principle is that believers do not shun social intercourse, but are careful with the snares of custom.[17] In *Paed.* 2:1.12.2–13.1 Clement sees a close link between gluttony (ὀψοφαγία, λαιμαργία, γαστριμαργία) and 1 Cor. 11:17–34 on the Lord's Supper. This is, according to Clement, a text about

---

[15] The Greek text has ἐπὶ γαστέρας ἕρποντες (see above as well); the cognate words for this participle refer to reptiles or snakes; see Lampe, *Lexicon* and LSJ s.v.

[16] The opposite of serving the belly (δουλεύειν) is expressed by the Greek terms βασιλεύειν and κατακυριεύειν.

[17] The question of how to conduct oneself at feasts is followed up in *Paed.* 2:4. Clement calls the banquets 'theatres of drunkenness' (θέατρον μέθης, *Paed.* 2:4.2).

gluttony. He is thinking of this Pauline passage when he addresses the
need to control the belly. In other words, it is in his view related to the
two belly-texts in Phil. 3:19 and Rom. 16:18.[18]

In an almost creed-like form, Clement says that there is one God, who
feeds birds, fishes and all animals. Since, however, lavish food is taken
not for the sake of necessity but for enjoyment only, that is, to eat without being hungry, Christians must be on guard against food bewitching
the appetite (γοητεύοντα τὰς ὀρέξεις) (*Paed.* 2:1.15.1). Clement is here
speaking of food with a verb usually associated with leading astray. The
aspect of being led astray by the stomach is continued when Clement
speaks of those who are seated around the inflammatory tables as ruled
by the belly-demon (κοιλιοδαίμων) (*Paed.* 2:1.15.4), which is the worst
of all demons. The Greek δαίμων is here properly rendered 'god' or
'divinity'.[19] This is confirmed in this text, where Clement says that a
person ruled by the belly-god is ἐγγαστρίμυθος, a ventriloquist as well.

At the very end of his instructions on food matters Clement returns to
the question of being ruled by abundance of food. This is, he says, typical
of Gentiles who are without αὐτάρκεια. They have buried their mind in
the belly:

> Such are the men who believe in their belly (οἱ εἰς γαστέρα
> πεπιστευκότες), 'whose God is their belly, whose glory is in their
> shame, who mind earthly things'. To them the apostle predicted
> no good when he said 'whose end is destruction'.
>
> (*Paed.* 2:1.19.4)

Clement thus ends his instruction on food by quoting Phil. 3:19 in full. He
introduces this Pauline passage as a dictum about those who 'believe in
the stomach'. He here coins a term which nicely picks up Paul's argument:
the belly replaced Christ and became the focus of life. 'Believing in the
belly' is idolatry, worshipping one's own pleasures and the easy life of
the loaded table, in short, gluttony.

11.2   Tertullian (c. 160–c. 225)

In his treatise on fasting (*De Ieiunio*), Tertullian argues from the first
commandment mentioned in the Bible, which is not to eat (*Ieiun.* 3:2).
He takes this as an admonition to fast. Tertullian advocates the need

---

[18] Cf. our exegesis of the same passage in chap. 10.2.

[19] See LSJ s.v. and Lampe, *Dictionary*, s.v. Some Patristic references related to the
Pauline belly-dicta are also found in Joh. Caspari Suiceri, *Thesaurus* Vol. 2, pp. 119–20 cf.
Vol. 1, pp. 737–9.

for fasting over against 'the Physics', whom he considered to have a lax attitude to fasting. Tertullian considered the Physics to be mediocre Christians who were not yet spiritual. His ironical tone is clearly seen in *Ieiun.* 12:3 where he mentions Pristinus, 'your well-known martyr'.[20] He blames the Physics for setting up cook-shops in the prison, which is probably a reference to the practice of feeding the martyrs undertaken by the church.[21] For Pristinus the result was, according to Tertullian, that he was stuffed (*fartum*) while in prison.

The Physics have, according to Tertullian, a whole worship focused on the belly: the stomach is itself god, the appetite is a sacrifice, the lungs a temple, the paunch[22] a sacrificial altar and the cook acts as priest. The smell from the fragrant food works like the Holy Spirit, the condiments as spiritual gifts and the belching as prophecy (*Ieiun.* 16:8). Tertullian's rhetoric is quite exaggerated. He uses it as an indictment of his adversaries; he depicts their preoccupation with food in devotional terms. Disagreement on food matters, i.e. fasting, becomes the launch-pad for an entire belly-rhetoric. Rhetoric is here no portrait of historical realities, but it still needs to be said that this rhetoric is triggered by matters of food and eating. In other words, the belly-rhetoric might well be a pejorative instrument, but it still takes food matters as its point of departure.

Chap. 17 brings this treatise to a conclusion. The belly-worship of the Physics brings to mind Esau, the hunter of wild beasts. Tertullian dwells on this analogy for some lines. The features which Esau and the Physics have in common are the following:

- both are indulgent to appetite (*gulae*)
- both sell their heritage for food
- both are lax in mind and spirit
- both are coming from the field; Esau from hunting, the Physics from the fields of lax discipline

Tertullian makes his point from the Esau story: if a paltry lentil-menu is presented to a belly-worshipper, he would sell all his birthright immediately (*Ieiun.* 17:2)! Tertullian is here close to Philo's exegesis of this biblical passage; Esau represents belly-worship.

Gluttony (*gulae*) leads the way to sexual sin, and Tertullian claims that this is so also with his adversaries (17:3). Being aware of this connection,

---

[20] The Latin text is found in *CCL* 2. For an English translation see ANF Vol. 4.

[21] For the expectation that prisoners would be fed by family, friends and relatives, see Karl Olav Sandnes, *A New Family*, pp. 165–70 and Brian Rapske, *Roman Custody*, pp. 370–92.

[22] *Aqualiculus* means 'belly' or 'maw'.

the Apostle warned against revelling, drunkenness, debauchery and licentiousness (Rom. 13:13). The Physics preach 'Let us eat and drink,
for tomorrow we die' – a message which echoes 1 Cor. 15:32. As for
himself Tertullian would preach instead 'Let us fast, brethren and sisters,
lest tomorrow perchance we die.' He quotes Rom. 8:8 that those who are
in the flesh cannot please God. This does not mean, he says, to be in the
substance of flesh, but to be in its care, affection, work and will.

From this Tertullian draws a very practical lesson: to enter through the
narrow gate is easier if one has a slim body; i.e. a body familiar with
fasting (*Ieiun.* 17:7). He considers fasting as training and preparing the
soul for times of trial to come.[23] With a clear reference to the trials he
has in mind, Tertullian brings his treatise on fasting to an ironical end:
the glutton will be more attractive to the animals in the arena than to God
(*Ieiun.* 17:9).

In *Ad Uxorem* 1:8,[24] Tertullian concludes his instructions to the women.
He has argued that although marriage is lawful and blessed, celibacy is
preferable. In the concluding chapter of this treatise he makes use of the
admonition concerning the widows in 1 Tim. 5:13. Widows are urged to
avoid wine-bibbing and to seek company which does not stir up curiosity
and emulation. This may cause *libido* (lust), and women with *libido* do
not speak of the good in having a single man (*univiratus*), 'for their god,
as the apostle says, is their belly, and so, too, what is neighbour to the
belly (*quae ventri propinqua*)' (*Ad Uxorem* 1:8.5).[25]

Tertullian is clearly quoting from Phil. 3:19 and applying belly-worship
to a sexual lust that is out of control. This is probably what he has in mind
in his argument for the veiling of the virgins (*De Virginibus Velandis*) as
well. In chap. 14:2.11[26] Tertullian quotes from Phil. 3:19: *aliquando et
ipse venter deus earum*. He does not in any way comment upon this, which
means that we have to guess what he had in mind. This is, however, not
difficult, taking into account the whole of chap. 14. Tertullian is addressing
the problem of women who were unwilling to wear the veil. He depicts
them as liberated in an indecent way, seeking to please men. In other
words, having the belly as god here has a primarily sexual reference.

In his *De Resurrectione Mortuorum* 49:13[27] eating and drinking are
said to be against the faith in resurrection. For obvious reasons 'eating and

---

[23] Tertullian's emphasis on fasting has an intense awareness of the eschaton as its background; see Eric Osborn, *Tertullian*, pp. 232–63.

[24] For the Latin text see *CCL* 1.

[25] In *De Monogamia* 16:5, Tertullian quotes 1 Cor. 15:32 in a discussion of second
marriage.

[26] For the Latin texts see *CCL* 2.   [27] For the Latin text see *CCL* 2.

drinking' here has a reference beyond being fed or nourished. The two appear as a common catchword for an Epicurean lifestyle, whose creed Tertullian finds in 1 Cor. 15:32 ('let us eat and drink, for tomorrow we die'). He reminds his readers that the Apostle had addressed this directly in his discussion on the resurrection. What we found to be implicit in the Pauline material is here openly declared by Tertullian.

11.3   Origen (c. 185–c. 254)

In his *Homily* 5:2 on Jeremiah, Origen comments on Jer. 3:22 on God calling His people to repent, and the response of the people (5:2.30–1 and 5:2.43–8):[28] 'You are our Lord (σὺ κύριος ὁ θεὸς ἡμῶν) and we belong to you (ἐσόμεθά σοι)' (*Hom. Jer.* 5:2.46–8). This creed is elaborated in the following passage 5:2.54–65, which is remarkable both for its style and content. The style is very much like a creed, which is emphasized also by Origen, who mentions Eph. 4:6 in the same breath. But the creed has its negative side as well, namely what believers are supposed to renounce. Nothing must be made into God since they know only One God. Some of the options on which the believers turn their back are mentioned:

- οὐ τὴν κοιλίαν ὡς οἱ γαστρίμαργοι, ὧν ὁ θεὸς ἡ κοιλία
- οὐ τὸ ἀργύριον ὡς οἱ φιλάργυροι
- καὶ τὴν πλεονεξίαν, ἥτις ἐστὶν εἰδωλολατρία

Origen focuses on gluttony, love of silver or money and greed. The belly is the god of the gluttons, as is witnessed in Phil. 3:19. The stomach or eating might acquire a devotional status. He considers this in the framework of belief in One God. Although Origen reserves the word 'idolatry' for greed here, the entire logic of this passage strongly suggests that belly-worship is idolatry as well.

Hom. Jer. 7:3.16–35 confirms and develops exactly this perspective. Origen here comments on Jer. 5:19 about the people who forsook God to serve foreign gods. The passage is almost like an extended exposition of *Hom. Jer.* 5:2. Origen introduces his comment on the biblical text by stating that everyone who makes himself a god is actually worshipping foreign gods. There follows, in the form of questions:

(A1)   · do you make a god of eating and drinking?
(A2)   is your god the belly?

---

[28] References from *SC* 232.

(B1)   do you consider silver and riches from here below a supreme good?

(B2)   do you have Mammon as Lord?

The first parts of the questions (A1 and B1) are expressed in everyday language, while the second parts (A2 and B2) develop them with the help of biblical texts. In other words, Origen is interpreting Phil. 3:19 and Jesus' remark about Mammon (Matt. 6:24). Furthermore, Origen quotes Jesus saying that one cannot serve two masters. Origen gives more attention to love of wealth in this text, which he defines as seeking honour and taking pride in riches as well as in neglecting the poor. The passage closes with a judgement introduced by ἐάν: if there is anyone obeying (προσκυνήσῃ) foreign gods in the church, he shall be expelled. Accordingly, judgement is pronounced on the money-lover and the glutton: the money-lover is to be shut out from the church (ἔξω ... ἐκβληθείς). The glutton is to be excluded from the church (ἔξω γενόμενος). The way Origen here juxtaposes love of money and gluttony demonstrates that he considers 'having the belly as god' as a kind of food-greed which is incompatible with the Christian devotion to the One God.

In his *Homilies on Jeremiah*, Origen thus widens the meaning of 'god'; gluttony, money-love and greed might well function as gods. He writes in a way which brings to mind Martin Luther's explanation of the first commandment in his Small Catechism. The first commandment has to do with trusting God, thus putting one's trust in no one and nothing else. God can, however, be replaced by many things. It all depends on how the person involved relates to things of this world, such as food, money etc. This can be applied to Origen's commentary on Matt. 15:10–20, found in his *Comm. Matt.* 11:14 as well. A person who does not know the spirit of the adopted ones (cf. Rom. 8:15) may even hold the 'god of this world' (2 Cor. 4:4) or 'the ruler of this world' (John 16:11) to be his god. Similarly, the belly who by no means is a god (ὡς γὰρ μὴ οὖσα θεός), becomes a god to those who love pleasure rather than God (φιληδόνων μᾶλλον ἢ φιλοθέων) (*Comm. Matt.* 11:14.3–6/p. 56).[29] Phil. 3:19 is here applied in a context discussing God in terms of 'what one puts one's trust in'.

Origen comments on Rom. 1:8 in his *Comm. Rom.* 1:9. Paul, who gives thanks to 'my God' (τῷ θεῷ μου), makes Origen reflect on this testimony of the apostle: this is the creed of believers (*sancti*), as it was to Abraham, Isaac and Jacob. It is a creed which cannot be uttered by those

---

[29] For the Greek text see *GCS* (Origenes Vol. 10).

- for whom the belly is God
- for whom avarice is God
- for whom glory is of the world
- and pomp is mundane
- or the power of perishable things is God (*cui venter Deus est,*[30] *cui avaritia Deus est, aut cui gloria saeculi, et pompa mundi, aut potentia rerum caducarum Deus est*)

Origen brings this list to an end, by pointing out that it is, in fact, open-ended: those things which one worships (*colit*) beyond other things become one's god (*Comm. Rom.* 1:9/*PG* 14.854–5).[31] For Origen, Paul has written Phil. 3:19 in a style that is proper to creeds, and it is from this observation that he understands the text. Origen uses Phil. 3:19 as an example of people who are opposed to the true creed. What, then, is the nature of belly-worship according to these texts? The examples which Origen places next to 'having the belly as god' (avarice and position in this world), are various modes of self-centredness. 'Having the stomach as god' is to be interpreted along the same lines; it is the self-pleasing life, manifesting itself particularly in excessive eating and drinking.

In *Comm. Rom.* 9:42, Origen gives an exposition of Rom. 14:14–15 (*PG* 14.1245–50), that is, of a Pauline text on the question of clean and unclean food. Origen mentions Jewish observance of purity laws as well as Pauline passages of relevance. He says that the Jews consider themselves superior to other people owing to their practice of abstaining from certain food. He then introduces Phil. 3:19 (*quorum Deus venter est*), but in a somewhat surprising way. In contrast to Jewish observance of food laws there exists a true observance of law (*vera observantia*). People who are practising this true worship cannot be said 'to have the belly as god (*Vera observantia est ubi ita sumitur cibus, et ita aguntur omnia, ut non de talibus dicatur: Quorum Deus venter est*)' (*Comm. Rom.* 9:42/*PG* 14.1248).[32] This means, according to Origen, to keep away from food stirring up *libido*, and eating moderately as well.

---

[30] Origen comments on Ps. 5:1–3 (ὁ βασιλεύς μου καὶ ὁ θεός μου) in his *Homily on Psalms* 5:1–3/*PG* 12.1167–8. This creed could not be uttered by 'those whose god is their belly', he says.

[31] Theresia Heither, *Translatio Religionis* does not comment upon the texts I am here discussing. A German translation with Latin text is available; see Theresia Heither, *Origenes, Römerbriefkommentar* Band 2/1.

[32] A German translation is available; see Theresia Heither, *Origenes, Römerbriefkommentar* Band 2/5.

Modern exegetes of this text might say that since Origen's logic implies a contrast to Jewish customs, this must apply to his reading of Phil. 3:19 as well. In other words, Origen is using Phil. 3:19 against the Jews who observe the dietary laws; 'having the belly as god' is to observe the food laws. Although this reasoning at first sight appears probable, it is nevertheless mistaken. Origen cites Phil. 3:19 with no echo of the question of food laws addressed in Rom. 14. True versus false *observantia* is certainly an implied contrast, but Phil. 3:19 is explained, not by the preceding passage, but rather by what follows. *Vera observantia* in contrast to Jewish food laws consists in abstaining from food that enhances desire and lust (*concupiscentia et libido*), in short, in avoiding luxury (*luxus*). What matters, Origen says, is not only what one eats, but the quantity as well. This demonstrates that excessive eating and drinking, not Jewish dietary laws, is the proper reference for Origen's use of Phil. 3:19 in this text.

Paul's warning against false teachers in Rom. 16:17–20 is, according to Origen, addressed to all believers (*ad omnes credentes*) (*Comm. Rom.* 10:35–7/*PG* 14.1283–7). He sees the Pauline text as revealing the nature of false teachers: they are not peace-makers (*beati pacifici*) (Matt. 5:9); they cause strife, quarrels, and dissension in the church. Origen provides a list of terms describing this activity: *dissensiones, scandala, certamina, jurgia, lites, studia contentionis* – all referring to activity tearing a fellowship apart. Of people involved in such activities Origen says that they 'do not serve Christ our Lord, who is our peace (*pax*), but their own stomach' (*Comm. Rom.* 10:35/*PG*14.1283). Naming Christ 'our peace' underscores the logic of the whole passage: falsehood and dissension versus truth and peace.

What is then the reason for quarrels and strife in the church? Origen poses this question and gives the answer himself: *ventris gratiae; hoc est, quaestus et cupiditas* (*PG* 14.1283); the belly is the reason for dissensions because it stirs up desire, gain and profit. The stomach is bent on gain and satisfying the desires. In this way false teachers who are serving their belly cause the fellowship to be torn apart, owing to their belly, i.e. their self-satisfaction. There is no mention of food in this text. The belly is a force undermining unity and peace for personal gain and satisfaction. Origen is here close to the political use of the belly-*topos* in antiquity.

In *Comm. Rom.* 10:36/*PG* 14.1286, Origen returns to 'the belly-servants'. He quotes from Rom. 16:18: *huiusmodi enim Christo Domino nostro non serviunt*. While many expositors in the Early Church say that 'worshipping the belly', is typical of Gentiles, Origen makes a distinction here. These are not people who would say of themselves that they were not serving Christ. However, their way of living shows them to be such.

They are betrayed by their way of life.[33] This means that according to this text false teaching is no mere doctrinal matter. Living according to the demands of the belly means a practical denial of Christian faith (*regula*). It is impossible, Origen continues, to serve two masters, both Christ and the belly; either desires or God will receive due honour (*non enim videtur simul quis et Christo servire posse et ventri ac voluptatis pariter amator esse et Dei*). To support his interpretation of Rom. 16:17–18, Origen quotes Matt. 6:24, saying that God and Mammon cannot be served at the same time. In other words, Origen in this text as well speaks of 'belly-worship' in terms applied to love of money in the Gospel tradition.

In *Hom. Gen.* 3:6 Origen interprets circumcision in a spiritual, but still very practical way. It is necessary for all the limbs of the body to be properly circumcised. The feet should be circumcised, so they should not 'be swift to shed blood (Isa. 59:7) and lest they enter the council of the wicked (Ps. 1:1)'. The eyes are in need of circumcision, so they should not look at a woman with lust (Matt. 5:28). Those who eat and drink to the glory of God (1 Cor. 10:31), have circumcised taste. Eating and drinking to the glory of God means to eat with moderation. This is evident from what it means not to have one's taste circumcised. When one holds the belly as god and turns to excessive eating (*suavitatibus gulae deservit*) (*Hom. Gen.* 3:6/p. 48.1–3),[34] one has an uncircumcised taste. In a context where circumcision is at the centre of Origen's thinking, and where the dictum from Phil. 3:19 on 'having the belly as god' is mentioned, one would expect this to be used polemically against Jews and Judaizers, but it is aimed instead at gourmandizers.

11.4   Cyprian (d. 258)

In his third book to Quirinus (*Ad Quirinum*) (*Treatises or Testimonies*), in 120 brief paragraphs or heads Cyprian gives a summary introduction to Christian faith and living. Chap. 60 is on the danger of desire for food (*concupiscentia ciborum*).[35] The paragraphs form a collection or catena of texts relevant to this issue.[36] Cyprian puts together the following texts: Isa. 22:13: *manducemus et bibamus, cras enim moriemur* (cf. 1 Cor.

---

[33] The Latin text has *rebus ipsis ostendit se Christo Domino non servire*. Theresia Heither, *Origenes, Römerbriefkommentar*, Band 2/5 p. 267 renders this in the following way: 'und durch die Taten zeigen, dass sie Christus, unserem Herrn, nicht dienen'.

[34] For the Latin text see *GCS* (Origenes Vol. 6). For an English translation see *FC* 71.

[35] For the Latin text see *CCL* 3/1. An English translation is available in ANF Vol. 5.

[36] On Cyprian as an expositor of the Bible, see Michael Andrew Fahey, *Cyprian and the Bible*.

15:32). He proceeds to Exod. 32:6 (which Paul quotes in 1 Cor. 10:7): *et consedit populus manducare et bibere, et surrexerunt ludere*. Cyprian then quotes 1 Cor. 8:6; 11:33–4; Rom. 14:17; and finally John 4:32,34. The texts are not commented upon; this is simply a text-collage. The texts can, however, be divided into two groups. Some describe the misbehaviour Cyprian is warning against; i.e. Isa. 22:13; Exod. 32:6; 1 Cor. 11:33–4. The others portray the constructive part of the instruction Cyprian gives. This cluster of texts is worth noting since it concurs with core-texts in our investigation.

In *Ad Quirinum* 3:11 Cyprian speaks of believers who have abandoned their old ways of life. They have set their mind on celestial and spiritual things. He quotes from a number of biblical passages, one of which is a combination of Phil. 2:21 and 3:19–21. The two Pauline passages are connected since both concern 'seeking one's own'. Cyprian interprets Phil. 3:19 in the light of 2:21, mentioning 'those who are seeking their own ends rather than those of Christ'. 'Having the belly as god' refers, then, to a lifestyle incompatible with setting the mind on celestial things. The following sentence makes this very clear: 'Our conversation, however, is in heavenly things (*nostra autem conversatio in caelis est*)' (*Quirinum* 3:11.44). Belly-worship is, then, according to this text, a self-centred life seeking one's own ends. This is characteristic of the life the believers have left behind.

In *De Duplici Martyrio* 24–5, Cyprian deals with the creed: *credo in unum Deum*.[37] This is a creed which cannot be recited by those who serve avarice, pleasure and luxury (*servit avaritiae aut libidini aut luxui*) (24:19). Calling upon God is a matter of doing what pleases Him (Matt. 7:21). Cyprian then quotes Tit. 1:16 on those who profess to know God, but who deny Him with their actions. The issue is the consequences of confessing belief in one God in the daily life of believers. Believing in one God is by no means merely a doctrinal matter; one's creed is manifested in how one lives.

Cyprian gives some examples of a lifestyle militating against this creed; in fact, nullifying it:

- neglecting one's family: the proof text is 1 Tim. 5:8[38]
- honouring Mammon: the proof text is Col. 3:5
- honouring the belly: the proof texts are: Phil. 3:19 and Rom. 16:18

---

[37] For the Latin text see *CSEL* (Cyprian Vol. 3/1).

[38] Probably a reference to selfishness; cf. Chrysostom's exegesis of 1 Tim. 5:8; *Hom.* 14/*PG* 62.571–80.

Chap. 24:12 mentions Mammon and belly in tandem. Chap. 25 pays particular attention to the view that avarice and Mammon are idolatry. Cyprian asks rhetorically; if a curse is laid upon those who prostrate themselves to the image of Diana, how much more will it be laid on those who whole-heartedly worship Mammon and sacrifice to him on a daily basis?[39]

From this text we can deduce that Cyprian considers Phil. 3:19 and Rom. 16:18 to be concerned with misbehaviour, not with false doctrines as such. Belief in the One God is nullified and, in fact, denied, by the lifestyle of the stomach. Although he does not say directly what this is, the way he mentions avarice, Mammon and belly-worship together makes it likely that he is thinking in terms of a greedy appetite; i.e. gluttony or gourmandizing and the way of life associated with it. Furthermore, 'belly-worship' is understood within a framework of the basic Christian creed and the first commandment (one God) (cf. our presentation of Origen above). The lifestyle associated with excessive eating is therefore considered idolatry. Finally, Cyprian follows Origen who sees the belly-dicta of Paul as developments of Jesus' sayings on Mammon and the impossibility of serving two masters.

11.5   Novatian (d. 257–8)

This Roman presbyter, who became the leader of the so-called Novatianists and caused a rigorist schism after the Decian persecution, wrote a treatise on Jewish foods (*De Cibis Iudaicis*).[40] Novatian reminds his readers that he has given his presentation of circumcision and the Sabbath elsewhere. Now he wants to address the question of food, which is a source of the Jews' feeling of superiority to other people. Novatian's basic principle of interpretation is that the Law is spiritual and must be understood accordingly. An example of this approach is given in *Cib.* 3:6–7, where laws on clean and unclean animals are seen allegorically to portray human traits, deeds and acts.

Chap. 5 speaks of the coming of Christ as the end of the Law (*finis legis Christus*), which also meant that the food laws were abrogated. In favour of this view Novatian cites 1 Tim. 4:1–3 and 1 Cor. 10:25, both of which take a critical stance towards the Jewish customs of distinguishing between clean and unclean foods: 'Accordingly, it is evident that all these

---

[39]   *Execramur eos qui procumbunt ad Dianae simulacrum: quanto iustius eos execramur, qui toto pectore serviunt mammonae, qui illi quotidie sacrificant?*

[40]   For the Latin text see *CCL* 4. An English translation is available in *FC* 67.

foods enjoy again the blessings they received at their creation, now that the Law has ended, and that we must not return to legal prohibition of foods commanded for certain reasons, and which evangelical liberty (*libertas evangelica*), setting us free from its bondage, has now discontinued' (*Cib.* 5:6). Novatian quotes 1 Cor. 6:13 and proceeds to an allusion of Phil. 3:19: 'the man who worships God with food is almost like one who has God as his belly (*nam qui per escas Dominum colit prope est, ut Deum habeat ventrem suum*)' (*Cib.* 5:9).

The immediate impression is that Novatian is here applying Phil. 3:19 to those who were agitating for Jewish food laws to be observed also by Christians; they are 'belly-worshippers'. Chap. 5 is throughout dealing with what Novatian considers as self-imposed slavery to Jewish practices. He claims – in a very Pauline way – that these practices do not apply to those who have been baptized. This lends support to this interpretation of Novatian's use of Phil. 3:19: 'the belly-devotees' are those who have missed the fact that the food laws have been abrogated by the coming of Christ.

Novatian's interpretation is, however, more complex than suggested by this initial reading of chap. 5. A slightly different interpretation will now be advocated. A close look at *Cib.* 5:9 makes it evident that Novatian is aware of the difference between food law proponents and 'belly-worshippers'. He makes a comparison between the two, and concludes that there is a similarity between them. His point can be paraphrased in this way: 'Worshipping the belly' is indeed something different from observing food laws, but the two can still be compared since both have to do with misconduct in terms of eating. This distinction is indicated in *Cib.* 5:9, where Novatian says: *Deus ventre non colitur nec cibis*, 'God is worshipped neither by belly nor by food.'

This distinction, which is indicated, although not emphasized, in chap. 5, is, however, spelled out elsewhere in his treatise. According to *Cib.* 4:1–3, the food laws were imparted to the Jews as a means of frugality and moderation in eating (*frugalitas decebat et gulae temperantia*).[41] Now that the food laws have been done away with, the demand for moderation in eating is still in force: 'Since certain privileges are granted regarding foods, one must not be quick to conclude that sensuality (*luxuria*) is permitted, or that moderation (*continentia*) in food and drink is abolished because the Gospel now treats us with more liberality' (*Cib.* 6:1). Abolition of the food laws is thus by no means a catering for the belly

---

[41] Cf. the interpretation of food laws in the Hellenistic-Jewish material, and in Philo in particular (see chaps. 6 and 7.8 of this study).

(*non . . . ventri procuratum est*). The rest of chap. 6 is then about the need for moderation in eating and drinking. Novatian says that no one attacked gluttony (*gulae*) as strongly as did Jesus. He said that the wealthy were wretched for their serving the dictates of the belly and gluttony (*quibus ad imperium ventris et gulae servientibus*) (*Cib.* 6:3). 'Serving the belly' is here evidently connected with gluttony.

It is therefore misleading to say that Novatian identifies observance of food laws with belly-worship. The two are not identical; on the contrary, the dietary laws were means of fighting belly-worship. But after the coming of Christ, this end is not catered for by the food laws. Continuing to observe them is, therefore, a misunderstanding in terms of food, and thus to be compared to belly-worship. All this means that Novatian is not only addressing Jewish food-customs, but luxury in eating and drinking as well. In *Cib.* 5:9 he brings the two together, saying that they are similar. But this does not mean that Phil. 3:19 is applied to the food laws as such. Novatian considers belly-worship and gluttony to be identical, but he is comparing the Jewish preoccupation with what to eat with the attitude of the gluttons. Both ways of living are unspiritual.

11.6   Methodius of Olympus (d. c. 311)

This bishop of Lycia wrote a treatise on the resurrection. In this discussion he also addresses the practical consequences of believing in the resurrection of the body. In *De Resurrectione* 1:60,[42] he argues from the Pauline conviction that God will raise the believers from the dead, as he did for Jesus, and also that their limbs belong to Christ (τὰ μέλη ὑμῶν μέλη Χριστοῦ ἐστίν) (*Res.* 1:60.4/325.9–10). From these basic assumptions, Methodius draws the lesson that faith in the resurrection has consequences for how to deal with the body. Bodily matters are not irrelevant to faith in the resurrection of the body. Believers must live a life worthy of Christ also in bodily matters. Believing in the resurrection makes the difference to how Christians use their body.

Methodius emphasizes the question of eating. He says that the law of God provides the necessary σωφροσύνη, which he defines with reference to the Apostle who urged his converts to subdue τὸ φρόνημα τῆς σαρκός (*Res.* 1:60.3/324.19). Gluttony (γαστριμαργία) and incontinence (ἀκρασία) must be swept away, desires (ὀρέξεις) and pleasures (ἡδοναί) destroyed (*Res.*1:60.4/324.21–325.1). Methodius cries shame on those who revel in food and luxury (τρυφή): 'They hold the belly as their God,

---

[42] For the Greek text see *GCS* (Methodius).

saying "let us eat and drink, for tomorrow we will die" (οἳ θεὸν ἡγοῦνται τὴν κοιλίαν, φάγωμεν καὶ πίωμεν, αὔριον γὰρ ἀποθνήσκομεν)' (*Res.* 1:60.4/325.2–3).[43] Methodius combines Phil. 3:19 and 1 Cor. 15:32 as both addressing a way of life associated with gluttony, and as a practical denial of faith in the resurrection of the body. The slogan quoted in 1 Cor. 15:32 is the creed of the belly-worshippers. Methodius also adds 1 Cor. 6:13 as a proof text, which then takes him to a topic associated with gluttony, that of πορνεία (*Res.* 1:60.4/325.5–18).

11.7   Ambrosiaster (c. 300)

The Latin commentaries on Paul's letters traditionally ascribed to Ambrose are now commonly ascribed to Ambrosiaster, but the identity of this ancient expositor of Paul's thirteen letters is unknown.[44]

His comments on Rom. 16:18 have nothing to say on 'serving the belly'. Ambrosiaster takes it as a passage addressing in a general way questions of genealogy and other Jewish traditions. He takes Rom. 16:18 as summarizing the warnings Paul issued against Jewish customs throughout the letter. The Jews 'empty God's grace around themselves – as I have said above – introducing issues of genealogy, putting them together to suit themselves and thus recommending their own traditions by which they seduce those of a simple heart (*Hi enim cogebant credentes Judaizare, ut Dei beneficium circa se inanirent, sicut supra memoravi; compositis enim genealogiae verbis, tractatus sibi coaptabant ad commendationem traditionis suae, per quos simplicium corda deciperent*)' (*PL* 17.181).

It is likely that in the traditions to which he refers Ambrosiaster would include food laws as well. But he leaves the phrase 'serving the belly' in the Pauline passage without comment. This Ambrosiaster text can, therefore, only indirectly be considered a proof text for the food law interpretation of Rom. 16:18.

According to Ambrosiaster, in Phil. 3:19 (*PL* 17.417) Paul has in mind the opponents who turned Galatia upside down, itinerant missionaries

[43] In *Res.* 2:17.9–10/367.18–24 (which *GCS* renders only in German since the text has survived only in Slavonic), 'having the belly as god' sums up the list of vices in 1 Cor. 6:9–10. Such people are living according to the flesh, and are likened to the animals. The comparison with the animals, which we have found to be common in texts using the belly-*topos*, Methodius develops in *De Lepra* 18:1–3/47–3. Belly-worshippers are here said to act like animals bowing down to the earth, unable to look upwards to God the Creator of all things.
[44] See Alfred Stuiber, 'Ambrosiaster' and Alexander Souter, *Earliest Latin Commentaries*, pp. 39–42.

who destroyed God's church with deception. In the name of Christ they preached Judaism, as though Christ were given to them:

> He [i.e. Paul] mentions them with tears; because they obstructed salvation for believers, by raising questions on food to be eaten or avoided, as though salvation consisted in food, or the belly were God. They thought God took pleasure in pure food, according to the Law, and they glorified in circumcised genitals; which is to set the mind on earthly things. But they who set the mind on spiritual things, they have pride in faith, hope and love. And to this place it does [not][45] apply as he said – for the sake of gain and gluttony: 'whose god is the belly'.

The Latin text goes like this: *Quos cum lacrymis memorat; quia saluti credentium obsistebant, de cibis edendis, et non edendis quaestiones moventes, quasi salus in esca sit, aut venter Deus, quem juxta legem mundis escis delectari putabant, gloriantes in pudendis circumcisis; hoc est terrena sapere: qui autem spiritualia sapit, in fide, in spe, in charitate gloriatur. Ad locum autem hunc non pertinet, ut quaestus causa aut gulae dixerit: Quorum Deus venter est.*

Ambrosiaster reads Phil. 3:19 in the light of Paul fighting Jewish opponents elsewhere as well.[46] This makes his reading of this Pauline passage into a general dictum on Jewish attempts to put obstacles to the believers. Imposing observance of food laws was an important tool in this endeavour, as witnessed particularly in Galatians and Romans. Hence 'having the belly as god' is linked to food laws. This is spelled out more explicitly here than in any of the other texts we have investigated. None the less, the belly is still, even in this text, primarily related to gluttony. In the last sentence quoted above, 'having the belly as god', relates to the acquisition of wealth (*quaestus*) and gluttony (*gulae*). Ambrosiaster indirectly says that Jews who are imposing food law observance on Christians are doing so out of their gluttony and self-interest. This is the reason why Paul says

---

[45] The Migne edition mentions that omission of '*non*' is attested; this makes better sense.

[46] Another ancient expositor of Pauline epistles is Marius Victorinus of Africa (fourth century). His commentaries are very much marked by his anti-Arian christology. Werner Erdt, *Marius Victorinus Afer*, speaks of the 'Christocentrik' which is characteristic of Victorinus' comments; see also pp. 123–5, 209–10, 215–16. Victorinus' commentaries are so steeped in the christological controversies that he actually leaves unnoticed large parts of the Pauline texts. This is also the case with his comments on Phil. 3:19 (*PL* 8.1224–5) where 'those who have the belly as god' has become a pejorative description of the heretics. His comments focus on *inimici crucis Christi*, and *deus venter est* in Paul's text is actually not commented on. He merely renders this as a name suitable for those who are teaching falsely about Christ. The Latin text is also available in Albrecht Locher, *Commentarii ad Epistolas Pauli*.

they have their belly as god. In other words, this refers not to the food laws as such, but to the motivation behind their preoccupation with food, which is their being obsessed with gain leading to gluttony.

11.8   Pelagius (late fourth and early fifth centuries)

Pelagius was a British theologian and exegete who taught in Rome. His commentary on Phil. 3:17–19[47] speaks of those who have given up the hope of suffering like Christ, and who have exchanged this for the legalistic ceremonies. An example is Jovinian (see below), who has changed the afflictions of fasting and physical suffering into luxury and feasting (*in luxuriam et epulas*). The god of this people is their belly. They think they serve God, but they gourmandize and do not listen to the words of the prophet, saying 'And when you eat and when you drink, do you not eat and drink only for yourselves (*si manducaueritis [et biberitis],* *nonne vobis manduca[b]itis[et bibetis]*)?' Paul's words about his opponents who glory in their own confusion (*et gloria in confusione ipsorum*) refers, according to Pelagius, to physical circumcision. He thinks that Jewish customs and gluttony are associated. Bringing the two together is surprising to a present-day reader. But we have already seen that Novatian and Ambrosiaster are thinking along these lines. We will elaborate on this below.

In his *Expositio* to Romans 16:18 Pelagius says that the belly-servants are the circumcised Jews of Paul's time who did away with fasting and abstinence. Disagreeing with the apostolic preaching, they preached new moons, sabbaths and other feast-days for the belly's sake: *De illis dicit* *qui ex circumcisione illo tempore venerant, ieiunia et abstinentiam de* *struentes, neomenias et sabbata et ceteras ferias ventris gratia praedica* *bant . . .* (*Expositio Rom.* 16:18). Pelagius says that Jewish customs were imposed for the sake of the stomach.

The way he is here bringing together Jewish practices with what is usually a reference to gluttony is surprising. Jewish customs such as food laws put restrictions on what to eat, while gluttony refers to an unlimited and excessive quantity of food. It is not obvious how the two can be combined in the way Pelagius is doing here. Alternatively, *ventris gratia* refers to the food laws themselves. But this runs contrary to our findings on the belly throughout this study. Furthermore, this makes Pelagius say that

---

[47] For the Latin text see Alexander Souter, *Pelagius's Exposition of Thirteen Epistles of* *St Paul*. An English translation is available in Theodore Bruyn, *Pelagius' Commentary on* *St Paul's Epistle to the Romans*.

food laws stirred up the pleasures, which is exactly the opposite of what might be expected from the Hellenistic-Jewish material presented above. Philo, for instance, thought the other way around: God put restrictions on just those foods that were prone to enhancing pleasure. Pelagius' reason for speaking of those coming from among the circumcised as 'belly-servants' is, therefore, hardly the question of food laws.

What causes him to speak of Jewish customs as belly-service is that they have done away with fasting and abstinence. This is the precise reference of the belly in this text, and it makes perfect sense within this text as well as continuing what we saw in his comments on Phil. 3:19 above. A cross-reference between Rom. 16:18 and Phil. 3:19 is made explicit by Pelagius himself in his exposition of the last-mentioned text. People (Jewish-Christians?) agitating for Jewish piety have, according to Pelagius, set fasting and abstinence aside. He therefore considers them devoted to the belly.

11.9   Jerome (c. 345–420)

Jerome preached ascetism and lived accordingly.[48] This is very obvious in his refutation of Jovinian (died about 405), an unorthodox monk who denied that virginity as such was a higher state than marriage, and that abstinence as such was better than thankful eating. This monk had undergone a complete change. He abandoned celibacy, developed a taste for good food, frequented public baths and mixed freely with the ladies.[49] Jovinian's writings are lost, but Jerome provides a brief review of his position before refuting it (*Jov.* 1:3/*PL* 23.222–4). Jovinian was finally condemned at two synods, thanks not least to the works which both Jerome and Augustine wrote against him. Jerome's refutation of him is found in Books 1 and 2 of his *Adversus Jovinianum* (AD 393).[50]

Jerome turns directly from a presentation of Jovinian's view to mentioning the Serpent in Gen. 3. The temptation of the snake was a temptation to eat; it promised eternal life to Eve if she ate. Jerome considers his own writing a Christian antidote to the poisonous words of the Devil (*Jov.* 1:4/*PL* 23.224–5).[51] The art of the Devil (*artes diaboli*), who is the old Serpent (*haec sunt serpentis antiqui*), is the desires of Gentiles.

---

[48]   For an introduction to his life and work see J. N. D. Kelly, *Jerome*.

[49]   Ibid. pp. 180–1.

[50]   See ibid. pp. 182–9 on how Jovinian's view challenged Jerome's theology. For a presentation of Jovinian's case and Jerome's attack on his position, see David G. Hunter, 'Virginal Ideal'.

[51]   An English translation is available in NPNF Vol. 6.

Jovinian's teaching resembles this art of the Serpent. It is, therefore, the task of Jerome to search out the snakes of Jovinian, hiding in their holes (*Jov.* 1:3/*PL* 23.224). It is not the business of Christians to perpetuate themselves by having heirs, says Jerome, for their longing is to be with Christ for ever (1:48/*PL* 23.291–3). Marriage grows out of adultery (1:49/*PL* 23.293–6).

In Book 2 he tackles the question of food and brings forward various arguments from the Scriptures in favour of eating. In chap. 6 he presents the counter-arguments, namely that fasting is pleasing to God. Christ laid down two sets of laws, one for soldiers and publicans, the other for the perfect,[52] mandating an ascetic life. This is where Jerome's heart lies: 'If you wish to be perfect, it is good not to drink wine, and eat flesh. If you wish to be perfect, it is better to enrich the mind than to stuff the body (*melius est saginare animum, quam corpus*)' (*Jov.* 2:6/*PL* 23.307). The person who loves food and dainties remains like a child:

> ... eat and drink, and if you like, with Israel rise up and play and sing: 'Let us eat and drink, for tomorrow we shall die.' Let him eat and drink, who looks for death when he has feasted (*post cibos*), and who says with Epicurus, 'There is nothing after death, and death itself is nothing.' We believe Paul when he says in tones of thunder: 'Meats for the belly, and the belly for meats. But God will destroy both them and it.'   (*Jov.* 2:6/*PL* 23.307)

This passage brings together, as into a cluster, 1 Cor. 10:7; 15:32; 6:13 and the doctrine of Epicurus. It is all part of a strategy of staying away from dainty food and of fasting instead. By means of fasting, the soul is like a charioteer enabled to control the wild horses; i.e. the bodily desires. Jerome is here using the old philosophical simile to explain his view (*Jov.* 2:10/*PL* 23.312–13).

An ascetic life is a means of devoting oneself to wisdom. 'For nothing is so destructive to the mind as a full belly' (*Jov.* 2:12/*PL* 23.315). Jerome thinks like a Stoic; the belly weighed down by food endangers the life of the soul. The full belly is to him a result of participating in *epulae*, dinner-parties at which one eats so much that not even a day and night is sufficent to digest it (cf. *Jov.* 2:11/*PL* 23.313–14). Paul's saying on being content with food and clothing (1 Tim. 6:8) is Jerome's guide (*Jov.* 2:11/*PL* 23.314). Repletion is by all means to be avoided. Avarice and lust are nursed by luxury of all kinds: 'Take away the luxurious feasting and the gratification of lust, and no one will want riches to be used either in

---

[52] Jerome speaks of *perfectus esse* which is a translation of τέλειος εἶναι in Matt. 19:21.

the belly or beneath it' (*Jov.* 2:11/*PL* 23.314). Food, according to Jerome, fuels sexual lust.[53]

Jerome fiercely attacks Jovinian for supporting his case with the tradition that Jesus was a glutton and wine-bibber (*voratorem et potatorem vini*). Jerome comes very close to denying this piece of evidence by calling upon other traditions, such as

- Jesus, who fasted for forty days
- Jesus said he had food which his disciples did not know
- Jesus called those who hungered and thirsted blessed
- Jesus said Lazarus was in the bosom of Abraham owing to his abstinence during his lifetime

Jesus was therefore not a glutton. Although food must be taken as nourishment, Jesus preferred fasting and virginity (*Jov.* 2:17/*PL* 23.324–6).

Jerome's strategy is to present Jovinian as an advocate of sexual freedom and excessive eating, very much in the Epicurean spirit. The very first words of his refutation of Jovinian go like this: *Epicurus Christianorum* (*Jov.* 1:1/*PL* 23.221); he considers himself to fight the 'Epicurus of the Christians'. Jerome makes a distinction, however, between Epicurus himself, who lived a simple life, and his role as an encourager of pleasure (*voluptatis assertor*)[54] (*Jov.* 1:48/*PL* 23.292 and 2.11/*PL* 23.314, cf. 2:12/*PL* 23.315). For Jerome Epicurus and gratifying of the stomach were symbols of indulgence, of pleasure in excessive eating and drinking. His strategy is to make Epicurus' philosophy a subtext to his refutation of Jovinian. This becomes evident in *Jov.* 2:36/*PL* 23.349, where his enemy is described as 'our modern Epicurus wantoning in his gardens with his favourites of both sexes'. In *Jov.* 1:4/*PL* 23.225, Jerome speaks of Jovinian's writings as vomit which has been thrown up, which is a code-word for what he considered to be an Epicurean lifestyle enjoyed at banquets. Jovinian is throughout depicted as the Epicurus of the Christians.

Jerome coins a slogan which he puts in the mouth of Jovinian's disciples: 'We follow vice, not virtue; Epicurus not Christ; Jovinianus not the Apostle Paul' (2:36/*PL* 23.349). Jerome considers this a creed echoing

---

[53] Teresa M. Shaw, *The Burden of the Flesh*, says that 'underlying Jerome's defence of fasting is his understanding of the connection between the pleasure of eating and sexual desire' (p. 101). How according to many writers in the Early Church repletion in food entices towards sexual intercourse, has been worked out in detail by Shaw; see e.g. pp. 81–96, 99, 101–2, 124–8, 145–7.

[54] In *Jov.* 1:4/*PL* 23.225, Jerome calls Jovinian a most voluptuous preacher (*voluptuosissimum concionatorem*).

the call of the Jerusalem mob to crucify Christ. The belly-philosophy of Epicurus has become a means of discrediting an adversary. None the less, there is still a link to the unholy trinity we have discovered throughout this study, excessive eating and drinking leading to unlawful sex – from the viewpoint of Jerome. The polemic tells us more about Jerome's rhetoric than it does about Jovinian.

From Jerome's ascetic point of view, Jovinian was living an Epicurean kind of life. His purpose in invoking the belly-philosophy of Epicurus is not merely rhetorical. It is perfectly clear that his use of this rhetoric does not contribute very much to a historical description of Jovinian's view. It is useful, however, to note that gluttony, at least from Jerome's point of view, was at the centre of this debate.[55] Although Jerome quotes neither from Phil. 3:19 nor from Rom. 16:18 in this treatise, he here provides a framework within which these texts were certainly at home. His use of some texts we have labelled the Corinthian belly-dicta related to Epicurus' pleasure-philosophy, suggests that Jerome would consider Phil. 3:19 and Rom. 16:18 as appropriate for fighting Jovinian as well. This assumption is justified by some of his letters, to which we now turn.

In his *Epistle* 7:5/*PL* 22.338–41, Jerome speaks of those who have their belly as god (*deus venter est*). He does not introduce this as a scriptural saying, but a reference to Phil. 3:19 is nevertheless likely. In this letter the phrase describes how people live as barbarians. They live only for the day at hand; they have no future horizon for their living. Their final aim is to become richer. Lupicinus is their priest. It is obviously Jerome's aim to discredit this fellow Christian, about whom we have no further information. The LCL translator suggests that 'he was at variance with Jerome probably because he opposed monasticism'.[56] 'Having the belly as god' is here a reference to living for the moment and for immediate satisfaction.

Epistle 14/*PL* 22.347–55 speaks of martyrdom and being prepared to let the dead bury the dead (14:3/*PL* 22.348–9). Jerome imagines an interlocutor saying that this is well enough, if one is a martyr (14:4/*PL* 22.349). To Jerome, however, there is no time when a Christian is not suffering. The sufferings he has in mind are the temptations of the Devil. He finds himself surrounded by self-indulgence, avarice and lust. His belly wants to replace Christ and become his god (*venter meus vult mihi*

---

[55] J. N. D. Kelly, *Jerome*, p. 181 says of Jovinian that 'he was evidently a serious thinker whose critique of celibacy and fasting, indeed the whole conception of a more perfect life attainable by ascetic practices, stemmed from a high estimate of baptismal regeneration and an interpretation of Christianity completely at variance with current orthodoxy'.

[56] The LCL edition p. 24.

Deus esse pro Christo). The pleasures of the belly all aim at driving away the Spirit who dwells in the believer and to violate His temple. Jerome is here alluding to 1 Cor. 3:17 and 6:19. This means that it is a matter of proper worship. Belly-devotion is indeed idolatry.

Epistle 22/*PL* 22.394–425 speaks of fasting and gives examples from the Old Testament heroes who led a simple life (22:9/*PL* 22.400). The Scriptures generally condemn gluttony (*gula*). Jerome reminds his addressee, the virgin Eustochium, that Adam, the first man, obeyed his stomach rather than God (*primus homo, ventri magis obediens quam Deo*) (*Epistle* 22:10/*PL* 22.400). The fall had to do with eating and obeying the belly. It is typical of Satan to tempt with food since he pursued the same approach with Christ; he was tempted with food as well (Matt. 4:1–3).[57] Jerome proves his point by quoting in tandem 1 Cor. 6:13[58] and Phil. 3:19. Phil. 3:19 was spoken to people who lived in luxury (*de luxuriosis*). It was repletion, the appetite for more and for forbidden food, which had human beings expelled from Paradise.[59] Return was possible only through abstinence and fasting. Belly-worship is, then, the result of having yielded to Satan's temptation to luxurious eating and drinking. In a way which recalls Philo, Jerome links this to Gen. 3 and the Serpent. To anyone who is drawn to this way of living, Jerome says: 'Live then by your own rule, since you cannot live by God's' (*Epistle* 22:11/*PL* 22.400–1). An empty and rumbling stomach is the only way to preserve chastity (*pudicitia*). A stuffed stomach is a sign of Satan's temptations, while a rumbling belly indicates piety. The belly is truly a sign in this literature.

In *Epistle* 123:18/*PL* 22.1059, Jerome comments on widows seeking a second marriage. He quotes 1 Tim. 5:13 about women wandering from house to house gossiping. 'Their god is their belly, their glory is in their shame', he says. Their knowledge of the Scriptures is limited to texts favouring a second marriage by which they justify their desires (*sua desideria*). Belly-worship is here an obvious reference to sexual desire.

---

[57] In Philo's appropriation of the belly-*topos*, Satan holds a key position. We saw this particularly in his exegesis of Gen. 3. This is a motif which we have uncovered in Rom. 16:17–20 as well.

[58] In *Epistle* 55:2/*PL* 22.561–2, Jerome quotes 1 Cor. 6:13 as a dictum against excess in eating. It has relevance to the question of fornication as well since excess in eating is the mother of sexual lust (*luxuria mater libidinis est*), according to Jerome: 'a belly that is distended with food (*ventremque distentum cibo*) and saturated with draughts of wine is sure to lead to sensual passion'; quoted from NPNF Vol. 6.

[59] Teresa M. Shaw, *The Burden of the Flesh*, pp. 161–219 has demonstrated that among Christian ascetics fasting was quite commonly seen as a means of returning to Paradise. See also Elizabeth A. Clarke, *Women in the Early Church*, pp. 115–55.

In *Epistle* 147/*PL* 22.1195–1204, Jerome addresses a deacon, Sabinianus, who had committed adultery, and whom he now tries to bring to repentance. To Jerome the deacon's refusal to repent is to Jerome a sign that his mind is earthly. He refuses to rise; his eyes are not lifted to heaven. We recognize here the motif of earthly versus heavenly which is often associated with the idiom 'serving the belly'. In this letter, Jerome quotes the parable of the prodigal son (Luke 15) who ate the husks given to the swine, together with Phil. 3:19: 'You make your belly your God instead of Christ; you are a slave to lust (*servus libidini*); your glory is in your shame' (*Epistle* 147:1/*PL* 22.1195–6). By reading Phil. 3:19 in the light of the prodigal son who ate husks, Jerome draws upon another motif associated with belly-worship, namely the animal-like character of the belly-devotees. The reference of worshipping the belly is sexual appetite and fornication in particular.

In his commentary on Philippians, Jerome briefly comments on Phil. 3:19 (*PL* 30.889) as well, a text which he connects with Rom. 16:17. Belly-devotion refers to people who think they serve God, but who are in fact gluttons; they have not heard what the prophet (Zech. 7:6) said: And when you eat and when you drink, do you not eat and drink yourselves? (*si manducaueritis et biberitis, nonne vos manducatis et bibitis?*)' 'Those who glory in their shame and who are of the earth', refers to those who honour circumcision: *in circumcisione verecundi membri*. Jerome's comments are almost identical with those of Pelagius, even in wording.[60]

In his commentary on Romans, Jerome says that Rom. 16:18 is about those circumcised who are destroying both fasting and restraint (*ieiunia et abstinentiam destruentes*) (*PL* 30.744–5). They prescribe new moons, sabbaths and other festivals – 'for the sake of the belly' (*ventris gratia*). They are abandoning the apostolic doctrine and preparing a stumbling-block for the brethren. Jerome's comments run in tandem with Pelagius' exposition of this text, even in its wording (see above). Like Pelagius, Jerome connects the belly and Jewish piety. Jerome says that Jewish practices are caused by the belly, without giving any explanation for this. Food laws are not mentioned, but judging from the context, they would fall within the framework of Jerome's interpretation, but not as a reference for *ventris gratia*. As we pointed out in the presentation of Pelagius' commentary, *ventris gratia* is explained by the mention of doing away with fasting and abstinence. This gives to *venter* the meaning we have found throughout our investigation.

---

[60] The comments of Pelagius and Jerome on the two Pauline sayings are almost identical (see above).

We have, however, already seen that Novatian, Ambrosiaster and Pelagius link belly-worship in terms of gluttony and food laws without necessarily claiming that the two are interchangeable. We will later see (particularly in John Chrystostom) that Jews were presented as gluttons. Judging from the material presented above, as well as from Jerome's preoccupation with food, it is not justified to take his comments on Rom. 16:18 as mere pejorative rhetoric. *Ventris gratia* certainly has a reference to food matters, which in this text means the doing away with fasting and abstinence. The Jews are belly-worshippers since they impose upon the believers practices that imply abandonment of Christian fasting.

11.10   John Chrysostom (c. 347–407)

John Chrysostom was one of the ablest expositors of the Early Church.[61] His *Homilies* on biblical texts provide an interesting view of early Christian exegesis. *Homily* 32 is on Rom. 16:17–18/*PG* 60.675–82. Chrysostom makes it his point of departure for speaking about false teaching in general. The nature of false teachers is to cause divisions. He emphasizes the unity of the church, a unity manifested in the teaching of the apostles. The best means of fighting false teaching is to remain united in one body. This creates an obstacle to the Devil's penetrating the church with false teaching (*Hom.* 32:1/*PG* 60.675–7). Chrysostom then proceeds to ask from where false teachings come. The answer is that they are introduced by 'those who are serving their belly' as well as other passions (ἀπὸ τοῦ γαστρὶ δουλεύειν καὶ τοῖς ἄλλοις πάθεσιν) (*Hom.* 32:1/*PG* 60.675–7). Serving the belly results in divisions, and neglect of the fellowship. Belly-devotion is not good for the church as a fellowship. Chrysostom here applies a common motif in the ancient critique of Epicureanism: belly-devotion: it is detrimental to the common good.

Chrysostom quotes Phil. 3:19 in his comments on Rom. 16. This further strengthens the identification of the false teachers as belly-devotees (*Hom.* 32:1/*PG* 60.676). He claims that Phil. 3:19 is about Jews who were gluttons (γαστριμάργοι). This claim is supported by a number of references to greed headed, however, by Tit. 1:12, which he sees as evidence for the Jews being γαστέρες. The scriptural references which support this reading of Tit. 1:12 are Matt. 23:14; Deut. 32:15; 6:11–12;[62] John 2:18 and 6:30. These texts are about Israel's enjoying fat and wine and food

[61] See J. N. D. Kelly, *Golden Mouth.*

[62] This text shows that having a full belly was considered a situation in which one was liable to succumb to temptations. Deut. 32:15 and 6:12 are examples of the temptation of eating which the Jews faced when they entered the promised land. The two texts are

in their land, as well as the manna in the desert. This text-collection is rounded off with a rhetorical question: 'How then comest thou not to be ashamed at having slaves of the belly (δοῦλοι κοιλίας) for thy teachers, when thou art a brother of Christ?' (*Hom.* 32:1/*PG* 60.676).[63] Then he proceeds to ask by what means these false teachers are attacking the church. The answer is summed up in one word, flattery (κολακεία). What Paul is describing in Rom. 16:18 is false teachers deceiving the believers by means of flattery. Chrysostom's way of summing up Paul's text in terms of κολακεία, is, in fact, what we argued in our exegesis of the same text.[64]

In this exposition, Chrysostom states that Jews were gluttons. He follows a view which we have found in Novatian, Ambrosiaster, Pelagius and Jerome (see also further examples later). But no one expresses this so emphatically as does Chrysostom. He describes the Jews as drunkards as well, and the synagogues as drinking-places. In *Jud.* 1:2/*PG* 48.845–7, he calls the Jews gluttons who live only for their bellies. Robert L. Wilken has investigated Chrysostom's comments on the Jews in the light of common rhetorical practice in his time.[65] Wilken argues that the rhetoric of the belly is here a tool of polemic and a pejorative description of an adversary, devoid of any historical reality.

It is necessary to urge a distinction here between how Jews actually lived, and how Chrysostom and other ascetic Christians were liable to see them. But the rhetoric of the belly cannot work properly if it is entirely out of touch with any historical reality. The rhetorical force of the belly-*topos* depends on its being rooted in reality, at least as some people see it. From the perspective of Chrysostom and many other ascetic writers the Jewish preoccupation with food, the importance of food in Jewish piety, and their common thanksgiving for food might well have served as points of departure for seeing them as gluttons. The Jewish joy in food is witnessed in many places.[66] Furthermore, as we noted above, Chrysostom supports his case with a Scriptural catena, in which the call for food in the

mentioned together with Phil. 3:19 and Luke 6:25 in *De Poenitentia* II:8/*PG* 60.697. Deut. 32:15 is to Chrysostom a comment on Israel's (Jacob's) love of fat food.

[63] The English translation is taken from NPNF Vol. 11.

[64] See chap. 9.2 in this study.

[65] Robert L. Wilken, *John Chrysostom and the Jews*; see particularly pp. 116–23. See also Marcel Simon, *Verus Israel*, pp. 217–23.

[66] The joyous meal as part of worship is well-known in the Old Testament. This is envisaged e.g. in the verb שׂמח, which refers to festival-meals enjoyed 'before the Lord'; see especially Deut. 12:18; 14:26; 27:7 where this verb appears synonymously with אכל (to eat) cf. 16:11, 14; 26:11. Deut. 14:26 mentions meat, wine and whatever is desired to be on the menu.

wilderness plays a major role. This means that the rhetoric of the belly in his writings is not a source as to how Jews were in fact living. It is, of course, a true source as to how Chrysostom the ascetic viewed them in the light of Scripture, and furthermore, that this rhetoric is especially associated with matters of food. They are not words to be used against just any opponent. The Jews were not ascetics. To many Patristic Fathers this justified calling them belly-worshippers; they were carnally minded, as witnessed in the wilderness-traditions as well as in their preoccupation with food laws.

In his *Homily* 13/*PG* 62.275–82, Chrysostom comments on Phil. 3:18–19. He proceeds verse by verse, but still considers the text as a unit in which the different parts shed light on each other. This is obvious, since some of the main thoughts appear throughout his exegesis. This is particularly so with the thought introducing the homily: it is not proper for a Christian to seek ease and rest (ἄνεσιν καὶ ἀνάπαυσιν ζητεῖν)[67] (*Hom.* 13:1/*PG* 62.275). He repeats this many times. Seeking an easy and comfortable life is contrary to the cross of Christ. Hence believers who seek these things become enemies of the cross. Chrysostom gives two reasons for this interpretation. One appears later in this *Homily* when Chrysostom is commenting on the heavenly πολίτευμα; rest is to be sought where one's home is, and that is not on earth. In this way the question of an easy life permeates Chrysostom's whole exegesis of Phil. 3:18–19.

The second reason is elaborated on at length. A believer who loves Christ will die his death. To prove this he quotes from Gal. 6:14 about being crucified to the world as well as Matt. 16:24 on taking up the cross to follow Jesus.[68] These quotations urge the believer to be prepared for death. Being a friend of delicious food (τρυφῆς φίλος), safety (ἀσφαλεία), of life and body (φιλόζωοι καὶ φιλοσώματοι), means enmity with the cross (*Hom.* 13:1/*PG* 62.277). God's plans for the Christians are not eating and drinking, but crowning them in the stadion. The athletic imagery here takes on a martyrological meaning.[69]

In *Hom.* 13:1/*PG* 62.275–8, Chrysostom comments directly on 'having the belly as god', although he has anticipated this throughout the homily. These are people saying 'let us eat and drink', which is a short form of

---

[67] Migne's Latin text has *requiem et otium quaerere*.

[68] For the martyrological interpretation of discipleship, see Eric Esborn, *Ethical Patterns*, pp. 122–8. Chrysostom's interpretation of Phil. 3:17–19 brings to mind how Ernst Lohmeyer reads Philippians. 'Those having the belly as god' refers to people who by all means attempt to avoid martyrdom.

[69] See John Alexander Sawhill, *Athletic Metaphors*. Unfortunately, this book has not been available to me.

1 Cor. 15:32, and which he cites in full later in the *Homily*. While some hold their wealth (χρήματα or *pecunia*) as god, some have the stomach. Both are idolatry of the worst kind.[70]

The glory of belly-devotees who eat and drink is in their shame. Chrysostom is aware that some take this as a reference to circumcision. Thus Chrysostom provides indirect evidence for a common interpretation of this part of the Pauline dictum, reaching back into the early history of Christian exegesis. Speaking for himself, however, he does not think so. It is a general reference to shameful things and behaviour. They have exchanged what is honourable for what is demeaning or shameful. Chrysostom's reference is basically in accordance with his exposition of Rom. 16:18 (see above), which he takes to refer to Jewish gluttony. In this text, however, the particular mention of Jews is left out.

His exegesis now takes quite a self-critical turn. Belly-worship does not apply only to the readers of Paul's time; on the contrary, it is even more relevant in our day, says Chrysostom. It applies to 'us'. He wishes that no one he knew was affected by this worship. But that is not the case, since belly-devotion is relevant to us (οἱ δὲ παρόντες ἡμῖν . . . πρὸς ἡμᾶς / Latin: *ad nos pertinere . . . in nos*) (*Hom.* 13:1/*PG* 62.277–8). Servants of the belly are not only found among outsiders; the stomach has its devotees within the Christian community as well. What makes Chrysostom say so? He gives the answer in a rhetorical question: 'For when one consumes his whole life[71] in drinking and revelling (ἐν πότοις καὶ κώμοις), and expends some small trifle on the poor, whilst he consumes the larger portion on his belly, will not these words with justice apply to him?' (*Hom.* 13:1/*PG* 62.278). Gluttony is here seen as a special form of greed, the reluctance to share with the needy (cf. *Hom.* 13 on 1 Tim. 4:11–14/*PG* 62.569–70). Excessive eating and drinking are in themselves selfish actions. Chrysostom knew that this was not a way of life with which Christians themselves were unfamiliar.

[70] In the treatise on Chrysostom's life (*PG* 47.44), Palladius interprets Tit. 1:5 and 1 Tim. 1:4 on fighting the false teachers in the light of Tit. 1:12. Those who were leading astray were the gluttons of this text, whose concern was with eating and drinking. They were belly-servants (κοιλιολάτραι), people to whom John the Baptist was addressing his message. These were people of the *symposia*, whose voice speaks in the injunction of Exod. 32:6 as well as in Exod. 32:1: Δεῦτε, ποιήσωμεν θεούς, οἵτινες προπορεύσονται ἡμῶν. Palladius sees this attitude as exemplified in 1 Cor. 15:32 ('let us eat and drink for to-morrow we will die'), which is contrasted to Jesus talking about spiritual food in John 6:27. We notice again that the belly-rhetoric includes a cluster of the Pauline texts we have investigated.

[71] The Greek text has πάντα τὸν βίον . . . ἀναλίσκῃ τις, which is a metaphorical way of speaking about life; life is seen as something to be eaten or consumed; see LSJ s.v.

In *Hom.* 13:2/*PG* 62.278, Chrysostom quotes Phil. 3:19 almost in full, thus demonstrating that all his comments apply to this whole verse. He now asks who are the worshippers of the belly. The answer is not given in historical terms, i.e. he is not identifying any particular group or persons. He proceeds rather by way of characterizing them. They care for earthly things. This earthly attitude is exemplified in the following sayings:

- let us build houses – on the earth
- let us purchase fields – on the earth
- let us obtain power – on the earth
- let us gain glory – on the earth
- let us enrich ourselves – on the earth

In all examples the limited horizon is expressed in terms of 'on the earth'. About people who live like this, Chrysostom says: οὗτοί εἰσιν ὧν ὁ θεὸς ἡ κοιλία(*Hom.* 13:2/*PG* 62.278). Their concern is not with spiritual things because they are preoccupied with their belongings and reputation; in short, their belly. In particular, luxurious eating makes the soul heavy and earth-hugging. He therefore quotes 1 Cor. 15:32, which applies to the belly-servants he has just presented.

But the stomach was given to feed us. Chrysostom now addresses his readers directly, urging them to master the stomach, lest it becomes the mistress of the house (δέσποιναν).[72] The stomach needs to be controlled, to be put under restraint (αὐτάρκεια). He makes his point in an analogy. The sea, when kept within its boundaries, does not cause as much harm to the earth as the belly does to the soul, when it breaks out of its limits. As with the sea, how much more is the stomach in need of restraint and moderation (σωφρονίσαι).[73] In *Hom.* 13.1/*PG* 62.278), Chrysostom ponders on what it means to worship or to be enslaved (δουλεύειν)[74] by the belly, since this is what it means to have it as god. The gluttons are worshipping the stomach by being its slaves, carrying out what it demands. This is the nature of belly-worship according to Chrysostom.

In his *Homily* 21 on Matt. 6:24/*PG* 57.293–300 ('you cannot serve two masters'), Chrysostom says that calling Mammon a master (κύριος) is by no means a reference to his true nature. Similarly, the belly is not called a god because it is worthy of this name, 'but from the wretchedness of them that are enslaved (ἀλλ᾽ ἀπὸ τῆς τῶν δουλευόντων ἀθλιότητος)' (*Hom.* 21:2/*PG* 57.296). A combination of the belly-*topos* and Christ's

---

[72] Migne's Latin text has *non ut dominum habeas*.
[73] Migne's Latin text has *moderari*.   [74] Migne's Latin text has *servire*.

words about Mammon is, as we have seen, quite common in Patristic literature.[75] Both are examples of enslavement which justifies calling them idolatry. In this *Homily*, enslavement to the belly is described in terms of πορνεύειν, μεθύειν, τρυφᾶν, which corresponds to the unholy trinity of eating, drinking and sex.

In his *Homily* 29 on Hebrews/*PG* 63.203–8, Chrysostom comments on Heb. 12:4–6. Discipline or παιδεία is necessary to remain on the narrow way. He gives some examples of people who have chosen the wrong one:

- those who live in luxury (ἐν τρυφῇ)
- the rich man (Luke 16:19–31)[76]
- the Jews who live for the belly, having the belly as their god (οἱ τῇ γαστρὶ ζῶντες Ἰουδαῖοι, ὧν ὁ θεὸς ἡ κοιλία)[77]

Before proceeding with this list of examples of belly-devotees, he briefly explains why the Jews belong in this list. This is the question we have grappled with above. While in the wilderness, the Jews always sought an easy life (ἄνεσις) (*Hom.* 29:3/*PG* 63.206). This explanation picks up the theme of *Homily* 13 on Phil. 3:18–19 (see above); seeking an easy earthly life is typical of belly-worshippers. This the Jews did in the wilderness. He does not elaborate on this here, but from some of his homilies (see below) we know that he is thinking of the yearning for food and drink which is so clearly witnessed in the biblical Exodus-traditions. It is worth noticing that the desert-traditions about Israel are summarized in the belly-*topos*; an easy life with food available at all times. Exodus traditions are here the major scriptural basis for calling the Jews gluttons enslaved by their belly.[78]

[75] Further references are given in this chapter; see also Chrysostom in his commentary on 2 Cor. 4:1, *Hom.* 8:2/*PG* 61.455–6 where Mammon as κύριος and belly as θεός are mentioned in tandem, as examples of who 'the god of this world' is. Similarly in *Hom.* 13:3/*PG* 60.511, where Matt. 6:24 and Phil. 3:19 are combined as outstanding examples of 'the law warring against the law of my mind' (Rom. 7:23).

[76] Chrysostom mentions this rich man in his *Hom.* 13:5 on Matt. 4:1/*PG* 57.214. He puts in his mouth something like a creed: 'Let me enjoy all things present for a time, and then I will consider about things out of sight: I will gratify my belly (χαρίσομαι τῇ γαστρί), I will be a slave to pleasures (δουλεύσω ταῖς ἡδοναῖς), I will make full use of the present life; give me to-day, and take to-morrow'; quoted from NPNF Vol. 10, where this text is found in *Hom.* 13:7. This 'creed' sounds very much like the Epicurean slogan quoted by Paul in 1 Cor. 15:32, and brings to mind the saying of the rich farmer as well (Luke 12:19).

[77] In his *Hom.* 14 /*PG* 62.571–80, Chrysostom says apropos of 1 Tim. 5:8 that the women who neglected their own household were living in luxury; i.e. living for the belly (ἡ γὰρ τῇ γαστρὶ ζῶσα). He paraphrases this dictum of Paul by means of the belly-*topos*, which in this text takes on the meaning of selfishness, neglecting the family for one's own pleasure.

[78] Cf. our exegesis of 1 Cor. 10:7 in chap. 10.

Chrysostom continues his list of people who have chosen the wrong way:

- the generation of Noah who sought an easy life
- people in Sodom, owing to their gluttony (γαστριμαργία)[79]
- Esau who was a man of an easy life (ἄνεσις)
- the giants who looked on women (Gen. 6)
- those who were maddened by lust for men
- kings of the nations
- Babylonians and Egyptians (*Hom.* 29:3/*PG* 63.206)

'Having the belly as god' is here embedded in a context speaking of luxury in food, gluttony, riches, an easy life, and illicit sexual relationships.

That the Exodus traditions in particular provide scriptural basis for calling the Jews belly-worshippers is evident from Chrysostom's comments on John 6:41–2 in his *Hom.* 46:1/*PG* 59.257. His commentary starts by quoting from Phil. 3:19: 'whose god is their belly and whose glory is in their shame'. This applies to the Jews. To Chrysostom that the Jews fell into this category was obvious both from their history and from what they said about Christ. That the Jews were devoted to their belly, he further substantiated with reference to the narrative in John 6. When Jesus filled their bellies (τὴν γαστέρα ἐνέπλησε), they hailed him as a prophet. But when Jesus was talking about spiritual food, they began to murmur. They honoured Jesus as the provider of bread, but not for the heavenly food he brought (*Hom.* 46:1/*PG* 57.257). The narrative followed by the dialogue in John 6 is significant because Chrysostom here finds evidence of Jewish preoccupation with food joined to a lack of understanding of spiritual or heavenly things. In other words, the belly-*topos* works itself out in his exegesis of this text. Together with Exodus traditions, John 6 then provides a basis for Chrysostom's rhetoric of the Jews as gluttons whose minds were set only on earthly things. For Chrysostom this was more than pejorative rhetoric; it was scriptural interpretation as well.

Chrysostom touches on the same topic in his homily on 1 Corinthians, *Hom.* 34:6/*PG* 61.294, commenting on 1 Cor. 13:8.[80] The Jews knew only the things of sense (τὰ αἰσθητά), he says. He substantiates this by quoting Ps. 77:20: 'Can you give us bread also? Our fathers did eat manna in the desert – whose God is their belly' (*Hom.* 34:6/*PG* 61.294). The Isrealites' yearning for food is to Chrysostom an example of whom they

---

[79] Ezek. 16:49 on the fullness of bread in Sodom justifies this interpretation.
[80] NPNF Vol. 12 has this text in *Hom.* 34:10.

served in the desert, who their real God was. The Jews' whole mind was carnal.

Chrysostom comments on the saying that greed is idolatry in Eph. 5:5–6 (*Hom.* 18/*PG* 62.121–8). Idolatry does not necessarily involve altar, sacrifice, libations or foreign gods, he claims. Idolatry includes not only Aphrodite or Ares (Venus or Mars), but also not mastering

- the passions (μὴ τοῦ πάθους κρατῶν)
- pleasure (ἡδονή)
- wrath (θυμός)
- Mammon (πλεονεξία)

A Christian would object that he never bows down (προσκυνεῖν) to these things. Chrysostom responds that the higher worship (μείζων ἡ προσκύνησις) is the deeds and practice (διὰ τῶν ἔργων καὶ τῶν πραγμάτων) of a person (*Hom.* 18:2/*PG* 62.123). *Hom.* 18:3/*PG* 62.124–5 mentions 'those having the belly as god' as well. These are flatterers (κόλακες) deceiving people so as to continue with idolatrous activities, such as venerating the picture of a deceased daughter (cf. Wisd. 14:15–16). The text is not very forthcoming with information on our topic, but it places Phil. 3:19 within the framework of idolatry and mastering the desires.

We have seen that for Chrysostom a full belly makes a person prone to be tempted by the Devil. This is the interpretation of Jesus' temptation (Matt. 4:1) found in Chrysostom's *Homily* 13 (*PG* 57.207–18). From this it follows naturally that fasting is the most powerful shield against the Devil.[81] Fasting characterizes the life of the believers while luxury, drinking and a loaded table are characteristics of life before baptism (*Hom.* 13:1/*PG* 57.209),[82] a life which, in short, is described as τὸ γαστρὶ δουλεύειν. It was the belly which caused Adam to be thrown out of Paradise, Noah's flood was due to the stomach, and God's punishment of Sodom was caused by the belly of the inhabitants.[83] The Devil causes

---

[81] In his *Hom.* 10/*PG* 53.81–90 on Gen. 1:27, Chrysostom accepts that not all are able to fast. For these he prescribes participation in the real fast, namely almsgiving, fervent prayers and listening enthusiastically to divine sayings (see *Hom.* 13:3/*PG* 53.84–5).

[82] NPNF Vol. 10 has this text in *Hom.* 13:2.

[83] Chrysostom gives Ezek. 16:49 as Scriptural proof of Sodom. This text speaks of the richness of food in that city. For Chrysostom this is a text which he draws upon elsewhere in presenting the Jews as gluttons; so also in this text, where he immediately says that the Jews were tempted by drinking and luxury (ἀπὸ τῆς μέθης καὶ τρυφῆς) (*Hom.* 13:1/*PG* 57.209–10). This is also the case in his *Hom.* 13:4 on Matt. 17:10/*PG* 57.563–4. The madness of the Devil caused, with help of the belly, Israel to commit idolatry (Exod. 32:6) and the people of Sodom to burn in unlawful lust (Tim. 16:49).

his victims to fall by targeting the stomach. So he did with Jesus as well; he began with the necessities of the belly (*Hom.* 13:2/*PG* 57.210–11). The strategy of the Devil is deceit (δόλος), which means tempting the incontinence of the stomach (τῆς κατὰ τὴν γαστέρα ἀκρασίας). In this way the Devil will bring people to obey (πείθεσθαι) him. It is obvious that Gen. 3 is a subtext of Chrysostom's exposition of Matt. 4:1 and his presentation of the strategy of the Devil. In *Hom.* 13:3/*PG* 57.211 he quotes directly from Gen. 3:5, thus making this connection obvious. The Devil, Gen. 3 and the belly-*topos* are here woven together.[84]

11.11   Augustine of Hippo (354–430)[85]

Among the letters of Augustine is also one to Bishop Alypius of Tagaste (*Epistle* 29)[86] written AD 395. The letter concerns the feast-day of Leontius, a former bishop of Hippo who died as a martyr. The celebration at the tomb of the dead martyr developed into banquets and drinking-bouts (*Epistle* 29:2).[87] A custom enhancing the pleasures of the body had been established within the 'walls' of the church; the celebration had beome a day for which the throats and stomachs were prepared (*fauces ventresque se parare*) (*Epistle* 29:8). Most of the letter reproduces the sermon given on this occasion in order to rectify this practice.

The sermon draws heavily on biblical material, mostly New Testament texts. The main texts are the following:

- the cleansing of the temple
- 1 Cor. 5:11 not to eat with Christians who live like pagans
- 1 Cor. 6:9–11 a list of vices excluding from the kingdom of God
- 1Cor. 11:21–22 the practice of eating excessively in Corinth while celebrating the Lord's Supper
- Matt. 7:16 a tree is known by its fruits
- Gal. 5:19–21 the works of the flesh
- 1 Pet. 4:1–3 life of indulgence belongs to the past

The sermon is embedded in biblical thinking throughout. The letter gives a very interesting glimpse into practical compromises the church had to accept. The practice of celebrating the martyrs is explained as a pagan

---

[84] Cf. our presentation of Philo (chap. 7.3) and Rom. 16 (chap. 9.2).
[85] For a biography of Augustine, see e.g. Peter Brown, *Augustine of Hippo*.
[86] According to the LCL edition.
[87] Cf. *Epistle* 22:6 speaking of the drunken revels and sumptuous meals taking place in the cemeteries, a practice which Augustine strongly denounces.

custom brought into the church to attract Gentiles. But to cling to a custom introduced for strategic purposes no longer makes sense (*Epistle* 29:9). The sermon urges a different kind of banquet, aiming at eating the sweetness of the Lord in singing and praising: 'For each man is made to share the fate of that which he worships (*eius rei quam colit*), and such people have been mocked by the Apostle in the words, "whose god is their belly"' (*Epistle* 29:11). This saying from Phil. 3:19 is immediately followed by 1 Cor. 6:13, paving the way for the conclusion; i.e. not to follow the belly, but to bring this practice to an end. In this text, then, Phil. 3:19 is an obvious reference to participating in sumptuous banquets, to be drunk; in short to live like Gentiles. The letter brings Phil. 3:19 together with other biblical passages in a strategy to rectify eating practices in the African church.

Augustine's *Sermo* 150/*PL* 38.807–14 on Paul's Areopagus speech (Acts 17:18–34) gives his view on Greek philosophy in general and the Epicureans in particular. The philosophers and the Christians have in common that they speak of the happy life (*vita beata* or *summum bonum*).[88] Augustine approaches this fundamental issue of ancient philosophical thought, and this is – as we have noted throughout – the larger framework within which the belly-*topos* works.

The Epicureans placed the happy life in bodily pleasures, while Stoics found it in the mind. To Augustine both of them are confined to the human (*Sermo* 150:5/*PL* 38.809–11).[89] He then considers how Paul would view the two. Augustine's interest lies primarily with refuting Epicurean thinking. Paul would never, according to Augustine, locate the Good in the body. The logic is the following: the Epicureans deny the resurrection. Augustine quotes from 1 Cor. 15:32 ('let us eat and drink, for tomorrow we will die') (*Sermo* 150:6/*PL* 38.811). This slogan quoted by Paul is a precise description of the Epicurean lifestyle and philosophy, and therefore it serves as as a good point of departure for presenting Epicureanism. Furthermore, this philosophy is selfish and leads to a contempt for the poor – of which the rich man in the parable in Luke 16:19 is an example. A Christian rewriting of 1 Cor. 15:32 is suggested: 'Let us fast and pray, for tomorrow we shall die' (*Sermo* 150:7/*PL* 38.811–12). The aim of

[88] In his *Epistle* 118 to Dioscorus (*PL* 33.431–49), Augustine speaks of the Greek philosophies. He says that the ashes of Stoics and Epicureans 'are not warm enough to strike out a spark against the Christian faith' (*Epistle* 118:12/*PL* 33.437–8). But Augustine is still very much involved with them in the letter. As for the Epicureans he says that they defined *summum bonum* as located in the pleasures of the human body (*Epistle* 118:13–14/*PL* 33.438–9). For an English translation of this letter see *FC* Vol. 18.

[89] For an English translation see Edmund Hill, *Sermons* III.5, pp. 30–7.

fasting is to relieve the hunger of the poor. It is quite clear that Augustine considers the Epicurean lifestyle – as expressed in 1 Cor. 15:32 – to be a justification for selfishness. *Sermo* 150:6–7 repeatedly quotes this Pauline text.

The Stoics are then briefly refuted (*Sermo* 150:8/*PL* 38.812). His argument is that placing the Good in virtue is tantamount to placing hopes in oneself, regardless of man's better part. He asks questions of the two philosophies, as well as of Christian faith: ' "Tell, Epicurean, what thing makes one blessed." "Bodily pleasures (*voluptas corporis*)", he replies. "Tell us, Stoic." "A virtuous mind." "Tell us, Christian." "The gift of God." ' (*Sermo* 150:8/*PL* 38.812.). According to Augustine, 1 Cor. 15:32 is, therefore, firmly rooted in Paul's way of refuting a lifestyle which defines *summum bonum* in pleasure, and thus represents a practical denial of resurrection in faith and the sharing lifestyle deriving from this faith.

Sermo 51/*PL* 38.332–54 is on the genealogy of Jesus. Chap. 14.23–4/*PL* 38.346–7 is of relevance for our study. Augustine speaks of two ways by which the human race keeps going; i.e. by eating and drinking (nourishment) and sex. These things should be taken according to duty (*officium*) not lust (*cupiditas*). The pious of the Old Testament preferred procreation without intercourse as well as staying alive without eating and drinking. In both cases, however, Augustine seems to admit that they cannot be partaken of without some pleasure. He draws a distinction between the people of duty and those of lust and greed.

In *Sermo* 51:24/*PL* 38.346–7 he addresses himself to eating in particular. 'How many people plunge ravenously into the business of eating and drinking, staking their whole lives on it as though it were the very reason for living! While in fact the reason they eat is to live, they think the reason they live is to eat' (*Sermo* 51:24/*PL* 38.347).[90] They come to the table to satisfy the lust of flesh; to participate in *epulae*;[91] i.e. sumptuous meals. Augustine applies Phil. 3:19 ('whose god is their belly') to such people: gluttons, drunkards and guzzlers (*edaces, ebriosi, helluones*). The reference of Paul's text is obvious here; it refers to people whose mind is set on the lavish tables to satisfy their lust.

Augustine comments on Rom. 16:17–18 in his *Expositio ad Romanos* 84/*PL* 35.2088.[92] His exposition consists almost entirely of other passages from Paul in which he addresses opponents. Firstly, he quotes from 1 Tim. 1:3–4 on Timothy's mandate to put things right in Ephesus after

---

[90] For an English translation, see Edmund Hill, *Sermons* III, p. 35.

[91] For the meaning of *epula*, see e.g. Origen, *Hom. Exod.* 2:1.25–27 (*GCS* Origen Vol. 6) where it is mentioned alongside banquets and sexual impurity.

[92] For the text see also Paula Fredriksen Landes, *Augustine on Romans*, pp. 48–9.

false teachers have sown confusion there. He then proceeds to Tit. 1:10–12 on the deceivers, especially the Jews (*ex circumcisione*). About these, one of their prophets says: Cretans are always liars, vicious animals, lazy gluttons (*ventres pigri*). The two texts from the Pastoral Epistles provide fresh illustrations of what Rom. 16:17–18 is about. Augustine then quotes v. 18: *Hi enim Christo domino non serviunt sed suo ventri.* This applies in particular to Jews whose false teaching is motivated by their desire for filthy lucre (*turpis lucri gratia*).

To this he adds that Paul in another place (i.e. Phil. 3:19) says *quorum deus venter est.* Tit. 1:12, Rom. 16:18 and Phil. 3:19 all speak about the belly. To Augustine, the two Pauline belly-sayings represent an extension of what Tit. 1:12 already implied. From Augustine's quoting of Rom. 16:18 and Phil. 3:19 nothing much can be said beyond the fact that he brings the two together in a common saying on gluttony; i.e. Tit. 1:12. This is, however, a clear indication of what Augustine had in mind here. Furthermore, Augustine is here close to Chrysostom (and others) who see this as typical of Jews who were deceiving the believers. How Augustine would further view the two Pauline sayings emerges from the following two examples.

In his writing on *The Usefulness of Fasting* (*De Utilitate Ieiunii*), Augustine speaks – in relation to Phil. 3:12–14 – about the two kinds of food, earthly and heavenly (*Ieiun.* 2:58). The earthly food is simply what life depends on, while the latter is what supports the life of angels.[93] Paul found himself caught in between the life of angels and the life of those who *ventri serviunt* (*Ieiun.* 2:70). The context is heavily dependent on Phil. 3; it is therefore natural to see this as a free rendering of Phil. 3:19, possibly influenced by the wording of Rom. 16:18. For this reason, Paul said that he was not yet perfect. In fasting, the believers, who are caught in the middle just like Paul, create obstacles for the flesh that draws them downwards. A believer who ridicules the practice of fasting is called *servus ventris* (*Ieiun.* 3:93). Augustine makes use of the common metaphor of riding a wild horse to refute believers who think like this. Such a person has no concern for taming the beast, and in accordance with the implications of the metaphor, he will fall off; i.e. be enslaved to the desire for food. Augustine thus sees Phil. 3 in the light of the mastery of desire by means of fasting.

In *The Teacher* (*De Magistro*), Augustine speaks of the glutton (*vorator*), a worshipper of the stomach (*ventris cultor*), who lives for the sake of eating, as stated by the apostle. In short, it is the matter of attending

---

[93] For the Latin text see *CCL* 46.

epulae (*Mag.* 9:26). Augustine quotes the apostle in a free way, but leaves no doubt that the issue addressed is the question of excessive eating at banquets.[94]

11.12   Severian of Gabala (fl. c. 400)

Severian was an exegete of the Antiochene school who commented on the Pauline Epistles. Of his extant fragments one is of interest for our study, namely his comments on 1 Cor. 6:12–13.[95] He says that Paul writes to urge ἐγκράτεια: 'Knowing that the stomach was the cause of their greed – for most are bold enough for everything for the sake of the pleasures of the stomach – he teaches that it is harmful to serve the belly.' The Greek text runs: εἰδὼς δὲ ὅτι τῆς πλεονεξίας αὐτῶν ἡ γαστὴρ αἰτία – οἱ γὰρ πολλοὶ πάντα τολμῶσιν διὰ τὰς τῆς γαστρὸς ἡδονάς – διδάσκει ὡς ἀσύμφερόν ἐστι δουλεύειν τῇ κοιλίᾳ. Severian understands 1 Cor. 6:12–13 within the framework of how to master the desires, among which the belly holds a key position. The phrase 'serving the belly' echoes Rom. 16:18.

11.13   Tyrannius Rufinus (c. 345–411)

In his exposition of the apostolic creed, Rufinus quotes Paul and Acts regarding circumcised Jews who pretended to be apostles of Christ, but did not teach according to Christian tradition. They did so for the sake of personal gain or for the belly's sake (*lucri alicuius vel ventris gratia*) (*Expositio Symboli* 2:20).[96] Rufinus here brings together 2 Cor. 11:13 and Rom. 16:18, and reads them in the light of Acts 15:1 about the Pharisees who were converted and demanded that Gentile-Christians observe Jewish customs. The belly is to be seen as a reference to their motives, not to what they taught. The primary reference is to Jewish selfishness.

11.14   Theodore of Mopsuestia (c. 350–428)

Theodore was an Antiochene exegete and theologian.[97] He wrote commentaries on the Pauline Epistles, of which some fragments are extant.

---

[94] For the Latin text see *CCL* 29. A French translation is available in Bernhard Jolibert, *De Magistro*.

[95] For the Greek text see Karl Staab, *Pauluskommentare*, pp. 246–7.

[96] For the Latin text see *CCL* 20. For an English translation see J. N. D. Kelly, *Rufinus*.

[97] For a general presentation of Theodore's exposition of Biblical texts, see Rudolf Bultmann, *Theodor von Mopsuestia*.

In his commentary on Phil. 3:19 he says: '. . . they are accustomed to eat not this, but this, not considering that the very thing which they eat, becomes faeces, which they feel ashamed even to see. Behold, that is the end of their zeal' (*PG* 66.926). The Greek text runs like this: νομίζουσιν τὸ μὴ τάδε φαγεῖν, ἀλλὰ τάδε, οὐκ ἐννοοῦντες ὅτι κόπρος γίνεται ὅπερ ἂν φάγωσιν, ἣν καὶ ὁρᾶν αἰσχύνονται. ἰδοὺ τῆς σπουδῆς αὐτῶν τὸ τέλος. Migne's Latin reconstruction goes like this: *Magnum putant, ait, non hoc, sed illud manducare, non cogitantes omnia stercus fieri quae-cunque manducaverint, quod vel respicere erubescunt. Ecce quis finis istorum studii.*

Theodore clearly sees Phil. 3:19 as a text on Jews or Jewish-Christians who were imposing observance of food laws on Christians. Modern inter-preters have (see above) mentioned this text to show that belly-worship referred to observing food laws. Although the text does not explain why Theodore connects observance of dietary laws and belly-service, he con-siders Phil. 3:19 as addressing those who are imposing food laws upon the believers.[98] It is, however, by no means obvious that Theodore is implying that imposing food laws on the Christians is in itself serving the belly. The text is too brief to suggest a clear conclusion. Our study of the Patristic writings so far has impelled us to make a distinction between food laws as a reference to belly-worship as such, and the reason for being preoccupied with food matters. Jewish preoccupation with food laws might well be one example of the carnal mind of belly-worshippers, without being itself the precise reference of belly-enslavement. Belly-worship can be defined in terms not only of quantity but also in terms of the obsession with food.

From his exegesis of Rom. 16:18, however, it becomes obvious that Theodore is not thinking of observance of food laws as such. Even in Phil. 3:19 he is thinking of luxurious eating. In his commentary on Rom. 16:18 (*PG* 66.875–6), Theodore says that Paul is talking about the flat-tery (κολακεία) of Jews travelling everywhere, trying to convince Gentile believers to observe the laws. He has sufficiently refuted them by saying: 'they do not serve Jesus Christ our Lord, but their own belly'. This is explained by claiming that the Jews not only know how to lead astray, but even more they do everything to fill their own stomach (*PG* 66.875–6). The Greek text goes like this: . . . εἴ γε ὑπὲρ τοῦ ἀπατῶντας δύνασθαι τὴν ἑαυτῶν γαστέρα πληροῦν πάντα ποιοῦσιν; while Migne's edition suggests the following in Latin: . . . *quando nil intentantum relinquunt ut alios seducendo ventrem suum compleant.* Even the food laws are a matter of filling the stomach.

---

[98] For the emphasis on Jewish customs in Phil. 3:19, see also H.B. Swete, *Theodori Episcopi Mopsuesteni* Vol. 1, pp. 242–3.

This text is often referred to as a piece of Early Church exegesis supporting the view that the question of food laws is at stake in the belly-*topos* (see above). According to Theodore, Rom. 16:18 is about Jews imposing food laws on Gentile-Christians. When it comes to the question of the precise meaning of belly-worship, however, his comment is not about distinguishing between lawful and forbidden food, but on the desire to fill the stomach. Hence the text is similar to what we have found extensively witnessed; the Jews are gluttons, even in their attempts to impose food laws on others. This is, however, not to say that belly-service is in itself a reference to dietary rules.

11.15   Theodoret of Cyrrhus (c. 393–c. 460)

In his commentary on Phil. 3:19 (*PG* 82.583–4), Theodoret says that the enemies of the cross are those who teach that salvation is not obtainable without observance of the law (δίχα τῆς νομικῆς).[99] Paul's saying on having the belly as god follows immediately, and thus comments directly on those who demand observance of the law, i.e. the Jews. Theodoret takes this to be an accusation of gluttony (τῆς γαστριμαργίας κατηγορῶν).[100] It is stated explicitly that having the belly as god means gluttony. In Phil. 3:19 Paul, according to Theodoret, is writing about Jews who are imposing legalism on Christians, a true act of gluttony. Theodoret joins the many writers in the Early Church who claim that Jewish customs were means of gluttony. He gives a reason why Phil. 3:19, a dictum on gluttony, applies to the Jews: 'For the Jews pay especially much attention to food, and they think of the luxury of Sabbath as a standard of righteousness. They regard as a glory that which one ought to be ashamed of.' The Greek text goes like this: Διαφερόντως γὰρ οἱ Ἰουδαῖοι πολλὴν ποιοῦνται τροφῆς[101] ἐπιμέλειαν, καὶ δικαιοσύνης ὅρον νομίζουσι τὴν ἐν Σαββάτῳ χλιδήν· δόξαν ταῦτα ὑπολαμβάνοντες ἐφ' οἷς ἔδει αἰσχύνεσθαι. Migne's suggestion for the Latin is: *Judaei enim praecipue victus impensam curam gerunt, et finem justitiae putant profusum in Sabbato luxum: gloriam ista existimantes, propter quae oporteret pudore affici.*

Theodoret provides a strong case that belly-service is manifested in Jews demanding that Christians observe the Law, probably the food laws in particular. This demand is due to the gluttony of the Jews. Belly-worship manifests itself in imposing food laws, but it is not the dietary

---

[99] Migne's Latin goes like this: *sine legali observatione*.
[100] Migne's Latin text has *eorum taxans ingluviem*.
[101] Another reading is τρυφῆς, which means excessive eating.

laws themselves. Jewish food laws are caused by gluttony; and this is the reference of 'having the belly as god'.

As for Rom. 16:18 Theodoret says that it is obvious that 'those who are serving their own belly' refers to Jews (*PG* 82.223–4). This is obviously so (Καὶ ἐντεῦθεν δῆλον) since Paul 'always accuses them of gluttony (ἀεὶ γὰρ αὐτῶν τῆς γαστριμαργίας κατηγορεῖ)'. The proof-text is Phil. 3:19 (ὧν θεὸς ἡ κοιλία). To Theodoret γαστριμαργία is a proper circumscription for 'having the belly as god' or 'serving it' in the Pauline texts, and Jewish preoccupation with dietary laws is an example of this.

11.16   Peter Chrysologus (c. 400–450)

Peter Chrysologus was archbishop of Ravenna.[102] He earned his epithet 'The Golden Orator' through his sermons. Although Chrysologus does not quote either of the Pauline texts presented in this study, his *Sermo* 5 is still of relevance.[103] The sermon takes the parable of the Prodigal Son (Luke 15) as its point of departure, and treats the two sons as representing Gentiles and Jews: 'Prudent knowledge of the Law made the Jewish people His elder Son, and the folly of paganism made the Gentile world His younger Son' (*Sermo* 5:2.20–2). In 5:5 Chrysologus pities the Gentiles who had to fill their stomach with pods that were the food of swine. At this point in his exposition, Chrysologus brings in the Epicureans. They knew the poor situation in which people found themselves, and they took advantage of it. Hence 'they offered themselves to Epicurus, the most recent promoter (*voluptatis auctor*) of despair and pleasure. And they ate pods. In other words, they opened their mouths wide to the sinfully sweet pleasures of the body' (*Sermo* 5:5.72–4). Chrysologus takes Luke 15:16 as a short description of paganism; it is about eating, filling the stomach, stirring up the pleasures, and Epicurus. In other words, the Epicurean lifestyle of being devoted to the belly is seen as a characteristic of Gentiles.

11.17   Gennadius of Marseilles (fl. 470)

Gennadius, best known as a patriarch of Constantinople, wrote a number of commentaries on the Pauline Epistles. The surviving sections are mostly in catenae. One of the extant texts is a comment on Rom. 16:17–18 (*Fragm. in Epist. ad Rom.* 16:17–18/*PG* 85.1727–8). His commentary

---

[102] For his life see *FC* Vol. 17, pp. 5–6.   [103] For the Latin text see *CCL* 24.

is brief, but quite explicit. Paul's text is seen as a warning against Jewish teaching misleading believers by urging them to keep food laws. 'They place all piety in the observance of food laws.' The Greek text says that their εὐσέβεια consists ἐν τῇ παρατηρήσει τῶν βρωμάτων ὁρίζεσθαι. As for Latin, Migne suggests *omnem pietatem in observatione ciborum*[104] *ponentes*. Thus they do not serve Christ, but their belly, says Gennadius. Being on guard against this Jewish teaching means preserving the traditions of Peter. Nothing in Gennadius' comments on Rom. 16:18 suggests that 'serving the belly' has any reference other than the food laws themselves, unless it is to be found in the idiom itself. It seems that Gennadius is defining belly-worship as observance of food laws without any indication that this is motivated by the gluttony of Jews; at least this is not spelled out. Among the fragments of his biblical expositions, none on Philippians has been found.

11.18   Antiochus, the Patriarch of Antioch (d. 598)

Antiochus devotes his *Homily* 4 (*PG* 89.1443–6) to the question of gluttony (περὶ γαστριμαργίας). The *Homily* starts in this way: 'It is necessary to all to overpower and control the belly. Most important is to wish to serve God (Πᾶσι μὲν ἀναγκαῖόν ἐστι τὸ βιάζεσθαι καὶ κρατεῖν γαστρός. Μάλιστα δὲ τοῖς θεῷ δουλεύειν ἐθέλουσι). The Latin text of Migne urges the need for moderation: *Nulli non hominum apprime necessarium sit vim inferre ventris edacitati, eamque justa temperie moderari: in primis tamen eos addecet, quibus curae est pia servitute colere Deum.*

Antiochus says that the body needs τροφή not τρυφή, αὐτάρκεια and not πολυτέλεια. He makes a word-play on alternatives; food or nourishment and excessive eating, as well as on sufficiency and lavishness. Too much food stirs up the pleasures; it is like adding wood to the fire. If the stomach is not brought under control, one becomes a slave to the belly (κοιλιόδουλος). This happened to Israel in the wilderness, of whom it is said that 'the people sat down to eat and drink, and rose up to play' (Exod. 32:6 and 1 Cor. 10:7). Antiochus then gives a catena of biblical texts (mostly from the New Testament) that he considers relevant to the topic of gluttony. The texts are the following, and they appear in this order (in the Greek text): Phil. 3:19; 2 Cor. 6:13; 1 Cor. 8:13; Rom. 16:18; Rom. 8:6; Heb. 13:9; Rom. 14:17; Isa. 5:5; John 6:26–7. Texts and biblical traditions holding a key position in our study are on this list, and are thus

---

[104] The plural of *cibus* ('food', 'nourishment'; see *Oxford Latin Dictionary* s.v.) is here to be rendered 'things of food'; i.e. food laws.

recognized as having a prominent place in a biblically-based refutation of γαστριμαργία.

11.19   John Climacus (c. 570–c. 649)

In his *Climaci* (*Ladder of Divine Ascent*) 14 (*PG* 88.863–72) John speaks of γαστριμαργία, 'gluttony', which he defines as hypocrisy of the belly (γαστριμαργία ἐστὶν κοιλίας ὑπόκρισις). Migne suggests the following Latin text: *Gula est hypocrisis ventris*. Gluttony also becomes the father of πορενία.[105] Then the belly is in charge and rules a person (κρατεῖν) (*PG* 88.865). An example of this is the Jews celebrating the Sabbath and their festivals with delicious food, thus making them festivals of γαστριμαργία.[106] Thus they live like κοιλιόδουλοι, enslaved by their passions (πάθους δοῦλος) (*PG* 88.864). It is the Jewish festivals with their emphasis on food and joy which caused John to call the Jews 'slaves of their belly'.

11.20   Summary

We have found that the belly-*topos*, Phil. 3:19, Rom. 16:18 and related texts were used in various ways by Christian writers. Within the variations, however, we have seen that it is justified to speak of a relatively fixed meaning of the Pauline belly-dicta: in the minds of Paul's first expositors these texts refer to excessive eating and drinking as well as to illicit sexual lust. They refer to a lifestyle contrasted with the ascetic life honoured by many Christians at this time. Opposition to belly-worship in terms of gluttony comes out very clearly in this material. The texts have been used to justify ascetic life far beyond what is implied in the Pauline texts themselves.

Having the belly as god is very often seen in tandem with the term 'Mammon'; i.e. having money and gain as god, which is seen as the worst form of idolatry. This means that belly-devotion appears as a kind of greed. It is, therefore, not surprising that the belly-dicta sometimes refer to selfishness and self-centredness. This figurative meaning is, however, entirely subordinate to the critique of gluttony. A number of biblical texts shed light on Phil. 3:19 and Rom. 16:18, among which the texts presented in this study have a prominent place. 1 Cor. 6:13; 10:7; 11:21–2, 33–4 and 15:32 were all seen as related to the belly-*topos*.

---

[105] This is emphasized also in the *Scholia* following John's treatise on gluttony, see especially *Scholion* 4; 10; 18 (*PG* 88.871–80).

[106] Migne's Latin suggestion has *gulosus*.

Serving the belly was incompatible with believing in Christ. This is only natural, since the Patristic writers discuss belly-enslavement in terms of worship, as did Paul. The Gentiles *believed* in the stomach. Still, some writers emphasized that the question of controlling the belly was a problem within the Church as well. Basically, our findings on the Pauline material, when seen in the light of the ancient discussion on mastery of passions, have been substantiated, confirmed and strengthened by the Patristic material.

Johannes Behm's position that having the belly as god was a reference to food laws in the Early Church is, in my view, no longer tenable. This position lacks evidence. It must be admitted, however, that it is a surprise that Judaism and food laws were by many expositors seen as examples of gluttony. Food laws were seen as belly-worship since they expressed the Jews' preoccupation with food. It is, however, a misreading of the evidence to argue that observing the food laws *as such* meant belly-worship. Preoccupation with food was not distinguished from gluttony; hence food laws were conceived of as serving the belly. In their criticism of Jewish dietary laws, Patristic writers depicted them as leading to enslavement to the carnal belly. The main perspective is not that of Paul's Galatian crisis, namely observation of food laws versus faith. The framework within which Patristic writers conceive of the belly-texts and the Jews is the spiritual versus the carnal attitude. Jewish preoccupation with food laws is an example of a carnal attitude; hence it is called belly-service. The Patristic evidence here differs from Paul. As we have argued, he would not claim that food laws were a means of gluttony. In the eyes of Christian ascetic writers Jewish emphasis on food matters was a sign of gluttony. This view was supported by Biblical references as well, among which Exod. 32:6 (1 Cor. 10:7); Deut. 32:15; Ezek. 16:49 and John 6 were the prominent examples.

The claim that Jews were gluttonous thus reflects Scriptural interpretation of the wilderness-tradition in particular, elaborated by ascetic writers. They thus turned the tables on the Jews; the dietary laws which in Jewish thinking, even in Paul, were given in order to restrain pleasures, have now themselves become examples of food-greed. Belly-worship manifests itself in food laws, but the reasoning of this claim is very different from what we found in Paul's letters. At the end of the day, however, the Patristic evidence still views belly-service as gluttony, but considers Jewish observation of food laws to be an example of it. Thus this material basically confirms carnal gluttony to be the primary reference of belly-worship.

PART 6

Conclusions

12

CONCLUDING REMARKS

12.1   Paul's critique of belly-worship in an ancient setting

At the beginning of our study we noted the uncertainty among New Testament scholars as to the precise meaning of 'belly' in Phil. 3:19 and Rom. 16:18. Owing to the brevity of the two dicta, I claimed that an adequate understanding was accessible only through uncovering the cultural competence of Paul's readers. This has taken us down the path of ancient moral philosophy as well as to the agenda of banquets. It has led us to abandon the common view that Paul had in mind Christians who continued to observe Jewish dietary laws. This view fails to account for the analogies with Paul's expression of 'having the belly as god', whether these analogies are Graeco-Roman or Jewish. A closer look at the Patristic evidence demonstrated that to many writers of the Early Church, Jews were seen as gluttonous, as preoccupied with food. This allegation looked beyond dietary laws, and belonged to a polemic of ascetics.

Plato's anthropology was the basis for the thinking of most moral philosophers. Reason and mind represented a divine element or kinship in human beings, while desires were located in the stomach and the organs below it, i.e. the genitals. These parts of the human body were marks of an earthly identity. The desires of the unruly belly had therefore to be mastered. Mastery of desires became a philosophical commonplace in antiquity, designed to keep the desires of the belly, such as eating, drinking and copulating, under control. All these passions would keep on demanding, take hold of a person and rule him. The unceasing demands of the stomach would take control of the whole life, although, as one of the authors put it, it took only some hours to satisfy it. This could be expressed in terms of enslavement to the belly or serving its demands. We even found some close analogies to Paul's vocabulary of 'belly-god'. In some instances, the stomach was praised in devotional terms. In quite a few of the relevant texts, Epicureanism was targeted; in defining pleasure as the supreme good, Epicurus and his followers were often seen as paving the way for the demands of the belly. The way of life associated with the belly manifested itself in lavish and indulgent banquets, at which excessive eating, drinking, and sexual 'after-dinners' showed what belly-enslavement was all about. Of course, this material primarily reflects life among the social elite, the upper stratum of society. Nevertheless, it was practised commonly enough to be noted and for a rhetoric of the belly to be developed.

Our investigation has demonstrated that the stomach was a cultural commonplace of the philosophical discussion on how to master the desires. It had become a stock accusation against a person hooked on eating, drinking and sex. That we are talking of a cultural stereotype has been confirmed by the fact that proverbial gourmandizers were associated with this material. The cluster of ideas, or the pattern, which has emerged in the material is the following.

(1) Belly-devotion, as we have defined it, reveals the earthly nature of a person. Such a person serves his most earthly needs, seeks instant gratification, and has no horizons beyond that.

(2) This is an animal-like way of living. Animals live to eat and reproduce themselves. Some philosophers hold that human beings hooked on the belly are worse than animals, since the latter, although they have no horizon beyond satisfying their needs, still obey the Law of Nature, while human beings stuff themselves far beyond these demands of nature.

(3) Persons living like this become selfish and egoistic, their main concern becomes to satisfy their own belly. The belly-*topos* often described a self-centred person, therefore. This figurative extension of the physiological reference of the belly was frequently attested in the material. Such an extension, however, was entirely dependent upon a common image of the glutton. The minds of the gluttons were set on food; they were preoccupied with food. This was, however, not only a matter of the quantity of food, but also their obsession with it. This explains why some Early Christian writers depicted the Jews as gluttons. Their food laws appeared to these writers as food-obsession.

(4) Belly-devotees were likened to flatterers or parasites. They want to eat but not to pay. They love soft living, but they evade costs and demands. A figurative extension of this was demonstrated in the ancient material.

(5) Belly-enslavement can therefore be seen in a political perspective as well. A person gorging, bibbing and copulating sets his mind on his own cravings, serves his own ends, and will neglect his *polis*. The common interest is not among the priorities of a belly-devotee, and so such a citizen is not to be relied upon in times of crisis. Furthermore, soft living does

not prepare a person for the hardships and war which the *polis* might sometimes require of its citizens.

(6) Belly-servants are often contrasted with athletes. Athletes submit to hardships to achieve their goals. They are men of *agôn*, seeking long-term goals and working hard to attain them.

It is this cluster of ideas that constitutes the belly-*topos* in ancient moral philosophy. Not all elements are necessarily extant in all texts. This pattern has been appropriated either in full or partly in Jewish sources as well as in Pauline letters. Philo in particular has appropriated the *topos* and embedded it into his Scriptural interpretation, centred around his allegorical interpretation of the Serpent in Gen. 3 and Egypt. The use of the belly-*topos* in Jewish sources facilitates a reading of the relevant Pauline texts. The only point which is entirely missing in the apostle's epistles is no. (2) above. It must, however, be emphasized that Paul has considerably reshaped this material according to his own theology.

Like the moral philosophers Paul speaks about self-control in, among other things, eating. But he defines self-control and self-sufficiency in terms of trusting God, relying on His providence in all circumstances. The wilderness generation, as well as some among his Corinthian converts who joined the pagan meals in the temple, did not consider God's providence sufficient. They devoted themselves to immediate satisfaction of their belly, and thus lacked faith in God's providence. Paul is here continuing traditions elaborated in Philo's writings.

Throughout the ancient texts we have seen that some shadow-figures are at work, even in Paul's sayings. Paul's belly-dicta are informed by Epicurus' philosophy, or rather, the lifestyle that came to be associated with this doctrine. The Pauline texts are informed by proverbial figures of gourmandizers, such as Sardanapalus, and the agenda of banquets as well. These are all parts of the cultural competence which shaped the belly-*topos*. Furthermore, we found that Epicurean philosophy and lifestyle, Sardanapalus and banquets are all frequently mentioned in Patristic literature when the relevant Pauline texts are under discussion. But Paul himself does not mention them, albeit he may possibly have assumed his readers' familiarity with them. The model which he brings out explicitly, in order to explain what belly-worship is all about, is the desert-generation. On a continuous basis they demanded food, and longed for the flesh-pots of Egypt. Finally, they devoted themselves to idolatry, in whose wake followed eating, drinking and copulation. The major contrast-figure was neither athletes nor Paul himself, but Christ. The way the model of Christ works in Philippians makes it clear that self-renunciation is the master-model for the contrast to serving oneself and one's stomach.

The biblical wilderness traditions probably justified Paul's adoption of devotional language about the stomach. This language had its predecessors in Graeco-Roman sources, Euripides in particular. But Paul strengthened and developed this further. Paul does not only say that idolatry is accompanied by the desires of the belly. He puts it differently; the danger of idolatry comes from within a human being. This danger from within has an ally in Satan, the Old Serpent from Gen. 3. In the words of Clement of Alexandria, one might live a life which is adequately described only in terms of 'believing in the stomach'. Hence it is either Christ or the stomach.

Throughout the material we have seen that belly-enslavement was a characteristic of earthly kinship as opposed to the divine. We called this a philosophy of identity. Paul adopted this discourse in his own terms in Phil. 3. The believer's heavenly citizenship could be jeopardized by giving way to the earthly needs of the belly. Citizenship demands responsible living. This is also the case with the heavenly *politeuma*, which also seems to impose suffering on its members. The heavenly identity of which Paul speaks is rooted in the resurrection of the body. In keeping with this hope, believers cannot echo the Epicurean creed of 'let us eat and drink, for tomorrow we will die', i.e. let us join in the life of banquets, since there is no tomorrow. Hope in the bodily resurrection is a barrier against hedonism. Faith in the resurrection thus underpins how Christians should live. Since their bodies are for the future, this conviction carries moral demands for the present. Ergo the stomach matters.

We saw that Paul's belly-dicta, particularly Rom. 16, had obvious repercussions for Rom. 6:1–20 on the believers being crucified and raised with Christ. The common denominator was the question of proper worship or service. Paul argued that the liberty he proclaimed should not become a licence for indulgence. He urged the Christians to be slaves of righteousness, obedience, and of Christ (Rom. 14:18). Being crucified and raised with Christ must be worked out in a commitment to a new way of life; i.e. enslavement to sin, body and desires belonged to the past. Devoting oneself again to the power of the belly was thus tantamount to nullifying Christ's crucifixion with which the believer was associated in baptism. Belly-devotees are necessarily enemies of the cross.

To Paul, then, Christian faith and obedience have outward expressions, one of which is to turn away from the selfish life associated with the belly. At the end of the day, therefore, Paul's rhetoric approaches his notion of flesh, 'the earthbound humanity from which the believer has been rescued into the humanity of Christ'.[1] But it certainly contributes to a more practical picture of this heavy theological notion.

Although the cluster of ideas related to the belly-*topos* is to a large extent common ground for Paul and the ancient texts, this is restated within his theology and so modified by it. Paul has a body theology. In this perspective, the dicta of Phil. 3:19 and Rom. 16:18 do not appear marginal and accidental, as they do to many scholars. They are by no means mere polemic against opponents. The polemic has been integrated into Paul's instruction, and is based on fundamental theological convictions. Advocates of the view that these two texts which *expressis verbis* address belly-worship, are no more than a rhetorical attempt to blacken opponents, have not noticed to what extent these dicta are deeply embedded in the strategy of the individual letters. Furthermore, they have neglected to observe that in these Pauline passages belly-worship appears within a set of ideas, such as participation or enmity with Christ, the identity of believers, idolatry and true worship, conduct, transformation of the body. Finally, they have failed to recognize that Paul's critique of the belly draws on his own theology of the body.

12.2   Belly-worship and body in Paul's letters

As I walked down King's Parade in Cambridge, I noticed a T-shirt on display, differing from the many University shirts on sale there. The shirt had the following text: 'My body is not a temple, it's an amusement park.' Paul's belly-dicta operate from an entirely different point of view. His dicta have as their target philosophies of pleasure and self-pleasing. Paul would certainly have turned the slogan of this T-shirt the other way around. The body is a temple; it is the place where God's Spirit dwells. It is therefore an instrument for glorifying God and serving the good.

According to Paul this temple is not without outward signs. There exists an outward appearance by which faith can be judged and corrected. To the ancient physiognomists, the stomach was a sign by which the inner quality of a person might be measured. Bodily form, including the belly, was seen as an index of human character. Physiognomics does not appear as a point of departure in Paul's letters. Indeed, the power of the belly outweighs the question of its size and form. However, Paul has retained one basic insight of physiognomics. Body and character do belong together, not in the sense that the depths of human character can be inferred from the

---

[1] Peter O' Brien, *Philippians*, p. 456.

outward appearance of the body, but in the sense that lifestyle, which also includes matters of food, drinking and sex, represents a yardstick by which the spiritual life may be measured, judged or corrected. Faith was to Paul not purely a matter of the heart, invisible to all but God. Faith worked itself out also in body and stomach.

Why did Paul regard belly-worship as incompatible with Christian identity? The answer to this is not that it might affect health and cause diseases, that it brought social shame, or that it involved misuse of nature and animals. All these reasons are attested in the relevant ancient material. Paul's primary concern with body and belly was religious. He conceived of the body and bodily activities in a strictly *religious* perspective. The body-theology which we have unravelled as forming the bedrock of Paul's critique of belly-worship, can be summarized in terms of transition, participation, transformation, worship, and redemption – all in relation to the body.

Paul's theology is borne aloft by the conviction that God's sending of Jesus Christ (Gal. 4:4) marked a distinction between before and now. With the coming of Christ and faith an age of salvation for all, Jews and Gentiles alike, had dawned. This basic structure forms a pattern of *transition* in which Paul casts the life and identity of believers. They have turned away from their pagan past, and Paul urges them to conduct their lives accordingly. Theological conviction and matters of conduct merge in a way which makes the question of 'who the Christians are' crucial to how the body is perceived.

Their new identity is cast in terms of being united with Christ, participating in his crucifixion and resurrection. In Rom. 6, Paul argues that believers should not continue to sin, since they participate in Christ. From this emerges a body-theology, which is clearly expressed also in the immediate context of Phil. 3:17–21; 1 Cor. 6:12–20; 11:17–34 and 15:32. *Participation* in Christ is the nucleus of Paul's thoughts on the body, since this is the motif which bridges the present body and the future transformed body. Sharing in Christ's sufferings implies not only bodily decay, which applies to all human beings, but taking his unselfish suffering as an example. The self-pleasing attitude which marks belly-worship is, therefore, tantamount to enmity to Christ's death. Furthermore, participation with Christ means sharing in his glorious body through the indwelling Spirit. In Rom. 6:4 this sharing is cast in terms of 'walking', i.e. conduct. Thus both sharing in Christ's sufferings and sharing in his being raised involve demands on the body, and for this reason Paul continues in Rom. 6 to depict the body of believers as involved in bodily struggle and service.

Since believers share in the Spirit which is characteristic of Christ's resurrected body, the future transformed body which Paul depicts in 1 Cor. 15 is already on the way. The heavenly body is, therefore, present in an inner renewal and in the lifestyle of Christians. The *transformation* of the body to become like Christ's accordingly has strong repercussions for bodily activities. Believers must not be involved in bodily conduct which is inappropriate for a body destined to be fully transformed. Furthermore, being the dwelling-place of the Spirit, the body of the individual participates in Christ as well. There is then a danger of violating Christ himself by bodily conduct. That bodily transformation is under way implies that the present body is characterized by the apocalyptic dualism of earthly and heavenly. This leads Paul to emphasize the body as an arena where the two are competing for control. The question of how to master the desires is, therefore, a significant part of his body-theology.

Worship and rituals are essential for the cohesion of religious groups. Temple and sacrifices were, of course, essential for the identity of Israel in Old Testament times. So it was to Paul and the groups whose identity he shaped. Paul took up cultic terms, but redefined them: 'The sacrifice God looks for is no longer that of beast or bird in temple, but the daily commitment of life within the constraints and relationships of this bodily world.'[2] We found this clearly expressed in e.g. Rom. 12:1–2 (cf. Rom. 6) and in Phil. 1:20. Both texts addressed the body as involved in worship, as a vehicle for glorifying God. This formed a clear contrast to making a god of the belly.

Paul redefines worship and cult by transposing these terms to body and conduct. He did not think of worship only in terms of an inner commitment without outward appearances. The notion of worship was surely all-embracing, including a daily commitment of all parts of life, but the bodily aspect of this is prominent in the texts. Worship embodied in conduct can hardly be without outward characteristics. Bodily worship means that the body belongs fully to the Lord; it does not exist for itself or with itself as an end in itself. Furthermore, worship implies a separation from other cults. Believers, whose body is a vehicle for praising God, have cut themselves off from worshipping the belly. Finally, the notion of body as an instrument for worshipping God implies that the body will be consumed. This follows by implication from the notion of bodily sacrifice. Self-centredness, which ancient texts depict so vividly in the glutton and the loaded table, and which Paul picks up in the rhetoric of belly-worship, is to be given up. Paul speaks of a worship which consists

---

[2] James D. G. Dunn, *Romans 9–16*, p. 717.

in self-sacrifice. We found that living to please oneself (*sua causa facere*) was a common shorthand for an Epicurean lifestyle, and that Christ's self-emptying (Phil. 2:4.21; 1 Cor. 10:24; Rom. 14:7; 15:1,7) represented the opposite. He gave an example which believers had to follow, lest they be enslaved by their belly. Sacrificing self-centredness and egoism was, therefore, how believers should respond to the demands of the belly.

Perceiving the body in terms of worship implies that it is faced with dangers of pollution and idolatry. Defilement called for protection in terms of firm boundaries, to isolate the dangers from outside. Paul was certainly concerned with keeping the body holy and undefiled. This led him to emphasize a lifestyle which separated his converts from pagans. Idolatry, which came from the inside, from the belly, could not, however, be coped with by firm boundaries. This leaves us with a somewhat complex picture: the identity of Christians was constantly endangered from both the outside and inside.

From Paul's notion of the present body as being both earthly and heavenly follows his firm hope that the body was to be fully redeemed. His admonitions on bodily activities were deeply influenced by his conviction that the body was destined for *redemption*. Participation in the Spirit that raised Christ from the dead guaranteed a full redemption. Paul thought of this in terms of a body transformed to a spiritual and glorious body, and thus appropriate to God's presence. In heaven, the body appears in a different kind of bodily existence; it has become heavenly all over. This redemption marks the end of a process in the believers. The question of living appropriately with the body is therefore a demand even at present. Since the body was to be fully redeemed, the present body mattered to Paul.

What becomes of the belly in the transformed body? The topic of this investigation has been limited to negative texts about the stomach. We have seen that belly-worship represents gluttony or a figurative extension of this, manifesting itself in utter selfishness. Belly-worship becomes meaningful against the background of the lifestyle associated with the loaded tables. As part of this rhetoric, the belly will not be raised and transformed. Belly-worship is closely associated with 'flesh' in Paul's theology. The resurrection includes σῶμα but not σάρξ. Paul insists on a body in heaven, but it differs from the earthly body. The body as it will become in heaven (σῶμα ἐπουράνιον) is contrasted with the present σῶμα ἐπίγειον (1 Cor.15:40 cf. vv. 47–49). The present body is earthly, owing to its inappropriateness in the presence of God. Paul here thinks of the mortality and weakness of the body; it is destined to perish, subject to death and decay (1 Cor.15:53–4, cf. Rom. 8:20–6). The transformed body is stripped of the perishable nature in which human beings are embodied. Being both mortal and weak, the body easily becomes a gate-way for temptations, according to Paul. Provision for bodily needs might be carried out in a way which allows desires to seize control. The earthly nature of the body then turns out to be highly sinister. This is what happens in Phil. 3:19 where belly-worship as well is said to be ἐπίγειος.

Is there a difference between the mortal body, inappropriate for heaven, and the belly – both being called earthly? Belly-worship, as we have seen, represents the earthly in a sinister sense, since the earthly here marks fundamental orientation. Belly-worshippers set their mind on earthly things, which brings to mind texts such as Rom. 8:5–7 (cf. Col. 3:2), where earthly orientation marks enmity to God. Their identity is exhausted in the present. Paul therefore issues warnings against this attitude and lifestyle. But his injunctions never address the mortality and perishable nature of the body as such. In other words, the mortal body is not appropriate for the heavenly body; it needs to be transformed. This includes the stomach as well. Belly-worship, however, is not only inappropriate; it marks fundamental enmity to God's ways.

Present-day readers might well think of the relevance of Paul's belly-dicta and his body-theology in ways which Paul and his first interpreters did not. To us it probably appears somewhat ironic that in ancient writings, including those of Paul, athletes were cast as the opposite of belly-worshippers. It appears to us that athletes may be among those whose concern with the body is most blatant. In our eyes, belly-worship in terms of self-centredness, self-concern and self-obsession might possibly apply to athletes as well. Modern athletics is obsessed with self and body. Inspired by Dante, Larry Niven and Jerry Pournelle have written a popular science fiction book, entitled *Inferno*. This is the story of Allen Carpentier's descent into the abyss of Hell. As he is accompanied through Infernoland, he meets Petri, 'a long-haired blond man built like an Olympic athlete',[3] a man who sought his 'salvation' through health and who 'used to run ten miles a day'.[4] Carpentier is surprised to meet Petri here: 'What are you doing here? You're no glutton.'[5] Petri responds:

> 'I'm the least gluttonous man who ever lived', he said bitterly. 'While all of these creeps were swilling down anything that came near their mouths, from pig meat to garden snails – and you too, for that matter, Allen – I was taking care of myself. Natural foods. Organic vegetables. No meat. No chemicals. I didn't drink. I didn't smoke. I didn't – ' He caught himself up.[6]

---

[3] Larry Niven, Jerry Pournelle, *Inferno*, p. 49.   [4] Ibid. p. 50.   [5] Ibid. p. 49.
[6] Ibid. p. 49.

Petri sees himself as opposed to the company of PIGS, 'the Prestigious International Gourmand Society, whose purpose in life was to go out and eat together'.[7] He emphatically denies that he belongs among the gluttons. Benito, Carpentier's guide through Hell, addresses him sadly: 'Gluttony is too much attention to things of the earth, especially in the matter of diet. It is the obsession that matters, not the quantity.'[8] As Carpentier and Benito continued, they heard Petri saying to himself: 'At least I am not *fat* like those animals. I take *care* of myself.'[9] The traditional contrast between athletes and belly-worshippers here appears in a light that differs from most of the material in this study. Belly-worship and body-centredness is indeed applicable in ways of which ancient sources seem unaware, but these ways can still be argued from how they conceived of gluttony.

In a similar way, the critique voiced in the Patristic literature by some ascetics might cause a modern reader to have second thoughts. If belly-worship is not necessarily a reference to quantity of food but to its obsession as well, what then about extreme ascetism? It may be that some of the Christian ascetic texts we have come across should fall under their own critique of gluttony, owing to their preoccupation with food. Belly-worship, as it appears in this investigation, therefore, is a never-ending story about self-gratification finding expression in various ways.

[7] Ibid. p. 49.   [8] Ibid. p. 50.   [9] Ibid. p. 50.

BIBLIOGRAPHY

Works of reference

Bauer, Walter, William, F., Gingrich, F. Wilbur, Danker, Frederick W., *A Greek–English Lexicon of the New Testament and Other Early Christian Literature* (Chicago and London: University of Chicago Press 1979)

Blass, F., Debrunner, A., Funk, Robert A., *A Greek Grammar of the New Testament and Other Early Christian Literature* (Cambridge, Chicago, Illinois: Cambridge University Press, University of Chicago Press 1961)

Borgen, Peder; Fuglseth, Kåre; Skarsten, Roald, *The Philo Index, A Complete Greek Word Index to the Writings of Philo of Alexandria Lemmatised & Computer-Generated*, UNITREL Studieserie 25 (Religionsvitenskapelig institutt, University of Trondheim 1997)

Brown, Frances, Driver, S. R., Briggs, Charles, *Hebrew and English Lexicon of the Old Testament* (Oxford: Clarendon Press 1929)

Computer-Konkordanz zum Novum Testamentum Graece (Berlin, New York: Walter de Gruyter 1985)

Cross, F. L., Livingstone, E. A., *The Oxford Dictionary of the Christian Church* (Oxford: Oxford University Press 1997)

Denis, Albert-Marie, *Concordance Grecque des Pseudépigraphes d'Ancien Testament, Concordance, Corpus des Textes, Indices* (Louvain-la-Neuve: Université Catholique de Louvain 1987)

Elliger, K., Rudolph, W., *Biblia Hebraica Stuttgartensia* (Stuttgart: Württembergische Bibelanstalt 1969)

Hatch, Edwin; Redpath, Henry, *A Concordance to the Septuagint and Other Greek Versions of the Old Testament (Including the Apocryphal Books)*, Vols. 1–3 (Oxford: Clarendon Press 1897–1906)

Hornblower, Simon; Spawforth, Anthony, *The Oxford Classical Dictionary*, 3rd edition (Oxford, New York: Oxford University Press 1996)

Lampe, G. W. H., *A Patristic Greek Lexicon* (Oxford: Clarendon Press 1961)

Lewis, Charlton T.; Short, Charles, *A Latin Dictionary* (Oxford: Clarendon Press 1879)

Liddell, Henry George; Scott, Robert; Jones, Henry Stuart, *A Greek–English Lexicon* (Oxford: Clarendon Press 1996)

Louw, Johannes P.; Nida, Eugene A., *Greek–English Lexicon of the New Testament Based on Semantic Domains*, Vols. 1–2 (New York: United Bible Societies 1988)

Oxford Latin Dictionary, Vols. 1–2 (Oxford: Clarendon Press 1968–1976)

Ralphs, Alfred, *Septuaginta*, Vols. 1–2 (Stuttgart: Württembergische Bibelanstalt 1952)

Wiles, James W., *A Scripture Index to the Works of St Augustine in English Translation* (Lanham, New York, London: University Press of America 1995)

Sources

André, Jacques, *Anomyme Latin, Traité de Physiognomonie*, Collection des Universités de France (l'Association Guillaume Budé) (Paris: Société d'éducation: 'Les Belles Lettres' 1981)

Arnim, Hans von, *Stoicorum Veterum Fragmenta*, Vols. 1–4 (Leipzig: B. G. Teubner 1905–1924)

Bailey, Cyril, *Epicurus, The Extant Remains* (Oxford: Clarendon Press 1926)

Beard, Mary; North, John; Price, Simon, *Religions of Rome*, Vol. 2: *A Sourcebook* (Cambridge: Cambridge University Press 1998)

Berger, Klaus, *Die Weisheitsschrift aus der Kairoer Geniza, Erstedition, Kommentar und Übersetzung*, Texte und Arbeiten zum Neutestamentlichen Zeitalter (TANZ) 1 (Tübingen: Francke Verlag 1989)

Bruyn, Theodore de, *Pelagius' Commentary on St Paul's Epistle to the Romans* (Oxford: Clarendon Press 1993)

Charles, R. H., *The Apocrypha and Pseudepigrapha of the Old Testament in English*, Vols. 1–2 (Oxford: Clarendon Press 1913)

The Assumption of Moses, Translated from the Latin Sixth Century MS, The Unemended Text of which is Published herewith, together with the Text in its Restored and Critically Emended Form, Edited with Introduction, Notes and Indices (London: Adam and Charles Black 1897)

Charlesworth, James H., *The Old Testament Pseudepigrapha*, Vols. 1–2 (London: Darton, Longman & Todd 1983–1985)

Cramer, John Anthony, *Catenae in Sancti Pauli Epistolas ad Corinthios, ad Galatas, Ephesios, Philippenses, Colossenses, Thessalonicenses, ad Timotheum, Titum, Philemona et ad Hebraeos, ad Romanos*, 4 Vols. (Oxford 1841–1844)

Daumas, F., Miguel, P., *De Vita Contemplativa*, Les Œuvres de Philon d'Alexandrie 29 (Paris: Cerf 1963)

Edmonds, John Maxwell, *The Fragments of Attic Comedy after Meinecke, Bergk, and Kock, Augmented, Newly Edited with their Contexts, Annotated and Completely Translated into English Verse*, Vols. 1–3b (Leiden: E. J. Brill 1957–1961)

Foerster, Richard, *Scriptores Physiognominici Graeci et Latini*, Vols. 1–2 (Leipzig: B. G. Teubner 1893)

Gaskin, John, *The Epicurean Philosophers*, Everyman Library (London, Vermont: J. M. Dent, Charles E. Tuttle 1995)

Heither, Theresia, *Origenes, Römerbriefkommentar*, Fontes Christiani 2/1 (Freiburg: Herder 1990)

Origenes, Römerbriefkommentar, Fontes Christiani 2/5 (Freiburg: Herder 1996)

Translatio Religionis, Die Paulusdeutung des Origenes im seinem Kommentar zum Römerbrief, Bonner Beiträge zur Kirchengeschichte 16 (Cologne: Böhlau 1990)

Hill, Edmund, *Sermons III (51–94) on the New Testament*, The Works of St Augustine, A Translation for the 21st Century (New Rochelle, New York: New City Press 1991)

    Sermons III/5 (148–183) on the New Testament, The Works of St Augustine, A Translation for the 21st Century (New Rochelle, New York: New City Press 1992)

Jolibert, Bernard, *Saint Augustin, De Magistro, 'Le Maître'*, Philosophie de l'éducation (Paris: Editions Klincksieck 1988)

Jonge, M. de, *Testamenta XII Patriarcharum, Edited According to Cambridge University Library MS Ff I.24 fol 203a–262b*, Pseudepigrapha Veteris Testamenti Graece 1 (Leiden: E. J. Brill 1964)

Kelly, J. N. D., *Rufinus, A Commentary on the Apostles' Creed*, Ancient Christian Writers (New York: Newman Press 1954)

Klauck, Hans-Josef, *4. Makkabäerbuch*, JSHRZ III/6 (Gütersloh: Gerd Mohn 1989)

Kock, Theodorus, *Comicorum Atticorum Fragmenta*, Vols. 1–3 (Leipzig 1880–1887)

Kohlenberger III, John R., *The Precise Parallel New Testament, Greek Text, King James Version, Rheims New Testament, Amplified Bible, New International Version, New Revised Standard Version, New American Bible, New American Standard Bible* (New York, Oxford: Oxford University Press 1995)

Landes, Paula Fredriksen, *Augustine on Romans, Propositions from the Epistle to the Romans, Unfinished Commentary on the Epistle to the Romans, Text and Translation*, Text and Translations 23, Early Christian Literature Series 6 (Chico, California: Scholars Press 1982)

Locher, Albrecht, *Marii Victorini Afri, Commentarii in Epistulas Pauli Ad Galatias, Ad Philippenses, Ad Ephesios*, Bibliotheca Scriptorum et Romanorum Teubneriana (Leipzig: B. G. Teubner 1972)

Lutz, Cora E., *Musonius Rufus 'The Roman Socrates'*, Yale Classical Studies 10 (New Haven: Yale University Press 1947)

Mercier, Charles, *Quaestiones et Solutiones in Genesim I–II e versione Armeniaca*, Les Œuvres de Philon d'Alexandrie 34A (Paris: Cerf 1979)

    Quaestiones et Solutiones in Genesim III, IV, V, VI e versione Armeniaca, Les Œuvres de Philon d'Alexandrie 34B (Paris: Cerf 1984)

Mozley, J. H., 'The Vita Adae', *JTS* 30 (1929) pp. 121–49

Pellétier, André, *Lettre d'Aristée à Philocrate*, SC 89 (Paris: Cerf 1962)

Petit, Françoise, *Quaestiones In Genesim et in Exodum, Fragmenta Graeca*, Les Œuvres de Philon d'Alexandrie 23 (Paris: Cerf 1978)

Nehamas, Alexander; Woodruff, Paul, *Plato, Phaedrus, Translated with Introduction and Notes* (Cambridge, Indianapolis: Hackett Publishing Co. 1995)

Rüger, Hans Peter, *Die Weisheitsschrift aus der Kairo Geniza: Text, Übersetzung und philologischer Kommentar*, WUNT 53 (Tübingen: J. C. B. Mohr (Paul Siebeck) 1991)

Savinel, Pierre, *Philon d'Alexandrie, De Somniis 1–2*, Les Œuvres de Philon d'Alexandrie 19 (Paris: Cerf 1962)

Souter, Alexander, *Pelagius' Exposition of Thirteen Epistles of St Paul*, Text and Studies 9.2 (Cambridge: Cambridge University Press 1926)

278   Bibliography

Staab, Karl, *Pauluskommentare aus der griechischen Kirche, Aus Kathenen gesammelt und herausgegeben*, NTAbh 15 (Münster: Verlag Aschendorff-schen Verlagsbuchhandlung 1933)

Suiceri, Joh. Caspari, *Thesaurus Ecclesiasticus, E Patribus Graecis Ordine Alphabetico*, Vols. 1–2 (Amsterdam: R & J Wetstenios & Gul. Smith 1728)

Swete, H. B., *Theodori Episcopi Mopsuesteni in Epistolas B. Pauli Commentarii, The Latin Version with the Greek Fragments*, Vols. 1–2 (Cambridge: Cambridge University Press 1880–1882)

Tischendorf, Constantinus, *Acta Apostolorum Apocrypha* (Leipzig: Avenarius et Mendelsohn 1851)

Usener, Hermann, *Epicurea*, Studia Philologica 3 (Rome: L'erma di Bretschneider 1963) (originally published in 1887)

Secondary literature

Alexander, Philip S., 'Physiognomy, Initiation, and Rank in the Qumran Community', in *Geschichte – Tradition – Reflexion, Band I, Judentum*, Festschrift für Martin Hengel (Tübingen: J. C. B. Mohr (Paul Siebeck) 1996), pp. 385–94

Andersen, Øyvind, *I Retorikkens Hage* (Oslo: Universitetsforlaget 1995)

Arrichea, Daniel C., Hatton, Howard A., *A Handbook on Paul's Letters to Timothy and to Titus*, Helps for Translators (New York: United Bible Societies 1995)

Asmis, Elizabeth, 'Seneca's *On the Happy Life* and Stoic Individualism, in Martha C. Nussbaum, *The Politics of Therapy, Hellenistic Ethics in its Rhetorical and Literary Context* (Edmonton, Alberta: Academic Printing & Publishing 1990), pp. 219–55

Aune, David C., 'Mastery of the Passions: Philo, 4 Maccabees and Earliest Christianity', in Wendy E. Helleman, *Hellenization Revisited, Shaping a Christian Response within the Graeco-Roman World* (Lanham, New York, London: University Press of America 1994), pp. 125–57

Aune, David E., '*De Esu Carnium Orationes* I and II' in Hans Dieter Betz, *Plutarch's Ethical Writings and Early Christian Literature*, SCHN 3 (Leiden: E. J. Brill 1975), pp. 301–16

Barclay, John M. G., 'Mirror-reading a Polemical Letter: Galatians as a Test Case', *JSNT* 31 (1987) pp. 73–93

Obeying the Truth, Paul's Ethics in Galatians (Minneapolis: Fortress Press 1988)

Jews in the Mediterranean Diaspora from Alexander to Trajan (323 BCE – 117C.E.) (Edinburgh: T & T Clark 1996)

'Paul and Philo on Circumcision: Romans 2.25–29 in Social and Cultural Context', *NTS* 44 (1998) pp. 536–56

Barr, James, *The Semantics of Biblical Language* (Oxford: Oxford University Press 1961)

Barrett, Charles K., *A Commentary on the First Epistle to the Corinthians*, Black's New Testament Commentaries (London: A & C Black 1968)

A Commentary on the Epistle to the Romans, Black's New Testament Commentaries (London: A & C Black 1991)

Barton, Tamsyn S., *Power and Knowledge, Astrology, Physiognomics and Medicine under the Roman Empire* (Ann Arbor: The University of Michigan Press 1994)

Behm, Johannes, 'κοιλία', *TDNT* 3, pp. 786–9

Bekken, Per Jarle, *The Word is Near You, A Study of Deuteronomy 30:12–14 in Paul's Letter to the Romans against the Background of Philo's Exposition in De Virtutibus and De Praemiis et Poeniis*, Doctoral thesis (NTNU Trondheim 1998)

Berger, Klaus, 'Die impliciten Gegner, Zur Methode des Erschliessens von "Gegnern" in neutestamentlichen Texten', in Dieter Lührmann, Georg Strecker, *Kirche*, Festschrift für Günther Bornkamm (Tübingen: J. C. B. Mohr 1980), pp. 373–400

Billerbeck, Margarethe, *Epiktet vom Kynismus, Herausgegeben und übersetzt mit einem Kommentar* (Leiden: E. J. Brill 1978)

Bloomquist, L. G., *The Function of Suffering in Philippians*, JSNT Suppl. Series 78 (Sheffield: Sheffield Academic Press 1993)

Bockmuehl, Markus, *The Epistle to the Philippians*, Black's New Testament Commentaries (London: A & C Black 1997)
 Jewish Law in Gentile Churches, Halakah and the Beginning of Christian Public Ethics (Edinburgh: T & T Clark 2000)

Booth, A. Peter, 'The Voice of the Serpent: Philo's Epicureanism', in Wendy E. Helleman, *Hellenization Revisited, Shaping a Christian Response within the Graeco-Roman World* (Lanham, New York, London: University Press of America 1994), pp. 159–72

Booth, Alan, 'The Age of Reclining and Its Attendant Perils', in William J. Slater, *Dining in a Classical Context* (Ann Arbor: The University of Michigan Press 1991), pp. 105–20

Borgen, Peder, 'Philo of Alexandria, A Critical and Synthetical Survey of Research since World War II', *ANRW* II.21.1 (Berlin, New York: Walter de Gruyter 1984), pp. 98–154
 Philo, John and Paul, New Perspectives on Judaism and Early Christianity, Brown Judaic Studies 131 (Atlanta: Scholars Press 1987)
 'Philo of Alexandria – A Systematic Philosopher or an Eclectic Editor? An Examination of the Laws of Moses', *SO* 71 (1996) pp. 115–34
 '"Yes", "No", "How Far"?: The Participation of Jews and Christians in Pagan Cults', in his *Early Christianity and Hellenistic Judaism* (Edinburgh: T & T Clark 1996), pp. 15–43
 Philo of Alexandria, An Exegete for His Time, NovTSup 86 (Leiden, Cologne, New York: E. J. Brill 1997)

Bormann, Lukas, *Philippi – Stadt & Christengemeinde zur Zeit des Paulus*, NovTSup 78 (Leiden, New York, Cologne: E. J. Brill 1995)

Braun, Herbert, *An die Hebräer*, HNT 14 (Tübingen: J. C. B. Mohr (Paul Siebeck) 1984)

Brewer, David Instone, *Techniques and Assumptions in Jewish Exegesis before 70 CE*, Texte und Studium zum Antiken Judentum 30 (Tübingen: J. C. B. Mohr (Paul Siebeck) 1992)

Brown, Peter, *Augustine of Hippo, A Biography* (London: Faber & Faber 1967)
 The Body and Society, Men, Women and Sexual Renunciation in Early Christianity (London and Boston: Faber & Faber 1988)

Bultmann, Rudolph, *Theology of the New Testament*, Vol. 1 (New York: Scribner 1951)

    Der zweite Brief an die Korinther, MeyerK (Göttingen: Vandenhoeck & Ruprecht 1976)

    Die Exegese des Theodor von Mopsuestia (Stuttgart: Kohlhammer 1984)

Byatt, Anthony, *New Testament Metaphors, Illustrations in Word and Phrase* (Edinburgh etc.: Pentland Press 1995)

Byrne, Brendan '"Sinning Against One's Own Body": Paul's Understanding of the Sexual Relationship in 1 Corinthians 6:18' *CBQ* 45 (1983) pp. 608–16

Castelli, Elizabeth A., *Imitating Paul, A Discourse of Power*, Literary Currents in Biblical Interpretation (Louisville, Kentucky: Westminster/John Knox Press 1991)

Chadwick, Henry, 'St Paul and Philo of Alexandria', *BJRL* 48 (1965–66) pp. 286–307

Ciampa, Roy E., *The Presence and Function of Scripture in Galatians 1 and 2*, WUNT II/102 (Tübingen: J. C. B. Mohr (Paul Siebeck) 1998)

Clark, Elizabeth A., *Women in the Early Church*, Message of the Fathers of the Church 13 (Collegeville: The Liturgical Press, Michael Glazier 1983)

    Reading Renunciation, Ascetism and Scripture in Early Christianity (Princeton: Princeton University Press: 1999)

Clarke, Andrew D., *Secular & Christian Leadership in Corinth, A Socio-Historical & Exegetical Study of 1 Corinthians 1–6* (Leiden, New York, Cologne: E. J. Brill 1993)

Collange, Jean-François, *The Epistle of Saint Paul to the Philippians* (London: Epworth Press 1979)

Collier, Gary D., '"That We Might Not Crave Evil", The Structure and Argument in 1 Corinthians 10, 1–13', *JSNT* 55 (1994) pp. 55–75

Conzelmann, Hans, *1 Corinthians, A Commentary on the First Epistle to the Corinthians*, Hermeneia (Philadelphia: Fortress Press 1975)

Costa, C. D. N., *Seneca, 17 Letters With Translation and Commentary* (Warminster: Aris & Phillips 1988)

    Four Dialogues, De Vita Beata, De Tranquillitate Animi, De Constantia Sapientis, Ad Helviam Matrem, de Consolatione (Warminster: Aris & Phillips 1994)

Countryman, L. William, *Dirt, Greed & Sex, Sexual Ethics in the New Testament and their Implications for Today* (London: SCM Press 1989)

Courtney, E., *A Commentary on the Satires of Juvenal* (London: The Athlone Press 1980)

Cranfield, C. E. B., *The Epistle to the Romans*, Vols. 1–2, ICC (Edinburgh: T & T Clark 1975–1979)

Crombie, I. M., *An Examination of Plato's Doctrines*, Vol. 1: *Plato on Man and Society* (London, New York: Routledge & Kegan Paul, The Humanities Press 1962)

Dalby, Andrew, *Siren Feasts, A History of Food and Gastronomy in Greece* (London and New York: Routledge 1996)

Davidson, James, *Courtesans and Fishcakes, The Consuming Passions of Classical Athens* (London: Fontana Press 1997)

Deidun, T. J., *The New Covenant Morality in Paul*, AnBib 89 (Rome: Biblical Institute)

Dibelius, Martin, *An die Thessalonicher I–II, An die Philipper*, HNT 11 (Tübingen: J. C. B. Mohr (Paul Siebeck) 1925)

Dobbin, Robert F., *Epictetus, Discourses Book I, Translated with an Introduction and Commentary*, Clarendon Later Ancient Philosophers (Oxford: Clarendon Press 1998)

Dodd, Brian J., 'Paul's Paradigmatic "I" and 1 Corinthians 6.12', *JSNT* 59 (1995) pp. 39–58

   Paul's Paradigmatic 'I', Personal Example as Literary Strategy, JSNT Sup 177 (Sheffield: Sheffield Academic Press 1999)

Donfried, Karl P., Marshall, I. Howard, *The Theology of the Shorter Pauline Letters*, New Testament Theology (Cambridge: Cambridge University Press 1993)

Doughty, Darrell J., 'Citizens of Heaven, Philippians 3.2–21', *NTS* 41 (1995) pp. 102–2

Dunn, James D. G., 'The New Perspective on Paul', *BJRL* 65 (1983) pp. 95–122

   Romans 1–8, WBC 38A (Dallas: Word Books 1988)

   Romans 9–16, WB 38B (Dallas:Word Books 1988)

   The Theology of Paul the Apostle (Grand Rapids, Cambridge: Wm B. Eerdmans 1998)

Edwards, Catharine, *The Politics of Immorality in Ancient Rome* (Cambridge: Cambridge University Press 1993)

Elgvin, Torleif, ' "To Master his Own Vessel", 1 Thess 4.4 in Light of New Qumran Evidence', *NTS* 43 (1997) pp. 604–19

Engberg-Pedersen, Troels, 'Stoicism in Philippians', in id., *Paul in His Hellenistic Context*, Studies of the New Testament and its World (Edinburgh: T & T Clark 1994), pp. 256–90

Erdt, Werner, *Marius Victorinus Afer, Der erste lateinische Pauluskommentar, Studien zu seinem Pauluskommentaren im Zusammenhang der Wiederentdeckung des Paulus in der abendländischen Theologie des 4. Jahrhunderts*, Europäische Hochschulschriften Reihe 23 Theologie 135 (Frankfurth am Main: Peter Lang 1980)

Erler, Michael, 'Epikuros', *Der Neue Pauly* 3, pp. 113–40

Evans, Elizabeth C., *Physiognomics in the Ancient World*, Transactions of the American Philosophical Society, New Series Vol. 59, Part 5 (Philadelphia 1969)

Ewald, Paul, *Der Brief des Paulus an die Philipper*, Kommentar zum Neuen Testament 11 (Leipzig: A. Deichertsche Buchhandlung Werner Scholl 1917)

Fahey, Michael Andrew, *Cyprian and the Bible, A Study in Third-Century Exegesis*, Beiträge zur Geschichte der Biblischen Hermeneutik 9 (Tübingen: J. C. B. Mohr (Paul Siebeck) 1971)

Fee, Gordon D., *The First Epistle to the Corinthians*, NICNT (Grand Rapids: Wm B. Eerdmans 1987)

   Paul's Letter to the Philippians, NICNT (Grand Rapids: Wm B. Eerdmans 1995)

Ferguson, John, *Moral Values in the Ancient World* (London: Methuen & Co 1958)

   Clement of Alexandria (New York: Twayne Publishers 1974)

Finsterbusch, Karin, *Die Thora als Lebensweisung für Heidenchristen, Studien zur Bedeutung für die paulinischen Ethik*, SUNT 20 (Göttingen: Vandenhoeck & Ruprecht 1996)

Fiore, Benjamin, *The Function of Personal Example in the Socratic and Pastoral Epistles*, AnBib 105 (Rome: Biblical Institute Press 1986)

'Passion in Paul and Plutarch, 1 Corinthians 5–6 and the Polemic against Epicureans' in David L. Balch, Everett Ferguson, Wayne A. Meeks, *Greeks, Romans, and Christians, Essays in Honor of Abraham J. Malherbe* (Minneapolis: Fortress Press 1990), pp. 135–43

Fisk, Bruce N., 'Eating Meat Offered to Idols: Corinthian Behavior and Pauline Response in 1 Corinthians 8–10 (A Response to Gordon Fee)', *Trinity Journal* 10 (1989) pp. 49–70

'ΠΟΡΝΕΥΕΙΝ As Body Violation: The Unique Nature of Sexual Sin in 1 Corinthians 6.18', *NTS* 42 (1996) pp. 540–58

Fitzgerald, John T., *Cracks in an Earthen Vessel: An Examination of the Catalogues of Hardships in the Corinthian Correspondence*, SBLDS 99 (Atlanta: Scholars Press 1988)

(ed.), *Friendship, Flattery, and Frankness of Speech, Studies on Friendship in the New Testament World*, NovTSup 82 (Leiden, New York, Köln: E. J. Brill 1996)

'Philippians in the Light of some Ancient Discussions of Friendship', in id. (ed.), *Friendship, Flattery, and Frankness of Speech, Studies on Friendship in the New Testament World*, NovTSup 82 (Leiden, New York, Köln: E. J. Brill 1996), pp. 141–60

Fitzmyer, Joseph A., *Romans, A New Translation with Introduction and Commentary*, AB 33 (New York etc.: Doubleday 1993)

Fowl, Stephen E., *The Story of Christ in the Ethics of Paul, An Analysis of the Function of the Hymnic Material in the Pauline Corpus*, JSNTSup 36 (Sheffield: Sheffield Academic Press 1990)

Franzmann, Martin H., 'Exegesis on Romans 16:17ff', *Concordia Journal* 7 (1981) pp. 13–20

Gardner, Paul Douglas, *The Gifts of God and the Authentication of a Christian, An Exegetical Study of 1 Corinthians 8–11:1* (Lanham: University Press of America 1994)

Garland, David E., 'The Composition and Unity of Philippians, Some Neglected Literary Features', *NovT* 27 (1985) pp. 141–73

Garvie, A. F., *Aeschylus Choephori, With an Introduction and Commentary* (Oxford: Clarendon Press 1986)

Geoffrion, Timothy C., *The Rhetorical Purpose and the Political and Military Character of Philippians, A Call to Stand Firm* (Lewiston, Queenstown, Lampeter: Mellen Biblical Press 1993)

Geytenbach, A. C. van, *Musonius Rufus and Greek Diatribe* (Assen: Van Gorcum 1962)

Gigon, Olof, *Kommentar zum ersten Buch von Xenophons Memorabilien*, Schweizerische Beiträge zur Altertumswissenschaft 5 (Basel: Friedrich Reinhard 1953)

Kommentar zum zweiten Buch von Xenophons Memorabilien, Schweizerische Beiträge zur Altertumswissenschaft 7 (Basel: Friedrich Reinhardt 1956)

Gleason, Maud, W., 'The Semiotics of Gender: Physiognomy and Self-Fashioning in the Second Century C.E.', in David M. Halperin, John J. Winkler, Froma

J. Zeitlin, *Before Sexuality, The Construction of Erotic Experience in the Ancient Greek World* (Princeton, New Jersey: Princeton University Press 1990), pp. 389–415

Making Men, Sophists and Self-Presentation in Ancient Rome (Princeton, New Jersey: Princeton University Press 1995)

Gnilka, Joachim, *Der Philipperbrief*, HTKNT 10 (Freiburg, Basel, Vienna: Herder 1968)

Gooch, Peter D., *Dangerous Food, 1 Corinthians 8–10 in its Context*, Studies in Christianity and Judaism 5 (Waterloo, Ontario: Wilfrid Laurier University Press 1993)

Gosling, J. C. B., Taylor, C. C. W., *The Greeks on Pleasure* (Oxford: Clarendon Press 1982)

Gowers, Emily, *The Loaded Table, Representations of Food in Roman Literature* (Oxford: Clarendon Press 1993)

Grässer, Erik, *An die Hebräer (Hebr 10, 19–13, 25)*, EKK 17/3 (Zürich, Neukirchen-Vluyn: Benziger, Neukirchener Verlag 1997)

Grimm, Veronica E., *From Feasting to Fasting, The Evolution of a Sin, Attitudes to Food in Late Antiquity* (London, New York: Routledge 1996)

Gundry, Robert H., *Sôma in Biblical Theology, With Emphasis on Pauline Anthropology*, SNTSMS 29 (Cambridge: Cambridge University Press)

Hadas, Moses, *The Third and Fourth Books of Maccabees* (New York: KTAV Publishing House 1953)

Hafemann, Scott, 'The Golden Calf and the History of Israel's Hard-Heartedness in Post-Biblical Judaism: Israel's Problem Behind Paul's Solution (2 Cor. 3:14–15)', unpublished paper presented in Oslo April 1998.

Hannestad, Niels, *Roman Art and Imperial Policy*, Jysk arkæologisk selskaps skrifter 19 (Aarhus: Aarhus University Press 1986)

Hawthorne, Gerald F., *Philippians*, WBC 43 (Waco: Word Books 1983)

Hays, Richard B., *First Corinthians*, Interpretation, A Bible Commentary for Teaching and Preaching (Louisville: John Knox Press 1997)

Henderson, Jeffrey, *The Maculate Muse, Obscene Language in Attic Comedy* (New Haven and London: Yale University Press 1975)

Hengel, Martin, *Judentum und Hellenismus, Studien zu ihrer Begegnung unter besonderer Berücksichtigung Palästinas bis zur Mitte des 2. Jh.s v. Chr.*, WUNT 10 (Tübingen: J. C. B. Mohr (Paul Siebeck) 1973)

Hoek, Annewies van den, *Clement of Alexandria and his Use of Philo in the Stromateis, An Early Christian Reshaping of a Jewish Model*, SupVC 3 (Leiden: E. J. Brill 1988)

Hunter, David G., 'Resistance to the Virginal Ideal in Late-Fourth-Century Rome, The Case of Jovinian', *TS* 48 (1987) pp. 45–64

Hurd, Jr, John Coolidge, *The Origin of 1 Corinthians* (London: SPCK 1965)

Jewett, Robert, 'The Epistolary Thanksgiving and the Integrity of Philippians', *NovT* 12 (1970) pp. 40–53

'Conflicting Movements in the Early Church as Reflected in Philippians', *NovT* 12 (1970) pp. 362–90

Paul's Anthropological Terms, A Study in their Use in Conflict Settings, AGJU 10 (Leiden: E. J. Brill 1971)

Johnson, Luke Timothy, 'The New Testament's Anti-Jewish Slander and the Conventions of Ancient Polemic', *JBL* 108 (1989) pp. 419–41

Jones, Christopher P., 'Dinner Theater' in William J. Slater, *Dining in a Classical Context* (Ann Arbor: The University of Michigan Press 1991), pp. 185–98

Jones, Howard, *The Epicurean Tradition* (London, New York: Routledge & Kegan Paul 1989)

Käsemann, Ernst, *An die Römer*, HNT 8a (Tübingen: J. C. B. Mohr (Paul Siebeck) 1974)

Kee, Howard C., 'The Linguistic Background of "Shame" in the New Testament', in Matthew Black, William A. Smalley, *On Language, Culture, and Religion*, In Honor of Eugene A. Nida, Approaches to Semiotics 56 (The Hague, Paris: Mouton 1974), pp. 133–47

Kelly, John Norman Davidson, *Jerome, His Life, Writings, and Controversies* (London: Duckworth 1975)

  Golden Mouth, The Story of John Chrysostom – Ascetic, Preacher, Bishop (London: Duckworth 1995)

Kidd, Reggie, M., 'Titus as Apologia: Grace for Liars, Beasts, and Bellies', *HBT* 21 (1999) pp. 185–209

Klauck, Hans-Josef, *Herrenmahl und Hellenistischer Kult, Eine religionsgeschichtliche Untersuchung zum ersten Korintherbrief*, NTAbh NF 15 (Münster: Aschendorff 1982)

Klijn, A. F. J. 'Paul's Opponents in Philippians 3', *NovT* 7 (1964/65) pp. 278–84

Koester, Helmut, 'The Purpose of the Polemic of a Pauline Fragment (Philippians III)', *NTS* 8 (1961–62) pp. 317–32

Lampe, Peter, 'The Eucharist, Identifying with Christ on the Cross', *Int* 48 (1994) pp. 36–49

Larsson, Edvin, *Christus als Vorbild, Eine Untersuchung zu den paulinischen Tauf- und Eikontexten* (Copenhagen: C. W. K. Gleerup Lund, Eknar Munksgaard 1962)

Lella, Alexander di, *The Wisdom of Ben Sira, A New Translation with Notes*, AB (New York: Doubleday 1987)

Leyerle, Blake, 'Clement of Alexandria on the Importance of Table Etiquette', *Journal of Early Christian Studies* 3 (1995) pp. 123–41

Licht, Hans, *Sexual Life in Ancient Greece* (London: Routledge & Kegan Paul 1931)

Lightfoot, J. B., *Saint Paul's Epistle to the Philippians* (London, New York: Macmillan and Co. 1891)

Lissarrague, François, *Un Flot d'Images, Une Esthétique du Banquet Grec* (Paris: Adam Biro 1987)

Loh, I-Jin; Nida, Eugene A., *A Translator's Handbook on Paul's Letter to the Philippians*, Helps for Translators 19 (Stuttgart: United Bible Societies 1977)

Lohmeyer, Ernst, *Der Brief an die Philipper*, MeyerK (Göttingen: Vandenhoeck & Ruprecht 1964)

Lukinovich, Alessandra, 'The Play of Reflections between Literary Form and the Sympotic Theme in the *Deipnosophistae* of Athenaeus', in Oswyn Murray, *Sympotica, A Symposium on the Symposion* (Oxford: Clarendon Press 1990), pp. 263–71

MacKendrick, Paul, *The Speeches of Cicero, Context, Law, Rhetoric* (London: Duckworth 1995)

Malherbe, Abraham J., 'Hellenistic Moralists and the New Testament', *ANRW* II.26.1, pp. 267–333

'The Beasts at Ephesus', *JBL* 87 (1968) pp. 71–80

Social Aspects of Early Christianity (Baton Rouge and London: Louisiana State University Press 1977)

Moral Exhortation, A Graeco-Roman Sourcebook, Library of Early Christianity (Philadelphia: The Westminster Press 1986)

Malina, Bruce J., *The Palestinian Manna Tradition, The Manna Tradition in Palestinian Targums in its Relationship to the New Testament Writings*, AGJU 7 (Leiden: E. J. Brill 1968)

Marcel, Simon, *Verus Israel, A Study of the Relations Between Christians and Jews in the Roman Empire (135–425)*, The Littman Library of Jewish Civilization (Oxford: Oxford University Press 1986)

Marshall, Peter, *Enmity in Corinth: Social Conventions in Paul's Relations with the Corinthians*, WUNT II/23 (Tübingen: J. C. B. Mohr (Paul Siebeck) 1987)

Martin, Dale B., *Slavery as Salvation, The Metaphor of Slavery in Pauline Christianity* (New Haven and London: Yale University Press 1990)

The Corinthian Body (New Haven and London: Yale University Press 1995)

'Paul Without Passion: On Paul's Rejection of Desire in Sex and Marriage', in Halvor Moxnes (ed.), *Constructing Early Christian Families, Family as Social Reality and Metaphor* (London, New York: Routledge 1997) pp. 201–15

Martin, Ralph P., *Philippians*, NCB (London: Marshall, Morgan & Scott 1976)

Mayor, John E. B., *Thirteen Satires of Juvenal, With a Commentary* (London and Cambridge: Macmillan and Co. 1881)

Mearns, Chris, 'The Identity of Paul's Opponents at Philippi' *NTS* 33 (1987) pp. 194–204

Meeks, Wayne A., ' "And Rose Up to Play": Midrash and Paraenesis in 1 Corinthians 10:1–22', *JSNT* 16 (1982) pp. 64–78

'The Social Context of Pauline Theology', *Int* 36 (1982) pp. 266–77

Meggit, Justin J., *Paul, Poverty and Servitude* (Edinburgh: T & T Clark 1998)

Mendelson, Alan, *Philo's Jewish Identity* (Atlanta: Scholars Press 1988)

Mengel, Berthold, *Studien zum Philipperbrief, Untersuchungen zum situativen Kontext unter besonderer Berücksichtigung der Frage nach der Ganzheitlichkeit eines paulinischen Briefes*, WUNT II/8 (Tübingen: J. C. B. Mohr (Paul Siebeck) 1982)

Mesk, Josef, 'Die Beispiele in Polemons Physiognomik', *Wiener Studien* 50 (1932) pp. 51–67

Meyer, Heinrich August Wilhelm, *Critical and Exegetical Handbook to the Epistles to the Philippians and Colossians* (Edinburgh: T & T Clark 1875)

Michaels, J. Ramsey, 'The Redemption of Our Body: The Riddle of Romans 8:19–22' in *Romans and the People of God*, Essays in Honor of Gordon D. Fee (Grand Rapids: Wm. B. Eerdmans 1999) pp. 92–114

Michel, Otto, *Der Brief an die Römer*, MeyerK 6 (Göttingen: Vandenhoeck & Ruprecht 1978)

Miles, Christopher; Norwich, John J., *Love in the Ancient World* (London: Weidenfeld & Nicolson 1997)

Mitchell, Margaret M., *Paul and the Rhetoric of Reconciliation, An Exegetical Investigation of the Language and Composition of 1 Corinthians* (Louisville, Kentucky: Westminster, John Knox Press 1991)

Mitsis, Phillip, *Epicurus' Ethical Theory, The Pleasures of Invulnerability*, Cornell Studies in Classical Philology 48 (Ithaca, London: Cornell University Press 1988)

Moo, Douglas J., *The Epistle to the Romans*, NICNT (Grand Rapids: Wm B. Eerdmans 1996)

Moore, Stephen D.; Anderson, Janice Chapel, 'Taking it Like a Man, Masculinity in 4 Maccabees', *JBL* 117 (1998) pp. 249–73

Muecke, Frances, *Horace, Satires II with Introduction, Translation and Commentary* (Warminster: Aris & Phillips 1993)

Müller, Ulrich B., *Der Brief des Paulus an die Philipper*, ThHK 11/1 (Leipzig: Evangelische Verlagsanstalt 1993)

Musorillo, Herbert, 'The Problem of Fasting in the Greek Patristic Writers', *Traditio, Studies in Ancient and Medieval History, Thought and Religion* 12 (1956) pp. 1–64

Mussies, G., *Dio Chrysostom and the New Testament, Parallels Collected*, SCHNT 2 (Leiden: E. J. Brill 1972)

Nanos, Mark D., *The Mystery of Romans, The Jewish Context of Paul's Letter* (Minneapolis: Fortress Press 1996)

Newman, Barclay M.; Nida, Eugene A., *A Translator's Handbook on Paul's Letter to the Romans*, Helps for Translators 14 (London: United Bible Societies 1973)

Newton, Derek, *Deity and Diet, The Dilemma of Sacrificial Food at Corinth*, JSNTSup 169 (Sheffield: Sheffield Academic Press 1998)

Neyrey, Jerome H., 'The Form and Background of the Polemic in 2 Peter', *JBL* 99 (1980) pp. 407–31

   Paul in Other Words, A Cultural Reading of His Letters (Louisville, Kentucky: Westminster/John Knox Press 1990)

Niven, Larry, Pournelle, Jerry, *Inferno* (New York: Pocket Books, Simon & Schuster 1976)

Nussbaum, Martha C., *The Therapy of Desire, Theory and Practice in Hellenistic Ethics*, Martin Classical Lectures New Series 2 (Princeton, New Jersey: Princeton University Press 1994)

O'Brien, Peter, *The Epistle to the Philippians, A Commentary on the Greek Text*, NIGTC (Grand Rapids: Wm. B. Eerdmans 1991)

O'Connor, Jerome Murphy, 'Corinthian Slogans in 1 Cor. 6:12–20', *CBQ* 40 (1978) pp. 390–6

   St Paul's Corinth, Texts and Archaelogy, GNS 6 (Wilmington, Delaware: Michael Glazier 1983)

Olson, Stanley N., 'Epistolary Uses of Expressions of Self-Confidence', *JBL* 103 (1984) pp. 585–97

O'Neill, Edward, 'De Cupiditate Divitiarum (Moralia 523c–528b)', in Hans Dieter Betz, *Plutarch's Ethical Writings and Early Christian Literature*, SCHNT 4 (Leiden: E. J. Brill 1978), pp. 289–362

Osborn, Eric, *Ethical Patterns in Early Christian Thought* (Cambridge: Cambridge University Press 1976)

   Tertullian, First Theologian of the West (Cambridge: Cambridge University Press 1997)

Pellizer, Ezio, 'Outlines of a Morphology of Sympotic Entertainment', in Oswyn Murray, *Sympotica, A Symposium on the Symposion* (Oxford: Clarendon Press 1990), pp. 177–84

Perkins, Pheme, 'Theology for the Heavenly *Politeuma*', in Jouette M. Bassler, *Pauline Theology*, Vol. I (Minneapolis: Fortress Press 1991), pp. 89–104

Perrot, Charles, 'Exemples du Désert (1 Co. 10.6–11)', *NTS* 29 (1983) pp. 437–52

Peterlin, Davorin, *Paul's Letter to the Philippians in the Light of Disunity in the Church*, NovTSup 79 (Leiden, New York, Cologne: E. J. Brill 1995)

Peterman, G. W., *Paul's Gift from Philippi, Conventions of Gift-Exchange and Christian Giving*, SNTSMS 92 (Cambridge: Cambridge University Press 1997)

Pfitzner, Victor C., *Paul and the Agon Motif, Traditional Athletic Imagery in the Pauline Literature*, NovTSup 16 (Leiden: E. J. Brill 1967)

Pilhofer, Peter, *Philippi, Band I: Die erste christliche Gemeinde Europas*, WUNT 87 (Tübingen: J. C. B. Mohr (Paul Siebeck) 1995)

Portefaix, Lillian, *Sisters Rejoice, Paul's Letter to the Philippians and Luke-Acts as Received by First-Century Philippian Women*, ConBNT Series 20 (Uppsala: Almquist & Wiksell International 1988)

Preisker, H., 'μέθη', *TDNT* 4, pp. 545–8

Pretorius, E. A. C., 'New Trends in Reading Philippians: A Literature Review', *Neot* 29 (1995) pp. 273–98

Rapske, Brian, *The Book of Acts and Paul in Custody*, The Book of Acts in its First-Century Setting, Vol. 3 (Grand Rapids, Carlisle: Wm B. Eerdmans, Pater Noster Press 1994)

Reed, Jeffrey T., *A Discourse Analysis of Philippians, Method and Rhetoric in the Debate over Literary Integrity*, JSNTSSup 136 (Sheffield: Sheffield Academic Press 1997)

Renehan, Robert, 'The Greek Philosophical Background of Fourth Maccabees', *Rheinisches Museum für Philologie NF* 115 (1972) pp. 223–38

Rengstorf, Karl H., 'δοῦλος', *TDNT* 2, pp. 261–80

Robertson, Archibald; Plummer, Alfred, *First Epistle of St Paul to the Corinthians*, ICC (Edinburgh: T & T Clark 1929)

Rosner, Brian S., *Paul, Scripture and Ethics, A Study of 1 Corinthians 5–7*, AGJU 22 (Leiden, New York, Köln: E. J. Brill 1994)

'Temple Prostitution in 1 Corinthians 6:12–20', *NovT* 40 (1998) pp. 336–51

Runia, David T., *Philo of Alexandria and the Timaeus of Plato*, Philosophia Antiqua 44 (Leiden: E. J. Brill 1986)

Philo in Early Christian Literature, A Survey, CRINT, Section III, Jewish Traditions in Early Christian Literature 3 (Assen, Minneapolis: Van Gorcum, Fortress Press 1993)

Sandmel, Samuel, *Philo of Alexandria, An Introduction* (New York, Oxford: Oxford University Press 1979)

'Philo Judaeus, An Introduction to the Man, His Writings, and His Significance', *ANRW* II.21.1 (Berlin, New York: Walter de Gruyter 1984), pp. 3–46

Sandnes, Karl Olav, *Paul – One of the Prophets? A Contribution to the Apostle's Self-Understanding*, WUNT II/43 (Tübingen: J. C. B. Mohr (Paul Siebeck) 1991)

A New Family, Conversion and Ecclesiology in the Early Church with Cross-Cultural Comparisons, Studies in the Intercultural History of Christianity 91 (Bern: Peter Lang 1994)

'Omvendelse og gjestevennskap, Et bidrag til noen Lukas-Acta tekster', in

Ad Acta, Studier til Apostlenes gjerninger og urkristendommens historie, in honour of Edvin Larsson (Oslo: Verbum 1994), pp. 325–46

'Prophecy – a Sign for Believers (1 Cor. 14, 20–25)', *Bib* 77 (1996) pp. 1–15

I tidens fylde, En innføring i Paulus' teologi (Oslo: Luther forlag 1996)

'Kroppen som tegn hos Paulus, Om magens sug', *Tidsskrift for Teologi og Kirke* 71 (2000) pp. 83–95

Sawhill, John Alexander, *The Use of Athletic Metaphors in the Biblical Homilies of St John Chrysostom* (Princeton 1928)

Schenk, Wolfgang, *Die Philipperbriefe des Paulus, Kommentar* (Stuttgart, Berlin, Cologne, Mainz: W. Kohlhammer 1984)

Schlier, Heinrich, *Der Römerbrief*, HTKNT 6 (Freiburg, Basel, Vienna: Herder 1977)

Schmid, Wolfgang, 'Epikur', *RAC* 5, pp. 681–819

Schmithals, Walter, 'Die Irrlehrer von Rm 16,17–20', *ST* 13 (1959) pp. 51–69

Der Römerbrief, Ein Kommentar (Gütersloh: Gerd Mohn 1988)

Schotter, David, *Suetonius, The Lives of Galba, Otho, Vitellius, Edited with Translation and Commentary* (Warminster: Aris & Phillips 1993)

Schrage, Wolfgang, *Der Erste Brief an die Korinther (1 Kor 6,12–11,16)*, EKK VII/2 (Solothurn, Düsseldorf, Neukirchen-Vluyn: Benziger Verlag, Neukirchener Verlag 1995)

Schreiner, Thomas R., *Romans*, Baker Exegetical Commentary on the New Testament (Grand Rapids: Baker Books 1998)

Schroer, Silvia and Staubli, Thomas, *Die Körpersymbolik der Bibel* (Darmstadt: Wissenschaftliche Buchgesellschaft 1998)

Schwankl, Otto, '"Lauft so, dass ihr gewinnt", Zur Wettkampmetaphorik in 1 Kor 9', *BZ* 41 (1997) pp. 174–91

Schweizer, Eduard, 'σῶμα', TDNT 7, pp. 1024–94

Seaford, Richard, *Euripides' Cyclops, Edited with Introduction and Commentary* (Oxford: Clarendon Press 1988)

Sevenster, J. N., *Paul and Seneca* (Leiden: E. J. Brill 1961)

Sharp, Douglas S., *Epictetus and the New Testament* (London: Charles H. Kelly 1914)

Shaw, Teresa M., *The Burden of the Flesh, Fasting and Sexuality in Early Christianity* (Minneapolis: Fortress Press 1998)

Shelton, Jo-Ann, *As the Romans Did it, A Sourcebook in Roman Social History*, 2nd edition (Oxford, New York: Oxford University Press 1998)

Shimoff, Sandra R., 'Banquets: The Limits of Hellenization', *JSJ* 27 (1996) pp. 440–52

Silva, David A. de, 'No Confidence in the Flesh: The Meaning and Function of Philippians 3:2–21', *Trinity Journal* 15 (1994) pp. 27–54

4 Maccabees, Guides to Apocrypha and Pseudepigrapha (Sheffield: Sheffield Academic Press 1998)

Silva, Moisés, *Philippians*, Baker Exegetical Commentary on the New Testament (Grand Rapids: Baker Book House 1992)

Simon, Marcel, *Verus Israel, A Study of the Relations between Christians and Jews in the Roman Empire (135–425)* (Oxford: Oxford University Press 1986)

Skarsaune, Oskar, *The Proof from Prophecy, A Study in Justin Martyr's Proof-Text Tradition: Text-Type, Provenance, Theological Profile*, NovTSup 56 (Leiden: E. J. Brill 1987)

Sly, Dorothy, *Philo's Perception of Women*, BJS 209 (Atlanta: Scholars Press 1990)

'The Plight of Woman: Philo's Blind Spot', in Wendy E. Helleman, *Helleniza-tion Revisited, Shaping a Christian Response within the Greco-Roman World* (Lanham, New York, London: World University Press of America 1994), pp. 173–87

Smolar, Leivy and Aberbach, Moshe, 'The Golden Calf Episode in Postbiblical Literature', *HUCA* 39 (1968) pp. 91–116

Souter, Alexander, *The Earliest Latin Commentaries on the Epistles of St Paul* (Oxford: Clarendon Press 1927)

Spicq, Ceslas, *Saint Paul, Les Epîtres Pastorales*, Tome 1, Etudes Bibliques (Paris: J. Gabalda 1969)

'γαστήρ', in id., *Theological Lexicon of the New Testament*, Vol. 1 (Peabody: Hendrickson 1994) pp. 293–5

Starr, Chester G., 'An Evening with the Flute-Girls', *La Parola del Passato, Rivista di Studi Antichi* 33 (1978) pp. 401–10

Stein, S., 'The Dietary Laws in Rabbinic and Patristic Literature', in Kurt Aland, F. L. Cross, *Studia Patristica* II, TU 64 (Berlin, Akademie Verlag 1957), pp. 141–54

Stowers, Stanley K., '4 Maccabees', in James L. Mays, *Harper's Bible Commentary* (San Francisco: Harper & Row 1988) pp. 922–34

'Friends and Enemies in the Politics of Heaven: Reading Theology in Philippians', in Jouette M. Bassler, *Pauline Theology* Vol. I, pp. 105–21 (Minneapolis: Fortress Press 1991)

A Rereading of Romans, Justice, Jews, and Gentiles (New Haven & London: Yale University Press 1994)

Stuiber, Alfred, 'Ambrosiaster', *TRE* 2, pp. 356–62

Stuhlmacher, Peter, *Paul's Letter to the Romans, A Commentary* (Edinburgh: T & T Clark 1994)

Taylor, A. E., *A Commentary on Plato's Timaeus* (Oxford: The Clarendon Press 1928)

Tellbe, Mikael, *Paul Between Synagogue and State, Christians, Jews, and Civic Authorities in 1 Thessalonians, Romans, and Philippians*, CBNT 34 (Stockholm: Almquist & Wiksell International 2001)

Terian, Abraham, 'A Critical Introduction to Philo's Dialogues', *ANRW* II.21.1 (Berlin, New York: Walter de Gruyter 1984) pp. 272–94

Theissen, Gerd, *The Social Setting of Pauline Christianity* (Philadelphia: Fortress Press 1982)

Thurén, Lauri, 'Hey Jude! Asking for the Original Situation and Message of a Catholic Epistle', *NTS* 43 (1997) pp. 451–65

Toit, Andrie du, 'Vilification as a Pragmatic Device in Early Christian Epistolography', *Bib* 75 (1994) pp. 403–12

Tomlin, Graham, 'Christians and Epicureans in 1 Corinthians', *JSNT* 68 (1997) pp. 51–72

Vincent, Marvin R., *The Epistles to the Philippians and Philemon*, ICC (Edinburgh: T & T Clark 1979)

Volf, Judith M. Gundry, *Paul and Perseverance, Staying in and Falling Away*, WUNT II/37 (Tübingen: J. C. B. Mohr (Paul Siebeck) 1990)

Vollenweider, Samuel, *Freiheit als neue Schöpfung, Eine Untersuchung zur*

Eleutheria bei Paulus und in seiner Umwelt, FRLANT 147 (Göttingen: Vandenhoeck & Ruprecht 1989)

Wallace-Hadrill, Andrew, *Suetonius, The Scholar and His Caesars* (London: Duckworth 1983)

Walter, Nikolaus, Reinmuth, Eckhart, Lampe, Peter, *Die Briefe an die Philipper, Thessalonicher und an Philemon*, NTD 8/2 (Göttingen: Vandenhoeck & Ruprecht 1998)

Watson, Duane F., 'A Rhetorical Analysis of Philippians and its Implications for the Unity Question', *NovT* 30 (1988) pp. 57–88

Weiss, Hans Friedrich, *Der Brief an die Hebräer*, MeyerK (Göttingen: Vandenhoeck & Ruprecht 1991)

Weiss, Johannes, *Der erste Korintherbrief*, MeyerK (Göttingen: Vandenhoeck & Ruprecht 1925)

Weissbach, 'Sardanapal', *PW* II/1, pp. 2436–75

Westman, Rolf, *Plutarch gegen Kolotes, Seine Schrift 'Adversus Colotem' als Philosophie-geschichtliche Quelle*, Acta Philosophica Fennica 7 (Helsingfors: Akateeminen Kirjakauppa 1955)

Wette, W. M. L. de, *Kurze Erklärung der Briefe an die Korinther* (Leipzig: Weidmannsche Buchhandlung 1841)

White, L. Michael, 'Morality Between Two Worlds: a Paradigm of Friendship in Philippians', in David L. Balch, Everett Ferguson, Wayne A. Meeks, *Greeks, Romans, and Christians, Essays in Honor of Abraham J. Malherbe* (Minneapolis: Fortress Press 1990), pp. 201–15

Whittaker, Molly, *Jews & Christians: Graeco-Roman Views*, Cambridge Commentaries on Writings of the Jewish & Christian World 200 BC to AD 200, Vol. 6 (Cambridge: Cambridge University Press 1984)

Wilckens, Ulrich, *Der Brief an die Römer (12–16)*, EKK VI/3 (Zürich, Neukirchen-Vluyn: Benziger, Neukirchener 1982)

Wilken, Robert L., *John Chrysostom and the Jews, Rhetoric and Reality in the Late 4th Century* (Berkeley, Los Angeles, London: University of California Press 1983)

Willis, Wendell Lee, *Idolmeat in Corinth, The Pauline Argument in 1 Corinthians 8 and 10*, SBLDS 68 (Chico: Scholars Press 1985)

Winston, David, 'Philo's Ethical Theory', *ANRW* II.21.1 (Berlin, New York: Walter de Gruyter 1984), pp. 372–416

Winter, Bruce W., 'The Lord's Supper at Corinth: An Alternative Reconstruction', *The Reformed Theological Review* 37 (1978) pp. 73–82

'Theological and Ethical Responses to Religious Pluralism in 1 Corinthians 8–10', *TynB* 41 (1990) pp. 209–26

Seek the Welfare of the City, Christians as Benefactors and Citizens, First-Century Christians in the Graeco-Roman World (Grand Rapids, Carlisle: Wm B. Eerdmans, Pater Noster Press 1994)

'Gluttony and Immorality at Elitist Banquets, The Background of 1 Corinthians 6:12–20', *Jian Dao* 7 (1997) pp. 77–90

After Paul Left Corinth: The Impact of Secular Ethics and Social Change (Grand Rapids: Wm B. Eerdmans 2001)

Witherington, III, Ben, *Friendship and Finances in Philippi: The Letter of Paul to the Philippians* (Valley Forge: Trinity Press International 1994)

Conflict & Community, A Socio-Rhetorical Commentary on 1 and 2 Corinthians (Grand Rapids, Carlisle: Wm B. Eerdmans, Pater Noster Press 1994)

Witt, Norman Wentworth de, *St Paul and Epicurus* (Minneapolis: University of Minnesota Press 1954)

Wolfson, Harry Austryn, *Philo, Foundations of Religious Philosophy in Judaism, Christianity, and Islam*, Vol. 1 (Cambridge, Massachusetts: Harvard University Press 1947)

Yeo Khiok-Khng, *Rhetorical Interaction in 1 Corinthians 8 and 10, A Formal Analysis with Preliminary Suggestions for a Chinese Cross-Cultural Hermeneutic*, Biblical Interpretation Series 8 (Leiden, New York, Köln: E. J. Brill 1995)

Zanker, Paul, *The Power of Images in the Age of Augustus*, Jerome Lectures 16 (Ann Arbor: University of Michigan Press 1988)

Ziesler, John, *Paul's Letter to the Romans*, TPI New Testament Commentaries (London and Philadelphia: SCM Press and Trinity Press International 1989)

Yardly, John C., 'Symposium in Roman Elegy', in William J. Slater, *Dining in a Classical Context* (Ann Arbor: The University of Michigan Press 1991) pp. 149–55

INDEX OF MODERN AUTHORS

Aberbach, M., 207
Alexander, Ph. S., 24
Andersen, Ø., 139
Anderson, H., 98
Anderson, J. C., 101, 102
Andrè, J., 27, 28, 31
Arrichea, D. C., 1
Asmis, E., 72
Aune, D. C., 101, 111, 112
Aune, D. E., 53

Barclay, J. M. G., 108, 111, 128, 156, 159, 194
Barr, J., 13, 169
Barrett, C. K., 169, 204
Barton, T. S., 24, 26, 34
Beard, M., 67
Behm, J., 7, 8, 146, 217, 262
Bekken, P. J., 130
Berger, K., 107, 156
Billerbeck, M., 51
Bloomquist, L. G., 136, 137, 139, 142
Bockmuehl, M., 5, 107, 144, 157, 158, 160, 176
Booth, A., 45, 80, 114
Borgen, P., 108, 111, 118, 126, 128, 208
Bormann, L., 139
Braun, H., 120
Brewer, D. I., 109
Brown, P., 15, 22, 252
Bultmann, R., 16, 256
Byrne, B., 192, 197

Castelli, E. A., 158
Chadwick, H., 109
Charles, R. H., 98
Ciampa, R. E., 4
Clark, E. A., 218
Clarke, A. D., 154, 196
Collange, J. F., 153
Collier, G. D., 200, 203, 205, 215, 216

Conzelmann, H., 7, 187
Costa, C. D. N., 72, 83
Countryman, L. W., 191, 192
Courtney, E., 88, 89
Cranfield, C. E. B., 8, 169, 170, 217
Crombie, I. M., 41

Dalby, A., 55, 77, 83
Davidson, J., 48, 208
Deidun, T. J., 16, 176
Dibelius, M., 10
Dobbin, R. F., 49
Dodd, B. J., 151, 192, 217
Donfried, K. P., 7
Douglas, M., 212
Dunn, J. D. G., 8, 15, 16, 17, 20, 169, 170, 176, 179, 271

Edwards, C., 82, 88
Elgvin, T., 9
Engberg-Pedersen, T., 142
Erdt, W., 236
Erler, M., 65
Evans, E. C., 24, 26, 27, 28
Ewald, P. E., 60, 137

Fahey, M. A., 230
Fee, G. D., 5, 8, 9, 137, 139, 148, 160, 182, 187, 188, 192, 193, 196, 200, 210, 217
Ferguson, J., 148, 219, 221
Finsterbusch, K., 178
Fiore, B., 139, 141, 192, 196
Fisk, B. N., 200, 213
Fitzgerald, J. T., 135, 151
Fitzmyer, J. A., 169
Foerster, R., 25, 28, 29, 30
Fowl, S. E., 142

Gardner, P. D., 200, 211
Garland, D. E., 136, 139, 157
Garvie, A. F., 38

Gaskin, J., 61, 62
Geoffrion, T. C., 139
Geytenbach, A. C. van, 47
Gigon, O., 43
Gleason, M. W., 24, 28, 30
Gnilka, J., 8, 160
Gooch, P. D., 200, 206
Gosling, J. C. B., 61
Gowers, E., 36, 79, 82, 88
Grimm, V. E., 218
Grässer, E., 121
Gundry, R., 16

Hadas, M., 98, 100, 101, 103
Hafemann, S., 207
Hannestad, N., 26
Hatton, H. A., 1
Hawthorne, G. F., 7, 144, 146, 153, 217
Hays, R. B., 195
Heither, T., 228
Henderson, J., 82
Hengel, M., 109
Hoek, A. Van den, 219
Hunter, D. G., 238
Hurd Jr, J. C., 192

Jewett, R., 10, 15, 16, 136, 146, 155, 160, 178, 210
Johnson, L. T., 14
Jones, C. P., 81
Jones, H., 65, 77

Käsemann, E., 8
Kee, H. C., 153
Kelly, J. N. D., 238, 241, 244
Kidd, R. M., 1
Klauck, H.-J., 101, 203, 210
Klijn, A. J. F., 155
Koester, H., 7, 155

Lampe, P., 144, 188
Larsson, E., 21
Lella, A. di, 97
Leyerle, B., 221
Licht, H., 81
Lightfoot, J. B., 137, 146
Lissarrague, F., 83
Lohmeyer, E., 10, 151, 246
Louw, J. P., 1, 7, 171
Lukinovich, A., 55
Lutz, C. E., 47

MacKendrick, P., 70, 71
Malherbe, A. J., 12, 36, 68, 183, 184

Malina, B. J., 200
Marshall, I. H., 7
Marshall, P., 54, 172
Martin, D. B., 17, 18, 19, 21, 22, 31, 41, 153, 167, 184, 196, 197, 212, 214
Martin, R. P., 7
Mayor, J. E. B., 68
Mearns, C., 9, 97
Meeks, W. A., 36, 199, 203, 204
Meggit, J. J., 36
Mendelson, A., 128, 129, 130, 131
Mesk, J., 33
Meyer, H. A. W., 137
Michaels, J. R., 19
Michel, O., 169, 173
Miles, C., 82
Mitchell, M., 204
Mitsis, Ph., 65
Moo, D. J., 166, 169, 173, 174
Moore, S. D., 101, 102
Muecke, F., 87
Müller, U. B., 144, 146
Musorillo, H., 218
Mussies, G., 47

Nehamas, A., 39
Newman, B. M., 5, 171
Newton, D., 201, 206
Neyrey, J. H., 5, 181, 212, 213
Nida, E. A., 1, 5, 7, 171
Niven, L., 273
North, J., 67
Norwich, J. J., 82
Nussbaum, M., 65

O'Brien, P. T., 8, 137, 139, 142, 144, 148, 155, 156, 161, 217
O'Connor, J. M., 188, 193, 195
Olson, S. N., 138
O'Neill, E., 148
Osborn, E., 220, 225, 246

Pellizer, E., 80
Perkins, Ph., 151
Perrot, C., 199
Peterlin, D., 137, 139, 144, 157
Peterman, G. W., 148
Pfitzner, V. C., 52, 103, 111, 141, 200
Pilhofer, P., 151
Plummer, A., 185
Portefaix, L., 154
Pournelle, J., 273
Preisker, H., 188

Pretorius, E. A. C., 139
Price, S., 67

Rapske, B., 224
Reed, J. T., 136, 144, 145
Reinmuth, E., 144
Rengstorf, K. H., 168
Robertson, A., 185
Rosner, B., 10, 36, 106, 107
Rüger, H. P., 107
Runia, D. T., 40, 109, 113, 120

Sandmel, S., 108, 109
Sandnes, K. O., 4, 12, 18, 130, 133, 151,
    187, 188, 192, 206, 224
Savinel, P., 116
Sawhill, J. A., 246
Schenk, W., 60, 137, 153, 155
Schlier, H., 8
Schmid, W., 65, 77
Schmithals, W., 155, 169, 173, 174
Schotter, D., 34
Schrage, W., 199, 211
Schreiner, T. R., 5, 165, 169, 170
Schroer, S., 5
Schwankl, O., 200
Schweizer, E., 16, 21
Seaford, R., 37
Sevenster, J. N., 72
Sharp, D. S., 50
Shaw, T. M., 2, 34, 52, 129, 218, 240,
    242
Shelton, J.-A., 82
Shimoff, S., 81
Silva, D. A., de, 101, 102, 139, 157
Silva, M., 8, 155
Simon, M., 245
Skarsaune, O., 203
Sly, D., 116
Smolar, L., 207
Souter, A., 237
Spicq, C., 36
Starr, C. G., 82
Staubli, T., 5
Stein, S., 129

Stowers, S. K., 18, 19, 36, 101, 133, 134,
    151, 158
Stuhlmacher, P., 166, 169, 170, 173
Stuiber, A., 235
Swete, H. B., 257

Taylor, A. E., 41
Taylor, C. C. W., 61
Tellbe, M., 139, 156
Terian, A., 108
Theissen, G., 36, 187
Thurén, L., 14
Toit, A. du, 14
Tomlin, G., 184, 187, 196

Vincent, M. R., 58, 142, 146, 217
Volf, J. G., 201
Vollenweider, S., 142, 200

Wallace-Hadrill, A., 34
Walter, N., 144
Watson, D. F., 136, 138, 139
Weiss, H. F., 120
Westman, R., 76
Wette, W. M. L. de, 184
White, L. M., 151
Whittaker, M., 99, 129
Wilckens, U., 166, 169
Wilken, R. L., 245
Willis, W. L., 200, 202, 206
Winston, D., 111, 115, 132
Winter, B. W., 2, 80, 82, 84, 89, 154, 185,
    188, 192, 194, 206
Witherington III, B., 7, 139, 187, 210
Witt, N. W. de, 137, 138
Wolfson, H. A., 111, 129
Woodruff, P., 39

Yardly, J. C., 82
Yeo, K. K., 199, 203

Zanker, P., 26
Ziesler, J., 166, 170

INDEX OF GRAECO-ROMAN SOURCES

Adamantius
14   30
44   30–31

Aeschylus
Choephori
244   38

Alciphron
Epist.
1:15.2   91
1:16.2   91
2:6.1   91
2:21   91
3:3.2   91
3:4.3–6   91
3:15.21   91
3:19.8   90
3:25.3   91
4:13.13–14   90
4:13.18   90
4:14.3   91
4:14.4–6   91
4:19.15   58

Andronicus
SVF   3/96–7   39

The Anonymous Latin Physiognomy
3–8   28
64   31

Aristotle
Analytica Priora
70b   25, 26

Eud. Eth.
1215b   46
1216a   207
1221b   45
1231a   45, 46, 96

Historia Animalium
488b   25

Magna Moralia
1212a   152
1212b   152

Nic. Eth.
1118a   45, 96
1118b   45
1123b   25
1128a   25
1152b   46
1152b–1154b   46
1154a   46
1169a   152
1168b   152
1172a   46
1172a–1181b   46
1179b   46
1180a   46
1180b–1181b   46

Parts of Animals
675b   31

Problems
896a   2
949a–950a   45
950a   46, 96

Rhet.
1357a   25
1368a   139
1402b   25
1418a   140

Vices and Virtues
1250a   45
1250b   45

Ps.-Aristotle
Physiognomonica
805a   25
805b   25
806a   26, 28, 32, 33
806b   26, 32, 33
806b–808b   26
807a   25, 27
807b   27, 32, 33
808a   33
809b–810a   27
810a   25
810a–814b   26
810b   28
813b   27
814b   27

Rhet. Alex.
8 (1429a)   140
32 (1439a)   140

Athenaeus
Deipn.
1:3f   55
1:7a   59, 220
1:28f   90
2:44f   55, 189
3:96f   55
3:97c   56, 59
3:100b   59
3:125b   55
4:129a   89
6:228d   56
6:236d–262a   56
6:239a–c   57
6:240d–e   57
6:243b   57
6:244b–d   57
6:246b–c   57
6:248c   56
6:248f   38
6:254c   56
6:254e   56, 172
6:260a–261b   56
6:262a   56
6:270b   90
6:270c   90
7:279a–280c   55
7:279f   55
8:336a–b   66
8:336c   67
8:336e   199
8:336f   55, 66
10:428a–c   81

10:435a–f   189
10:436b   55
12:529d   67
12:529d–530c   67
12:529f–530a   67
12:530b   67
12:530f   55
12:531c   55
12:532c   82
12:549d–550f   55
13:55a–612f   89
13:556d   55
13:573c–574d   211
13:599f   38
13:607b–c   89
13:607b–f   89
13:608b   89
15:675b–c   81

Cicero
De Natura Deorum
1:112   73
1:113   69

Fin.
1:13   68
2:6   68
2:7   68
2:12   68
2:18–19   68
2:20–2   68
2:23   68, 84, 85
2:36–7   68
2:49   63
2:58–60   68
2:60–3   69

In Pisonem
17   69
22   69
24   69
37   69
39   69
40   69
41   69
42   69
59   69
62   69
66   69, 70
68   69
69   70
70   70
84   69
85   69

85–91	70	9	189
92	69	9:3	189
		9:9	189
Pro Sestio		30:30–44	47
20–5	70	30:33–9	188, 189
23	70	32:90	46
26	70	33:33	189
		33:52–6	26
Off.		55:21	47
1:100–6	69	77/78:4	82
1:102	69	77/78:28–9	66, 82
		77/78:29	67
Tusc. Disp.		80:7–10	47
1:77	63		
2:7–8	63, 65	Diodorus Siculus	
2:18	65	8:18	220
3:41–3	65	8:18–19	59
3:49	65		
4:6–7	63	Diogenes Laertius	
5:73	65	*Philosophers*	
5:101	66	10:6	64, 73
		10:6–7	64
Ps.-Cicero		10:16–22	61
Rhet. Her.		10:131–2	63
4:1–7	140	10:132	63
		10:138–54	62
Cleanthes			
Hymn to Zeus		Dionysius Halicarnassus	
*SVF*1/537	38	*Rom. Ant.*	
		2:19.2	211
Demosthenes			
De Corona		Epictetus	
83–6	149	*Diss.*	
285–305	149	1:4.20	48
286	150	1:4.20–1	52
286–7	150	1:9.3–12	51
289	150	1:9.11–13	51
291	150	1:9.16	51
291–2	150	1:9.26	50, 51
292	150	1:13.1	48
295	150	1:16.8	50
296	149	1:16.17	50
298	150	1:19.11	152
301	150	2:8.11–23	51
321	150	2:8.12	48
		2:9.4	51
Dio Chrysostom		2:18.27–9	52
Orat.		2:20	76
6:36	189	2:20.10	50
8:11–14	52	2:20.16	50
8:20	183	2:20.21–7	50
8:21	183	2:20.26	149
8:25	183	3:1.19	51
8:36	183	3:1.24	51

3:1.36–37	51
3:7.3	50
3:7.19	50
3:7.21	51
3:15	52
3:18.1–4	51
3:21.1–10	52
3:21.11–24	51
3:22.23	51
3:22.45–9	51
3:22.53	51
3:22.56	51
3:22.86–9	52
3:25.1–5	52
4:8.20	48

Encheiridion
41	197

Eupolis
Fragm. nos.
172–3	59

Euripides
Alcestis
780–9	185

Cyclops
220–1	37
239–49	37
303–4	37
310	37
316	38
316–45	37
323–41	38
345–6	38
409	37
415–17	37
505–6	37

Helen
940–3	141

Herodotus
Hist.
2:78	185

Hesiod
Theogony
26	1, 50

Homer
Odyssey
6:133	40
18:2	40
21:287–94	119

Homeric Hymns
23	38

Horace
Epist.
1:15.32	87

Odes
2:3	185

Sat.
1:1.102	73
1:8.11	73
2:1.22	73
2:2.1	86
2:2.39–52	86
2:2.40	87
2:2.43	87
2:2.77–9	87
2:2.110–11	86
2:2.118–36	87
2:7.102–18	87
2:7.111	87

Isocrates
Demonicus
32	80

Against the Sophists
16–18	141

Juvenal
Sat.
5:24–37	85
5:49	85
5:80–3	85
5:92–102	85
5:114–19	85
5:146	85
6:293	87
6:298–305	88
6:314	88
6:314–34	88
6:329	88
6:335	87
6:419–33	88
6:432	88
10:356	67
10:360–2	67
10:362	68

11:11	88
11:39–40	88
11:162–82	89
11:170	89
11:183–92	87
14:96–106	129

Livy
Ab Urbe Condita

34:4	83
39:8–18	75

Lucian
Anacharsis

14–15	143
20	143
24	143
30	143

Fug.

16	64
18	64
19	64

Patr. Laud.

10	150

Saturn.

4	91

Symp.

1	81
3	81
33	81
47	81

Ps.-Lucian
Erôtes

42	92, 96

Martial
Epigrams

47:5–6	84

Menander
Thais

Fragm. 218	184

Musonius Rufus

3	47
7	47
18a	48
18a–b	47
18a–20	48

18b	48, 49, 96, 188, 194
20	48, 49

Ovid
The Art of Love

1:229–52	82
603–30	82

Petronius
Satyricon

34	185

Plato
Laws

1:637a	83

Phaedo

80a–b	40
80c–81c	40
81e	40
81e–82a	25

Phaedrus

237a–242a	39
238a	39
238c	39
238e	39
241a	39

Protagoras

353a–356c	40
353c	40

Republic

519b	41
573e	40
575a	40

Symp.

176a	81
176e–177e	81
178a	38
180b	38
189c	38

Timaeus

44d	41
69c	41
70d–e	111
70d–71a	41
72e–73a	41
74e	41
75c	41
82a	41

86b–c	41
87e	41
90a	41
90b	41
91c	41
91d–92a	40
92a	116

Pliny
Nat. Hist.

11:200	31
14:138–9	88
14:410	82
26:36	73

Pliny the Younger
Epist.

15	84

Plutarch
Cato the Younger

56:4	81
67:1	81

Marcus Cato

9:5	150

Mor.

13f	148
49d	54
51b–c	172
52c–f	172
53d	172
53f	172
53f–54a	172
54b	54
55e	54
60b	54
61e–f	54
64e–f	54
68c–d	197
123e–f	52
128b	52
128f	52
330f	66
336e	67
336d–e	66
346b	76
413f	148
428e–f	140
433c	76
434d–e	39

435b	39
437e	76
443c–d	198
523d–f	148
639e–f	140
644b–c	188
710a–713f	81
751b	76
758e	76
760a	82
821d	140
990d–991a	53
991c	53
991d	53
994e	53
996d	53
996d–e	53
1086d	76
1089f–1091b	76
1097d–1099d	76
1098c	75
1098d	75, 76
1099b	76
1100d	65, 75, 76
1102b	76
1105c	76
1108c	76
1124d	74
1124f–1125a	95
1125a	74
1125a–b	75
1125d	75
1128b	152
1129b	75

Polemon

14	28
16	29
23	33
25:7–9	29
35:14–15	29
40	29
61	33

Polybius
Hist.

31:25.2–8	86

Quintilian
Inst.

5:11.1–2	140
11:6.38	140
12:4.1–2	140

Seneca
Ben.
7:26.4 — 73

Const.
9:5 — 74

Helv.
10:2 — 85
10:2–6 — 85
10:3 — 85
10:5–6 — 85
10:8–11 — 73, 85
10:11 — 86

Ira
2:14.2 — 74

Mor. Epist.
8:7–8 — 64
15:5 — 74
18:1 — 91
21:9 — 64
21:10 — 74
21:11 — 73
47:2 — 84, 194
47:5–6 — 84
47:8 — 84
60:4 — 85
78:16 — 74
79:15 — 64
80:1–5 — 74
89:22 — 74
92:25 — 72
95:13 — 83
95:15–16 — 84
95:16 — 84
95:19 — 84
95:21 — 83
95:23–4 — 83
95:24 — 84
95:25 — 83
9:27–9 — 83
108:15–16 — 74
110:12–20 — 84
110:15 — 84
110:16 — 85
114:25–7 — 74
119:14 — 74

Tranq.
3:1 — 74
9:4 — 74

Vit. Beat.
4:4 — 72
5:4 — 80
7:1 — 72
7:3 — 80
9:1–4 — 72
9:4 — 72
10:1 — 72
10:3 — 73
11:4 — 73
12:3–4 — 72
13:1 — 71
13:1–3 — 71
14:1–2 — 73
20:5 — 73

Sextus Empiricus
Pyrrhonism
1:64–8 — 25
1:85 — 25

Strabo
Geography
14:5.9 — 66

Suetonius
Vita Caesarum
Aug.
79 — 27

Caligula
3 — 27
50 — 27

Claud.
8 — 27
31–3 — 27

Domitian
18 — 34

Nero
1–7 — 32
8–19 — 32
19:3 — 32
20–50 — 32
20:1 — 32
25:3 — 32
45–50 — 33
49:4 — 32
51 — 27
51–7 — 32

Tib
68   27

Titus
2   34

Vitellius
13   34
17:2   33

Tacitus
Hist.
5.4   67

Theophrastus
Characters
11:7   81
20:10   81

Thucydides
Peloponnesian War
2:53   185

Vatican Fragments (Epicurus)
33   62
59   62
409   76

Xenophon
Cyropaedia
1:2.8   42

Mem.
1:2.23   43
1:5.1   42, 43
1:5.1–6   43, 150
1:5.4   42
1:5.5   42
1:6.1–3   42
1:6.3   141
1:6.8   42
2:1.1–2   43
2:1.2–9   43
2:1.21–33   44
2:1.23   44
2:1.24   44
2:1.25   44
2:1.28   44
2:1.30   45
2:1.33   45

Symp.
2:1   81
9:2   199
9:7   82

INDEX OF OLD TESTAMENT, APOCRYPHA, PSEUDEPIGRAPHA AND OTHER JEWISH WRITINGS

The Old Testament

Gen
2:10	110
3	169, 170, 238, 242
3:1	170
3:5	252
3:11	115
3:13	170
3:14	117, 119, 131
3:14–15	114
3:14–17	114
3:15	169, 170, 172
6:14	118
7:2–3	131
8:21	117
9:20	111
17:10–11	128
25:25	118
26:8	199
26:34–5	121
27:8–10	120
27:15	120
27:30	147
27:42–5	118
28:6–9	121
32:3	118
36:8	118
37:33	131
39:7	121
39:12	121
40:1–23	122
42:36	122
47:3	112

Exod.
12:8	111
13	204
14	204
15:24	205
15:25	112
16	204
16:2–3	205
16:3	204
16:4	114, 205
16:7–8	205
16:8	205
17	204
17:2	205
17:3	204, 205
20:27–9	204
23:33	168
24:11	111
25:30	111
27:1	128
32:1	247
32:6	190, 199, 202, 204, 206, 210, 231, 247, 251, 262
32:20	113
32:27–9	207

Lev.
9:14	117
11:42	117
19:5–6	129

Num.
11	204, 208, 209
11:1	205
11:4	204, 205
11:4–5	205
11:13	204
11:34	208, 215
14	204
14:2	205
16	204
16:11, 41	205
16:13–14	204
17	204
20:17–20	118

21	204, 210
21:5	204
25	204
25:1–5	210

Deut.

1:27	205
6:10–12	209
6:11–12	244
21:18–21	147
23:17–18	196
28:64	168
30:11–14	130
32:15	244

Josh

9:18	205

Judg.

2:7	168
10:6	168
10:13	168
10:16	168

1 Sam (1 Kgs LXX)

2:24	168
12:14	168
26:19	168

2 Sam (2 Kgs LXX)

7:12	9
16:11	9

1 Kgs (3Kgs LXX)

9:6	168
16:31	168
22:54	168

2 Kgs (4 Kgs LXX)

10:18	168
17:41	168
21:3	168

2 Chr.

7:22	168
24:18	168
30:8	168
33:3	168
33:16	168
33:22	168
34:33	168

Job

20:12–15	95
24:19	96

Ps.

1:1	230
5:1–3	228
5:10	95
9:28	95
10:3–5	95
10:7	95
22:14	95
27:2	95
33:4–5/LXX	160
39:17/LXX	160
53:5 = 14:4	95
56:11/LXX	160
68:30–31/LXX	160
73:4–6	95
77 LXX	204
77:20	250
78(77):18–20	205
91:12	170
95:5 LXX	203
105 LXX	204
105:14 LXX	204
105(106):15	205
106:39	210
110:1	169

Prov.

1:12	96
19:28	95

Isa.

5:5	260
5:14	96
22:13	37, 183, 184, 190, 215, 231
30:12	205
40:19–20	203
41:6–7	203
44:12–17	203
58:9	205
59:7	230
65:2	168

Jer.

1:15	4
2:20	168
3:22	226
5:19	168, 226
8:2	168
10:3–5	203

11:10	168	6:25–7	100
13:10	168	6:32–6	99
16:11	168	6:36	99
22:9	168	7:1–9	100
25:6	168	7:10–11	98, 100
42:15 LXX	168	7:11	100
51:34	95	7:16	100
		7:18–20	99
Lam.		7:21	100
3:46	95		
		4 Macc.	
Ezek.		1:1	101
16:49	250, 251	1:2–5	101
		1:3	101
Dan.		1:13–3:18	101
7:23	95	1:25–30	101
		1:27–35	101
Hos		1:33–5	97
1–3	210	2:7	101
		3:5	103
Jonah		3:18	103
2:3	96	4:26	99
		5:3	101
Micah		5:6	99
3:2–3	95	5:14	101
		5:20–1	101
Mal.		5:25–38	101
1:5	160	6:10	103
		6:18–21	101
		8:2	101
		9:1–2	101
		9:8	103
Old Testament Apocrypha		9:23–4	103
		11:20–3	103
Bar.		12:13	103
4:7	203	13:1–5	102
		13:13–15	103
1 Macc		15:29	103
1:62	99	16:14	103
		16:16	103
3 Macc.		17:11–16	103
2:31	100	18:23	103
2:31–3	99		
3:2–10	99	Sir.	
3:3	100	18:30	97
3:4	99	19:12	97
3:7	99	23:6	97, 192
3:7–9	100	23:16(23:17 LXX)	97, 192
3:23–4	100	36:18–19	97
3:26	100	51:5	96
5:3	99		
5:16–17	99	Wisd.	
5:36	99	2:5–9	183
6:6–7	99	13:10–19	203

| 14:17–21 | 203 |
| 14:22, 27 | 210 |

**Old Testament
Pseudepigrapha**

Adam and Eve
| 9:1–5 | 170 |

Apoc. Mos.
15	171
16	171
17	171
19:3	171

Enoch
| 19:1 | |

Ep. Arist.
128–66	99
135–9	105
139	105
140–1	104
142	105
144	105
146–50	105
153–5	129
163–6	105
169	105
187–294	104
221–4	104
237	104
256	104
277–8	104

Jub.
| 21:8 | 4 |

T. Levi
| 18:12 | 170 |

T. Mos.
7:2–4	105
7:8	106
8:2–3	106

T. Rub.
2:1–3:8	97
2:7	98
3:2	98
3:3	98

T. Sim.
| 6:6 | 170 |

T. Zeb.
| 9:8 | 170 |

Other Jewish Writings

Cairo Geniza Wisdom
14:6–8	106
15:1	106
15:7	106
17:2–8	106
17:5	106

Josephus
Ag. Ap.
2:79–81	67
2:137–42	129
2:154–6	108
2:182–3	108
2:220–4	108
2:256–7	108
2:180	78
2:291–5	108

Ant.
7:169	97
10:277–8	78
18:65–80	211
19:32	78
20:34–48	158

Philo
Abr.
3–6	140
57	111
119	108
135	131
149	120
226	116
276	140

Agr.
35–8	112
38	110
41	112
66	120
88	112
97	116
142	129
145	129

Cher.
84–97	124
91–3	124
93	124
94	125
94–7	124
98–107	111
100–2	111

Congr.
61–2	121
83–4	112
192	108

Contempl.
34–90	125
48–56	125
50–1	82
53–4	125
55	125
54	82, 84
74	120

Decal.
1	140
134	111
149	116

Det.
32	152
32–4	155
33	121, 154, 196
33–4	154, 166
34	152
38	185
45	121
113	116
156–7	152

Deus
15	153
16–18	153
143	118
144	118
180	118

Ebr.
9–10	147
15	147
20–1	147
20–2	147
21	147
27	147
69–70	208

82–3	111
95	207
95–6	147
95–100	207
124	207
127	207
206	123
208–24	123
210	122
212–13	122
214	122
217–19	123
220	123
221–2	123

Fug.
23–43	118
31	119
31–2	119
35	119
90–2	207
124	108
208	111

Gig.
18	110
29–31	153
60–1	105

Her.
51	111
79–80	208
169	147
238	114, 116
315–16	112

Ios.
1–3	112
61–3	172
135	116
151–6	122
154	122

Leg.
1:63–73	110
1:70–1	110
1:82	176
2:9–15	115
2:59	120
2:71–85	116, 210
2:72	114
2:74	210
2:84	114
2:95	176

3:2	120
3:49	113
3:61	115
3:65–119	117
3:67–8	115
3:76	114
3:86	114
3:114–17	110
3:137	176
3:138	117
3:138–9	176
3:139	117
3:141	117
3:144	111
3:145	117
3:147	111, 117
3:149	117
3:151–9	111
3:156	119
3:157	116
3:159	117
3:162	114
3:182	172
3:191	118
3:236	122
3:237–40	196
3:239–40	121
3:239–42	121
3:242	121

Legat.
361	129

Migr.
14–15	112
18	112
19–21	121
39	111
64–7	117
77	112
86–93	128, 158
151–2	112
153	120
154	112
155	208
160	112
201	111
202	112
204	116

Mos.
1:28–9	194
1:78	116
1:160	116

1:191–5	209
2:17–20	127
2:17–24	127
2:23	110, 127
2:159–73	207
2:162	207

Mut.
81–2	111

Opif.
77–81	113
153–69	115
156–66	114
157	114
158	114, 115
160	115
165–6	115

Plant.
36–8	112
105–6	172

Post.
74	116
96	112
121	152
155	112, 116, 207
155–9	112
158–9	207
162–3	207
180–1	153

Praem.
15	130
15–21	130
43–4	111
99	194

Prov.
2:18	118

QE
1:14	111
2:39	111
2:100	128
2:72	111

QG
1:12	110
1:33	115
1:47	114, 171

1:48	114, 171
2:12	131
2:67	111
3:46–7	128, 158
4:160	120
4:160–245	119
4:161	120
4:164	119
4:171	119
4:189	120
4:191	120
4:198	120
4:200	120
4:201	120
4:203	120
4:204	120
4:206	120
4:215	119
4:225	119
4:227	120
4:233	119
4:234	119
4:238	120
4:245	119

Sacr.

3	152
17–18	118
19–33	115, 152
33	152
48	112
49	112
52	152
81	118
130	207
135	121
136	176

Spec.

1:1–11	128, 158
1:21–2	147
1:22	147
1:147–50	127
1:148	120
1:149	128
1:174–6	127
1:176	127
1:192–3	124
1:200	115
1:206	117
1:220–3	129
1:280–2	196
2:42–5	124

2:46–51	176
2:49–50	124
2:145–9	113
2:147	113
2:148	113
2:163	124
2:193	126
2:193–203	126, 211
2:195	126
2:195–9	209
2:197	126
2:198	127
2:199	127
3:1	116
3:8–82	208
3:43	131
3:124–7	207
3:125–6	207
4:79–131	208
4:91	116, 128, 209
4:92–4	110
4:94	120, 208
4:96–7	128, 208
4:97	209
4:97–131	128
4:99	126, 128, 209
4:100–2	129
4:101	128, 209
4:102	111
4:105–98	129
4:112	116
4:113	116, 117, 118, 209
4:113–27	152
4:122	68
4:124	111
4:126	209
4:126–31	208
4:127	207
4:130	208
4:131	152

Somn.

1:49	111
1:120–6	115
1:121	122
1:122	116
1:124	115
1:171	111
2:25	176
2:48–67	131
2:51	131
2:63	131
2:105	116
2:116	116

2:132	116	208	118
2:155–63	122	210	118
2:177	111		
2:181	122	Ps.-Philo	
2:205	122	*Lib. Ant.*	
2:206–14	122	9:2	4
		9:5	4
Virt.		22:3	4
5–6	194		
134–6	128, 130	Ps.-Phocylides	
175–86	130	69	194
178–227	117	223	194
181–2	130		
182	130, 167	Qumran	
183	130	4Q 186	24
207–10	118	4Q 561	24

INDEX OF NEW TESTAMENT AND EARLY
CHRISTIAN WRITINGS

The New Testament

Matt.

3:7	219
4:1	249, 251
4:1–3	242
5:28	230
6:24	227, 230, 248, 249
7:13–14	117
7:16	252
7:21	231
15:10–20	227
16:24	246
19:21	239
23:14	244

Luke

1:46	160
1:50	160
6:25	245
12:19	50, 186, 249
13:23–4	117
14:8	222
14:10	222
14:12–13	222
14:16	222
15	243
15:16	259
16:19–31	249

John

1:43–51	121
2:18	244
4:32	231
4:34	231
6:26–7	260
6:27	247
6:30	244
6:41–2	250

Acts

10:47	160
15:1	256
17:18–34	253
19:17	160
24:25	135

Rom.

1:1	167, 175
1:8	227
1:18–23	17
1:18–32	17, 175
1:18–3:20	18
1:24	17, 175, 176, 177, 197
1:25	168, 175
1:26	176
1:26–7	154
1:27	17, 97, 176
3:8	173, 174, 179
3:10–18	96, 134
3:30	175
6:1	173
6:1–20	167, 174, 268
6:3–9	167
6:4	143, 178, 270
6:5	20
6:6	167, 174, 178
6:12	174, 178
6:12–14	18, 177
6:13	177
6:14	174
6:16–17	167
6:17	166, 173
6:18	167
6:19	174, 177
6:20	167
6:22	167
7:5	18
7:7–13	18, 175

7:14–25	18	**1 Cor.**	
7:23	249	1:11	191
7:24	17, 178	3:3	143
8:2	178	3:16	197
8:3	18	3:16–17	15
8:4	143	3:17	242
8:4–5	17	4:11–13	160
8:6	260	5:1	210
8:8	225	5:1–8	192
8:10	20	5:1–11	210
8:11	20	5:1–13	16
8:12	18	5:1–6:20	191
8:13	20, 178	5:7	198
8:17	178	5:7–8	198
8:18–30	178	5:9–11	192, 210
8:21–3	19	5:11	188, 252
8:23	178	6:1–8	192
8:29	15, 20, 178	6:9	210
9:33	168	6:9–10	235
10:21	168	6:9–11	17, 192, 193, 252
12:1	16, 17, 177	6:10	188
12:1–2	16, 132, 160, 177, 271	6:11	196, 198
		6:12	144, 154, 192, 196
12:2	20	6:12–14	195
13:11–14	19	6:12–20	19, 192, 194, 197, 198, 210, 212, 213, 215, 270
13:13	19, 143, 188, 225		
13:13–14	174		
13:14	19	6:13	4, 13, 191, 192, 193, 194, 195, 197, 199, 210, 221, 233, 235, 239, 242, 253, 261
14:1–15:13	172		
14:2	193		
14:2–3	104		
14:14–15	228	6:13–14	196
14:15	143	6:13–20	181
14:17	104, 193, 231, 260	6:14	196
14:17–18	173	6:15	212
15:14	138	6:15–16	210
16:17	165, 166, 173, 243	6:15–20	193
16:17–18	230, 255	6:18	197, 210
16:17–20	115, 171, 172, 173, 175, 198, 229	6:18–20	197
		6:19	197, 242
16:18	1, 4, 5, 6, 7, 8, 13, 23, 35, 36, 47, 53, 85, 107, 135, 165, 166, 167, 168, 170, 171, 173, 175, 176, 179, 180, 217, 219, 223, 229, 231, 232, 235, 238, 241, 243, 244, 245, 255, 256, 257, 258, 259, 260, 261, 265, 269	6:19–20	15, 198
		6:20	197, 198
		7:2	210
		7:5	21, 192
		7:9	192
		7:17	143
		7:23	198
		7:36	192
		8:1–13	199
		8–10	19, 195, 200, 212, 222
16:19	173	8:1–10:22	199
16:20	165, 169, 170	8:1–11:1	181
16:27	175	8:6	231

8:8	104, 193	11:33–4	190, 231, 261
8:10	200	11:34	188, 190
8:13	205, 260	13:8	250
9:1–23	200	14:20	190
9:24	200	14:26	190
9:24–7	19, 135, 177, 200,	15:23	186
	201, 213	15:29	182, 186
9:26–7	201	15:29–32	182, 186
9:27	19	15:29–34	181, 184, 186
10:1	200	15:32	13, 37, 67, 181, 182,
10:1–5	202		183, 184, 185, 187,
10:1–13	200, 201, 203, 208		190, 195, 209, 212,
10:1–22	199, 201		215, 216, 225, 231,
10:5	200, 202		235, 239, 247, 248,
10:6	202		249, 253, 254, 261,
10:7	13, 67, 147, 181,		270
	190, 199, 200, 202,	15:32–4	182, 186, 187
	203, 204, 206, 215,	15:33	184, 185
	216, 231, 239, 260,	15:33–4	182, 187
	261	15:34	187
10:8	202, 210	15:36–41	21
10:9	202, 203	15:40–51	162
10:10	202, 205	15:48–50	21
10:11	202	15:49	20
10:12	200, 201, 202	15:50	212
10:13	203	16:9	184
10:14–22	200, 202	16:13	135
10:14	201		
10:15–17	191	2 Cor.	
10:19–21	203	1:8–11	184
10:21	200	1:22	19
10:23	192	2:3	138
10:23–11:1	200	3:9	154
10:24	272	3:18	20
10:25	200, 232	4:1	249
10:25–7	104	4:2	144, 153, 154
10:26	22, 201	4:7–12	16, 160
10:27	200	4:10–11	20
10:30	22	4:16	20
10:31	230	4:16–17	20
11:1	19, 20, 142	4:16–5:5	20
11:2–16	190	5:1–10	162
11:17–34	181, 190, 195,	5:5	19
	212, 213, 222,	5:7	144
	270	6:13	260
11:17	190	6:14–16	16
11:18	190	6:16	15
11:20	190	7:1	160
11:21	188	10:2	17
11:21–2	190, 252, 261	10:2–3	144
11:22	188	11:3	170
11:27	189	11:13	256
11:29	190, 191	11:14–15	170
11:33	188	12:21	210

Gal.

1:15	4
1:23	17
4:19	20
5:1	135
5:13	19, 134, 159
5:13–6:10	159
5:16	144
5:16–17	19, 134
5:16–21	17
5:19–21	8, 252
5:21	188
5:23	134
5:24	19, 134, 178, 198
6:7–8	17
6:12	156
6:12–17	9
6:14	220, 246
6:17	160

Eph.

2:3	17
2:11–13	17
4:6	226
4:22	17

Phil.

1:2	148
1:3	148
1:3–11	138
1:6	138, 141, 144, 160
1:7	44, 139
1:9–11	138
1:11	148
1:20	16, 160, 161, 197, 271
1:24	160
1:25	138
1:27	135, 139, 151, 158
1:28	148
1:28–30	139
1:29–30	141
1:30	143
2:1–5	139
2:1–11	142
2:2	44
2:3	148
2:3–4	158
2:4	44, 139, 140, 151, 272
2:4–11	20
2:5	44
2:5–11	142
2:6	148

2:6–11	153, 161, 162
2:8	139, 142, 148, 151
2:9	148
2:11	148
2:12–13	138
2:13	148
2:14–16	139
2:15	148
2:15–16	160
2:16	138
2:17	16, 161
2:19–21	142
2:19–30	139, 142
2:21	142, 151, 158, 231, 272
2:22	142
2:24	138
2:27	148
2:30	139, 142, 161
3:1	136
3:1–2	145
3:1–4	159
3:2	138
3:2–3	7
3:2–4	155, 156, 157
3:2–6	156
3:3	148, 150, 158
3:3–4	151
3:5–11	157
3:6	159
3:7–9	158
3:8	155
3:9	148
3:10	20, 139, 141, 159
3:10–11	20, 141, 162
3:11	142
3:12	142
3:12–14	138, 255
3:12–16	141, 142, 177
3:14	148, 149
3:15	44, 138
3:17	44, 138, 139, 140, 141, 143, 150, 157, 178
3:17–18	10
3:17–19	161, 246
3:18	139, 142
3:17–21	136, 139, 140, 141, 146, 156, 162, 186, 187, 270
3:18–19	136, 137, 138, 140, 141, 142, 143, 144, 145, 146, 148, 151, 152, 153, 155, 156,

	157, 158, 162, 163,	5:13	4
	167, 246	5:23	15, 160
3:18–21	198		
3:19	1, 4, 5, 6, 7, 8, 10,	2 Thess.	
	13, 23, 35, 36, 40,	3:4	138
	42, 47, 53, 78, 107,		
	135, 137, 144, 147,	1 Tim.	
	148, 149, 150, 151,	1.3–4	254
	154, 155, 156, 158,	2:9	115
	159, 160, 161, 162,	4:1–3	232
	163, 169, 176, 180,	5:8	231
	187, 217, 223, 225,	5:13	225, 242
	226, 227, 228, 229,	6:8	239
	230, 231, 232, 233,	6:9	135
	234, 235, 236, 238,		
	241, 242, 243, 244,	2 Tim.	
	248, 249, 250, 251,	2:2	135
	253, 255, 257, 258,	3:6	135
	259, 260, 261, 265,		
	269	Tit.	
3:19–21	153, 231	1:10–12	255
3:20	49, 150, 186	1:12	1, 4, 36, 37, 50, 53,
3:21	20, 142, 146, 151,		56, 244, 247, 255
	153, 159, 161, 162	1:16	231
4:1	149, 160	2:12	135
4:2	44, 139	3:3	17
4:2–3	157		
4:3	139	Phlm.	
4:4	138	21	138
4:6	148		
4:7	148	Heb.	
4:8	138	12:14–17	120, 121
4:9	141, 142, 143, 157	12:16	121
4:10	44	13:9	260
4:11	138, 148, 220		
4:11–12	22	1 Pet.	
4:11–13	211	3:3	115
4:12	148	4:1–3	174, 252
4:14	139		
4:18	148		
4:19	148	**Early Christian writings**	
4:20	148		
		Ambrosiaster	
Col.		*PL* 17.147 (Phil. 3:19) 235	
3:1	135	*PL* 17.181 (Rom. 16:18) 235	
3:5	135, 231		
		Antiochus of Antioch	
1 Thess.		Hom. 4 (*PG* 89) 260	
2:10	160		
3:13	15, 160	Augustine	
4:3–8	17	*Epistle*	
4:4	9	22:6	252
4:5	21, 134	29:2	252
5:6–8	187	29:9	253
		29:11	253

Expositio ad Romanos (*PL* 35)
84   254

Ieiun.
2:58   255
2:70   255
3:93   255

Mag.
9:26   256

Sermo (*PL* 38)
51:24   254
150:5   253
150:6   253
150:6–7   254
150:7   253
150:8   254

Clement of Alexandria
Strom.
1:14   37
2:20   220, 221
4:16   219, 220

Paed.
2:1.1.4   221
2:1.2.1   221
2:1.3.1–4.2   221
2:1.4.1   221
2:1.4.2–3   221
2:1.7.1–5   222
2:1.7.2   222
2:1.7.3   222
2:1.9.2   222
2:1.9.4–12.1   222
2:1.12.2–13.1   222
2:1.15.1   223
2:1.15.4   223
2:1.19.4   223
2:4   222
2:4.2   222

Cyprian
Ad Quirinum
3:11   231
3:11, 44   231
3:60   230

De Duplici Martyrio
24–5   231
24:12   232
24:19   231
25   232

Did.
11–12   169

Gennadius of Marseilles
Fragm. in Epist. ad Rom. 16:17–18
(*PG* 85)   259

Jerome
PL 30.744–5 (Rom. 16:18) 243
PL 30.889 (Phil. 3:19) 243

Epistles
7:5   241
14:3   241
14:4   241
22:9   242
22:10   242
22:11   242
55:2   242
123:18   242
147:1   243

Jov.
1:1   240
1:3   238, 239
1:4   238, 240
1:48   239, 240
1:49   239
2:6   239
2:10   239
2:11   239, 240
2:12   239, 240
2:17   240
2:36   240

John Chrysostom
De Poenitentia (*PG* 60)
II:8   245

Hom. 13 (Phil. 3) (*PG* 62)
13:1   246, 247
13:2   248

Hom. 13 (Matt.) (*PG* 57)
13:1–3   251, 252

Hom. 18 (Eph.) (*PG* 62)
18:2–3   251

Hom. 21 (Matt. 6) (*PG* 57)
21:2   248

Hom. 29 (Hebrews) (*PG* 63)
29:3   249, 250

Hom. 32 (Rom. 16) (*PG* 60)
32:1   244, 245

Hom 34 (1 Cor.) (*PG* 61)
34:6   250

Hom. 46 (John 6) (*PG* 59)
46:1   250

Jud. (*PG* 48)
1:2   245

John Climacus
Climaci (*PG* 88)
4   261
10   261
14   261
18   261

Marius Victorinus
PL 8.1224–5 (Phil. 3:19)   236

Methodius of Olympus
De Lepra
18:1–3   235

De Resurrectione
1:60.3   234
1:60.4   234, 235
2:17.9–10   235

Minucius Felix
Octavius
8–9   67
9:5–6   75

Novatian
Cib.
3:6–7   232
4:1–3   233
5:6   233
5:9   233, 234
6:1   233
6:3   234

Origen
Comm. Matt.
11:14.3–6   227

Comm. Rom.
1:9   227, 228
9:42   228
10:35   229
10:35–7   229
10:36   229

Hom. Gen.
3:6   230

Homily to Jeremiah
5:2.30–1   226
5:2.43–8   226
5:2.46–8   226
5:2.54–65   226
7:3.16–35   226

Hom. Psalms
5:1–3   228

Pelagius
Expositio
Rom. 16:18   237

Phil. 3:17–19   237

Peter Chrysologus
Sermo
5:2.20–2   259
5:5.72–4   259

Tertullian
Ad Uxorem
1:8   225
1:8.5   225

De Monogamia
16:5   225

De Resurrectione Mortuorum
49:13   225

De Virginibus Velandis
14:2.11   225

Ieiun.
3:2   223
12:3   224
16:8   224
17:2   224
17:3   224

17:7   225
17:9   225

Theodore of Mopsuestia
Comm. Phil. 3:19 (PG 66) 257
Comm. Rom. 16:18 (PG 66) 257

Theodoret of Cyrrhus
Comm. Phil. 3:19 (PG 82) 258
Comm. Rom. 16:18 (PG 82) 259

Tyrannius Rufinus
Expositio Symboli
2:20   256